Maimonides for Moderns

Ira Bedzow

Maimonides for Moderns

A Statement of Contemporary Jewish Philosophy

Ira Bedzow
New York Medical College
White Plains, New York, USA

ISBN 978-3-319-44572-4   ISBN 978-3-319-44573-1   (eBook)
DOI 10.1007/978-3-319-44573-1

Library of Congress Control Number: 2016957562

Cover illustration: © Howard Grill/Getty Images

Printed on acid-free paper

This Palgrave Macmillan imprint is published by Springer Nature
The registered company is Springer International Publishing AG
The registered company address is: Gewerbestrasse 11, 6330 Cham, Switzerland

CONTENTS

CHAPTER 1

Introduction

The Current State of Affairs

For with stammering lips and with a strange tongue shall it be spoken to this people.[1]

When I think and talk about Jewish virtue ethics, I find that the terms that I use and the examples that I give are heavily dependent, though not exclusively so, on Maimonides' philosophy and, thus, the Aristotelian framework that he used to convey his Jewish ideas. Yet, despite my reliance on Maimonides' philosophy and ethics, his ultimately Aristotelian background no longer coheres with my contemporary view of the world and of human nature.[2] For example, many, including myself, agree with the general description of human moral development that Aristotle provides and that Maimonides adopts, namely, that people have a natural capacity to be good and, through continually performing good acts, a person will become the best person that he or she can be. Moreover, we might also recognize that ethics is as much about character as it is about actions, and that intellectual development is tied to moral development. Yet we are nevertheless left with only a superficial understanding, since many currently do not use the same terminology as Aristotle and Maimonides to describe the faculties of the soul, nor do most contemporary schools of psychology retain the same distinctions that they made between a person's intellect, imagination, and emotions. Many contemporary psychologists use a biological categorization of parts of the brain, whereas Aristotle and Maimonides use a functional categorization when they speak of parts of

© The Author(s) 2017
I. Bedzow, *Maimonides for Moderns*,
DOI 10.1007/978-3-319-44573-1_1

the soul. Also, with respect to differences in epistemology, Aristotelian epistemology is doxastic in that justification of belief is primarily explained in terms of the believer's faculties, virtues, and intellectual processes; contemporary epistemology, on the other hand, is propositional, in that justification is explained in terms of proof, demonstration, and evidence for the belief itself. Even virtue epistemologists who rely on Aristotle for a language and framework to talk about intellectual virtues share the assumption with other contemporary epistemologists that Aristotelian views of the relationship between intellectual and moral virtues is incorrect. Moreover, in an Aristotelian epistemology, knowledge is acquired when the thinking part of the soul receives intelligible forms from the Active Intellect; a person cannot actualize knowledge by himself or herself. Only the Active Intellect can turn the potential knowledge that the human mind possesses into actual knowledge.[3] Many contemporary philosophers no longer rely on this metaphysics. Aristotle's description of moral virtues faces similar challenges by contemporary philosophy and psychology, as will be demonstrated in this book.

It seems as if I—and those who share my frustration when using medieval terms to describe contemporary ideas—have reached an epistemological crisis,[4] in that the concepts that I use to explain my beliefs do not cohere with my view of the world or of my understanding of human nature. Moreover, it seems as if the tradition in which those ideas once made sense no longer allows for their understanding on more than a superficial level. It is not that Maimonides' concepts of moral development and habituation no longer hold sway; rather, their normativity is based on the authority of tradition and not on their ability to explain in any comprehensive way how moral development actually occurs based on today's science and philosophical descriptions of the world. This predicament is similar to the one that Alasdair MacIntyre describes in the beginning of *After Virtue*, where, in depicting the relationship of contemporary ethics to its medieval predecessor, he writes, "What we possess ... are the fragments of a conceptual scheme, parts which now lack those contexts from which their significance derived. We possess indeed simulacra of morality, we continue to use many of the key expressions. But we have—very largely, if not entirely—lost our comprehension, both theoretical and practical, of morality."[5]

My aim in this book is to construct a contemporary Jewish philosophy that accounts for virtue ethics—or, rather, to give Jewish virtue ethics a contemporary language for its expression. In doing so, I will draw significantly on the work of Moses Maimonides and his religio-philosophical explanation of Jewish ethics. However, I will move away from various aspects of both Maimonides' and Aristotle's biology, physics, and metaphysics, as well as their psychology. In providing a contemporary idiom for Jewish virtue ethics, my hope and objective is to take the normative principles of the Jewish tradition and make them my own by putting them in a contemporary language so as to integrate them into my everyday life, as well as edify those who find themselves in a similar position. As such, this project has a broader implication than just translating Jewish ethics from a medieval, Aristotelian framework into a contemporary one; it also is a means for Judaism to continue as a living tradition. The imperative to translate the Jewish tradition so as to effectively transmit it is described in the first Mishna in *Pirke Avot*: "Moses received (*kibbel*) the Torah from Sinai and handed it down (*mesarah*) to Joshua. Joshua [handed it down] to the Elders, the Elders [handed it down] to the Prophets, and the Prophets handed it down (*mesaruha*) to the Men of the Great Assembly." To receive (*kibbel*) is not a passive acceptance of something external and independent. Rather, it is a voluntary undertaking and adopting. It is making it one's own, in service to God and for the sake of oneself and one's neighbor.[6] Similarly, *mesarah* connotes a connection between giver and receiver; there exists a trust that the giver's intentions will remain with the receiver and that the receiver will stay sincere to the path laid out by the giver.[7] Just as *kibbel* conveys mutuality in the act of transmission, *mesarah* conveys a bond that joins the giver and the receiver together.[8] With this Mishna in mind, I hope to receive that which has been handed down to me in a way that I can make it my own, yet also in a way that joins me to those from whom I have learned, and will continue to do so. Of course, I hope that others may be able to learn from me as well.

BUILDING ON MAIMONIDES

The disciples of the wise increase peace in the world, as it says, "And all your children shall be taught of Hashem, and great shall be the peace of your children." Read not "your children (banayikh)" but "your builders (bonayikh)."[9]

I rely on Maimonides' philosophy as the conceptual foundation and starting point for a contemporary expression of Jewish philosophy because he is "the most influential Jewish thinker of the Middle Ages, and quite possibly of all time."[10] His legal and philosophical works have been the subject of study, they have provoked controversy, they have stimulated commentary and further analysis, and they have ultimately been affixed to the Jewish canon to the point that no Jewish philosopher can ignore them. Moreover, his ideas and explanations of Jewish concepts have reached such a level of authority that they are held to esteem similar to the original receipt of the Torah itself, as articulated by the adage, "From Moses [son of Amram] to Moses [Maimonides], there was none like Moses." Because of his stature in the Jewish tradition, any contemporary Jewish philosophy must be heavily referential if not dependent on Maimonides' teachings, though it need not be exclusively so since there are many normative voices in the Jewish tradition that have disagreed with his explanations of certain concepts and *halakhic* rulings.

Though Maimonides' teachings ground the normative religio-ethical premises of my expression of a contemporary Jewish philosophy, this does not mean that notions that are purely philosophical or explanations that endorse an Aristotelian perspective must be accepted without question. Rather, the authority of his teachings and the necessity to engage with them apply to cases where they affect the normative practices of Jewish life and law and not when a philosophical expression is devoid of an immediate practical ramification. This is in line with Maimonides' own statement in *Sefer HaMitzvot*, where he states, "We explained in our commentary on the Mishna that in any disagreement which deals only with theory and is not of practical importance, the Halakha is not decided."[11] While it is true that the formal principles of jurisprudence used to determine Jewish law are usually not applied to disagreements in Jewish philosophy, this applies to cases when philosophical views do not have practical consequences, and not *when they have normative practical ramifications* in Jewish law. In those cases, they should be considered in the same manner as his *halakhic* rulings.

By asserting my philosophical stance vis-à-vis the Jewish tradition and Maimonides' position in it, I am deliberately choosing what Michael Walzer calls the path of interpretation in moral philosophy. In contradistinction to the path of discovery,[12] where the philosopher approaches the subject from outside his or her social position so as to maintain a distanced objectivity, and the path of invention,[13] where the philosopher invents a morality that will achieve the end that he or she desires,[14] the path of interpretation is one in which the philosopher recognizes that the moral life is already being lived, and the goal is not to answer the question, "What is the right thing to do?" but rather "What is the right thing *for us* to do?"[15] The path of interpretation is a practical philosophy that seeks to clarify and explain the moral life of a living community rather than build or discover an abstract or ideal framework for any community. Because the morality of a community is based on historical ideals, foundational texts, practices, *and how the people explain and justify their behavior in light of them*, moral traditions are vulnerable to contradiction and incoherence when the people's explanations and justifications of behavior no longer conform to their understanding of the community's canon. Therefore, I am making it known at the outset that I am not creating a system of Jewish ethics *ex nihilo* nor am I rediscovering a Jewish ethics that has been lost. I am seeking new ways to explain and to justify behavior in light of the authority of historical ideals, foundational texts, and practices that are normative for Orthodox Judaism. As such, this project is one of *hiddush* (creative interpretation to understand something in a new way), which Rabbi Joseph Soloveitchik calls "the very foundation of the received tradition."[16] I am attempting to provide new ways of looking at the same ideas in order to find a new, contemporary way to discuss those ethical concepts found within the Jewish tradition which Maimonides, as well as other Jewish scholars, explained according to the discourse of his day and age.

A Contemporary Framework

There is a thing of which [someone] will say, "See this, it is new."—It has already been for ages which were before us.[17]

In translating Maimonides' religious and ethical concepts so that they are coherent in a contemporary framework, I intend to be Maimonidean in two respects. First, substantively, I will maintain the normative, religio-ethical aspects of Maimonides' theory, albeit now with greater understanding and coherence in my worldview. Second, methodologically, I will adopt his method of translating Jewish premises into the discourse of the philosophy of the day.[18] Translation is not only a process of converting a word from one language to another; it can also mean converting something from one form to another. Hence, translating medieval concepts into a contemporary schema is an act of maintaining the same or similar meaning while converting its form to fit into a new framework.[19] This is not a new challenge in the history of Jewish thought; Jewish philosophers often adapted secular terms and language so as to fit religious demands. Yet the contemporary challenge is a slightly different project since the translation is from Jewish framework$_{(medieval)}$ to Jewish framework$_{(contemporary)}$ rather than from secular framework$_{(medieval)}$ to Jewish framework$_{(medieval)}$.

To construct a contemporary Jewish philosophy, given the divergence between contemporary views of the world and an Aristotelian view, I will attempt to explain moral and intellectual development in terms of aspiration rather than actualization, that is, reaching perfection or excellence. Many contemporary aretological ethicists recognize that contemporary conceptions of nature are different from an Aristotelian worldview, in that they admit that humans do not have an innate inclination toward their *telos*.[20] In my account of how a person develops his or her moral and intellectual capabilities, I will use a social rather than metaphysical–biological teleology, where Jewish law provides certain practices, which are embedded within the narrative of aspiring to serve God fully as understood within the Jewish tradition.

One major point of divergence between Maimonides' philosophy and my theory of ethics is that Maimonides does not have an explicit place for practical reason in his philosophy while I explicitly incorporate it into mine. The divergence is not simply an addition, however. Rather, in dismissing the Aristotelian conception of practical reason as originating reasons in exchange for a conception of practical reason as responding to reasons, my inclusion of practical reasoning allows for a contemporary account of how a person can improve his or her intellectual and moral abilities. It also provides an answer to the deontological question of how a person can act voluntarily without his or her morality being self-legislated.

I also will reevaluate the relationship between the theoretical and the practical,[21] though Maimonides differed somewhat from Aristotle on this point already.[22] To do this, I must respond to the following challenges made by contemporary philosophers[23]:

1. There are no such things as global character traits[24]; and
2. Belief is not voluntary whereas action is.

It is also necessary to recognize how Maimonides incorporated Jewish law into his Aristotelian ethical framework so that I can similarly incorporate Jewish law into my contemporary theory of Jewish ethics.

* * * *

In the pages that follow, I attempt to lay out a contemporary Jewish philosophy and virtue ethics. I begin by setting a framework for a teleology of aspiration rather than of actualization, which will be based in

Maimonides' ethical framework for moral and intellectual development and which utilizes the ways in which he departs from Aristotle. I then provide a contemporary description of what should be a person's motivation and *telos* and the entelechy that a person attains when he or she achieves that *telos*. What follows this basic outline will be a further examination of the various components of that entelechy and how they interact with each other and relate to one's religious obligations.

More particularly, with regard to building upon Maimonides' teleology and his departure from Aristotle, I will argue that Maimonides' teleology does not fully accept Aristotle's notions of *ergon*, *telos*, and *entelecheia*; rather, his use of those terms must be understood in the context of how Jewish law and values influence the ways in which a person develops toward moral and intellectual perfection. Moreover, according to Maimonides, human perfection is a consequence of a religious goal and not a primary focus of motivation. I adopt the premise that moral and intellectual development is a consequence of a person's goal to serve God, yet my account recognizes that a person's "unique activity" is not intrinsic to his or her physical essence as a member of humanity, but rather it is based on how society and Jewish law situate him or her in a system of values. By living according to the law that God wills for him or her, a person will engender a disposition that allows him or her to recognize the values embedded within the law and will aspire to become the type of person the law is meant to assist the person in becoming. Normativity is a consequence of an external relationship between a person and the community in which he or she lives as it is structured by Divine commands, and a person's moral and intellectual growth is based on how he or she internalizes that relationship, not in how what is already internal becomes manifest.

Though Maimonides uses the term *eved Hashem* (servant of God) to describe a person who achieves his *telos*, in contemporary society the words used to translate *eved*, namely "slave" and "servant," frequently have negative connotations, which can affect their positive import when used to denote a theonomous relationship. Therefore, I attempt to provide a functional description for the term, through which one could recognize the importance of the Jewish tradition in influencing contemporary understanding in Jewish ethics, yet which would not be encumbered by a vocabulary that is no longer properly understood given changes in linguistic connotations. The starting point for my understanding of the ideal of being a "servant of God" is based on the Talmudic understanding of a verse in Habakuk and its subsequent discussion, that is, "the righteous shall live by his faith (*emunah*)." I will also give a contemporary definition of Maimonides' term for entelechy, that is, *Shlemut*.

After examining the difference between Aristotle and Maimonides with respect to their views on the role of the law in their theory of ethics, I will provide a contemporary explanation of how the law can instill practical and theoretical concepts in its adherents. In particular, I will show that the law shapes a person's mental processes and provides both theoretical and practical concepts which a person uses in his or her daily living through two mechanisms, namely, (1) by creating social categories through which a person comes to understand the world and (2) by integrating those concepts into a person's understanding of the world through their influencing daily behavior and in shaping a person's habits so as to be in line with legal norms.

Because Maimonides' conception of the law, given his acceptance of Aristotelian physics and metaphysics, disallows an explicit mention of practical reason from being part of his theory of ethics, I will provide an account of practical reasoning that differs from the Aristotelian as well as the Kantian conception of practical reasoning. By introducing a different view of practical reasoning into my conception of contemporary Jewish ethics, I part ways from Maimonides' framework. However, the inclusion of practical reasoning, which includes reasoning about legal facts and norms, allows for a Jewish virtue ethics that can account for the aretological question of how a person can improve his or her intellectual and moral abilities as well as account for the deontological question of how a person can act voluntarily without his or her morality being self-legislated.

I will then provide a discussion of virtues in light of contemporary epistemological and moral challenges. My theory of virtue is based in the identity of the agent rather than in his or her biology, and will be defined in terms of personal motivation and reliability of success rather than as excellences or perfections of a person. My account of a contemporary Jewish ethics will conclude with a discussion of moral motivation and the difference between a continent person and one who has attained *Shlemut*.

NOTES

1. Isaiah 28:11.
2. For an explanation of how there was a paradigm shift away from the Aristotelian framework in science, see Thomas S. Kuhn, *The Structure of Scientific Revolutions* (Chicago: University of Chicago

Press, 1996). For an explanation of how this paradigm shift has created differences between medieval and modern Jewish philosophy, see Aaron W. Hughes, "Medieval Jewish Philosophers in Modern Jewish Philosophy, *The Cambridge History of Jewish Philosophy: The Modern Era*, eds. Martin Kavka, Zachary Braiterman, and David Novak (Cambridge: Cambridge University Press, 2012) 224–251.

3. This description is general, and the specifics regarding how the Active Intellect imparts knowledge are subject to great debate among medieval philosophers.

4. See Alasdair MacIntyre, *Whose Justice? Which Rationality?* (Notre Dame: University of Notre Dame Press, 1984) 349–369.

5. Alasdair MacIntyre, *After Virtue: A Study in Moral Theory* (Notre Dame: University of Notre Dame Press, 1984) 2.

6. The root of the word "to receive" (*kibbel*) is used in the Bible to denote a matching of counterparts, such as when it is used to describe how the loops of the covers of the Tabernacle would fit together (Exodus 26:5, 36:12). Between people, it connotes willful acceptance, as when Mordechai refused to receive clothes from Esther: "And Esther's maidens and her chamberlains came and told it her; and the queen was exceedingly pained; and she sent clothes to Mordechai, to take off his sackcloth, but he did not accept (*kibbel*) it. (Esther 4:4.)"

7. This connotation stems from the fact that the root of the word *mesarah* denotes a yoke, chains, and chastisement, as well as surrendering something to another. Rabbi Judah Loewe, in his commentary on this Mishna, explains the word *mesarah* with a similar understanding. He writes, "*Mesirah* is used only when the thing still remains with the person [who gave it]. Therefore, it says, 'and he handed down' and did not say 'and he taught it' since the word taught could imply that he taught it and then forgot it, but to hand it down implies that he handed it but it still stayed with him. (*Derekh Hayyim*.)"

8. It is with this meaning that the expression *mesirat nefesh*, that is, giving up one's soul or sacrificing for a purpose, is not meant as the giving of one's soul independent of the connection between the giver and the purpose, but rather as trusting in oneself to uphold the values of the purpose for which one sacrifices as well as trusting in the values and purpose for which one sacrifices.

9. BT *Berakhot* 64a.

10. He was called this by Shlomo Pines, scholar of medieval Jewish philosophy and best known for his English translation of Maimonides' *Guide of the Perplexed*. See *Time* magazine, December 23, 1985. Jonathan Jacobs has similarly said that he is "surely the most influential and important medieval Jewish thinker (not just philosopher)." (Jonathan A. Jacobs, *Law, Reason, and Morality in Medieval Jewish Philosophy* (New York: Oxford University Press, 2010) 21.)

11. See Maimonides, *Sefer HaMitsvot*, Negative Commandment 133. See also his commentary on Mishna, *Sanhedrin* 10:3, *Sotah* 3:4–5, *Shevuot* 1:4. For others who express this view, see Rabbi Chaim Joseph David Azulai (*Hida*), *Responsa Hayyim Sho'el* 2:4; Rabbi Yom Tov Lipman haLevi Heller, *Tosafot Yom Tov, Sotah* 3:5; and Rabbi Mordechai Fogelman, *Responsa Bet Mordekhai* 2:40.

12. Walzer writes, "There are natural as well as Divine revelations, and a philosopher who reports to us on the existence of natural law, say, or natural rights or any set of objective moral truths has walked the path of discovery." (Michael Walzer, *Interpretation and Social Criticism*, [Cambridge: Harvard University Press, 1987] 5).

13. Walzer writes, "[M]ost philosophers who have walked the path of invention have begun with methodology: a design of a design procedure. (Ibid. 10)"

14. Ibid. 10.

15. Ibid. 23.

16. Joseph Dov Soloveitchik, *Halakhic Man* (Philadelphia: Jewish Publication Society of America, 1983) 81.

17. Ecclesiastes 1:10.

18. David Novak makes a similar claim in his article, "Can We Be Maimonideans Today?" in *Maimonides and his Heritage*, eds. Idit Dobbs-Weinstein, Lenn Evan Goodman, and James Allen Grady (Albany: State University of New York Press, 2009).

19. See my discussion about translation as it relates to this endeavor in the section on epistemic and moral objectivity.

20. For example, Alasdair MacIntyre, in adapting Aristotle's conception of the virtues to his own view of virtue ethics, admits that he diverges from Aristotle by exchanging a metaphysical–biological teleology for a social one and by accepting that the existence of conflicting goods may not just be a consequence of flaws in an individual's character.

For MacIntyre, the social nature of moral development consists of a three-stage approach. For the virtues to be properly conceived, as well as developed, they must first be embedded within practices. By practices, MacIntyre means established cooperative activities through which people make an effort to realize the goods internal to the activities while at the same time exerting themselves to achieve the standards of excellence in them (*After Virtue: A Study in Moral Theory*, 187). Participants of practices can aspire to receive two types of goods. The first are goods external to the practice itself, such as a reward for winning a game or recognition for being the best. As people engage in a given practice, however, goods internal to it become more of a primary focus. These goods are internal to the practice in a two-fold respect; they can only be understood within its structure and they can only be recognized through experience and participation. Initially, the achievement of excellence is a product of obedience to the practice's rules and acceptance of the authority of set standards. As a person's skills are developed, however, excellence results from the expansion of one's understanding and involvement in the practice beyond the confines of the general rules. An excellent participant is able to apply the rules in new and expansive ways that allow for superior performance. When a given practice pertains to moral life, the excellences acquired are the virtues and the internal goods acquired relate to human flourishing. They must also be accompanied with a narrative for a single human life that gives comprehensibility to those practices as a means to achieve human flourishing. This allows people to place different events in their life in an account that provides a unity of character and accountability. By setting practices within a narrative, the virtues that one acquires become more than just dispositions that sustain the practices; they become part of a broader scope and serve to allow a person to develop his or her life story as he or she searches for the good. Finally, both practices and the narrative must be part of a larger tradition. See Alasdair MacIntyre, *After Virtue: A Study in Moral Theory* (Notre Dame: University of Notre Dame Press, 1984) 195–196.

21. The primacy of reason and the ideal of a life of intellectual contemplation in an Aristotelian framework is a consequence of conflating a thing's form with its purpose, that is, that which makes a thing unique determines the activity which it is meant to pursue. Many

contemporary conceptions of identity, however, attribute many different abilities to human beings without conflating any of those abilities with the purpose of humanity.

22. For example, his notion of a person's *telos* is different from that of Aristotle, and his views of character development and practical reason differ from Aristotle despite the fact that he uses Aristotelian arguments to describe his views. His divergence from non-Jewish Aristotelian philosophy is due to his adherence to Jewish foundational premises, in particular his acceptance of the primacy of Jewish law in shaping one's character and reasoning.

   That Maimonides differs even from his Arabic contemporaries in the way he adopts an Aristotelian framework can be seen in the practical ramifications of their respective philosophies as it pertains to the supremacy of the prophecy of Moses for Maimonides and Muhammad for the Arabic philosophers and the authority of the law for the different philosophers. For example, Alfarabi, one of Maimonides' greatest influences, does not consider Muhammad's prophecy unique, and he holds that for the philosopher who has acquired true wisdom, observing the doctrines in the Qur'an would be superfluous at best and a diminishing of his wisdom at worst. Like Alfarabi, Avicenna asserts that it is possible to achieve perfection so as to become the type of prophet that Mohammed was, and, since the details of the Qur'an as told by the Prophet were relayed only with the intention that it best serve those unable to comprehend philosophic truth, for one who is philosophically gifted, it would be logically consistent to transgress *Shariah* yet claim to uphold the reality of the Qur'an as revealed to him personally. Maimonides, on the other hand, continually upholds the premise that Moses' prophecy is unique and that the law can never be abrogated, even by those who have become prophets themselves. These practical differences reflect a greater difference in the overall philosophical framework that each one developed. Of course, this premise is general, and Maimonides does provide an explanation for certain exceptions, where the law is abrogated temporarily, such as in the case of Elijah.

23. This is not to say that there are not contemporary philosophers who hold alternative or contrary views, but rather that these are dominant positions in contemporary philosophy.

24. A global character trait is one that exhibits both cross-situational consistency in a wide variety of circumstances and is stable in repeated instances of the same kind of circumstances.

CHAPTER 2

Teleology: One of Aspiration and Not Actualization

INTRODUCTION

The path of life goes upward for the wise.[1]

Moses Maimonides' ethics can be seen as a synthesis between Aristotelian virtue ethics and Divine command morality, where God's law[2] sets the terms for ethical action and Aristotle's philosophy provides the explanation for the process of moral development. However, Maimonides' ethics is not simply Jewish law dressed in Greek philosophical garb, nor is it Greek philosophical ethics residing within the four cubits of Halakha. Rather, Maimonides uses Aristotelian philosophical language to describe a Jewish ethics that emerges from Jewish law. Moreover, even though Maimonides uses an Aristotelian framework upon which to base his teleology, he does not do so in a way that would make a contemporary Jewish virtue ethics that builds on Maimonides dependent on Aristotelian physics and metaphysics. Therefore, in constructing a contemporary Jewish ethics, I can still rely on Maimonides' teleological account of ethical development without being constrained by an Aristotelian worldview.

The idea of a synthesis between virtue ethics and Divine command morality might seem to be a contradiction, both axiologically and ontologically. Axiologically, the contradiction lies in how a person recognizes and adheres to what is ethical. In the former, a person relies on his or her own wisdom to determine what is ethical, while in the latter, and especially in Jewish ethics, the person relies on God and an external law. G.E.M. Anscombe argues that the perception of ethics through

© The Author(s) 2017
I. Bedzow, *Maimonides for Moderns*,
DOI 10.1007/978-3-319-44573-1_2

a legal framework and the perception of ethics as a matter of attaining virtues are wholly distinct and that the attempt to combine ethical legalism and the virtues results in a confused moral theory. Anscombe admits that Aristotelian ethics has a sense of norms, but she denies that ethical norms are equivalent to law.[3] Norms, according to her understanding of Aristotle's ethics, are general descriptions of character traits which demonstrate that a person has a particular virtue. They are not prescriptive demands to be ethical; rather, they are descriptive criteria, which allow a person to be defined as such.

Others have argued that the idea of virtue is found in all ethical frameworks, and therefore, any claim to synthesize a virtue- and a law-based ethics is misleading.[4] However, while it is true that Kantian ethicists discuss the idea of virtue, its meaning is very different than what is meant by virtue ethicists because their ethical frameworks are inherently different. In a Kantian ethics, moral virtue is developed through one's ability to abide by a self-legislated, yet external law, for Aristotelians, virtue is developed alongside one's ability to ascertain what is good.

Anscombe is correct that for Aristotle the virtues are not directly related to a set of rules that prescribe actions in a way that Kantian ethics has rules or maxims, and that the definition, or description, of a particular virtue is not fixed, but is rather continually refined via experience. Yet the difference between the two types of ethical frameworks is not simply that virtue ethics focuses on the development of character traits while rule-based ethics focuses on particular actions. Rather, virtue ethics, as well as those religious ethical traditions such as Maimonides' which incorporate virtue ethics into their framework, subsumes the community and public laws into its ethics while rule-based ethics does not.[5] The laws of the community (and religious law) serve the dual function of prescribing actions and, through those prescriptions, intend for the individual to develop certain character traits.[6] Divine command morality can therefore allow for the incorporation of virtue ethics when Divine law is both personal and communal and when it focuses on the development of character traits in addition to focusing on particular actions.

In *The Fabric of Character*, Nancy Sherman explains how Aristotle conceives law to relate to the acquisition of the virtues. According to her, Aristotle believes that the law is a necessary, yet not sufficient, means to acquire the virtues. Its necessity stems from the fact that it establishes impartiality by ordering society according to "objective" practical reason. By "objective" practical reason, I mean that rationality of the law is based on the general consensus of the community and is not the product of any one individual. Its insufficiency stems from its inability to take into account the particularities of moral life. It must therefore be supplemented by a sense of equity to account for those particularities. Also, according to Aristotle, the law cannot influence the cultivation of dispositional capacities and must, therefore, be supplemented by social relationships, such as friendship. While I am not negating the need for friendship or recognition of the particular in a Maimonidean ethics, by the end of the book I will show that Maimonides differs with Aristotle on these two premises about the law.

For Aristotle, as well as Maimonides, civil law tries to regulate social life so that it is conducive for individuals to attain *eudaimonia*. It forms a continuing part of the education of character begun at home, where the political community serves the role previously played by parents. The law, therefore, not only compels just behavior but it also teaches people how to be just. The following passage from Aristotle demonstrates both the social nature and the teleological presupposition of his ethics, and the necessity of law for an individual's moral development:

> To obtain the right training for virtue from youth up is difficult, unless one has been brought up under the right laws. To live a life of self-control and tenacity is not pleasant for most people, especially the young. Therefore, their upbringing and pursuits must be regulated by laws; for once they have become familiar, they will no longer be painful. But it is perhaps not enough that they receive the right upbringing and attention only in their youth. Since they must carry on these pursuits and cultivate them by habit when they have grown up, we probably need laws for this, too, and for the whole of life in general.[7]

Aristotle does, however, recognize that people can act lawfully yet lack good character. The difference between Kant's and Aristotle's view of law and its relation to ethics is that for Aristotle ethics begins at the level of society, and it is society's conception of the good that shapes individuals' characters. For Kant, on the other hand, ethics begins at the level of the individual, and it is individuals' conceptions of the good which ultimately affect society's structure. Therefore, for Aristotle, the law is not set against ethics; rather, it is both a cause and a consequence of it. It is a cause by virtue of its effect on its adherents, and it is a consequence of ethics in that legislation and judicial decisions are made, and improved, by those ethical legislators and judges who have been shaped by the community's laws. As we will see, Maimonides has a more comprehensive role for the law, since it is a consequence of God's will and not ethical legislators and judges as Aristotle posits, yet his conception of the law still allows for a synthesis of virtue ethics and Divine command morality.

Ontologically, the seeming contradiction in creating a synthesis of virtue ethics and Divine command morality is that in Divine command morality, morality derives its authority from, and is based upon, Divine commands, while in virtue ethics "the good" is not based on a theological presumption. To avoid this tension and to mitigate the assumption that Divine command morality is arbitrary, some have tried to equate God with the good. This attempt, however, is unsatisfactory for a theology that admits that one cannot describe God essentially, except apophatically, even if it is possible to describe God's attributes of action. To dismiss the attempt to conflate God and the good, one could make mention that the prophet Isaiah, in recognizing that God created the world, has already circumvented the challenge posed in the *Euthyphro* when he states, "Thus says Hashem ... I form the light, and create darkness; I make peace, and create evil; I am Hashem that does all these things."[8] God's will does determine morality, yet morality is not arbitrary because of this. Rather, in creating the world, God created a morality that best suits it.[9] While one can still argue that morality might then be arbitrary, the verse in Isaiah can stop the infinite regress by allowing us to accept as a theological premise that God created a moral order for the world with the intention that it be good.[10]

Others have claimed that Divine commands do not make something right and wrong necessarily, nor are they sufficient to apply to all situations; therefore, there must be a combination of moral goodness and Divine command which allows a person to know the good in certain situations. This claim accepts Aristotle's critique of law, and it also allows for the notion that there is an ethics that is independent from Halakha. With respect to the argument that there must be a combination between moral goodness and Divine command due to the contingency of certain situations, Rabbi Aharon Lichtenstein, in his essay, "Does Jewish Tradition Recognize an Ethic Independent of Halakha?," argues that while there is an internal morality of the law, it is procedural rather than substantive and it intends for the law to reach excellence in its application.[11] The internal morality of the law is thus part of the law itself. A morality that is an external system has no place in influencing the Halakha. Rabbi David J. Bleich argues further, claiming that contingency does not mean that an independent ethics joins with Halakha, even if it is an internal one. Differing legal opinions can equally be expressions of the Halakha, and need not entail that jurists have differing moral or religious views from each other or from the law itself. Rather, disagreement lies in the application of internal rules of procedure. Therefore, despite the aspirational nature of Jewish law, Rabbi Bleich denies any relationship between Halakha and even an internal, independent (Jewish) morality.[12]

Though this will be discussed further in later sections, in brief, Maimonides claims that God's laws are equated with truth, thereby eliminating the tension between Divine command morality and virtue ethics. Also, though Maimonides believes that truth can be discovered through philosophical investigation, the moral weight of that truth comes from one's recognition that it is grounded in God's law and that one's ethical goal is to follow that law out of love for God. This can be shown in what Maimonides writes with respect to adherence to the Noahide laws,[13] yet it would certainly apply to the Jews' adherence to the Torah as well:

> Anyone who accepts upon himself the fulfillment of these seven command-ments and is precise in their observance is considered one of the pious among the gentiles and will merit a share in the world to come. This applies only when he accepts them and fulfills them because the Holy One, blessed be He, commanded them in the Torah and informed us through Moses, our teacher, that Noah's descendants had been commanded to fulfill them previously. However, if he fulfills them out of intellectual conviction, he is not a resident alien, nor of the pious among the gentiles, nor of their wise men.[14]

For Maimonides, Divine command is the source for the good on an onto-logical level and recognition that God commanded them is the source for the good on an epistemological and axiological level. Therefore, the Noahide laws, which David Novak calls the natural law component or the moral component of Jewish law,[15] have normativity solely by virtue of its legality.

While Maimonides' ethics, and my contemporary translation of it, posits that Jewish law constitutes what should be considered as moral action, his theory is different from many other Divine command theories of morality in that obedience to the law does not automatically mean that actions are morally ideal. The separation between what is legal and what is moral occurs because, as a legal system, Jewish law must accommodate a broad spectrum of society. Therefore, that which is generally permitted by the law sets the floor for moral action, but still may not be condoned as the highest ethical imperative.[16] Nor is the law impervious to people manipulating it in an immoral fashion. For example, Nahmanides, who agrees with Maimonides' premise that the law sets the floor for what constitutes moral behavior, writes that the Torah permits a person to have relations with his wife and to enjoy meat and wine, yet a person who is addicted to (permitted) sexual relations or who is a glutton (albeit who eats kosher food) is nevertheless a sordid person, despite acting within the strict boundaries of what is legally permitted.[17] Similarly, one who adheres to Jewish law for ulterior motives may act properly in the legal sense, yet he or she would nevertheless be lacking the proper motivation to be moral. Like most other forms of virtue ethics, right action alone is not sufficient to be considered moral. The actor must also act from a moral disposition or character.

****

The substantive differences between Aristotle's and Maimonides' ethics are readily apparent when one compares their respective arguments for what is, or, in Maimonides' case what should be, a person's motivation in life as well as their views on a person's ultimate purpose or life activity. Aristotle contends that people are ultimately motivated to pursue their own development, whereby a person's potential lies in an activity that is unique and innate to the person as a member of humanity (*ergon*),[18] and the achievement of excellence in that activity (*telos*) results in a person's achievement of perfection or completion (*entelecheia*). *Telos*, therefore, connotes a person's final cause, while *entelecheia* connotes a person's formal cause. To be more specific, *entelecheia* is related to *energeia* (both of which are translated as "actuality" as opposed to "potentiality/*dunamis*") in that it is the actualization of a person's potential with respect to his or her unique activity (*ergon*).[19] *Entelecheia* is also related to *telos* in that it provides the means to fully engage in one's unique activity successfully.

Entelecheia, therefore, has two connotations; either it can connote the form which allows for the activity to be performed properly (this connotation being more closely aligned with *telos* as its etymology makes clear) or it can connote the excellent performance of the activity itself (this connotation being more closely related to *energeia*). Aristotle recognizes these two connotations when he discusses the term *entelecheia* in *De Anima*. He writes with regard to the soul being the *entelecheia* of the body, "Now there are two kinds of *entelecheia* corresponding to knowledge and to reflecting. It is obvious that the soul is an *entelecheia* like knowledge; for both sleeping and waking presuppose the existence of the soul, and of these waking corresponds to reflecting, sleeping to knowledge possessed but not employed, and knowledge of something is temporally prior."[20] In this passage, the soul is an *entelecheia* as a formal cause; it is what enables a person to act but it is not acting per se. Yet because *entelecheia* has that second connotation, Aristotle acknowledges that the soul is only the first entelechy, and that the second entelechy of a person consists in his or her living an active life. James Hart explains the two connotations as follows:

> In Aristotle's primary sense, "entelechy" derives from the consideration of the action accomplished or brought to its term in contrast to action that is in the course of being realized. Thus entelechy (actualization) is *the perfection characteristic of the achievement* or the actual complete unity. Yet there is a second but not disconnected sense of entelechy: the form (*eidos*), or *the inherent principle of structure* or specific intelligibility that *enables a determinate actualization of a power*. Here entelechy refers to a formal-essential actuality that functions as the actuation of *hylē* and is therefore in regard to this functioning not yet complete or fully actual. Toward that end it works immanently in the realization of that *telos* or perfection. Entelechy in this sense is like actually possessed knowledge that precedes new acts of knowing.[21]

Because of the way in which physics and metaphysics interact in Aristotle's framework, the goals that people will come to endorse are those that they ultimately find in themselves. Moral and intellectual development is about actualization rather than aspiration, and normativity is a consequence of the inherent desire for personal growth and the understanding that a particular decision will help to achieve it.

Maimonides' account adopts Aristotle's language of actualization in describing moral and intellectual development, yet it replaces Aristotle's naturalistic description of a person's motivation with a religious one. The result of this inclusion is that Maimonides' ethics cannot be seen as fully accepting Aristotle's notions of *ergon*, *telos*, and *entelecheia*; rather, his use of those terms must be understood in the context of the religious worldview according to which a person develops toward moral and intellectual perfection. According to Maimonides, human perfection is a consequence of a religious goal and not a primary focus of motivation.

In giving my account for a contemporary Jewish virtue ethics, I will keep Maimonides' description of a person's source of motivation and his view of a person's ultimate purpose, yet I will not keep the Aristotelian idea of having a unique, species-wide function (*ergon*). By doing so, moral and intellectual development will not be a matter of actualization but rather of aspiration and of achieving one's goals.[22] Of course, one cannot say that Aristotle's teleology does not have an aspirational component, since his whole premise that *eudaimonia* is something that people want to attain presupposes that his teleology is at the same time natural/metaphysical as well as desired. By calling my teleology one of aspiration, I only mean to say that it does not include the notion of actualization in the Aristotelian sense. As such, my description will differ from Maimonides' theory as well, yet it will not contradict his general outline.

Even though my account is not teleological in the Aristotelian sense,[23] it is nevertheless teleological. Also, my account recognizes that while a person's "unique activity" is not intrinsic to his or her physical essence, a person nevertheless still has a definite "unique activity," albeit one that is based on how society situates him or her in a system of values. In other words, a person's goals and ideals are socially, rather than physically, established and they are understood through a person's recognition of causal relations as they are interpreted through a presupposed set of goals.[24] This view of teleology is in accord with John Searle's explanation of how purposes are found in nature. He writes,

> It is because we take it for granted in biology that life and survival are values that we can discover that the function of the heart is to pump blood. If we thought the most important value in the world was to glorify God by making thumping noises, then the function of the heart would be to make a thumping noise, and the noisier heart would be the better heart. If we valued death and extinction above all, then we would say that a function of cancer is to speed death. The function of aging would be to hasten death, and the function of natural selection would be extinction. In all these functional assignments, no new intrinsic facts are involved. As far as nature is concerned intrinsically, there are no functional facts beyond causal facts. The further assignment of function is observer relative.[25]

The goals which an individual aspires to achieve, and the ideals which a community upholds, are recognized through the values embedded in the community's institutions, namely in its laws and tradition. By living according to the law, a person will engender a disposition that allows him or her to recognize the values embedded within the law and will aspire to become the type of person the law is meant to assist the person in becoming. Normativity is a consequence of an external relationship between a person and the community in which he or she lives as it is structured by

Divine commands, and a person's moral growth is based on how he or she internalizes that relationship, not in how what is already internal yet in potential becomes manifest and actualized through a person's moral and intellectual development.[26]

In this chapter, I will briefly review Aristotle's *ergon* argument and his conception of *eudaimonia* as the actualization of a person's innate species-wide potential, and then I will show how Maimonides' adoption of Aristotle's language and general framework does not make his religious teleology dependent on his physics and metaphysics. I will conclude by discussing the implications of Maimonides' divergence from Aristotle for my own teleology of aspiration.

ARISTOTLE AND EUDAIMONIA

If a person tells you there is wisdom among the nations, believe him. If he tells you there is Torah among the nations of the world, do not believe him.[27]

Aristotle's account of natural development presupposes that everything in the world has a unique activity toward which it is primarily suitable, and the good for that particular thing constitutes the proper performance of that unique activity. Aristotle's biology, physics, and metaphysics presuppose that such natural development is due to the existence of four causes, namely, the material, the formal, the efficient, and the final cause. A cause is more than just a force that acts upon a body, as it is typically conceived in contemporary parlance; it includes the broader sense of being an explanation for how something has transpired and, therefore, includes reasons as a subset. While this may not have great import in Aristotle's physics, in my construction of an alternative view of practical reason, I will make a sharp distinction between reasons and causes. The material cause of something is its non-accidental potential, that is, the primary potential from which a thing would develop if left to its own accord under the right conditions. It is the aspect of a thing's natural development which is determined by the matter of which it is made. The formal cause is that which determines the specific arrangement, shape, or appearance according to which a thing will develop; it is what gives a thing its inherent structure according to its unique function.[28] What motivates a thing to move toward that aim or end is the efficient or intermediate cause. The final cause is that which is ultimately sought and for which everything is ultimately done.[29] The final cause is also intrinsic to a living being; it is the principle by which the being moves toward its end,[30] and in reaching it the thing attains completion and perfection vis-à-vis its unique activity.[31] The natural teleological process of each living thing is for the material cause of the thing to become perfected according to the dictates of its formal cause,[32] yet perfection is achieved through, or because of, the impetus of efficient causes.[33] Ultimately, though it is by no means inevitable,[34] the change toward which the thing will be directed is its final cause, thereby moving it from a state of potentiality to actuality. This process is innate, though efficient causes may be external, since the manner in which a thing will respond to external causes is based on its material and formal causes. Moreover, each thing has a strong teleological inclination toward its final cause.[35]

In his ethics, Aristotle starts with the premise that every activity[36] and every choice has a good[37] as its aim. Additionally, a good may either be intermediate, that is, for the sake of another good, or it can be final, for its own sake. After a brief survey investigating human motivation in the beginning of the *Nicomachean Ethics*, Aristotle argues that *eudaimonia*, that is, living well (*eu zēn*) and doing well (*eu prattein*) in the sense of living a life that fulfills one's humanity, is—or should be[38]—the chief good which people desire to attain.[39] The happiness of which *eudaimonia* consists, however, is not simply any kind of happiness. Rather, in addition to being that which motivates people, *eudaimonia* also perfects individuals,[40] by giving them the capacity to engage in their unique activity, that is, in using their intellect properly.[41] In other words, the happiness of *eudaimonia* consists of living a complete life of actively engaging in rational thinking.[42] Aristotle writes,

> For no function has so much permanence as excellent activities (these are thought to be more durable even than knowledge), and of these themselves the most valuable are more durable because those who are blessed spend their life most readily and most continuously in these; for this seems to be the reason why we do not forget them. The attribute in question, then, will belong to the happy man, and he will be happy throughout his life; for always, or by preference to everything else, he will do and contemplate what is excellent, and he will bear the chances of life most nobly and altogether decorously, if he is "truly good" and "foursquare beyond reproach."[43]

As Aristotle notes, rational activity only constitutes *eudaimonia* when it is the type of activity that is worthy to pursue in and of itself.[44] Also, rational activity is not a means to *eudaimonia*, where the possession of knowledge is the ultimate end. Nor should rational activity be for the sake of lesser goods, which themselves are sought for the sake of happiness.[45] Rather, even when seeking lesser goods through rational activity, the rational activity and the seeking of lesser goods are part and parcel with the person naturally fulfilling his or her unique activity in life.[46]

There are two types of rational activity, each corresponding to a different aspect of a person's soul. The rational component of the soul achieves excellence through intellectual activity, namely through engaging in theoretical wisdom. The appetitive component of the soul, that is, the will, on the other hand engages in practical wisdom and complies with it, and a person achieves excellence through moral activity, which helps to develop moral virtues. The moral virtues, however, do not consist solely of excellence of the appetitive part of the soul independent of any relationship with the rational part of the soul. On the contrary, there is a tight relationship between the moral virtues and reason (through the implementation of *phronesis*) as well as in the other direction between certain intellectual virtues, such as *phronesis* and deliberation, and the moral virtues.

In the *Nicomachean Ethics*, Aristotle seems to equate *eudaimonia* with the contemplative life (though this is subject to great debate),[47] since it is a life that most appropriately utilizes that which is uniquely human. He does, however, recognize that a life of constant contemplation is impossible. Therefore, though contemplative activity cannot be a constant pursuit, Aristotle, nevertheless, urges that one still attempt to engage in it to the best of his ability, since it allows for the achievement of perfection and one's *telos*.[48] Because people are not purely intellect, Aristotle recognizes that the moral life of practical wisdom is also a eudaimonic life, albeit to a secondary degree. Happiness comes from the activity of the moral excellences, yet it is of a secondary degree since such a life does not completely engage one's intellect, which Aristotle sees as something separate and as partly Divine. (Though Aristotle maintains that the soul in general cannot be separated from the body, since it is the first actuality/entelechy of a natural body or object,[49] with respect to the human intellect, however, Aristotle does maintain that a person's active intellect is immortal.[50])

MAIMONIDES AND SERVING GOD FROM LOVE

And I will delight myself in Your commandments, which I have loved.[51]

Maimonides accepts Aristotle's premise that what motivates people also gives them the ability to engage in their unique (species-wide) activity properly. Yet Maimonides does not adopt Aristotle's naturalistic teleology strictly; rather, he recognizes that humans have a religious priority and he thus incorporates a theological framework into Aristotle's ethical one. By doing so, Maimonides contends that a person's motivation is theological, and that moral and intellectual development is a consequence that supports a person's true aspirations (*telos*) rather than being primary motivations in and of themselves.

In describing the type of life a person should be motivated to pursue, Maimonides uses a modified version of Aristotle's *ergon* argument.[52] In the introduction to his *Commentary on the Mishna*, Maimonides rejects the simple understanding of the Talmudic expression, "The Holy One, blessed be He, has nothing in this world except for the four cubits of Halakha,"[53] (namely that Jewish law is the height of intellectual study and should be pursued at the expense of all other areas of knowledge) based on his acceptance of Aristotle's premise that humans have a unique activity or purpose. Moreover, the exercise of this unique (species-wide) activity is superior to learning Jewish law in the simple juridical sense.[54] Like Aristotle, Maimonides asserts that the prime uniqueness of human beings rests in their capacity for theoretical reasoning, and thus a person's perfection consists in acquiring the ability to contemplate theoretical wisdom properly.

Though the unique (species-wide) activity of human beings is engaging in theoretical reasoning, and thus their entelechy is in perfecting their intellect, Maimonides nevertheless does not describe the *telos* of the wise and good person as living a life solely engaged in theoretical speculation. On the contrary, his *telos* is to contemplate wisdom, by which he means grasping the principles of reality and how they relate to God's will, *as well as to engage in actions*, by which he means to engage properly in those actions which God commands.[55] It is true that Maimonides does at times emphasize contemplation, and because of this, many scholars have argued that Maimonides believes that the life of human perfection is a life of intellectual contemplation alone.[56] Yet, at other times, he writes that a life of action is the ideal. For example, at the end of *Moreh Nevukhim*, Maimonides writes regarding one who has attained perfection, "The way of life of such an individual, after he has achieved this [intellectual] apprehension, will always have in view loving-kindness, righteousness, and judgment, through assimilation to His actions, may He be exalted, just as we have explained several times in this Treatise."[57] Isadore Twersky, David Hartman, Lenn E. Goodman, and Menachem Kellner have argued that, in truth, Maimonides' ideal is achieved when contemplation and action are united. In Kellner's words, "while perfection of the intellect is surely to be prized above all other perfections, it is not in itself the final end of human existence but itself serves as a way of deepening, enriching, and elevating observance of the mitzvot."[58] The unity of intellectual apprehension and proper action as the ideal is different than Aristotle's claim, who also recognizes that acting, and not just contemplation, can lead to *eudaimonia*, since for Aristotle it is only to a secondary degree and not as an ideal.

Maimonides further distances his theory from Aristotle's in how he defines his terms. For Aristotle, a person's entelechy and *telos* refer to the same activity, albeit in different ways. For Maimonides, the term "entelechy (שלמות/כאמל)," which connotes a person's actualized ability, is defined as intellectual contemplation, while a person's "*telos* (תכלית/אלגאיה)," that is, the action of which humans are uniquely suited, is to serve God. The difference between Aristotle's conception of the relationship between *telos* and entelechy and Maimonides' is best exemplified in Maimonides' commentary on *Mishna Sanhedrin* 10:1. Maimonides, analogous to how Aristotle starts his *Nicomachean Ethics*, begins with a discussion of what is the proper conception of happiness. He uses as his starting point the premise that all actions are meant to aim at some good,[59] and he discusses various opinions regarding the type of happiness that comes from the fulfillment of the commandments as well as the manner of punishment that results from transgression. After noting a number of erroneous opinions, Maimonides quickly asserts that the error of all of the opinions he has brought, besides for confused theological notions, is that the motivation for each of them is to achieve a certain state of being and not the pursuit of a given activity. Therefore, the proposed motivations and the ultimate goals of these opinions disregard the value of the activity which they believe serves as the means to an ideal state of being. The error of these opinions is that they do not understand that the true good is an activity; therefore, they seek a good of lesser worth, whether it is physical reward[60] or the opportunity to become a leader or a judge so as to receive praise and honor. In both instances, a person's motivation is for something of less value and the person's development is considered to be inferior to the type of person that he will become by virtue of active engagement.[61]

The true ultimate goal for Maimonides is the acquisition of the wisdom of the Torah. He writes, "One should consider the only end of learning [Torah] is knowing it, and so the only true end is to know that it is true and that the commandments are true and thus their end will last." Moreover, he claims that the Torah is a great good, since it brings a person to perfection (שלמות/כאמל). Yet, unlike Aristotle's contemplation of the Divine, which comes with no prescriptive force except for that which is self-imposed and which directly relates to a person's motivation for self-actualization, the wisdom of the Torah possesses a normativity that is external to the intellectual understanding of the person and which should be fulfilled with deference to that external authority. Therefore, to return to his interpretation of the Talmudic expression brought above, that "The Holy One, blessed be He, has nothing in this world except for the four cubits of Halakha," Maimonides writes that a person fulfills his purpose when he contemplates the wisdom of God as it is manifest and as the person manifests it in the world through the four cubits of Halakha.

Maimonides confirms this relationship between practical activity and theoretical wisdom in the introduction to his *Commentary on Mishna Avot*. He writes that a person should direct all his powers of thought to knowing God to the best of his ability, and he also includes that one should direct all his actions as well as his speech toward the goal of knowing God.[62] Similarly, in the *Mishne Torah*, he writes that the path to attaining love of God is to contemplate "His wondrous and great deeds and creations and [to] appreciate His infinite wisdom that surpasses all comparison."[63] Even still, when a person has achieved perfection and truly serves God from love, his attention and contemplation of God pervades every action.[64]

Maimonides' differentiation between a person's *telos* and his entelechy is furthered by his replacing Aristotle's contention that a person's ultimate goal is to achieve *eudaimonia* for its own sake with the belief that acquisition of the wisdom of Torah and fulfillment of its commandments should not be for the sake of personal development but rather for the purpose of serving God from love. This purpose should also be one's sole motivation for acting.

Maimonides does accept the theological premise that the ultimate good and final end of a person is to participate in the World to Come. Though he calls it an essential good without comparison, the World to Come does not play a strong role in his description of a person's teleology. This is demonstrated by the fact that even though it is the ultimate good and though it is only attained through the performance of the commandments, Maimonides strongly asserts that it is not what should motivate a person to obey the Torah. Nor is it an activity which demonstrates that which is uniquely human. He writes,

The world to come is the ultimate end towards which all our effort ought to be devoted. Therefore, the sage who firmly grasped the knowledge of the truth and who envisioned the final end, forsaking everything else, taught: "All Jews have a share in the world to come." Nevertheless, even though this is the end we seek, he who wishes to serve God out of love should not serve Him to attain the world to come. He should rather believe that wisdom exists, that the wisdom is the Torah; that the Torah was given to the prophets by God the Creator; that in the Torah He taught us virtues which are the commandments and vices that are sins.[65] As a decent man, one must cultivate the virtues and avoid the sins. In doing so, he will perfect the specifically human which resides in him and will be generally different from the animals.[66]

Through serving God from love, a person will achieve perfection and will thus merit the World to Come, yet the activity of serving God is not for the sake of this future state of being. Maimonides' grounding for human moral and intellectual development thus differs from Aristotle's in that Aristotle maintains throughout his ethics that *eudaimonia* is both the *telos* and the motivation for human development. For Maimonides, on the other hand, a person's immediate and ultimate motivation should be to serve God from love, his entelechy is self-perfection through acquiring the wisdom of the Torah, and his *telos* is acting according to its commandments. The consequence of reaching one's *telos* of serving God properly is achieving the World to Come, which occurs after death.

Maimonides' teleology is very difficult to understand in the context of Aristotle's naturalistic framework, since a person's motivation and *telos* are different than the pursuit of the activity which is innately unique to human beings (*ergon*) and which is perfected by virtue of achieving his entelechy. From an Aristotelian standpoint, if serving God from love is one's immediate motivation for the sake of self-perfection, then serving God would be a lesser good than self-perfection, yet Maimonides explicitly calls serving God from love superior to self-perfection since serving God from love is sought for its own sake (while self-perfection is not). This difficulty, however, is based on the assumption that Maimonides wholly adopts Aristotle's naturalistic framework. Yet, for Maimonides, the uniqueness of a human being is not simply the potential to be a self-actualized rational person, but rather to be a true servant of God. For Maimonides, self-perfection is a consequence of serving God from love and the means by which one can best act as God's servant, yet self-perfection is never a goal or a good in and of itself.[67]

To accord with the Aristotelian premise that the highest good is sought solely for its own sake, one might think that Maimonides' distinction between self-development and serving God from love is a false dichotomy. One would then conflate seeking human perfection and serving God from love. Yet Maimonides seems to stand firm in his distinction between the two. This distinction is also accepted by later Jewish philosophers. For example, Rabbi Yosef Albo writes that the uniqueness of human beings lies in their intellectual capabilities, but that the actualization of their intellectual potential alone does not constitute human perfection. Rather, he writes explicitly that true perfection is achieved when a person acts with the intention of doing what is good and upright in God's eyes, and does not act to benefit oneself *or for any other intention at all*, whether that be wealth, strength, or even wisdom. One's ultimate goal should be only to live according to God's will.[68] Maimonides does recognize that serving God from love is itself a very difficult motivator. Even if one can understand it intellectually, he or she may still not be motivated by it, as it may not be viewed as a direct benefit.

A description of the same teleology is repeated in the *Mishne Torah*. Maimonides asserts in *Hilkhot Teshuva* that the ultimate good is the World to Come,[69] and that whoever fulfills the commandments of the Torah and comprehends its wisdom with complete and proper knowledge will merit it according to the magnitude of his deeds and the extent of his knowledge.[70] However, despite the fact that the World to Come is the ultimate good, a person should not be motivated by its attainment. Rather, proper motivation for fulfilling the commandments is to serve God from love.[71] In a similar vein as in his *Commentary on the Mishna*, he writes in the *Mishne Torah*,

> One who serves [God] out of love occupies himself in the Torah and the commandments and walks in the paths of wisdom for no ulterior motive: not because of fear that evil will occur, nor in order to acquire benefit. Rather, he does what is true because it is true, and ultimately, good will come because of it. This is a very high level which is not merited by every wise man. It is the level of our Patriarch, Abraham, whom God described as, "he who loved Me," for his service was only motivated by love. God commanded us [to seek] this rung [of service] as conveyed by Moses as [Deuteronomy 6:5] states: "Love Hashem, your Elohim." When a man will love God in the proper manner, he will immediately perform all of the commandments [and be] motivated by love.[72]

In contradistinction to his account in his *Commentary on the Mishna*, in the *Mishne Torah* Maimonides does not speak of self-perfection. This is possibly because the focus in the *Mishne Torah* is how to best fulfill the commandments, and thus it only discusses the direct relationship between a person's motivation and *telos*, and not the process of human development which is ancillary to it. The *Mishne Torah* is primarily a legal work, and any philosophical content that it contains is for the purpose of providing a proper perspective to ground observance. It is not a philosophical work meant to discuss the moral and intellectual effects the law has on a person who is engaged in the acquisition of wisdom.

Because Maimonides uses Aristotelian terms to describe his teleology, an ambiguity arises with respect to the relationship between performing the commandments from a motivation to serve God from love and performing them because they are right or true. This ambiguity relates to the question, discussed above, of how it is possible to synthesize Divine command morality with virtue ethics. To resolve this ambiguity, both in his *Commentary on the Mishna* and in the *Mishne Torah*, Maimonides cites as a proof-text for serving God from love the statement of Antigonos Ish Sokho, "Be not like a servant who serves his or her master for the sake of reward; but rather like a servant who does not serve his or her master for the sake of reward; and let the fear of Heaven be upon you."[73] In the *Mishne Torah*, he even concludes the quote in a way that insinuates that Antigonos' statement is a completely accurate description of what it means to serve God from love.[74] Yet as seen above in the quote from the *Mishne Torah*,[75] Maimonides also writes that the person who serves God from love does what is true because it is true. In his *Commentary on the Mishna*, he also defines serving God from love as believing in truth for the sake of truth.

This ambiguity became a point of contention among Maimonides' critics. For example, one medieval critic argued that the whole notion of being a servant is that one acts out of necessity and obligation and not for the benefit of acting, whether that benefit is a reward or is simply the benefit of acting on one's own convictions. Moreover, this critic contended that the assertion that one should act from conviction betrays a philosophical perspective which denies Divine providence over particular individuals, for otherwise the person's actions would be motivated by serving God and not by following truth.[76] Maimonides' critics fail to see, however, that he makes no distinction between what is true and what God wills. For example, in *Moreh Nevukhim*, he writes, "For only truth pleases Him, may He be exalted, and only that which is false angers Him. Your opinions and thoughts should not become confused so that you believe in incorrect opinions that are remote from the truth and you regard them as Law. For the Laws are absolute truth if they are understood in the way they ought to be."[77] As a result, the seemingly two reasons for acting, that is, from love of God and for the sake of truth, are actually one. There is thus no tension between serving God from love and acting out of conviction of the truth, since the recognition of God's will is also recognition of what is true in both the ontological and normative sense. Lenn E. Goodman has eloquently explained this idea as follows: He writes, "The Torah speaks of autonomy, not in Kant's language but in its own, when it calls on us to love God with all our heart, with all our soul, and with all our might (Deut. 6:5). What this means, as Maimonides explains, is that we serve God faithfully when we do what is right for its own sake. This honors God, by acknowledging the intrinsic goodness and wisdom of his commands."[78] Maimonides gives both reasons in his *Commentary on the Mishna* and in the *Mishne Torah* so as to explain what is meant by truth and what constitutes service from love.[79] Therefore, to act as a servant who does not expect reward is to act from love and from a voluntary commitment to God. Nevertheless, in order to remember the proper role one has in his or her relationship with God, so that one's actions are theonomously motivated and not autonomously legislated in the Kantian sense, the fear of Heaven should be upon the person.

****

Because Maimonides makes a distinction between a person's motivation and *telos*, on the one hand, and his or her capabilities and their actualization, on the other, my contemporary teleological account can adopt the theological part of Maimonides' framework while replacing the Aristotelian explanation with one more contemporary. The ability to do so is made easier by the fact that Maimonides' description of a person's motivation and *telos* is in terms of an external relationship, that is, between the person and God, and not in terms of an internal relationship between a person's potential and its actualization. Therefore, a contemporary teleology can explain how a person is better able to fulfill the demands of that relationship without needing to rely on the premise that the possibility of its fulfillment is innate.

Serving God from love demands desire, effort, experience, *and a proper understanding of what God wants of the person and not only what the person wants for himself or herself.* The two-sided nature of the relationship presupposes the idea that personal development is not wholly personal in that a person's goals are not simply based on the perfecting of the exercise of an activity that is unique to his or her constitution. Rather, a person's ultimate goal is to develop a relationship with God, which demands certain activities. Those activities may refine an individual,[80] but they do so not because they bring out a person's natural abilities. They do so because they strengthen the person's commitment to serving God with love. Also, once the goal is not self-perfection, the process of reaching one's goal can be described in terms of improving one's abilities to attain it rather than in terms of maturation or perfection.

As a broad stroke description, which will be further developed in the remainder of the book, a contemporary Jewish virtue ethics would have the following trajectory: A person would be instructed to adhere to the laws of the Torah from childhood, which would serve to inculcate proper moral habits. Education of the Torah would not only include instruction of how to act in a given situation but it would also include instruction in practical/juridical reasoning of the various laws as well as theoretical reflection on the Torah as a comprehensive system. The different levels of education will correspond to different levels of moral maturity. This education will serve to develop the person's intellectual virtues. It will also allow for the person to appreciate his or her obedience to the law as an end in and of itself rather than as a means to avoid punishment or receive reward. As the person continues to develop his or her moral and intellectual capabilities, loving adherence to the law will be perceived as a means to strengthen one's relationship to God. Therefore, adherence will become easier and internal conflict between personal desires and Torah values will diminish. Happiness/*simcha* will also become a natural consequence of daily living. As one can see, this broad stroke trajectory reflects a Maimonidean virtue ethics. The difference between Maimonides' trajectory and my contemporary version lies in the details of how this can be achieved and explained in a contemporary world.

NOTES

1. Proverbs 15:24.
2. Wherever I mention the law in reference to Maimonides' ethics, unless the context demonstrates otherwise, I mean Jewish law (Halakha).
3. G.E.M. Anscombe, "Modern Moral Philosophy," *Virtue Ethics*, eds. Roger Crisp and Michael Slote (Oxford: Oxford University Press, 2007) 40.
4. For example, in her essay, "Virtue Ethics: A Misleading Category?," Martha Nussbaum acknowledges that virtue ethics is predominantly considered a distinctive approach to utilitarian and Kantian ethics, yet she claims that this taxonomy is incorrect, since both utilitarianism and Kantianism speak of virtue. See Martha Nussbaum, "Virtue Ethics: A Misleading Category?" *The Journal of Ethics*, Vol. 3, No. 3 (1999) 165.
5. Even virtue ethicists, such as Iris Murdoch, who do not discuss the role of public rules for the achievement of the good still admit of their necessity. For example, Murdoch's comparison of aesthetics and ethics presupposes a set of rules to which the artist and moralist must adhere. Similarly, MacIntyre's discussion of practices as a means for moral education includes the need for practices to have well-defined rules.
6. Alasdair MacIntyre gives a similar critique as Anscombe regarding the incomprehensibility of modern rule-based ethics, yet, in contrast to Anscombe, he recognizes that Aristotelian ethics and religious, law-based ethics have a teleological presupposition. According to MacIntyre, both Aristotelian and religious, law-based ethics assume that people transition from an untutored state to a state where they have actualized their potential. Therefore, in religious, law-based ethics, God's laws are not only a command to service; they are also teleological injunctions which lead to the acquisition of good character traits. *After Virtue*, 53.
7. *Nicomachean Ethics*, 296.
8. Isaiah 45:7.
9. BT *Makkot* 23b.
10. BT *Sanhedrin* 38a; BT *Berakhot* 60b.
11. This is similar to the idea proposed by Lon Fuller where the internal morality of the law relates to the way in which a system of rules

should be constructed and administered in order for it to effectively govern behavior. It is a morality of aspiration rather than of duty, in that it attempts to shape the law based upon an idea of excellence while recognizing, at the same time, that under varying circumstances different principles will take precedence over others in order to ensure excellence in a given context. (Lon Fuller, *The Morality of Law* [New Haven: Yale University Press, 1964])

12. David Bleich, *Contemporary Halakhic Problems Volume 1* (New York: Ktav, 1977) xvi.

13. The Noahide laws are normative for non-Jews, and were prescriptive for Jews before the giving of the Torah (BT *Hullin* 100b). The Noahide legal system consists of seven general instructions concerning adjudication, idolatry, blasphemy, sexual immorality, bloodshed, robbery, and eating a limb torn from a living animal (Tosefta *Avoda Zara* 8:4–6; BT *Sanhedrin* 56a-b), and they are identified as being within the first commandment given to the first human being, "And Hashem Elohim commanded regarding the man saying, 'Of every tree of the garden you may certainly eat' (Genesis 2:16)." Even though the laws were given to the first human being, they are still called "Noahide laws," since mankind is considered to be descended from Noah after the Flood. The general nature of the Noahide laws allows for the existence of differences in moral temperament among different societies, even if the broader ethical outlines are the same. Given a certain location, customs may develop that may be different from those in other places due to the constraints of geography, demography, and economy. With varying customs will come varying social perspectives and, hence, different nuances in moral temperament. The relationship between law and ethics is therefore easier to see through a more comprehensive legal system, such as Jewish law, than through a more general one.

14. *Hilkhot Melachim* 8:11. This seems to be the correct version of this Halakha as supported by textual and contextual analysis. See, however, Schwarzschild, "Do Noachites Have to Believe in Revelation? (A Passage in Dispute between Maimonides, Spinoza, Mendelssohn and H. Cohen). A Contribution to a Jewish View of Natural Law: The Textual Question" and "Do Noachites Have to Believe in Revelation? (Continued)" for further discussion.

15. See his *Natural Law and Judaism.*

16. Walter Wurzburger explains Rabbi Soloveitchik's statement, "Halakhah is not a ceiling, but a floor," to mean that "Jewish piety involves more than meticulous adherence to the various rules and norms of religious law; it also demands the cultivation of an ethical personality…We are commanded to engage in a never-ending quest for moral perfection, which transcends the requirements of an 'ethics of obedience'…[The] halakhic system serves merely as the foundation of Jewish piety" (Walter Wurzburger, *Ethics of Responsibility: Pluralistic Approaches to Covenantal Ethics* (Philadelphia: Jewish Publication Society, 1994) 3).

17. Commentary Leviticus 19:2.

18. Christine Korsgaard explains this idea as follows: "So when Aristotle says that the function of a human being is the activity of the rational part of the soul, he does not mean simply that reasoning is the purpose of a human being. Nor does he mean merely that it is a characteristic activity of human beings, if we understand that to mean only that it is an activity which, as it happens, picks out the species uniquely. He means rather that rational activity is *how we human beings do what we do*, and in particular, how we lead our specific form of life." See Christine M. Korsgaard, *The Constitution of Agency: Essays on Practical Reason and Moral Psychology* (Oxford: Oxford University Press, 2008) 141.

19. Aristotle writes as follows: "τὸ γὰρ ἔργον τέλος (For the *ergon*" is the *telos*), ἡ δὲ ἐνέργεια τὸ ἔργον (and the *energeia* is the *ergon*), διὸ καὶ τοὔνομα ἐνέργεια λέγεται κατὰ τὸ ἔργον (hence the term "*energeia*" is derived from "*ergon*"), καὶ συντείνει πρὸς τὴν ἐντελέχειαν (and tends to have the meaning of "*entelecheia*")." *Metaphysics* 1050a21.

20. *De Anima* 412a22–26.

21. "Divine Truth in Husserl and Kant: Some Issues in Phenomenological Theology," *Phenomenology of the Truth Proper to Religion: Critical Essays and Interviews*, edited by Daniel Guerrière, 222.

22. If one replaces the notion of an objective, species-wide *telos* for a non-Aristotelian *telos* of aspiration, then any neo-Aristotelian aretology that does not recognize the weakness of a wholly internal validation of morality may risk turning moral objectivity and realism into moral subjectivity and relativism. In my framework, Jewish law plays a role in creating an objective moral standard. Through

fulfilling the commands of Jewish law, not only does each action have value in helping a person achieve his or her moral goal(s) but each action also has immediate moral relevance as a fulfillment of a Divine command.

23. Michael Bradie and Fred Miller have argued that, for Aristotle, accounts of a living being's development through natural necessity is essentially incomplete and must be supplemented by a metaphysical teleology. Not only does a being develop due to the constraints of its natural composition, but inherent in its being is a metaphysical *telos* toward which natural development progresses. For example, In *Physics*, Aristotle writes, "Now surely as in action, so in nature; and as in nature, so it is in each action, if nothing interferes. Now action is for the sake of an end; therefore the nature of things also is so (*Physics* 199a9-12)."

See Michael Bradie and Fred D. Miller, Jr., "Teleology and Natural Necessity in Aristotle," *History of Philosophy Quarterly*, Vol. 1, No. 2 (April 1984) 133. See also Allan Gotthelf, "Aristotle's Conception of Final Causality," *Philosophical Issues in Aristotle's Biology*, eds. Allan Gotthelf and James G. Lennox (Cambridge: Cambridge University Press, 1987) 204–242; David Charles, "Aristotle on Hypothetical Necessity and Irreducibility," *Pacific Philosophical Quarterly*, Vol. 69 (1988) 1–53; Susan Sauvé Meyer, "Aristotle, Teleology and Reduction," *Philosophical Review*, Vol. 101 (1992) 791–825; and Christopher V. Mirus, "The Metaphysical Roots of Aristotle's Teleology," The Review of Metaphysics, Vol. 57, No. 4 (June 2004), 699–724.

24. One may argue that a socially based *telos* may engender ethical relativism. See, however, my section below on epistemic and moral objectivity, where I try to respond to this challenge.

25. *The Construction of Social Reality*, 15–6.

26. Of course, it is not absolutely determined that a person will achieve his or her final end, nor is that end exactly the same for everyone, since physical limitations and functional advantage given those limitations will affect a person's trajectory. Also, the inevitability of reaching one's final end is always subject to the inexactitude of chance or, in the case of humans, luck. Of chance, Aristotle writes, "That there are principles and causes which are generable and destructible without ever being in course of being generated or destroyed, is obvious. For otherwise all things will be of necessity,

since that which is being generated or destroyed must have a cause which is not accidentally its cause (*Metaphysics* 1027a 29-32)." Luck, on the other hand, uniquely affects humans since it is specifically tied to the realm of action, which includes a deliberative component. As Aristotle writes, "Chance and what results from chance are appropriate to agents that are capable of good fortune and of action generally. Therefore necessarily chance is in the sphere of actions. This is indicated by the fact that good fortune is thought to be the same, or nearly the same, as happiness, and happiness is a kind of action, since it is well-doing. Hence what is not capable of action cannot do anything by chance (*Physics* 197b1-9; See also *Physics* II: 4–6)." As such, Aristotle denies any notion of strict determinism. Moreover, Aristotle is not a complete determinist because he held that even though all events have definable causes, he did not accept that there was a universal nexus of causes and effects. Also, because he believes that nature does not provide laws but rather norms that are accurate for the most part, indeterminacy is inherent in nature. See D.M. Balme, "Greek Science and Mechanism: II. The Atomists," *The Classical Quarterly*, Vol. 35, No. 1/2 (January–April 1941).

Aristotle was also not essentialist in his biology but rather recognized that natural necessity and functional advantage played a role in individual differences among animals in a species. Moreover, the inevitability of reaching one's final end is calculated differently for humans than for other living beings, since humans are measured on an individual scale, whereas everything else is measured on the scale of the species.

However, because Aristotle held that practical and theoretical wisdom was objective, and that people possessed a rational faculty to some degree, diversity would lie in limitations of one's rational faculty and not in the functional advantage of having a unique rational faculty. For information on Aristotle's biology not being essentialist, see D.M. Balme, "Aristotle's Biology was not Essentialist," *Archiv für Geschichte der Philosophie*, Vol. 62, No. 1 (1980) 1–12. Aristotle therefore had a monistic view of human flourishing, whereby ultimate actualization rests in theoretical contemplation and penultimate actualization is found in political activity. See below, however, where I show that this hierarchy is not so stark and that both activities are appropriate at different times. Because of his view of humanity's species-wide function, Lenn

Goodman explains, "Individuality, for Aristotle, in large part meant idiosyncrasy, accident, and contingency. Matter, differentiating, even isolating particulars, gave such free rein to welter the conflicting causes that the network of interactions readily escaped analysis, letting the unwary imagine that chance rules in nature." (Lenn Goodman, "Individuality," *Judaic Sources and Western Thought: Jerusalem's Enduring Presence*, ed. *Jonathan Jacobs* (Oxford: Oxford University Press, 2011) 248).

27. Ecclesiastes Rabba 2.

28. This differs from Plato's conception of forms, which are different from the objects that represent them. For Aristotle, a substance is a compound of matter and form; they are never separated even if they are distinguished. The form of a living being, for example, is what Aristotle calls its (first) entelechy or soul.

29. *Physics* II 2, 194a29–30; *Parts of Animals* I 1, 642a1.

30. *Physics* II 2, 199b15–16.

31. See *Metaphysics* 1012b33–24; *Physics* 194b16-195b30.

32. Though the final cause is a principle inherent to a living being, it should not be conflated with its formal cause. The formal cause is what makes an object what it is, that is, its blueprint or design, yet it continually changes as the being develops. The final cause, on the other hand, does not change. Also, unlike the final cause, the formal cause is not normative, that is, it does not direct a thing toward a particular goal; it, rather, enables the thing to progress toward that goal. Moreover, the formal cause is an immediate end of coming to be, while the final cause is the activity the thing performs when it comes to be.

33. *Physics* 192b21.

34. Reaching one's final end is always subject to the inexactitude of chance or, in the case of humans, luck.

35. See footnote 23.

36. According to Aristotle, there are four different types of goal-directed pursuits, namely, craft, inquiry, action, and decision. A craft is a type of production that is aimed at some goal beyond its own exercise. Similarly, an inquiry and a decision also aim at something beyond its own exercise. An activity, on the other hand, aims to pursue itself and does not seek anything further. An activity includes a decision to act as well as the action itself.

37. A good, according to Aristotle, is what is sought.

38. Aristotle begins his analysis by basing the premises of his ethical theory on the empirical observations of social life, yet he does not justify his theory or ground the normativity of his framework strictly on empirical data. My assertion that Aristotle bases the premises of his ethical theory on empirical observations of social life is based on the following statement: "Presumably, then, we must begin with things familiar to us. ... For the facts are the starting-point, and if they are sufficiently plain to him, he will not need the reason as well; and the man who has been brought up has or can easily get starting-points" (NE 1095b2–8). Yet, as Sara Broadie has shown, Aristotle's choice of reason as that which is uniquely human is based not only on the fact that people are able to reason but also from a normative judgment that reason is a person's most important characteristic, at least ethically speaking (Sarah Broadie, *Ethics with Aristotle* (New York: Oxford University Press, 1991) 36).

39. The reason why *eudaimonia* is considered the chief good, even though people also choose pleasure, honor, intelligence, or the virtues as goods, is that the latter four are also chosen for the sake of *eudaimonia*. *Eudaimonia*, on the other hand, is the only thing that is chosen as worthy of pursuit in and of itself. Aristotle gives the first three examples because he divides interpretations of the life of happiness (*eudaimonia*) into three categories, namely, the life of pleasure, the political life, and the contemplative life. The fourth example, that is, the virtues, is given because his theory is a virtue-based ethics and the option is involved in two of the three modes of living.

40. That is, it is the final cause. NE 1102a1–4.

41. Therefore, it is also related to a person's material and formal causes.

42. NE 1098a7–18. The end achieved via rational activity, however, is not automatic, despite the fact that it is natural. Unlike the final end for other species, human happiness through rational activity demands the possibility of failure as part of the requirement for success. Otherwise human excellence would not be uniquely human. This point is tied to Aristotle's view of luck and human responsibility. If achieving *eudaimonia* were automatic, then reason would not play a role in human excellence. If it were based on chance, Aristotle writes, "To entrust to chance what is greatest and

most noble would be a very defective arrangement (NE 1099b23-24)." Therefore, for human reason to be a factor in human excellence, it must be a factor in the choices that humans make toward achieving what is good. This does not preclude deleterious effects of luck on human fortune, which can hinder a person from achieving happiness due to actions that are outside of his or her control.

43. NE 1100a12–21.

44. A eudaimonic life is also a noble one, as Aristotle writes, "Happiness then is the best, noblest, and most pleasant thing and these attributes are not severed (NE 1099a24–25)."

45. For example, someone may seek intelligence to get a good job to earn a lot of money to have a happy lifestyle. Aristotle does admit, however, that to live a life of happiness it is oftentimes necessary to achieve a certain level of prosperity. It is not that external goods make a person happy; rather, they allow a person to achieve happiness by making it possible to live life in fulfillment of what truly makes the person human.

46. For example, though rational activity may be used to determine which lesser goods one should desire and in finding the best way to achieve them, it is through rationally trying to promote these lesser goods that a person achieves the chief good of *eudaimonia*. In other words, happiness comes by virtue of rational pursuit and not as a consequence thereof. A rationally active person seeks to attain these lesser goods because he or she understands that their pursuit is a good in and of itself, though in a different sense than the person's own *telos* is considered a good per se.

47. See footnote 61.

48. NE 1177b27-1178a8.

49. *De Anima* 412b5–15.

50. See *De Anima* III:5. Because his views in the *Nicomachean Ethics* seem to waver between the ideal of the contemplative life at the expense of everything else and the ideal of the contemplative life with the recognition that it cannot be the only activity in which one can engage at all times, there are three schools of thought as to how to understand Aristotle's view of the eudaimonic life. The exclusivist view contends that contemplation is the only ultimate cause worth pursuing. Every other pursuit is an intermediate cause whose ultimate goal is contemplation. The inclusivist view, on the other hand, argues that the eudaimonic life cannot consist of only

one activity; there must be a collection of activities which allow one to live well and be happy. The terms "exclusivist" and "inclusivist" were coined by W.F.R. Hardie in his book, *Aristotle's Ethical Theory* (Oxford: The Clarendon Press, 1968).

The third view describes the eudaimonic life as follows: Though social beings, what is most human about human beings is their capacity for rational thought, both theoretical and practical, of which the former is the superior of the two and can be performed solitarily. Similarly, both work and leisure are necessary components of life (See *Politics* 1337b33–4). Therefore, when one is working, the good life consists of practical activity consisting of moral excellence. At times of leisure, happiness consists of engaging in the best activity, that is, theoretical contemplation. Furthermore, when engaged in practical activity, the person of excellence will understand more than just the practical aspects of the activity. He or she will choose a certain action because it is both good and noble to do so (NE 1120a23), and in acting he or she will learn more than just the practical knowledge that the activity imparts. The reason for this is because the theoretical knowledge that he or she possesses will serve to ground practical reason in a grander vision of the world. The person is happiest in leisure, yet also lives well while having to engage in social life. This view attempts to reconcile Aristotle's position in the *Nicomachean Ethics* with his views in the *Eudemian Ethics* and in *The Politics* and it is similar to Sara Broadie's interpretation of the eudaimonic life as provided in Chapter 7 of *Ethics with Aristotle*. I believe this view also fits best with Maimonides' understanding and adaptation of Aristotle's framework for his own moral theory. See Lenn E. Goodman's *God of Abraham*, where he writes, "The great difference between Maimonides and Saadiah here, then, parallels that between Aristotle and Plato. For where Plato sees a competition among rival goods, which reason must adjudicate, Aristotle trusts the idea of organicism to arrange all the aims of a healthy life in the order most conducive to our highest aim, *eudaimonia*, in which contemplation is the noblest and freest but hardly the sole or all-sufficing activity. Maimonides, like Aristotle, sees the activities of life—waking and sleeping, eating, drinking, and making love—not as mere additive or partitive components of the good life but as organic constituents, means to an end, which life as a whole pursues, and which Maimonides, echoing Plato (*Theaetetus* 176), calls an approach to God. The quest is not a blinkered pursuit of mystical union, although its summit does promise contact or communion (*ittiṣāl*) with the divine. Rather, it is an inclusive, active, and practical, as well as speculative and contemplative, realization of human perfection that makes us akin to God. The singleness of our goal and the unity of the good life represent an organic rather than exclusive unity." (153)

51. Psalms 119:47.

52. In the same way that Aristotle's *ergon* argument necessitates acceptance of the premise that a person voluntarily chooses his or her trajectory, so does Maimonides accept the premise of free choice. See *Hilkhot Teshuva* 5:2–3, 5; 6:5. See also *Shemonah Perakim*, Chapter Eight. Though Shlomo Pines and Alexander Altmann have argued that Maimonides upheld the notion of determinism. See "Excursus. Notes on Maimonides' Views Concerning Free Will" in "Studies in Abul-Barakat al-Baghdadi's Poetics and Metaphysics," *Studies in Philosophy, Scripta Hierosolymitana*, Vol. 6 (Jerusalem: Magnes Press, 1960) 195–198, and "Free Will and Predestination in Saadia, Bahya and Maimonides," *Religion in a Religious Age*, ed. S.D. Goiten (Cambridge: Harvard University Press, 1974) 25–52. Gad Freundenthal accounts for Maimonides' acceptance of free will by distinguishing between a person's biological constitution, which determines one's propensity to act in a certain way, and a person's actual behavior, which is under the control of his or her intellect. See "Maimonides' Stance on Astrology in Context: Cosmology, Physics, Medicine, and Providence," *Moses Maimonides: Physician, Scientist, and Philosopher*, eds. Fred Rosner and Samuel S. Kottek (Northvale: Jason Aronson Press, 1993) 77–90.

53. BT *Berakhot* 8a.

54. Daniel Frank has shown that though Maimonides accepts Aristotle's premise that the uniqueness of human nature rests in the intellect, in *Shemonah Perakim* he differs greatly from Aristotle

with respect to the nature of the human soul and its similarity to animal souls. According to Aristotle, humans are rational animals, meaning that their uniqueness lies solely in their rational capacity; all parts of the human soul except for the intellect are the same as those possessed by animals. Maimonides, on the other hand, thinks that humans are wholly unique; the "animal" aspects of their souls, such as the nutritive, sentient, imaginative, and appetitive parts, are only analogous to those which are found in animals, but they are not the same (See *Shemonah Perakim*, Chapter 1). Frank notes, however, that Maimonides adopts Aristotle's conception of the human soul in *Moreh Nevukhim*, and he supports his assertion based on his reading of *Moreh Nevukhim* III:54. Yet, one need not accept, as Frank does, that Maimonides changed his view. In his discussion of true human perfection in *Moreh Nevukhim* he writes that corporeal perfection belongs to man qua animal, yet he continues to write that this is because man has this in common with animals. As such, one need not read the two sources as contradictory but rather they can be seen as consistent. For Frank's analysis, see Daniel Frank, "'With All Your Heart and With All Your Soul': The Moral Psychology of the Shemonah Peraqim," *Maimonides and the Sciences*, eds. R.S. Cohen and H. Levine (London: Kluwer Academic Publishers, 2000) 25–33.

55. The assumption that Maimonides does not intend that the ideal life be one of pure theoretical contemplation but still nevertheless contains theoretical contemplation as a dominant activity is supported by his immense aversion to the notion that Torah scholars be supported on account of their scholarship. In his commentary on *Mishna Avot*, which warns that whoever derives benefit from the words of Torah removes his life from the world, Maimonides admonishes those who advocate for communal support of Torah scholars and calls such an institution a desecration of God's name (*Mishna Avot* 1:7). In the *Mishne Torah*, his censure is even stronger (*Hilkhot Talmud Torah* 3:10–11).

56. MN III:8; MN III:27; MN III:51. Isaac Husik, Alexander Altmann, and Harry Blumberg, hold this position.

57. MN III:54; Pines, 638. Because of passages like this, scholars have argued that Maimonides' conception of the ideal life is either a

moral or a political one. Scholars who argue that the ideal is moral include Hermann Cohen, Julius Guttman, and Steven Schwarzschild. Scholars who argue that it is political include Leo Strauss and Lawrence Berman.

58. See Isadore Twersky, *Introduction to the Code of Maimonides* (*Mishneh Torah*), 363–4 n18; David Hartman, *Maimonides: Torah and Philosophic Quest*, 26; Lenn E. Goodman ("Happiness," *The Cambridge History of Medieval Philosophy, Volume 1*, 461; and Menachem Kellner, *Maimonides on Human Perfection*, 10. See also H.A. Wolfson, "Classification of Sciences in Medieval Jewish Philosophy," *Hebrew Union College Jubilee Volume* (Cincinnati: HUC Press, 1925) 263–315; and Shalom Rosenberg, "Ethics," *Contemporary Jewish Religious Thought*, eds. Arthur A. Cohen and Paul Mendes-Flohr (New York: Scribner, 1987) 195–202."

59. Compare NE 1095a16–30.

60. Compare NE 1095b19–22.

61. Compare NE 1095b22–30.

62. *Shemonah Perakim*, Chapter Five.

63. *Hilkhot Yesode HaTorah* 2:2.

64. See *Hilkhot Deot* 3:3; *Hilkhot Teshuva* 10:3.

65. In truth, Maimonides holds that virtues and vices are dispositions or character traits that are reinforced by observing the commandments or by sinning. The passage suffers from an ambiguous translation.

66. Commentary Mishna *Sanhedrin* 10:1, translation in Moses Maimonides and Isadore Twersky, *A Maimonides Reader* (New York: Behrman House, 1972) 416.

67. This interpretation of Maimonides' theological ethics is similar to the interpretation of Isadore Twersky, David Hartman, and Lenn E. Goodman. For example, Isadore Twersky writes, "The goal of all commandments is fear and love of God, but the consequence of this fear and love is not only the *vita contemplativa* but a deepened, more sensitive, highly motivated performance of laws. (*Introduction to the Code of Maimonides (Mishneh Torah)*, 363–4 n18)." David Hartman writes, "The primacy of action is not weakened by the contemplative ideal; a deeper purpose for the normative structure is realized instead once the philosophic way is

followed. The contemplative ideal is not insulated from halakha, but affects it in a new manner (*Maimonides: Torah and Philosophic Quest*, 26)." Similarly, Lenn E. Goodman writes, "Awareness of God's perfection is the ultimate object of the human quest. But that awareness does not compete with other human goals. Intellectual consumption spills over into holy acts of guidance and generosity ('Happiness,' *The Cambridge History of Medieval Philosophy, Volume 1*, 461)."

68. *Sefer Ikkarim, Maamar* 3, *Perek* 5.
69. *Hilkhot Teshuva* 8:1; 9:1.
70. *Hilkhot Teshuva* 9:1.
71. *Hilkhot Teshuva* 10:1.
72. *Hilkhot Teshuva* 10:2.
73. *Mishna Avot* 1:3.
74. See *Hilkhot Teshuva* 10:4, where he writes, "In a similar manner, the great Sages would command the more understanding and brilliant among their students in private: Do not be like servants who serve their master [for the sake of receiving a reward]. Rather, since He is the Master, it is fitting to serve Him; i.e., serve [Him] out of love."
75. *Hilkhot Teshuva* 10:2.
76. See Isaac Abravanel's *Nahalot Avot* on *Mishna Avot*.
77. MN II:48, Pines 409.
78. Lenn E. Goodman, *God of Abraham* (New York: Oxford University Press, 1996) 96–7.
79. See *Hilkhot Shehita* 14:16, where he writes, "For the commandments in and of themselves are not worthy of honor. Instead, [the honor is] due He, blessed be He, who commanded us to observe them and [thus] saved us from groping in darkness and thus granted us a lamp to straighten crooked paths and a light to illumine the upright ways. And so [Psalms 119:105] states: 'Your words are a lamp to my feet and a light for my ways.'"
80. "What does God care whether a man kills an animal in the proper Jewish way and eats it, or whether he strangles the animal and eats it? Will the one benefit Him, or the other injure Him? Or what does God care whether a man eats kosher or non-kosher animals?

'If you are wise, you are wise for yourself, but if you scorn, you alone shall bear it. (Proverbs 9:12)' So you learn that the commandments were given only to refine God's creatures, as it says, 'God's word is refined. It is a protection to those who trust in Him (2 Samuel 22:31)' (*Midrash Tanhuma, Shemini*)."

CHAPTER 3

Telos: To Be a Servant of God

INTRODUCTION

You are My witnesses, says Hashem, and My servant whom I have chosen; that
you may know and believe (ta'aminu) Me, and understand that I am He;
before Me there was no God formed, neither shall any be after Me.[1]

As with both Maimonides and Aristotle, I will begin my description of
moral and intellectual development with the goal for doing so, and I will
adopt Maimonides' goal that a person should aspire to serve God with
love. Different from Aristotle, yet still in line with Maimonides' philosophy, in my contemporary framework, a person's *telos* of serving God with
love is an externally imposed goal with which one identifies and internalizes. It is not based in an internal, essential part of human nature in the
same way that Aristotle describes the four causes.[2] After describing what
serving God with love means in practice, I will continue in the following
chapters to explain how doing so allows one to develop moral and intellectual virtues.

Though Maimonides uses the term *eved Hashem* (servant of God) to
describe a person who has achieved his *telos*, in contemporary society the
words used to translate *eved*, namely "slave" and "servant," frequently
have negative connotations,[3] which can affect their positive import when
used to denote a theonomous relationship. Moreover, the Biblical idea of
being a servant of God connotes a qualitatively different type of relationship than other forms of servitude found in the Bible. To explain, the
Bible discusses two types of servitude, that of an *eved Kena'ani* (Canaanite

© The Author(s) 2017
I. Bedzow, *Maimonides for Moderns*,
DOI 10.1007/978-3-319-44573-1_3

slave) and that of an *eved Ivri* (Israelite servant), yet neither model can serve as an analogy to inform what constitutes being a servant of God. The Torah permits a person to own a Canaanite slave,[4] and forbids a person to free his slave, except possibly for the sake of another commandment.[5] One is also not obligated to provide sustenance for his slave, and, according to the law, he may have him perform excruciating labor. Jews are nevertheless urged to treat their Canaanite slaves properly.[6] A Canaanite slave is not obligated to keep time-based positive commandments, since he has no control over his own time. This form of slavery is clearly different both in the manner of relationship and in the types of obligations imposed on the servant than that which is found with respect to the type of servitude that entails serving God from love. With respect to an Israelite servant, the Torah discusses this type of relationship in three different places.[7] In each place, the Israelite servant is described more in terms of a hired worker than as a slave. The relationship between master and servant is one of relative equality; the servant never loses his liberty and status as a free person but rather he only relinquishes it for a set period of time. The Torah also refers to the Israelite slave as "your brother," and the Talmudic Sages remark that "one who acquires an Israelite slave is like one who acquires himself a master."[8] This form of servitude also is clearly different in the manner of relationship and in the types of obligations imposed on the servant than the type of servitude that entails serving God from love.

In addition to the fact that other forms of servitude found in the Bible cannot serve as an explicatory model, when one looks to the Bible for examples of servants of God, such as Moses, Joshua, Caleb, Samuel, Ahiyah, Elijah, Jonah, Isaiah, Eliakim, Job, and Zerubabel,[9] one would not consider them as living lives of servitude given our contemporary language and understanding of the term. Moreover, each of these servants of God lived a different life than the others. Similarly, the first man was charged to serve (*l'avda*, related to word *eved*) and protect the Garden of Eden,[10] yet he was not a simple sharecropper who was charged to work the land.

To discontinue using the term "servant of God" would be ineffective, since the Jewish tradition gives the idea great weight as an ideal to which one should aspire. Nevertheless, due to the difficulty with which we can understand its meaning linguistically, even if we can appreciate the way those who were known as servants of God lived, it would be helpful to find a way to describe *how* a servant of God lives that is both conducive to contemporary language and loyal to its traditional meaning. Through the use of this functional description, one could recognize the importance of the Jewish tradition in influencing contemporary notions in Jewish ethics and philosophy, yet he or she would not be encumbered by vocabulary that is no longer properly understood given changes in linguistic connotations. Furthermore, the ideal of being a "servant of God" could be given a practical and efficacious definition for the contemporary world in which we live.

I will, therefore, provide the *definiendum*, "servant of God," with a *definiens* that bridges the understanding of the term in the Jewish tradition with contemporary language so that the intention for using the term is clarified. Unlike a dictionary definition, its meaning will not be rooted in the etymology of the term *eved* but rather in terms that are currently understood and demonstrable of what constitutes the responsibilities and ideals of being a servant of God. Also, the definition will not be a statement of the essence of a servant of God, since such a definition would cause me to slip into a naturalistic teleology. The starting point for my understanding of being a "servant of God" is based on the Talmudic understanding of a verse in Habakuk and its subsequent discussion, since the verse is used in the Talmud to describe the pinnacle of what it means to fulfill the Torah[11]—"the righteous shall live by his faith (*emunah*)."[12]

To Serve God from Love = To Live by Faith

...but the righteous shall live by his faith.[13]

Toward the end of his life, Moses gives a final message to the people and asks them, "And now, Israel, what does Hashem your God require of you, but to fear Hashem your God, to walk in all His ways, and to love Him, and to serve Hashem your God with all your heart and with all your soul; to keep for your own good the commandments of Hashem, and His statutes, which I command you this day?"[14] Though Moses reminds the people that there is only one purpose in life, namely to serve God through observing the commandments, he also describes a moral path which would enable a person to reach this goal as well as develop his or her character accordingly. One may see this by reading Moses' question to the people as follows: "What does Hashem your God require of you? [He requires you] to fear Hashem your God, to walk in all His ways, and to love Him, and to serve Hashem your God with all your heart and with all your soul. How does one serve God and what is the process for moral development? [One must] keep for your own good the commandments of Hashem, and His statutes, which I command you this day." To reach the point where one can serve with all one's heart and soul, one must first acquire a fear of God. One must then walk in His ways, which means to follow the commandments and imitate God's ways even if the person has not yet developed the ability to do so wholeheartedly. Through walking in His ways, the person will begin to love God and will eventually devote his heart and soul to serving Him. At this stage, the person has attained the ability to live a life according to his or her purpose (*telos*).

This process is not teleological in the Aristotelian sense because it denies that there is a paradigmatic biological or physical trajectory which can lead a person toward perfection, yet it is teleological in the normative sense in that the person develops into a more effective servant of God, as it is understood in the context of the verse above. A servant of God loves and fears Him, and walks in His ways through fulfilling the commandments and statutes that He has prescribed. Each descriptive component of the verse, however, is still pregnant with meaning that comes with their being embedded in previous schematic frameworks, and in the remainder of the chapter I hope to provide an appreciation of the terms that can bridge those frameworks with one more contemporary.

Similar to the Maimonidean view, fulfillment of the Torah is not a motivation for self-development, even if its attainment may be a consequence thereof. Rather, self-development serves the purpose of enabling one to better fulfill the Torah's commandments. Also, even if reward and punishment are associated with fulfillment or transgression of the Torah, relying on the words of Antigonos Ish Sokho, one should not be like a servant who serves his or her master for the sake of reward; but rather one should be like a servant who serves his or her master not for the sake of reward.[15] Though belief in the World to Come is a foundational theological premise, belief in it should not be a motivating reason to serve God.

Though the developmental process of attaining the ability to serve God wholeheartedly will be discussed in later chapters, it is important at this point to explain what is meant by fear of God, since it provides the theological grounding for any contemporary Jewish virtue ethics as well as the foundation for how I understand the way moral and intellectual development occurs. Love of God, on the other hand, is less difficult to understand, since there are many contemporary forms of love from which a person can draw an analogy, namely, spousal love, parental love, familial love, and friendship. Though each is different in its own way, each type of love is grounded in appreciating the other and being open to sacrificing for the other's benefit.[16]

Fear of God (Yirat Hashem)

In the Bible, there are two main words that denote fear, that is, *yirah* and *pahad*, yet they are not synonyms. Moreover, each word is associated with a different word for faith/trust, that is, *emunah* and *bitahon*, respectively, which are not true synonyms either.

Pahad is the type of fear that comes with instability; it is the opposite of *bitahon* (trust/security). Similarly, just as *bitahon* can be warranted or not,[17] *pahad* is a personal, subjective feeling of agitation and anxiety which may or may not be appropriate. The relationship between the two words is clear from Isaiah's statement, "Behold, God is my salvation; I will trust (*evtah*), and will not be afraid (*efhad*)."[18]Similarly, among the curses mentioned in Deuteronomy, there is a description of the potential lives of Jews who, if they do not observe God's law, will be scattered among the nations. Their lives are portrayed as hanging in doubt, they fear (*pahdeta*) night and day, and have no assurance of their lives.[19] In each of these examples, *pahad* refers to a sense of immediate anxiety over the insecurity of daily life.

When *Pahad Hashem* is used throughout the Bible, it refers to a fear that comes from a lack of wholehearted commitment. Thus, the person develops a fear that the relationship between him and God has become estranged and that the consequences of this alienation will be dire. For example, in I Samuel, the people have *Pahad Hashem* and follow King Saul after he sends a threatening message to them regarding what will happen if they do not follow him and Samuel the prophet.[20] In Isaiah, *Pahad Hashem* refers to the fear one has at the Day of Judgment.[21] In Hosea, after the Jews return to God, they tremble with fear (*pahdu*) since they are unsure of how God will respond to their return.[22]

Yirah, on the other hand, is the type of fear that comes from insight. For example, the first man becomes afraid (*ayra*) upon hearing God's voice in the Garden of Eden after realizing that he was naked.[23] Similarly, following the war between the kings, Abraham is told that he need not fear (*al tirah*), since his fear was based on incorrect inferences that he had made.[24] Sarah denied laughing over hearing that she would bear a child, since she became afraid (*yera'eh*) after fully understanding the situation.[25] For just one more example, the Israelites had fear (*va'yiru*) in God after they saw what occurred at the Sea of Reeds, yet along with this fear came faith and trust (*va'yaminu*) in God and in Moses, His servant.[26]

Yirat Hashem is therefore not a subjective fear and insecurity, which thereby motivates a person to follow God's commandments. Rather, it is recognition of the relationship one has with God and the corresponding sense of gravitas that such knowledge imparts. Serving God becomes motivation in and of itself, and any thought of the consequences of one's service is minimized. Having a broader respect for one's purpose through *Yirat Hashem* is epitomized by Isaiah's statement,

> And there shall come forth a shoot out of the stock of Jesse, and a twig shall grow forth out of his roots. And the spirit of Hashem shall rest upon him, the spirit of wisdom and understanding, the spirit of counsel and might, the spirit of knowledge and of *Yirat Hashem*. And his delight shall be in *Yirat Hashem*; and he shall not judge after the sight of his eyes, nor decide after the hearing of his ears; but with righteousness shall he judge the poor, and decide with equity for the meek of the land; and he shall smite the land with the rod of his mouth, and with the breath of his lips shall he slay the wicked.[27]

The notion that one is not motivated by consequences when acting from *Yirat Hashem* is further supported when the term is juxtaposed with the Biblical idea of *Pahad Hashem*. A fascinating example of this distinction is when King Jehoshaphat installed judges throughout the cities of the Kingdom of Judah. He told them that they should have *Pahad Hashem*. Yet to the Levites who were to judge in Jerusalem he said that they should have *Yirat Hashem*.[28] The difference between the two is that the judges in the cities in the surrounding areas in the Kingdom of Judah were not as safe as the judges who were in Jerusalem. They could not, therefore, judge the people without worry of social and political consequences, whereas the judges in Jerusalem did not have such a worry and could thus judge more securely.

Acquiring *Yirat Hashem* is the first step toward serving Him because, as King Solomon writes, it is the beginning of knowledge,[29] and wisdom.[30] King David also writes that it is the beginning of wisdom.[31] Though I will discuss the differences between knowledge and wisdom when I discuss intellectual virtues, the point of both statements is that theological awareness grounds moral and intellectual development, which is a premise that Maimonides also held. Moreover, moral and intellectual development cannot be taken for granted, since, as the Talmudic sages infer from Moses' final message to the people,[32] everything is in the hands of Heaven except the fear of Heaven.[33] Therefore, when considering how moral development occurs, one should consider the voluntariness of a person's beliefs and in how they motivate the actions with which they are associated, rather than any innate qualities that a person may possess.[34]

When the motivation for living life a certain way is one's *Yirat Hashem*, the manner in which one ultimately lives is by faith (*emunah*).[35] Not only is this idea supported by the association the two words have in the Bible but, as I will discuss below, it is also reinforced by Habakuk's overarching principle, "the righteous shall live by his faith (*emunah*)."[36]

To say that living by faith is the ultimate manner of living, however, is too broad a statement to be practical or even helpful in describing how those who live their lives as servants of God actually live. Therefore, to describe more clearly the purpose for which a person aspires to live, I will rely on the passage in the Talmud which recounts how various prophets attempted to amalgamate the 613 commandments of the Torah into fewer and fewer principles or categories in order to communicate the ultimate purpose(s) for the commandments.[37] Though the Talmudic passage proceeds to give fewer and fewer principles or categories, I will explain the passage in reverse, starting with the prophet who gives the fewest principles and working back to the 613 commandments, in order to show how the more numerous categories fit into the fewer ones.[38]

> *Habakuk reduced them [the commandments] to one principle, as it is said: But the righteous shall live by his faith (emunah).*[39]

The entire verse from Habakuk is, "Behold, his soul is defiant, it is unsettled in him, but the righteous shall live by his faith." A defiant soul is one that asserts independence and attempts to pursue what it wants without cognizance of what is best. This can be seen from the example of when the Jews defiantly[40] attempted to ascend the mountain against God's will and were then brutally destroyed by the Amalekites and Canaanites.[41] A defiant soul will always be in a state of opposition, and thus can never be settled; not only will there be external opposition, as the soul is defying its Maker, but it will also be at odds with itself, since it will have no anchor on which to ground its judgment and perspective.

The righteous, on the other hand, have faith (*emunah*). *Emunah* is neither blind nor fideistic, where one's belief is independent of his or her rationality; rather, like *yirah* (fear), it connotes understanding of that in which one has faith. *Emunah* is a reliance on something permanent and effective, such as the promises that God made to one who follows His will and who observes the Torah. It is not purely a propositional belief that justifies later action, though it does contain propositional content. The propositional component of faith can be explained through the linguistic relationship between *emunah* (faith) and *emet* (truth), which share a triliteral root. In order to explain the meanings of, and relationship between, *emunah* (faith) and *emet* (truth), I will first provide a linguistic examination of the two terms. Then I will show how their meanings reflect contemporary pragmatist views of truth and belief.

Explanation of the Term "Emunah"

When God is called a God of *emunah*, the context of the verse implies a consistency upon which one can rely so as to make decisions for the future. Moses calls God, "The Rock, His work is complete (*tamim*); for all His ways are justice; a God of *emunah* and without iniquity, just and right is He."[42] His meaning is as follows: Like a stone foundation of a building, the stability and strength of consistently applying a system of justice allows for people to rely on it. God is a God of *emunah* since He does not imperfectly apply His justice, and because of that He is righteous (*tzadik*) and upright (*yashar*).

God calls Moses *ne'eman* after exposing Aharon and Miriam to prophecy when they were not ready for it, thereby showing the difference between them and Moses. In this instance, *ne'eman* (faithful) connotes being constantly prepared and ready at any moment.[43] Similarly, Samuel is called *ne'eman* to be a prophet, because the people saw that everything he said came to fruition.[44] The Biblical commentators recognize that in this instance, *ne'eman* does not only mean reliable but also established; that is, Samuel was both established as a prophet and people relied on him as one because everything he said came to fruition. The common denominator for both connotations is the security that being established and being reliable entails.[45] For more general examples, in the Bible, a *bayit ne'eman*[46] is a poetic allusion for an established, lasting kingdom. A *makom ne'eman* is a secure place into which a peg may be fastened because it can withstand great weight.[47] A faithful priest is one that does what God wants him to do.[48] In all these cases, faith is steadfastness or loyalty to a relationship or to a manner of living. Therefore, when the righteous live by faith (*emunah*), they live wholeheartedly devoted to their purpose, which is based on their understanding of, and having respect for, the relationship upon which it is based. Their manner of living by faith is also a pedagogical paradigm upon which people can rely to instruct them correctly.[49] That faith is manifest in action and not only through cognition is demonstrated in the Bible when Moses incorrectly and out of anger struck the rock in order for it to release water. The Bible states,

> And Hashem spoke to Moses, saying: 'Take the rod, and assemble the congregation, you, and Aharon your brother, and speak to the rock before their eyes, that it give forth its water; and you shall bring forth water out of the rock for them; so you shall give the congregation and their cattle drink.' And Moses took the rod from before Hashem, as He commanded him. And Moses and Aharon gathered the assembly together before the rock, and he said to them: 'Hear now, you rebels; are we to bring forth water out of this rock for you?' And Moses lifted up his hand, and smote the rock with his rod twice; and water came forth abundantly, and the congregation drank, and their cattle. And Hashem said to Moses and Aharon, 'Because you did not believe (*he'emantem*) in Me, to sanctify Me in the eyes of the children of Israel, you shall not bring this assembly into the land which I have given them.'[50]

Because Moses and Aharon did not do as God commanded them, they demonstrated a lack of faith in God's instruction *and they risked teaching the children of Israel that it is acceptable not to sanctify God*. Moses' sin was not lack of belief (in a cognitive sense)—he was in steady communication with God "face to face."

In Biblical Hebrew, whenever the verb form of *emunah*, *he'emin*, is followed by a *b-*, it means that one believes in the person (as in "I believe in you") and, as a consequence, in what he says as well. On the other hand, when the verb *he'emin* is followed by a *l-*, it means that the person believes, or relies on, a particular statement that was made.[51] For example, Abraham believed in (*he'emin b-*) God in general[52]; he did not just believe God's statement that he will have offspring. Similarly, the Israelites believed in (*ya'aminu b-*) God and his servant Moses, after seeing what God did to the Egyptians.[53] Their belief in God was not only in what Moses said in His name; rather, it was trusting in the promise that Hashem will bring them and implant them on the mount of His heritage and the foundation of His dwelling place.[54] On the other hand, Jacob did not believe (*he'amin l-*) his sons when they told him that Joseph was still alive.[55] This is not to say anything about the relationship Jacob had with his sons; it only speaks of his reliance on this particular statement. Rabbi Samson Raphael Hirsch explains the meaning of *emunah*, in his commentary on the verse, "He had put his *emunah* in God and He counted this to him as *tzedaka*,"[56] as follows:

> *Emuna* is the essence of Judaism; but to define *emuna* as "belief" is to empty the term of its true content. Belief is an act of the mind, sometimes only an opinion. Every believer thinks his beliefs are true, based on the reasoning and assurances of someone else. Nowadays, religion is identified with belief, and belief is thought to be the essence of religion. A religious person believes in principles that cannot be grasped by the intellect. Thus, religion has been divorced from life and converted into a catechism of doctrines, a system of faith-slogans, required for admission to the hereafter.
>
> However, to put one's faith in the words of another is never expressed as *he'amin b'*, but as *heamin l'* ... *Emunah b'* is not merely theoretical faith, the subordination of one's own mind to the mind of another. Rather, *he'amin b'Hashem* means: to rely upon God, in theory and in practice; to take strength in Him and to follow Him.
>
> One who replies "*amen*" after a *berakha* does not merely declare the statement to be true; rather, he devotes himself to this truth, accepts it in his heart, and vows to adopt it as the guide for his conduct. *Amen* refers not to the content of the statement, but to the person who hears and accepts it.

Emunah as belief is thus not just a reliance on facts or theoretical statements. It also includes motivation for acting on reliance of those facts or statements. In the theological sense, it is the acceptance of the yoke of the Kingdom of Heaven and the yoke of the commandments, which binds the person in a relationship with God and His world.[57]

Explanation of the Term "Emet"

The most prevalent conceptual metaphor which the Bible uses in relation to *emet* is that of walking. One walks in *emet*,[58] yet *emet* can also describe the path one which on walks as well.[59] The most prevalent collocations in the Bible associate *emet* with *hesed* (loving-kindness),[60] *tzedaka* (righteousness),[61] *mishpat* (justice),[62] *temimiut* (completeness/wholeheartedness),[63] and *shalom* (peace).[64]

When associated with *hesed*, the two words are often built into the phrase, *hesed v'emet*. Only once is *emet* juxtaposed with *hasadim*, and only once does *emet* precede *hesed*. In all cases except for one, both *hesed* and *emet* are things that are done to another person. In the exception, both *hesed* and *emet* are used as descriptive designations for God, which are meant to describe God's actions and not His essence.[65] In the one case where *emet* precedes *hesed* in the sentence, *emet* is attributed to Jacob and *hesed* to Abraham[66]; therefore, if one puts the actions in chronological order, it is no longer an exception. To clarify the meaning of *emet* in relation to *hesed*, I will cite a few of the relevant verses in which they are juxtaposed, as well as the relevant rabbinical commentaries which attempt to explain the relationship between the two terms.

After Eliezer tests Rebecca to see whether she would be an appropriate wife for Isaac, and she successfully demonstrates her worthiness of character, he says, "Blessed is Hashem, the God of my master Abraham, who has not forsaken His *hesed* and His *emet* toward my master; as for me, Hashem has led me in the way to the house of my master's brethren."[67] Radak explains that pursuing the good as obligated is *emet*, and *hesed* is supererogation. According to Radak, therefore, the *emet* that God did toward Abraham was to allow Eliezer to find Rebecca and the *hesed* was for Rebecca to be a direct relative.

After Eliezer tells Rebecca's family what happened and asks for Rebecca to come back with him to marry Isaac, he says, "And now if you will do *hesed* and *emet* with my master, tell me; and if not, tell me; that I may turn to the right hand, or to the left."[68] Rabbi Abraham ibn Ezra explains that *hesed* is something that is not obligatory, and *emet* is to uphold that which is *hesed*. According to Rabbi Abraham ibn Ezra, Eliezer is asking whether Rebecca's family will agree to something of which they are not obligated and then uphold their agreement.

When Jacob returns from Laban's house and Esau advances toward him, he prays,

> O God of my father Abraham, and God of my father Isaac, Hashem, who said to me: Return to your country, and to your kindred, and I will do you good; I am not worthy of all the *hasadim*, and of all the *emet*, which You have shown to Your servant; for with my staff I passed over this Jordan; and now I am become two camps. Deliver me, I pray You, from the hand of my brother, from the hand of Esau; for I fear him, lest he come and smite me, the mother with the children. And You said: I will surely do you good, and make your seed as the sand of the sea, which cannot be numbered for multitude.[69]

Sforno explains that *hasadim* were those things of which Jacob was not worthy and *emet* is the good that was done due to the merit of Jacob's fathers. Similarly, Nahmanides explains that *hasadim* are the kindnesses that God did for Jacob without promising to do them and *emet* is the kindness which God promised to do and fulfilled.

Regarding God's attributes of *hesed* and *emet*,[70] Rashi explains that *hesed* is given to those without sufficient merit, and *emet* to those who obey His will. Based on the examples of this collocation of *hesed* and *emet*, *emet* refers to upholding a previously designated beneficence which originally was voluntarily undertaken. Similarly, when juxtaposed with *shalom*, *emet* is understood as long-lasting or permanent. Also, the Bible always juxtaposes the designation "men of *emet*"[71] with the fact that they are God-fearing, and the biblical commentators understand that the designation refers to the fact that they are trustworthy and that it is therefore appropriate to heed their words. When the Bible refers to God as *emet*,[72] the commentators understand it to signify God's ability to uphold His words. When it refers to the land[73] or to Jerusalem,[74] *emet* signifies steadfastness. When *emet* describes Torah, it is meant to signify that what is being taught is the same as what the teacher believes in his heart.[75]

In all of these cases, *emet* is used to reinforce a voluntarily accepted standard; it is not an external, objective evaluation of a standard. Furthermore, that standard which *emet* upholds is neither static nor strictly theoretical; it encompasses a position that a group takes, and it demands active engagement to fulfill the goals of that position. *Emet* cannot only refer to theoretical truth; it must also refer to truth in practice.[76]

In the rabbinic literature, the Sages infer that God's seal is *emet* from two accounts. The first account occurs during the creation of mankind.[77] The second account occurs during the days of Nehemiah, when the Jews recognized the destructive power of the urge toward idolatry and desired to eradicate it.[78] To explain why God's seal is *emet*, the Sages cite Rabbi Shimon ben Lakish's explanation as to how *emet* relates to God. Just as *emet* consists of the first letter of the alphabet, the last letter, and the middle letter, indicating that it incorporates all means of expressing reality, God is first, last, and there is none besides Him.[79]

The two accounts that demonstrate that God's seal is *emet*, and Rabbi Shimon ben Lakish's explanation for why *emet* should be God's seal, support the conclusion drawn from examining the biblical uses of the word *emet*, that is, that it connotes a truth which is determined by how a person carries out his or her beliefs in action. In the first rabbinic account, the angels recognize that humans perform acts of *hesed* and *tzedek*, but are composed of the opposite of *emet* and *shalom*. The argument between the angels, therefore, is not over the consequences that humans will affect in the world. Rather, it is a comment on God's proclamation to make humankind in His image and likeness. Humans may be able to walk in God's ways by performing deeds of *hesed* and *tzedek*. Yet by virtue of the fact the humans are created, they can never be similar in likeness or image to God. Their existence is finite and full of struggle. In response to the angels' challenge, God throws *emet*, yet not *shalom*, to the ground, proclaiming that it should rise from the same earth of which humans were to be formed. God's response is as if to say that though human life may be filled with strife by virtue of their physical nature, *emet* can be achieved when humans act in the manner which God prescribes, thus allowing them to imitate His image and likeness. Moreover, by throwing it to the ground, God's response indicates that, unlike *shalom*, which is static, *emet* requires continuous action to reinforce it.

In the second account, God again casts *emet* to the ground, yet this time it was to accede to the Jewish people's request to remove the inclination toward idolatry from them. The accession was not a recognition that the people's conclusion regarding the inclination toward idolatry was correct, since even after God's accession the Jews still feared that God would have pity on the inclination and they therefore continued to restrain it. Rather, the casting of *emet* to the ground signified that even the enticement of a potentially harmful lack of clarity does not serve a purpose. In other words, having a "devil's advocate" is not worth the reward of defeating it. Recognition of what is right is most clear when it is not contradicted. For even when false ideas are defeated, they tend to stay with us and make sport of us when we find ourselves in a vulnerable state.

Rabbi Isaac Hutner explains Rabbi Shimon ben Lakish's statement to mean that *emet* expresses the fact that the past is bound to the future through the present. This means that clarity on the present not only gives clarity to the past but it also provides clarity to foresee the future. In other words, *emet* is not an understanding of a moment in time; it is an understanding of how reality has progressed and will continue to progress in time.[80] Moreover, *emet*, as an expression of human language, and *emet*, as God's seal, is only analogous; the two do not equate to each other. Since human perception is myopic, human *emet* is primarily in understanding the past and the present and in having faith in God with respect to the future. The *emet* of God's seal, however, lies in God's faith in humankind's ability to tie the past to the teleological future; it is an *emet* that must be first cast to the ground in order for it to arise from the earth.[81] It is dependent on human action being in accord with God's will.

The word *emet*, therefore, connotes a truth which is determined by how a person carries out his or her beliefs in action. However, those beliefs are neither personal nor subjective; they are anchored by God's revelation and acquired through communal instruction in the Jewish tradition. To walk in *emet* is to live wholeheartedly dedicated to a worldview, with all the practical responsibilities that it entails, and to consider a thing as *emet* is to consider it as correctly situated in one's belief system.

Relationship of Emunah and Emet

As stated above, though *emunah* is not purely propositional, it does have a propositional component. In the Bible, the relationship of *emunah* to *emet* can be seen through the words of the Queen of Sheba, "True (*emet*) was the word that I had heard in my country about your words and your wisdom! I had not believed (*he'emanti l-*) the words until I came and my own eyes saw; and behold—even the half of it was not told to me."[82] The word she heard was not true in the propositional sense, since it was claimed that Solomon was only half as wise as he actually was. Rather, the truth of the word she heard was in its reliability; she did not have to see for herself if she would have only believed, or relied on, the report in the first place.

There is one place in the Bible where *emet* (truth) and *ne'eman* (faithful) are juxtaposed, which highlights the difference between the two. When the people come to Jeremiah the prophet and ask him to pray for them so that God will tell them what they should do, Jeremiah tells them that he will pray for them, and he will also tell them everything that God demands. To this, the people respond, "Let Hashem be a true and faithful witness against us, if we do not act according to everything that Hashem your Elohim tells you concerning us."[83] That God is a true witness (*l'ed emet*) is meant to affirm that the people will do everything that Jeremiah tells them that God demands of them. That God is a reliable witness (*v'ne'eman*) is meant to indicate that they know that He will make sure that the people will receive the warned consequences if they do not fulfill everything that they must do.[84] This explanation is consistent with the understanding of *ne'eman* in the verse, "Know therefore that Hashem your Elohim, He is God; the faithful (*ne'eman*) God, who keeps covenant and mercy with them that love Him and keep His commandments to a thousand generations."[85] He is faithful because He keeps His covenant, and so on. In the case of Jeremiah's statement, truth is not a description of circumstances but an acceptance of a normative obligation. Similarly, faithful is not a reliance on facts but a reliance on the proper response to a fulfillment or breaking of a commitment. The difference between *emet* and *ne'eman*, at least as it is conveyed in this exchange, is more a function of time and tense, and less a matter of justifiability.

Given this relationship between *emunah* and *emet*, the distinction between theoretical knowledge and practical knowledge, or propositional truth and normative truth, becomes less stark than is usually assumed. The relationship between *emet* and *emunah*, as well as "belief that" and "belief in," also tells as much about how a particular belief fits with other beliefs as it says about a person's stance toward a given piece of knowledge. For example, under this conception, it is not the case that a smoker believes the proposition "smoking kills" despite the fact that he or she does not stop smoking. Rather, what occurs is that the smoker's belief in the idea that smoking kills in general is overpowered by his or her belief in the idea that the next particular cigarette he or she will smoke will not do much damage. Both beliefs entail a certain action as a direct consequence, and, when they contradict, the idea with the greater weight will determine what the person will do. The person's behavior is based on how his or her beliefs are prioritized.[86]

The relationship between *emunah* and *emet* also means that the strength of one's reliance on a propositional truth influences the connection between a truth and its ultimate manifestation in a corresponding action of conviction no matter how many intermediate steps there may be between them. Thus, "believing that" (*he'amin l-*) is really only a subset of "believing in" (*he'emin b-*)—even though different beliefs at times may contradict each other—and belief in general should be seen in terms of how one acts on a truth rather than as a possession of it. Therefore, while it is the case that the righteous assert or assume (meta-)physical truths, the meaning of those truths for them is in how they relate to that truth. This will be discussed further when I examine the relationship between theoretical and practical wisdom, as well as in my discussion of the development of intellectual virtue.

A Jewish/Pragmatist Theory of Truth

The theory of truth that I am suggesting is different from the dominant conception of truth found in the modern epistemological tradition, which is grounded in foundationalism. Foundationalist theories of knowledge focus on the justification of belief and on certainty of the believer. The goal of contemporary epistemology is to clarify knowledge claims and to determine the degree of validity that knowledge claims could possess. This is true for both the rationalist school and the empiricist school; their differences are only over method. Rationalism posits that we gain knowledge through reasoning, while empiricism contends that we gain knowledge through sensory experience. The suggested theory that I am putting forth, however, has a strong similarity to the one accepted within the pragmatist school of philosophy. In order to explain its similarity and give my theory philosophical support, I will rely on the works of William James, Charles S. Peirce, and John Dewey.

According to William James, all philosophical systems are initiated by people who first have an experience and then inquire into its meaning,[87] yet James is not advocating for the empiricist theory described above. According to James, a person knows that he or she has achieved the goal of obtaining a rational conception of the world only when a feeling of ease, peace, and rest overcomes him or her. Rational comprehension is acknowledged by the transition from perplexity to relief.[88] James calls this alignment "the sentiment of rationality." Reasoning, whether practical or theoretical, therefore, does not begin *in abstracto*; it presupposes a general picture of reality as determined by one's experiences. Philosophy only puts into greater focus the picture the person already sees.[89]

Charles S. Peirce seconds James' view that what a person deems rational is a consequence of his or her sentiment; however, he is more concerned about the possibility that what a person deems rational is truly real. Peirce admits that people generally do reason correctly, by which he means in accord with reality, yet he maintains that it is not necessarily so. The veracity of a conclusion is independent of one's inclination to accept it, and its falsity is unrelated to a person's aversion to it. What does guide a person's inferences, if not the truth, is, according to Peirce, a habit of mind, whether inborn or acquired.[90]

Peirce's view that there is a distinction between truth in an ontological sense and truth in an epistemological sense supports the idea presented above in my discussion regarding how it might be possible for Maimonides to create a synthesis between virtue ethics and Divine command morality. Ontologically, truth is determined by God and equated with His will. Epistemologically, truth can be discovered through philosophical reflection or through study of the Torah. Axiologically, however, true moral value comes from one's relationship to God.

Moreover, Peirce's view can also provide philosophical support for the conception of *emet* explained above. If truth is defined as consistent with reality, it would be unattainable, since reality encompasses more than all of human experience, let alone an individual's experiences.[91] True knowledge would also not be able to justify itself,[92] since to judge knowledge as true one must use an external measure that can determine the veracity of its correspondence to reality. However, if truth/*emet* is defined as steadfast-ness to a belief or worldview, then even if truth in the ontological sense is unattainable, epistemologically and axiologically one can live faithfully according to that truth. This idea can be used to explain the statement in *Mishna Avot* that Moses received the Torah from Sinai rather than stating that God gave Moses the Torah. Because God's wisdom is greater than anything that Moses would be able to comprehend, the Mishna focuses on that which Moses received rather than on that which God could have conveyed. The rabbinic expression, "*Emet* is its own witness," is also comprehensible in light of this understanding, since the continuity of its existence testifies to its reliability and steadfastness.[93]

Pragmatist theories of truth also argue that belief and action are inti-mately related. According to John Dewey, beliefs are rules for action, since an acted-upon belief is a way to conceive of reality with the highest possi-ble conviction. Yet, the relationship between beliefs and actions is not uni-directional, the two influence each other and, in doing so, refine both.[94] As such, habituation is a process of action, experience, and reflection.

Though Maimonides has a very different epistemological framework, his response to the question of the veracity of creation can be used as an example of this notion of truth applied to the context of Jewish philoso-phy. He writes,

> Owing to the absence of all proof, we reject the theory of the Eternity of the Universe. ... For if the Creation had been demonstrated by proof, even if only according to the Platonic hypothesis, all arguments of the philosophers against us would be of no avail. If, on the other hand, Aristotle had a proof for his theory, the whole teaching of Scripture would be rejected, and we should be forced to other opinions.[95]

For Maimonides, belief in creation *ex nihilo* is valid—or one can rely on this premise—for two reasons. It is essential for the purpose of believing other ideas such as the history of miracles and the establishment of the Jewish people. Also, it is not contradicted by any other idea that makes up his worldview. Therefore, there is no reason for him to accept an alternative theory, especially one which does not cohere with the rest of his ideas. Since the Aristotelian theory of eternality has not been proven, its strength lies in the persuasiveness of the arguments for it and the ability for it to cohere with other beliefs that Maimonides' worldview demands. Because the theory disallows the acceptance of his foundational beliefs, such as the existence of miracles, Maimonides cannot accept it. On the other hand, the Platonic theory, which claims that the world was formed from a co-eternal primal matter, has likewise not been proven, yet its acceptance can still allow for the existence of miracles within a coherent worldview. Therefore, as opposed to the Aristotelian theory, the Platonic theory could be incorporated into a Jewish belief system.[96]

To live by one's faith, that is, to follow God's will by observing the Torah, can be expanded into two categories, as is noted by Isaiah.

Isaiah established two principles, as it is said: Thus says Hashem, (1) Guard justice (mishpat) and (2) perform righteousness (tzedaka).[97]

The entire verse from Isaiah is, "Thus said Hashem: guard justice (*mishpat*) and perform righteousness (*tzedaka*), for My salvation (*yeshuati*) is soon to come and My righteousness to be revealed." Though Isaiah said elsewhere, "For My thoughts are not your thoughts, nor are your ways My ways, says Hashem,"[98] the linguistic relationship in the verse allows for analogy.[99] In other words, the justice performed by the Israelites corresponds to God's salvation, just as the righteousness of the Israelites corresponds to God's actions of righteousness.

Mishpat is usually translated as justice and the plural (*mishpatim*) as "societal laws" (or laws of a just society). However, *mishpat* is not the same as contemporary conceptions of justice. In contemporary parlance, justice is often equated with fairness, due to the influence of John Rawls on contemporary political theory.[100] Justice is an institutional concept, whereby the rules of the society are known and accepted by all. Rawls even calls it, "the first virtue of social institutions."[101] Justice is therefore not about personal relationships, but rather one's affiliation to the organizing principle of the state. One may see this through the manner in which Rawls depicts the construction of a just society, even if it is only a thought experiment. Rawls asks us to conceive of a hypothetical scenario, which he calls the "original position." In this position, we are asked to allocate all of society's goods and responsibilities to people without knowing anything about them. More importantly, we do not know in which group or class we would fall, whether it will be the wealthiest strata of society or the lowliest. Under this "veil of ignorance," Rawls assumes that we would structure society in such a way that everyone would receive the allocation of goods and responsibilities needed for them to have a fair chance to succeed in life. Everyone has an equal chance because anyone could be the most dejected. It is a consideration of individuals through the medium of a political framework and not directly as human beings. Under this conception, we can adopt David Hume's description of justice as an "artificial virtue."

The virtue of justice in Rawls' political theory is similar to Kant's view of moral duty. According to Kant, duty is the necessity of action from respect for the law.[102] As Kant writes, "The pre-eminent good which we call moral can therefore consist in nothing else than the conception of law in itself, which certainly is only possible in a rational being, in so far as this conception, and not the expected effect, determines the will."[103] All that matters is a person's adherence to the law, and not loyalty to another person. He writes, "The object of respect is the law only, that is, the law which we impose on ourselves, and yet recognize as necessary in itself. As a law, we are subjected to it without consulting self-love; as imposed by us on ourselves, it is a result of our will. ... *Respect for a person is properly only respect for the law of which he gives us an example* [my italics]."[104]

Mishpat, on the other hand, has a personal, relational significance and it connotes salvation or societal improvement rather than a static ideal of societal welfare and its distribution. For example, in Psalms it states, "When God arose to *mishpat*, to save (*hoshia*) all the earth's humble."[105] Another example of the salvific aspect of *mishpat* is when David says to King Saul: "God therefore be judge (*dayan*), and judge (*shaphat*) between me and you, and see, and plead my cause, and deliver me (*v'yishpeteini*) out of your hand."[106] In this verse, a verbal form of *mishpat* (*v'yishpeteini*) is used to mean deliverance.[107] Also, in the Book of Judges, the leaders (*shophtim*) are clearly more than just magistrates, they are also saviors: "And God raised up judges (*shophtim*), who saved them (*v'yoshiyum*) out of the hand of those that spoiled them."[108] To guard justice is to make sure to provide for those who are oppressed in society on an institutional level, to save those of whom people take advantage from oppression.[109] Rabbi

Eliezer Berkovits explains the difference between *mishpat* and justice as follows:

> For the Western mind, he who exercises loving-kindness and practices charity foregoes the implementation of justice. *Hesed* and *mishpat*, *s'daqah* and *mishpat* are opposites within the frame of reference of practically all cultures and their religions. A judge is either just or merciful. One exercises either *hesed* or *misphat*. ... Not so in the Bible. The meaning of *mishpat* must be different in essence from that of justice, as the word is understood in most languages, if it is possible to say of God that he exercises lovingkindness, justice, and charity in the earth, for 'in these things he delights.'[110]

While *mishpat* is societal justice which ensures that life and community are in their proper order, righteousness (*tzedaka*) focuses on the individual person and is thus social in nature rather than societal. For example, when King Saul was in pursuit of David, David was able to stealthily enter King Saul's camp while he was sleeping, yet he nevertheless spared King Saul's life, even when Avishai, his commander, advised him to kill his enemy. When King Saul recognized that David had saved his life, David said to him, "And God will render to every man his righteousness (*tzidkato*) and his faithfulness (*emunato*); forasmuch as God delivered you into my hand today, I would not put forth my hand against God's anointed." David spares King Saul for two reasons, he acted in righteousness since he saw King Saul as a fellow person, and he acted in faith because King Saul is God's anointed. David also hopes that God will give him the same righteousness and save his life as he saved King Saul's. Moreover, on the verse, "And he [Abraham] believed (*he'emin*) in God; and He counted it to him for righteousness (*tzedaka*)," the Biblical commentators note that Abraham's righteousness was that he, as an isolated individual, went beyond the norm and sought to improve society, one individual at a time, by developing social bonds between himself and others, while acting based solely on his personal faith in God's will. Therefore, God made a personal covenant with him so that he would build a family, only after which a nation would develop from him. Righteousness (*tzedaka*) is similar to loving-kindness (*hesed*), which is a voluntary behavior that is not obligatory in the strictly legal and societal sense but is proper in the social sense, and thus prescriptive in the aspirational, religio-ethical sense.

Tzedaka is related to *hesed* in that both constitute giving for the sake of another in a way that is not based in reciprocity. Yet *tzedaka* differs from *hesed* in that it is a giving to another with whom one lives interdependently, so that the person might be able to return that *tzedaka* one day in the future. *Hesed*, on the other hand, is given to a person who can never (or is assumed never will be able to) return that *hesed* in the future. For example, a true *hesed* is one that is performed for a person after he or she has already died, such as the *hesed* done for Joseph when the Jews brought his bones from Egypt to Israel.[111] On a scale from reciprocity to complete one-sidedness, the three terms would be ordered as follows: *mishpat*, *tzedaka*, *hesed*.

Though the terms "social" and "societal" are often used interchangeably, I am decisively giving them "précising definitions" based on the dichotomy between *Gemeinschaft* and *Gesellschaft*, as proposed by the German sociologist Ferdinand Tönnies.[112] According to Tönnies, interpersonal ties can either be based on personal social interactions, roles, values, and the beliefs based on such interactions in a community (*Gemeinschaft*) or can be a consequence of indirect interactions, impersonal roles, formal values, and the beliefs based on such interactions in society (*Gesellschaft*). Though *Gemeinschaft* and *Gesellschaft* are usually translated as "community" and "society," respectively, when speaking of the relationships themselves I use "social relationship" rather than "communal relationship" in order to move away from contemporary communitarian notions that emphasize collectivity as well as to move closer toward the etymological meaning of *socius* (sharing, kindred, related, allied, united, companion), which I think better corresponds to the meaning of *tzedaka* that I am trying to develop. Societal relationships are those that are defined and determined by legal and politico-economic institutions, such as the laws of a state. Social relationships are defined and determined by private and personal interactions, such as giving a housewarming gift to a new neighbor. A person may participate in a number of communities, all of which are included within a society.[113] For example, a person can be a member of a family, a neighborhood, a synagogue, a basketball league, and so forth, which are all communities that lie within the American society. My reason for using these distinctive terms is because I want to emphasize that individuals live within many different types of communities at the same time, and not that they live only in a society while having different roles or functions within it.[114]

Both the social sphere and the societal sphere are extremely important but in different ways. In Abraham Maslow's terminology, society protects physiological needs and safety needs, whereas communities are meant to enhance love and belonging, esteem, and self-actualization. Notice that society "protects from," that is, enhances one's negative liberty, while communities "add to," that is, enhances positive liberty. Robert Putnam, in his book *Bowling Alone: The Collapse and Revival of American Community*, has argued that the development of communities and of social relationships benefits individuals, the local communities themselves, and the nations in which those communities reside in the following ways: Social groups allow their members to resolve collective difficulties more easily by mitigating the problem of the "free rider" who shirks responsibility because he or she gains more as an individual who can profit from the work of others. Social groups also allow for upward mobility for its members, since repeated interactions create a higher level of trust and sharing of information between its members while reducing the costs of doing business with each other (by reducing legal fees, etc.). Social groups even allow for their members to become more open-minded because they further an awareness of how the destinies of individuals are joined together. Putnam has shown how the connectedness of communities has a tangible benefit on child welfare and education, the health and happiness of the groups' members, and, even in the societal sphere, on democratic citizenship and government performance.

Each social group, as well as society, has its own priorities, and the interactions between them can create both tensions and systems to promote human flourishing most effectively. When social groups cooperate with society, the society sets the overarching framework, and the different social groups, and their respective interests, help to mitigate the potential abuse of power that society may exercise. Social groups also assist in establishing local, particular avenues for improving human welfare which the societal framework cannot do because of its size and jurisdiction, such as building soup kitchens and help shelters for local members.

Society creates an institutional framework whereby its members can live in an environment that maximizes relative welfare. This is often done by distributing political and economic benefits in a proportion predetermined as proper, and by restoring that distribution when it has been compromised. In other words, the foundation of society, properly understood, is justice, in the sense of *mishpat*. When considering the concept of justice, however, one must recognize certain vulnerabilities. While society may have a clear vision of the ideal to which it should aim and to strive continuously to attain, the correct proportion of economic and political benefit for which it may advocate is subjective.[115] For example, Michael Walzer writes,

> Justice is relative to social [according to my aforementioned definition, "societal"] meanings. Indeed, the relativity of justice follows from the classic non-relative definition, giving each person his due, as much as it does from my own proposal, distributing goods for "internal" reasons. ... A given society is just if its substantive life is lived in a certain way—that is, in a way faithful to the shared understanding of its members. (When people disagree about the meaning of social [societal] goods, when understandings are controversial, then justice requires that the society be faithful to the disagreements, providing institutional channels for their expression, adjudicative mechanisms, and alternative distributions.)[116]

Justice as fairness depends on how one defines treating like cases alike and how one determines what is similar, both in terms of cases and in terms of treatment. Also, justice, according to this definition, is not conceptualized in terms of the individual but rather in terms of classes found within society. This is because the law can only relate to the legal fiction of the "reasonable person," since the law requires an objective standard by which to apply societal justice.

One function of social groups, on the other hand, is to promote loyalty, or a voluntary and practical devotion of one individual to another. For example, in the Bible, when David was being pursued by King Saul, his son Jonathan stayed loyal to David and protected him, despite the fact that it undermined the monarchy. When King Saul understood that his son, Jonathan, the next in line to be king, had stayed loyal to David despite his own desire to kill him, King Saul said to his son, "For as long as the son of Jesse [David] lives on the earth, you will not be established nor your kingdom. Now send for him and bring him to me, for he deserves to die!" Jonathan could only respond, "Why should he be put to death? What has he done?"[117] This distinction between the function of society and of social groups is a broad generalization, since both justice and loyalty can have individual and collective expressions or dimensions, yet I use the terms "justice" and "loyalty" in this context to refer to justice to ideals and loyalty to people, respectively.[118] Loyalty, according to my definition, does not depend on defining the terms of a relationship or on identifying an abstract ideal that the relationship seeks to fulfill. Rather, loyalty develops through meaningful interaction between people that fosters mutual responsibility for the welfare of one's fellow. As such, social relationships demonstrate a greater willingness of people to give to one another solely for the other's sake. (The Sages remark that the love between David and Jonathan was the paradigm of unselfishness.[119]) In societal relationships, on the other hand, exchange is based on reciprocity and balancing the distribution of benefits and obligations. For example, the manner of interaction within a social group is comparable to that of family and friends, whereas the relationships within societal institutions are similar to those in a polity or a corporation. Another way to look at the difference between social and societal relationships is that social groups involve personal commitments whereas society is held together through institutions and not through personal connections.

When social organizations and societal institutions work together yet are kept separate, each can serve to complement the other in a way that can achieve the greatest and most equitable welfare for a community. Smaller social groups can combine resources, so that the economies of scale of society can create a positive sum game. Societal institutions are able to determine a just allocation of benefits and obligations, yet social groups can serve as natural systems of checks and balances, since active members of the community who feel a sense of responsibility for their fellow members will protest when they see that others are being treated unjustly. Because they have their own sphere of influence, social groups can also promote values that would be considered supererogatory when measured by societal norms.

The subsumption of social groups into society can weaken social relationships and threaten society in two ways. Because social groups are now perceived in terms of roles, the dynamic of the group changes from one that is based on loyalty among individuals to one that is based on a notion of justice among the group as a whole. Therefore, individual cohesion is lost. Second, since social groups maintain the façade of semi-independent existence, the social inclination attaches itself to the societal ideal. Society continues to be based on the predetermined ideal of justice, yet the ideal is now further reinforced by its members' loyalty. In this situation, loyalty compounds the vulnerabilities inherent in founding a society solely on the basis of a particular notion of justice, since now it is not only self-serving but also worthy of self-sacrifice.[120]

Superficially, one may not be able to distinguish between the realm of social groups and the realm of society, especially in a situation where the two have been conflated. Certain interactions between people, however, can still reveal the differences between the two types of relationships. Social relationships demonstrate a greater willingness of people to give to one another solely for the other's sake; in societal relationships, on the other hand, exchange is based on reciprocity and balancing the distribution of benefit and obligation.

The social aspect of *tzedaka* can be seen through the particular commandment that shares its name, which is translated as "charity" in contemporary English. For clarification, *tzedaka* as a concept is translated as "righteousness" while *tzedaka* as a commandment, that is, "to give *tzedaka*," is translated as "charity." I believe that the reason for this distinction is because the phrase "to give *tzedaka*" is a consequence of linguistic development, where the word *tzedaka* went from describing the act to describing the object that was given through the act. The result is that to give *tzedaka* now means to give money and not to give money *out of righteousness*. Thus, I believe that the expression "to give *tzedaka* to a person" should be translated as "to give something as an act of righteousness to a person." Even though *tzedaka* is an unselfish act of giving to another, the benefits are not one-sided. The Talmudic Sages note that more than the benefactor benefits the pauper through giving *tzedaka*, the pauper benefits the benefactor in providing an opportunity to give.[121]

According to Jewish law, there are eight different ways that a person can give *tzedaka*,[122] the highest level of which is to find some manner of employment for the one in need. This is not a societal correction of unemployment, but rather a social concern for another's welfare and stability. The social impetus of finding another person employment has been explained by sociologist Mark Granovetter. He distinguishes between "weak ties," which consist of those people who are less likely to be socially involved with one another, and "strong ties," that is, those among people who are close friends. His research shows that "weak ties" are more important than "strong tie" relationships with respect to helping people find employment. Those who share strong ties would know of the same opportunities as the one looking for a job, yet weak ties are able to facilitate more opportunities and to provide greater assistance by virtue of being outside the person's social nucleus.[123] By virtue of the *tzedaka* of helping another find a job, one also extends his or her social base and turns "weak ties" into "strong" ones, all for the purpose of helping another simply because he or she is in need.

Another concrete example of how social and societal interaction differs relates to how giving to another person occurs in the two frameworks. Social groups consist of relationships between people living a shared life, and people within them utilize gift-giving as a way of sharing. Societal institutions, on the other hand, are founded on the solidarity among people who share a common purpose; as such, in societal institutions only an exchange based on reciprocity is considered legitimate.

The bond that keeps communities, such as families and friends, together is based on affection and/or a sense of moral obligation. For example, in a study that measured people's intentions in gift-giving, the findings showed that even though the number of gifts given to friends was approximately the same as to extended family members, the predominant reason for giving to one's extended family was out of moral obligation while giving to friends was out of affection.[124] That is not to say that families do not give out of affection; rather it means that the familial bond is stronger than the benefit one may have from maintaining it.

Because friendships are voluntarily initiated, they are more fragile and more easily severable than familial bonds. Therefore, affection would naturally be a strong motivator for giving to a friend without expectation of return. Family relationships, on the other hand, supersede relationships based on affection, so maintaining the relational bond can be seen as an inherent obligation based on loyalty rather than choice.

The loyalty that one demonstrates to friends, however, may be strengthened so as to become as strong as that demonstrated to family members. For example, we often hear of the closeness of friends who say, "She is like a sister to me," or when children refer to their parents' friends as Uncle and Auntie. Some friendship bonds may even be maintained after affection is no longer present, as when one hears things like "We can't leave her out. She is like family." This strengthening of friendship bonds allows social groups to become more intimately connected and further reinforced.

Familial loyalty, however, cannot be taken for granted. Except for the situation of an immediate family with dependent children, familial bonds are reinforced by nothing but willing continuation of the relationship. As children become less dependent upon their parents, if the bond between parent and child does not evolve from a one-dimensional relationship, where the parent is dominant, to one that is multi-dimensional, where the child's maturation is recognized and his or her autonomy respected, the familial bond will naturally wither and the priority of family will be replaced by a different social group.

To separate social interaction from societal, it is important to examine exchanges based on societal roles. For example, a government tax rebate or a corporate year-end bonus is not an explicit exchange based on reciprocity, yet there is still an implicit intention to confer an obligation to the recipient of a rebate or a bonus. For example, the 2008 tax rebate was a gift, yet it was given for the purpose of bolstering economic performance in light of a downturn in economic activity. Similarly, year-end bonuses are often tied to a person's performance, which means that it is an incentive rather than a gift.

One could presume that promises between members of a societal institution could parallel gift-giving within a social group, since promises are commitments to act without placing conditions on another person for the commitment to stand. Within the American legal system, however, promises upon which the promisee does not justifiably rely or where there was no bargain for a mutual exchange of value, in other words gifts, are not legally binding. The reason for the necessity of clear reciprocity for a promise to be legally binding is due to the function that promises serve in society. Because societal relationships are contingent on political or economic goals, the function of a promise is transformed into that of a contract, and the reasons for gift-giving are transformed from being motivated by affection and moral obligation to being a means of bargaining for benefits and detriments.

The importance of the family for the development of one's sense of loyalty to others has long been established, and in noting this point, Eric Felton has written, "The family has long been seen as the training ground for loyal living: The commitments we learn to keep at home build up the moral muscles we use in our commitments to friends, to community, to country, to the truth."[125] Strong familial ties and their efficacy in instilling a sense of social loyalty that ensures societal justice may be one of the reasons why Abraham led a family before Moses led a nation. As Rabbi Samuel David Luzzatto writes in his *Yesodei HaTorah*,

> The people of Israel did not acquire their religion from Moses but had inherited it from their ancestors, Abraham, Isaac and Jacob. ... This religion was adequate for the Israelites as long as they constituted one family. However, when they became a great people and the time drew near to bring them to the land promised by God to their forefathers, the Lord realized

that they were in need of instruction, laws, education, and proper guidance, for the perfection of virtue and social welfare as well as for the maintenance of religion.[126]

When the Jewish polity and legal system were established by the Torah of Moses, the Jews in their righteousness continued to be known as the children of Abraham, Isaac, and Jacob. Even when the Jewish state was governed by kings, the prophets made sure that the poor individuals were neither forgotten nor abandoned.

When society is stable, the foundation upon which social groups flourish is loyalty and the ideal that it promotes is righteousness (*tzedaka*). Because loyalty develops through continual interaction, acting for the benefit of another person inculcates a sense of personal strength and ability, as well as intensifies the emotional connection between provider and beneficiary.[127] Moreover, continual interaction for the sake of another allows for the acceptance of changing realities without dissolving relationships because it fosters a sense of voluntary and mutual responsibility for the welfare of one's fellow. Acting through loyalty also creates a habit of action rather than habit of deference to formal structures. Though a society must have justice (*mishpat*) as a foundation, the righteous (*tzadik*) will live by his faith (*emuna*) so as to better the social world around him.

Serving God, therefore, has a double focus. One must look outward to improving society as a whole as well as inward to one's social community. To paraphrase Rabbi Samson Raphael Hirsch, rather than be a Jew in the home and a man in the street, one purpose's should be to strive to become a *Mensch-Jisroel*, who becomes the ideal of both in all areas of life. Rabbi Hirsch describes this ideal as follows:

The more the Jew is a Jew, the more universalist will be his views and aspirations, the less alien will he be to anything that is noble and good, true and upright in the arts and sciences, in civilization and culture. The more the Jew is a Jew, the more joyously will he hail everything that will shape human life so as to promote truth, right, peace and refinement among mankind, the more happily will he himself embrace every opportunity to prove his mission as a Jew on new, still untrodden grounds. The more the Jew is a Jew, the more gladly will he give himself to all that is true progress in civilization and culture—provided that in this new circumstance he will not only maintain his Judaism but will be able to bring it to ever more glorious fulfillment.[128]

The way in which one must balance these two priorities is dependent on the ideals of the society and the social groups in which the person lives and in how well they are being implemented. Yet, no matter what the case, the demand to one's family and one's social community for righteousness cannot be fulfilled without also carrying out the demands to one's society for justice as well. "Thus says Hashem, 'Guard justice (*mishpat*) and perform righteousness (*tzedaka*).'"[129]

> *Rabbi Simlai when preaching said: Six hundred and thirteen precepts were communicated to Moses, three hundred and sixty-five negative precepts, corresponding to the number of days in the solar year, and two hundred and forty-eight positive precepts, corresponding to the number of the parts of the human body.*

The importance of Rabbi Simlai's statement is not necessarily that 613 commandments were communicated to Moses, since in and of itself the number 613 has no independent meaning in the Jewish tradition other than the fact that God gave 613 commandments. Rather, its importance is in the order he describes them and the reasons behind this exact number. The order in which he describes the commandments corresponds to two different verses from Psalms. The first is, "Depart from evil, and do good; seek peace, and pursue it (*bakesh shalom v'radphehu*)."[130] The second is, "Depart from evil, and do good; and dwell for evermore (*shokhen l'olam*)."[131] The good to which the verses refer is not a *telos* in the Aristotelian sense nor is it a Platonic form; rather, it is the Torah and its commandments.[132] Yet the Torah does not only provide a direct means to pursue good but also allows the pursuit of good to be wholly efficacious through one's departing from evil as well. The reference to the calendar and the fact that the negative precepts are mentioned first conveys the idea that keeping away from evil is prior to doing good and that it is a daily imperative to remind oneself to do so. Moreover, Rabbi Simlai refers to the solar year, which is always 365 1/4 days, unlike the lunisolar Jewish calendar year whose length can range from 353 to 385 days. The reference to the stability of the solar calendar conveys that the negative commandments are meant to provide consistency so that one has a firm foundation upon which to develop morally and to do good. The positive commandments correspond to the number of the parts of the body to inform that adherence to the Torah demands that one's entire being be involved in the process. The commandments are not merely mechanical, and religious contemplation is not exclusively in the realm of the spirit; serving God from love demands that the person be wholly attuned to one's purpose and in harmony toward its attainment in every endeavor. If one pursues this path and lives by his or her faith, then he or she will ultimately dwell in God's house for evermore, yet will seek peace and pursue it in the meantime.

NOTES

1. Isaiah 43:10.
2. That it is not an innate development is demonstrated by the many times in the Bible where idolatry is depicted as a fallback position and serving God as a result of intentional desire to do so.
3. The contemporary view of slavery, at least in the United States, can be seen by the US Victims of Trafficking and Violence Protection Act of 2000. This act, which opposes both slavery and involuntary servitude, states that:

   (1) As the 21st century begins, the degrading institution of slavery continues throughout the world. Trafficking in persons is a modern form of slavery, and it is the largest manifestation of slavery today…

   (22) One of the founding documents of the United States, the Declaration of Independence, recognizes the inherent dignity and worth of all people. It states that all men are created equal and that they are endowed by their Creator with certain unalienable rights. The right to be free from slavery and involuntary servitude is among those unalienable rights. Acknowledging this fact, the United States outlawed slavery and involuntary servitude in 1865, recognizing them as evil institutions that must be abolished. Current practices of sexual slavery and trafficking of women and children are similarly abhorrent to the principles upon which the United States was founded.

4. Leviticus 25:44–46.
5. BT Gittin 41ab.
6. *Hilkhot Avadim*, Chapter 9.
7. Exodus 21:1–6; Leviticus 25:39–46; and Deuteronomy 15:12–18.
8. BT *Kiddushin* 20a.
9. Nebuchadnezzar, the Babylonian king who destroyed the First Temple in Jerusalem, is also given this honorific.
10. Genesis 2:15.
11. BT *Makkot* 23b–24a.

12. Habakuk 2:4.
13. Habakuk 2:4.
14. Deuteronomy 10:12–3.
15. *Mishna Avot* 1:3.
16. For examples of how sacrifice is a component of love, see *Duties of the Heart, The Gate of Love of God*, Chapter 4; *Moreh Nevukim* [MN] 3:24; and the commentary of Rabbi Bahaye ben Asher on Genesis 22.
17. See Genesis, Chapter 34, regarding Shimon and Levi attacking the city of Shekhem to avenge the defilement of their sister Dina. Genesis 34:25 states, "And it came to pass on the third day, when they were in pain, that two of the sons of Jacob, Shimon and Levi, Dinah's brothers, took each man his sword, and came upon the city *betah*, and slew all the males." There is a disagreement among the Biblical commentators whether the city had a false sense of security or whether the brothers came upon the city confident that they were correct. Their confidence, however, was not shared by their father, Jacob, who chastised them for their actions. Both interpretations, however, acknowledge that *betah* is a subjective sense of security or trust that may or may not be warranted.
18. Isaiah 12:2.
19. Deuteronomy 28:66.
20. I Samuel 11:7.
21. Isaiah 2:10.
22. Hosea 3:5.
23. Genesis 3:10.
24. Genesis 15:1.
25. Genesis 18:15.
26. Exodus 14:31.
27. Isaiah 11:1–4.
28. II Kings 19:4–11.
29. Proverbs 1:7. For a descriptive account to support then notion that fear of God, walking in His ways, and loving Him precede and lead to wisdom, see I Kings, chapter 3. Before Solomon asks for wisdom in a dream, he is described as one who loved Hashem and who walked in the statutes of David his father, meaning that he kept the commandments and was righteous like his father (3:3).
30. Proverbs 9:10.
31. Psalms 111:10.
32. Deuteronomy 10:12.

33. BT *Berakhot* 33b.
34. Thus the effort a person exerts to maintain his or her beliefs as well as have them influence his or her daily living is more a testament to moral progress than any professed moral declaration. As William James eloquently writes, "Thus not only our morality but our religion, so far as the latter is deliberate, depends on the effort which we can make. '*Will you or won't you have it so?*' is the most probing question we are ever asked; we are asked it every hour of the day, and about the largest as well as the smallest, the most theoretical as well as the most practical, things. We answer by consents or non-consents and not by words (*Briefer Course*, 426)."
35. There are two more expressions for fear of God in the Bible, namely *Pahad Elohim* and *Yirat Elohim*. *Pahad Elohim* maintains the idea of fear as a sense of insecurity, yet the term connotes a different aspect of God toward which one has fear. For example, when King Yehoshafat went to war against the surrounding nations and Hashem did battle against them, *Pahad Elohim* came upon all the kingdoms of the lands. The reason why the nations had *Pahad Elohim*, even though Hashem was doing battle, is that the nations did not recognize Hashem as Elohim (as Pharoah declares in his first conversation with Moshe). They therefore could not have *Pahad Hashem*, but only *Pahad Elohim* (II Chronicles 20:29). After he had conquered them, however, they had *Pahad Hashem*, since they recognized the God of the Israelites (II Chronicles 17:10). *Yirat Elohim* connotes a fear that consists of temporal loss, even when acting in service of God. For example, when Abraham, Sifcha and Puah served God with *Yirat Elohim*, their fear was predicated on the possibility of losing one's son, in Abraham's case, or their own lives by the hand of Pharoah, yet they still continued to serve God. See also, Nehemiah 5:14–15.
36. Habakuk 2:4.
37. BT *Makkot* 23b–24a.
38. In order to avoid digression, I will discuss only the statements of Habakuk, Isaiah (the first one) and Rabbi Simlai in the body of the chapter and will mention the statements of Micah, Isaiah (the second one) and King David in the footnotes.
39. Habakuk 2:4.

40. The same word is used in both places.
41. Numbers 14:44–5.
42. Deuteronomy 32:4.
43. Numbers 12:7.
44. I Samuel 3:19–20.
45. See *Metsudat David, Metsudat Tsiyon*. Onkelos uses the same word in his translation in I Samuel 3:20.
46. I Samuel 25:28.
47. Isaiah 22:23–25.
48. I Samuel 2:35.
49. The purpose of this last statement is to emphasize that Jewish virtue ethics and moral development is based on a living tradition which must adapt its ideals to temporaneous practical living. Therefore, Jewish law cannot be learned solely from books. It must be learned from the people who observe it correctly.

    Similarly, the Talmudic Sages use the expression, "people of little faith" (*katane amanah*) to refer to people who lack "*emunah* in action" and not in cognitive belief. For example, those who are called people of little faith are those who have enough to eat today but still ask, "What will we eat tomorrow?" (*Mekhilta deRabbi Yishmael, Beshalah, Vayasa* 2). Also, Noah was called a person of little faith, since he did not enter the ark until the waters of the flood reached his legs (Midrash Aggada to Genesis, Buber edition, 7). See also BT *Sotah* 46b, 48b, Mishna *Sotah* 9:12.
50. Numbers 20:7–12.
51. See Shadal on Genesis 15:6.
52. See Nahmanides on Genesis 15:6.
53. Exodus 14:31.
54. Exodus 15:17.
55. Genesis 45:26.
56. Genesis 15:6.
57. BT *Berakhot* 14b.
58. I Kings 2:4, 3:6; II Kings 20:3; Isaiah 38:3; Psalms 25:5.
59. Genesis 24:48; Isaiah 59:14.
60. Genesis 24:27, 24:49, 32:11; Exodus 34:6; II Samuel 2:6; I Kings 3:6; Isaiah 16:5; Hosea 4:1; Micah 7:20.
61. Isaiah 48:1; Zecharia 8:8; Psalms 19:1.

62. Isaiah 42:3, 59:15, 61:8; Jeremiah 4:2; Psalms 19:1; Nehemiah 9:13.

63. Joshua 24:14; Judges 9:16,19.

64. Jeremiah 14:13, 33:6; Esther 9:30.

65. Exodus 34:6.

66. Micah 7:20.

67. Genesis 24:27.

68. Genesis 24:49.

69. Genesis 32:11–14.

70. Exodus 34:6.

71. Exodus 18:21; Nehemiah 7:2.

72. Jeremiah 10:10; Psalms 31:6.

73. Jeremiah 32:41.

74. Zecharia 8:3.

75. Malachi 2:6.

76. Samson Raphael Hirsch and Daniel Haberman, *The Hirsch Chumash: Sefer Bereshis* (New York: Feldheim; Judaica Press, 2000) 356.

77. See *Genesis Rabba* 8:5: When the Holy One, blessed be He, came to create Adam, the ministering angels formed themselves into groups and parties. Some of them said, "Let him be created," while others urged, "Let him not be created." Thus it is written, "*Hesed* and *Emet* have met each other, *Tzedek* and *Shalom* kissed." *Hesed* said, "Let him be created, because he will dispense acts of *hesed*." *Emet* said, "Let him not be created, because he is full of falsehood." *Tzedek* said, "Let him be created, because he will perform deeds of *tzedek*." *Shalom* said, "Let him not be created, because he is full of strife." What did the Lord do? He took *Emet* and cast it to the ground. The ministering angels said before the Holy One, blessed be He, "Sovereign of the Universe! Why do You despise Your seal?" [God replied,] "Let *Emet* arise from the earth!" Hence it is written, "Let *emet* spring up from the earth" (Psalms 85:12).

78. See BT *Sanhedrin* 64a; BT *Yoma* 69b: "And they cried with a loud voice unto the Lord their God." Now what did they say? Rav Yehudah, or as others maintain Rabbi Yonatan said, "[They cried this:] 'Woe, woe, is it that destroyed the Sanctuary, burnt the Temple, slew the righteous, and exiled Israel from their land;

and still it sports amongst us! Have You not set it before us that we might be rewarded [for withstanding its allurements]? But we desire neither temptation nor reward!' That too was after they were seduced by it. [Continuing Rav Yehudah's statement:] They fasted for three days, entreating for mercy; thereafter their sentence fell from Heaven, the word *emet* written upon it." Rabbi Hanina said, "This proves that the seal of the Holy One, blessed be He, is *emet*." The shape of a fiery lion's whelp issued from the Holy of Holies, and the Prophet said to Israel, "That is the Tempter of Idolatry." While they held it fast, a hair (of its body) fell out, and his roar of pain was heard for 400 parasangs. (In perplexity) they cried, "What shall we do? Maybe Heaven will pity him!" The prophet answered, "Cast him into a lead cauldron, and cover it with lead to absorb his voice, as it is written, 'And he said', This is wickedness; and he cast it into the midst of the *ephah*, and he cast the weight of lead upon the mouth thereof" (Zecharia 5:8).

79. BT *Shabbat* 55a; *Genesis Rabba* 81:2.
80. Isaac Hunter, *Pahad Yitzhak: Sukkot* (Brooklyn: Gur Aryeh Institute for Advanced Jewish Scholarship, 2003) 211.
81. Ibid. 213.
82. I Kings 10:6–7.
83. Jeremiah 42:5.
84. *Metsudat David.*
85. Deuteronomy 7:9; see also Isaiah 49:7.
86. A 2009 study found that to the extent that smoking is a source of self-esteem, warnings on cigarette packages, such as "Smoking kills," ironically stimulates smoking. On the other hand, cigarette package warnings such as "Smoking brings you and the people around you severe damage" and "Smoking makes you unattractive," reduces smoking for those who based their self-esteem on the habit. The scientists of the study explained this finding by the fact that the latter warnings may be particularly threatening to those who believe the opposite, namely that smoking raises their positive self-image. Death warnings, on the other hand, cause those with a high smoking self-esteem to use smoking as a strategy to buffer against existential fears provoked by the death warnings. See Jochim Hansen, Susanne Winzeler, Sascha Topolinski, "When the

Death Makes You Smoke: A Terror Management Perspective on the Effectiveness of Cigarette On-Pack Warnings," *Journal of Experimental Social Psychology*, Vol. 46, No. 1 (January 2010) 226–228.

87. William James, *Writings 1978–1899*, 563.
88. James *Writings 1978–1899*, p. 504.
89. To demonstrate that truth serves the teleological purpose of creating consistency and stability in a person's practical life, James uses the example of how children are generally more curious than adults. Children, who are still trying to understand their place in the world, typically possess a great amount of curiosity. Adults, on the other hand, who have already developed a routine in their daily lives, are not usually disposed toward discovering new truths (James and Kuklick 1992, p. 740). James calls this tendency to ignore new ideas, the acceptance of which would entail reinterpreting a person's belief system, "old fogyism" (James and Kuklick 1992, p. 803).
90. Peirce, *The Essential Pierce: Selected Philosophical Writings*, Volume 1, 112.
91. Joachim, 52.
92. Bradley, 33.
93. See also Appendix II, which gives a genealogy of the term *Moshe emet v'Torato emet*, which supports this view.
94. Dewey (2008), 115.
95. Moses Maimonides, Shlomo Pines, and Leo Strauss, *The Guide of the Perplexed* (Chicago: University of Chicago Press, 1963) 319.
96. There are contemporary scholars who argue that Maimonides did actually believe in the Aristotelian conception of the eternity of the world. See Norbert Samuelson's essay, "Maimonides' Doctrine of Creation," for a discussion and his rebuttal of the views of a few of those scholars. (Norbert Samuelson, "Maimonides' Doctrine of Creation," *The Harvard Theological Review*, Vol. 84, No. 3 (July, 1991) 249–271).
97. Isaiah 56:1.
98. Isaiah 55:8.
99. What I mean by noting that the linguistic relationship in the verse allows for a comparison is that in the verse, the Jews are told to (1) guard justice and (2) perform righteousness, so that Hashem will (1) bring salvation and (2) reveal righteousness. Though one

might say that God's salvation and righteousness are not like the justice and righteousness of human beings (MN III:20), one can still say that, from a human perspective justice and salvation are analogous, just as a human being's righteousness is analogous to God's acts of righteousness (MN I:53).

100. For Rawls, "a society is well-ordered when it is not only designed to advance the good of its members but when it is also effectively regulated by a public conception of justice. That is, it is a society in which (1) everyone accepts and knows that the others accept the same principles of justice, and (2) the basic social institutions generally satisfy and are generally known to satisfy these principles... Among individuals with disparate aims and purposes a shared conception of justice establishes the bonds of civic friendship; the general desire for justice limits the pursuit of other ends. One may think of a public conception of justice as constituting the fundamental charter of a well-ordered human association." (*A Theory of Justice*, 4–5.)

101. *A Theory of Justice*, 3.

102. *Fundamental Principles*, 18.

103. Ibid. 19. He defines respect as a rational concept whereby a person recognizes that his or her will is subordinate to a law without being affected by any other motivating factors or inclinations. A person cannot have respect for internal motivations for acting except for those which are based in reason, since all other motivations disallow for the subordination of self to the law. Only that which is rational can be considered necessary in the sense that it is not contingent on personal factors; therefore, only the principles derived from reason, that is, the moral law, can be truly obligatory or, in other words, a command that is worthy of respect.

104. Kant, *Fundamental Principles* 19.

105. Psalms 76:10.

106. I Samuel 24:15.

107. For more examples, see II Samuel 18:19, 31.

108. Judges 2:16.

109. Isaiah 1:17.

110. Eliezer Berkovits, *Man and God: studies in Biblical theology* (Detroit: Wayne State University Press, 1969) 236.

111. Genesis Rabba, Parshat Vayehi, 96.

112. Ferdinand Tönnies, *Gemeinschaft und Gesellschaft*, Leipzig: Fues, 1887.

113. The recognition that social communities and societal communities are different and that they can, in fact, clash is the reason for Aristotle's discussion in *Politics* over whether the virtue of a good man and a good citizen is the same or not.

114. For a complementary discussion of how the Torah aims at the construction of both a society and a community of social relationships, see Lenn E. Goodman's *On Justice*, Chapter 1.

115. By a clear vision of the ideal to which it should aim, I mean that there is a conception of the rule of law that relates to the essential legal principles administered by the courts, as opposed to just a set of mechanisms which allow society to function without taking into consideration the value of its functioning to its members. This view of justice is in line with Ronald Dworkin's "rights" conception of the rule of law. He writes, "The rule of law on this conception is the ideal rule by an accurate public conception of individual rights. It does not distinguish, as the rule-book conception does, between the rule of law and substantive justice; on the contrary it requires, as part of the ideal of law, that the rules in the rule book capture and enforce moral rights (*A Matter of Principle* (Cambridge, MA: Harvard University Press, 1985) 11–12)." This view is also in accord with John Rawls's theory of justice. See footnote 100.

116. Michael Walzer, *Spheres of Justice: A Defense of Pluralism and Equality* (New York: Basic Books, 1983) 312–313.

117. I Samuel 20:31–32.

118. I use the terms "justice" and "loyalty" to refer to ideas and people, respectively, in order to distance myself from views of loyalty, such *as that held by Josiah Royce in his The Philosophy of Loyalty,* where loyalty is the willing and practical and thoroughgoing devotion of a person to a *cause rather than to a person.*

119. *Mishna Avot* 5:15.

120. Without any intention of being political and solely for the purpose of giving a practical example that will relate to the discussion below, Arnold Brooks has found that American liberals, despite their reputation for being more compassionate, are personally less charitable than conservatives. The reason he discovered for this irony is not that liberals are disingenuous but rather because their political

ideology stands in place of their sense of need to give to others. Because liberals believe that redistribution of wealth and welfare for the poor are responsibilities of the state, their inclination to give charity personally is diminished and the satisfaction they would get from giving charity is now being provided by their belief that the state will give on their behalf as citizens. Though it is not the place to discuss it here, this relationship is an example of how thinking about something can bring as much satisfaction as actually doing it, thereby reducing the motivation to act. See Arnold Brooks, *Who Really Cares: The Surprising Truth About Compassionate Conservatism* (New York: Basic Books, 2006) 70.

121. Leviticus Rabba 34:8.
122. *Hilkhot Tzedaka* 10:7–14.
123. Mark S. Granovetter, "The Strength of Weak Ties," *American Journal of Sociology* (1973) 1360–1380; Mark S. Granovetter, "The Strength of Weak Ties: A Network Theory Revisited," *Sociological Theory*, Vol. 1.1 (1983) 201–233.
124. See Komter, Aafke and Wilma Vollebergh. "Gift Giving and the Emotional Significance of Family and Friends." *Journal of Marriage and Family*, Vol. 59, No. 3 (August 1997).
125. Eric Felten, *Loyalty: The Vexing Virtue* (New York: Simon & Schuster, 2011) 7.
126. See Noah H. Rosenbloom and Samuel D. Luzatto, *Luzzatto's Ethico-Psychological Interpretation of Judaism: A Study in the Religious Philosophy of Samuel David Luzzatto* (New York: Yeshiva University, Department of Special Publications, 1965).
127. Of course, as Timothy Jackson notes, for this to occur, self-sacrifice cannot be blind or self-destructive. One must recognize limits to proper self-sacrifice—for example, that it be kind (right motive), consensual (right form of action) and constructive (right consequence). For example, Jewish law discourages a person from giving more than a fifth of his income to *tzedaka*, lest he himself comes to be in need of charity (BT *Ketubot* 50a).
128. Samson Raphael Hirsch, *The Collected Writings VI* (New York: Feldheim, 1984) 123.
129. Before giving the statement of Rabbi Simlai, the Talmud cites three other statements where prophets have aggregated the commandments into smaller categories and explained what each set of categories entails.

Micah established three principles, as it is said: It has been told you, O man, what is good, and what does the Lord require of you, only (1) to do justly (*mishpat*), (2) to love loving-kindness (*hesed*) and (3) to walk humbly before your God (Micah 6:8). The additional category of "walking humbly before God" is meant to emphasize the fact that when a person does *mishpat* and *hesed* consistently, emergence occurs whereby the person becomes one who possesses the character trait of "walking humbly before God" which is different than a person whose specific actions are humble.

Isaiah established six principles, as it is written: (1) He that walks righteously and (2) speaks uprightly; (3) he that despises the gain of oppressions, (4) that shakes his hand from holding bribes, (5) that stops his ear from hearing blood and (6) shuts his eyes from looking upon evil (Isaiah 33:15). Isaiah distinguishes within the societal and social realms between different types of interactions, namely those of action and those of speaking. As with Micah's third category, Isaiah's first category is one of emergence. The Talmud explains that a person who walks righteously (*tzedakot*) is like Abraham, as it is written, "For I have known him, so that he may command him to guard the way of God, to do *tzedaka* and *mishpat* (Genesis 18:19)."

King David established 11 principles, as it is written: A Psalm of David. Hashem, who shall sojourn in Your tent? Who shall dwell upon Your holy mountain? (1) He that walks wholeheartedly, (2) practices righteousness and (3) speaks truth in his heart; (4) that has no slander upon his tongue, (5) nor does evil to his fellow, (6) nor tolerates an aspersion against his neighbor; (7) in whose eyes a vile person is despised, (8) but he honors them that fear Hashem; (9) he that swears to his own hurt and changes not; (10) he that puts not out his money on interest, (11) nor takes a bribe against the innocent. He that does these things shall never be moved (Psalm 15). King David distinguishes within the societal and social realms between different types of action, namely those of promotion and of correction. Again, the first category is one of emergence. The Talmud explains that he that walks wholeheartedly (*tamim*) is like Abraham, as it is written, "Walk before me and be wholehearted (*tamim*) (Genesis

17:1)." Rabbi Samson Raphael Hirsch describes *tamim* as follows: "A *tamim* unites all his aspirations and masters them from within himself. *One* moral will masters all his aspirations; external allurement will not remove them from his control, and his moral integrity cannot be impaired (*The Hirsch Chumash: Sefer Bereshis*, 175)."

Because both Isaiah's and King David's sets of principles use Abraham as a paradigm, it becomes clear that in achieving one's *telos* a person will come to recognize how his or her actions affect the greater narrative of life so that the true servant of God walks before his Master and not solely alongside Him. This is exemplified in the difference between Abraham, who walked before God, and Hanokh ben Yered, who walked with God. In walking with God, Hanokh, whose name ironically bears the connotations of education and training, nevertheless secluded himself from the people and had no influence on society. (This is in stark contrast to Hanokh ben Kayin. While the Hanokh ben Yered walked with God, yet taught no one, Hanokh ben Kayin, who did not walk with God, became one of the first city-builders.)

130. Psalms 34:15.
131. Psalms 37:27.
132. BT *Avoda Zara* 19b; the proof-text which the Talmud uses to equate good and Torah is "For a good taking I gave to you, My Torah do not forsake it (Proverbs 4:2)."

CHAPTER 4

Entelechy: *Shlemut*

INTRODUCTION

Jacob arrived whole...[1]
> *Whole in his body, for he was cured of his limp. Whole with his money, for he did not lose anything despite the entire gift [that he had given to Esau]. Whole with his Torah, for he had not forgotten [any of] his studies in Laban's house.*[2]

After providing a contemporary vision for what should be one's *telos*, that is, serving God, and of what that activity should comprise, that is, living by faith in pursuing *mishpat* and performing *tzedaka*, I will now provide a brief contemporary description of what the achievement of that *telos* accomplishes for such a person in terms of fully developing his or her moral and intellectual virtues. In later chapters, I will describe how the pursuit of that *telos* influences the development of those virtues, as well as return to discuss in greater detail the consequences of achieving their full development.

Shlemut, per se, is not an Aristotelian idea. It is a Jewish idea that has Biblical origins[3] and Talmudic precedent,[4] yet it has been adapted numerous times over the centuries to fit the various frameworks in which Jewish ethics has been discussed.[5] For example, Kabbalistic views of *Shlemut* differ from Jewish Aristotelian views, despite the fact that they developed over a similar period of time.[6] As a starting point for a contemporary definition, I will rely on Rabbi Samson Raphael Hirsch's definitions of the words *shalem* and *shalom*, which are as follows:

© The Author(s) 2017
I. Bedzow, *Maimonides for Moderns*,
DOI 10.1007/978-3-319-44573-1_4

Shalem is full, harmonious, undiminished completeness, not only physical completeness but also—and above all—moral integrity, in view of the moral dangers to which a person is exposed in the necessary struggle to attain material independence. *Shalem* denotes perfect harmony, especially the complete accord between the outer and inner aspects of things.

Hence *shalem* is related to *tzelem* (image). The form of a thing, the way a thing manifests itself—this is not merely something external. A form is the highest, most fitting embodiment of a thing's inner essence. Every form imposed by a creator represents mastery over external material for the sake of its higher perfection, all in accordance with the conditions dictated by the very nature of the material.

All perfection is the harmonious realization of an idea. All true peace that is worthy of the name *shalom*—and this applies also in communal life—is not fashioned in an exterior mold. Rather, it must emanate from within, in harmonious accord with the essence and ideal of communal life.[7]

When one achieves a state of *Shlemut*, he or she can truly act in the image of God (*b'tzelem Elohim*). This is not to imply that a person has spiritual value or is endowed with a sense of Godliness only when one achieves *Shlemut*. Everyone is endowed with a sense of Godliness whether the person acts accordingly or not, yet there is a distinction between who and what one is and what he or she does, which only becomes unified in *Shlemut*. Consistent with a Maimonidean negative theology, where God's essence cannot be known, the term *tzelem Elohim* connotes an activity and not an essence. To be created in the image of God means that one is created with a particular role in a relationship, to have dominion over the earth in a way that demonstrates compassionate justice and righteousness. Just as a person relates to God through a relationship structured by Divine commands, so does a person who embodies the image of God relate to the world by imposing a just and compassionate order upon it.[8]

My definition for *Shlemut* is as follows: *Shlemut is the active state of living with others, while committed to adhering to the four cubits of Jewish law and the teachings of the Torah, where all aspects of a person, his or her theoretical and practical understanding, emotions, dispositions, and actions, are in harmony.* The person who has achieved *Shlemut* achieves inner peace by virtue of the fact that he or she has no internal conflict; and he or she has attained undiminished completeness since the entire person is in harmony. The concept of *Shlemut* acknowledges that Jewish ethics is focused on more than Divine commands and lawful human action, since it includes notions of human development and social harmony.

My definition of *Shlemut* is similar to, yet not exactly the same as, Gabriel Taylor's and Lynne McFall's definitions of "integrity." Taylor defines integrity as being sincerely true to one's commitments and having the fortitude of will to stay committed to them. The person of integrity "will be rational in a number of related ways. He will not ignore relevant evidence, he will be consistent in his behaviour, he will not act on reasons which, given the circumstances, are insufficient reasons for action."[9] In having integrity, the person keeps himself or herself "intact." McFall defines integrity as the state of being undivided or as an integral whole. This entails having consistency within one's set of principles or commitments and having coherence between one's principles, actions, and the motivations behind them.[10]

There are two main differences between my definition of *Shlemut* and their definitions of integrity. The first is that *Shlemut* accounts for how Jewish law influences a person's commitments and motivations, as well as how a person's religious perspective affects how he or she will consider relevant evidence. A second difference between my view of *Shlemut* and their definitions of integrity is that integrity is often seen as a formal virtue of being "true to one's commitments," where the virtue is an intellectual steadfastness to one's inclinations without including the inclinations themselves. This view is consistent with that of many medieval philosophers, who made a distinction between the material element of a virtue and its formal element. For example, Aquinas writes regarding the moral virtues that "the material element in these virtues is a certain inclination of the appetitive part to the passions and operations according to a certain mode: and since this mode is fixed by reason, the formal element is precisely this order of reason."[11] As I will try to demonstrate below, reasoning cannot be analytically distinguished from one's affective processing; therefore, there cannot be a sharp distinction between one's inclinations and the "mode" (reason) through which those passions are directed. As such, *Shlemut* should not be seen either as a formal or as a material virtue; rather, it should be seen as a description of the harmony one attains when intellectual and moral virtues are properly inclined through the "mode" of Jewish law.

The person who has attained *Shlemut* endeavors to make all of his or her actions willingly fulfill a Divine command.[12] That is not to say that he or she is incapable of sin[13]; on the contrary, he or she retains free will[14] and is concerned that he or she will succumb to sin. Concern over the possibility to sin is based on the premise that self-control, or voluntary choice, is a matter both of physiology and psychology, and that one's resolve can weaken under stress or effort. This premise is supported by the research of neuroscientists who have discovered that willpower is similar to muscle strength in that the more effort one expends, the more fatigued the person gets and the less one is able to continue regulating himself or herself. Nevertheless, a person is able to increase the strength of his or her willpower through moral "exercise" and development.[15]

In normal, everyday circumstances,[16] the person recognizes that the content of his or her actions is an expression of the Divine will, and the volition to perform those actions is unencumbered by other internal motivations which either hinder the person's will to act or motivate the person to perform alternative actions.[17] While the following chapters discuss how *Shlemut* relates to a person's relationship to Jewish law and the development of virtues, to better understand the details of the following chapters, it would be helpful to give a bit more detail up front regarding *Shlemut* and its relation to theoretical understanding, the ethical aspect of Jewish law, and practical understanding.

THEORETICAL UNDERSTANDING

And the spirit of Hashem shall rest upon him, the spirit of wisdom and understanding.[18]

In accord with Maimonides' appreciation of the necessity for theoretical understanding to be a component of *Shlemut*, my contemporary definition of *Shlemut* requires a definite social and metaphysical orientation that is based on a person's understanding of the theoretical and practical concepts and values embedded in the Torah.[19] In terms of his or her metaphysical orientation, the person who has achieved *Shlemut* performs the commandments theonomously,[20] willingly fulfilling the Divine command.[21] This premise is based on the statement of the Talmudic Sages, "It says, 'The Tablets are God's handiwork and the script was God's script, engraved (*harut*) on the Tablets.' Do not read engraved (*harut*) but freedom (*herut*) for you can have no freer man than one who engages in the study of Torah."[22] *Herut* (freedom) is a different form of freedom than *Dror* or *Hofesh*. *Dror* is a form of political freedom; *Hofesh* is to be stripped of external encumbrances. *Herut*, as it is related to *Harut* and hence the exegetical pun, is the ability to act properly after being shaped, that is, positive liberty. This is not to say that he or she acts solely by virtue of his or her own rational justification independent of the normativity of the law. Rather, in recognizing that his or her rationality has been developed through a process of religious and moral development,[23] by which the law provides epistemic and normative facts and reasons, the person who has attained *Shlemut* acts in service to God with the trust that the Divine seeks to benefit the world. This idea of rationality is in line with a Maimonidean framework, and will be discussed below.

The demand for a metaphysical orientation in order to achieve *Shlemut* has Talmudic precedent, as seen through the following account: Rabbi Judah HaNassi said, "Great is circumcision, for [notwithstanding] all the commandments that Abraham our father fulfilled, he was not called *Shalem* until he circumcised himself, as it is written, 'Walk before Me, and be *tamim.*'"[24] The importance of the statement is not that Abraham performed an additional commandment; rather its importance is in the type of command he fulfilled and the manner in which it was commanded. It shows that *Shlemut* is not an autonomous, individual development of one's intellectual and moral virtues. On the contrary, *Shlemut* cannot be achieved unless the person is bound in a relationship that is greater than him or her. The Talmud recognizes the social and metaphysical requirements of *Shlemut* through Rabbi Judah's explanation of Rabbi Judah HaNassi's statement.[25] Rabbi Judah explains that when God said to Abraham, "Walk before me and be *tamim,*" Abraham was seized with trembling because he thought that there still might be something shameful in him. Only when God stated, "And I will make my covenant between Me and you," did Abraham become appeased.[26] In other words, only when Abraham could live by faith and have complete trust in his covenant with God could his habits reach a level of confidence such that he would not falter because of self-doubt even when he knew his choices were correct.[27]

THE ETHICAL ASPECT OF JEWISH LAW

Happy are they that are upright in the way, who walk in the law of Hashem.[28]

The premise that fulfillment of Jewish law affects the attainment of *Shlemut* challenges the Aristotelian idea that ethics is the means through which humans in general, yet as particular individuals, act so as to actual-ize the unique aspect of their humanity, whereas law, on the other hand, is the framework through which political leaders determine how people in particular, yet as a general populace, should act so as to maintain society.

This distinction between law and ethics, however, is not limited to an Aristotelian view. Rather, it has become a common distinction even among contemporary legal and moral philosophers.[29]

Yet medieval Jewish philosophers, and in particular Maimonides, have already proposed an alternative view of the relationship between law and ethics. As we will examine in the following chapters, Maimonides proposes a two-tiered conception of Jewish law,[30] where in the first tier the law serves as a tool for social stability and for moral development in the sense of habituating good actions yet not in the sense of being a means to actualize a person's potential. In the second tier, however, the law serves as a direct means to promote intellectual and moral development.[31]

PRACTICAL UNDERSTANDING

So that you make your ear attend to wisdom, and your heart incline to understanding.[32]

Much of the contemporary literature regarding ethics and law assumes that ethics is consistent with freedom of conviction and the proper will of the agent. In other words, ethics presupposes that one is able to grasp and to do what is right regardless of external threat or reward and that the person maintains authority over the principles by which he or she thinks and acts. The first presupposition, namely, the ability to grasp and do what is right, regardless of external threat or reward, has long been part of Jewish thought, even as it has been placed alongside the notion of obedience.[33] For just one medieval example: Rabbi Bahya ibn Pakuda writes in *Torat Hovot HaLevovot* (*Sha'ar Avodat Elohim, Perek* 3),

> Service is defined as the submission of a beneficiary to his benefactor, [which he expresses] by repaying him—to the best of his ability—for the favor [he received from him]. This submission is of two types: (1) submission out of fear and expectation, under compulsion and pressure; and (2) submission out of [a sense of] duty and [a sense] that it is right to exalt and glorify the individual one submits to. Of the first type is that submission to God which is prompted by an external stimulus (mentioned above), for it follows from the phenomenon of reward and punishment in this world and the next. The second type, however, is submission which is prompted by a stimulus embedded in the mind and implanted in the nature of man when his body and soul are joined together. ... The submission which is prompted by the [inner] urging of the mind and by rational demonstration is preferred by God and more acceptable.

The second presupposition, on the other hand, is what is meant by the Kantian notion of autonomy, and it is a relatively modern challenge to Jewish ethics and its relationship with Jewish law.[34]

To respond to the challenge that moral thinking requires that the agent has sole authority over his or her principles of rationality, I will provide an alternative view of practical (and theoretical) reasoning, whereby the agent responds to reasons that exist in the world rather than originating reasons for himself or herself. This alternative view allows for three consequences. First, it provides a means to maintain volition for the agent even when there exists an external normative framework by which he or she is obligated. Second, it offers the ability to construct a Jewish deontology that maintains that a person has autonomy of execution rather than of legislation. Third, it provides an account of rationality that is more amenable to my contemporary description of the development of intellectual virtue.

A practical example for how this alternative view of rationality allows one to explain the relationship between a person's will, his or her developing intellectual virtue, and an external normative framework which must be obeyed is when a person is faced with a Divine command which seems to contradict the person's moral sense. Because the person recognizes that his or her moral sense has been developed by virtue of observing Divine commandments, he or she appreciates the situation as one where the seeming contradiction is a consequence either of not knowing all of the details of the situation or of misinterpreting the particular command in light of its relationship with other Divine commands. When faced with this situation, the person who has attained *Shlemut* will approach the difficulty with a sense of epistemological humility[35] and with the motivation to find a (legally appropriate) interpretation of the seemingly immoral command that best fits with the moral sense that the other commandments provide.

Another example for how this view of rationality can explain the relationship between a person's will, his or her developing intellectual virtue, and an external normative framework which must be obeyed is when one acts *lifnim mishurat hadin. Lifnim mishurat hadin* is usually translated as supererogation either acting "beyond the letter of the law" or acting "within the limits of the law." The difference in the latter two translations is a consequence of which perspective to take vis-à-vis the law when translating the phrase, that is, the law is either the limit of what is acceptable or the limit of what is required. Though many have argued that when acting *lifnim mishurat hadin,* one acts from a moral duty that stands independent of any legal obligation,[36] the Talmudic sources seem to indicate that acting *lifnim mishurat hadin* should be conceived as voluntary obedience to the spirit of the law so as to allow for the manifestation of the ethical within the legal. While the concept of *lifnim mishurat hadin* will be discussed at length in Appendix I, I will provide the most oft-quoted example of the concept here to explain my point. Though the term is not explicitly mentioned, the *Rishonim* refer to it as a case of *lifnim mishurat hadin*. The case is as follows:

> Some porters [negligently] broke a barrel of wine belonging to Rabbah son of Rabbi Huna. Thereupon he seized their garments; so they went and complained to Rav. "Return them their garments," he ordered. "Is that the law?" he enquired. "Even so," he rejoined: "That you may walk in the way of good men." Their garments having been returned, they observed, "We are poor men, have worked all day, and are in need: are we to get nothing?" "Go and pay them," he ordered. "Is that the law?" he asked. "Even so," was his reply: "and keep the path of the righteous."[37]

Even though his actions were more than the basic law required, it is difficult to say that Rabba acted supererogatively and from a position of moral autonomy. Moreover, it is difficult to say that he acted ethically, in terms of acting independent of the law, since he acted upon the directive of Rav, whose order was made obligatory by virtue of his authority as a legal decisor and judge.[38]

∗ ∗ ∗ ∗

The following chapters examine, from different angles, how a person who achieves *Shlemut* forms his or her worldview and how he or she lives according to it. This formation is a result of a combination of factors, namely, one's societal and social environment (law), the manner of interpreting and responding to one's experiences (theoretical and practical reasoning), and the development of tools by which one can coherently and accurately interpret and act on one's understanding of the world (intellectual and moral virtues). Therefore, no single chapter alone can convey how *Shlemut* is achieved, since each chapter provides an account of how one of these interdependent components work. In order to understand how a person achieves *Shlemut* in terms of forming an appropriate worldview and acting properly according to it, one must look at all the chapters as a whole with various related parts.

NOTES

1. Genesis 33:18.
2. Genesis Rabbah 79:5; BT *Shabbat* 33b.
3. The Biblical roots of *Shlemut* can be seen through the meaning of two different Biblical expressions, namely "a whole heart (*lev/levav shalem*)" and "with all one's heart (*b'khol lev/levav*)." For a few examples of the use of the expression "a whole heart (*lev/levav shalem*)," see I Kings 8:61; 11:4; 15:3,14; II Kings 20:3; Isaiah 38:3; I Chronicles 12:39; 28:9; 29:9,19; II Chronicles 15:17; 16:9; 19:9; 25:2. For a few examples of the use of the expression "with all one's heart (*b'khol lev/levav*)," see Deuteronomy 4:29; 6:5; 10:12; 11:13; 13:4; 26:16; 30:2, 6, 10; Joshua 22:5; 23:14; I Samuel 12:20,24; I Kings 2:4; 8:23, 48; II Kings 10:31; 23:3, 25; Jeremiah 29:13; Psalms 9:2.

    Yoram Hazony correctly points out in *The Philosophy of Hebrew Scripture* that the word *lev* does not mean "heart" in the strict sense of either the organ or simply the seat of emotions in contradistinction to the "mind." Rather, the Biblical term *lev* encompasses a person's processes of thought and his or her emotions in one unified sense (171). This idea is extended to the Mishnaic meaning of the word *lev*, which encompasses how one perceives the world, acts toward his or her friends and neighbors, and considers the consequences of his or her actions (*Mishna Avot* 2:13).

4. See BT *Berakhot* 17a; BT *Sotah* 40a.
5. Rabbi Eliezer Berkovits explains the phenomenon of Judaism having multifarious forms in which it has expressed itself and the various frameworks that Jewish philosophy has taken as follows: "Ever since Sinai we have witnessed an entire series of Jewries, all based on Torah and Halakha, yet differing from each other in outlook, attitude, and their understanding of Judaism. Babylonian Jewry was not Spanish Jewry; and the Spanish Jewry of Gabirol, the Ibn Ezras, of Hisdai Ibn Shaprut, Halevi and Maimonides, was not the Central European Jewry of the authors of the Tosafot. Nearer to our own times, the halakhic Jewries of Eastern Europe were not the halakhic Jewries of a Samson Raphael Hirsch or an Ezriel Hildesheimer. There were vast differences between them in the understanding of Halakha, in the philosophical interpretation of the teachings and faith of Judaism; considerable divergences in

their respective attitudes toward the outside world, far-reaching ideological disagreements concerning secular studies and professional pursuits ('Authentic Judaism and Halakha,' 66)." As Rabbi Berkovits notes, as long as a Jewish philosophy incorporates the normative premises of the reality of God, Israel, and the Torah, it is an authentic Jewish philosophy, regardless of the schematic framework in which ideas are explained.

6. Elliot R. Wolfson, "Light through Darkness: The Ideal of Human Perfection in the Zohar," *The Harvard Theological Review*, Vol. 81, No. 1 (January 1988) 73–95.

7. Samson Raphael Hirsch, *The Hirsch Chumash: Sefer Bereshis* (New York: Feldheim Publishers, 2005) 675–676.

8. For an extensive account of my understanding of *tzelem Elohim* in contradistinction to Rabbi Soloveitchik's description, see *Halakhic Man, Authentic Jew: Moderns Expressions of Orthodox Thought*, 28–42.

9. Gabriele Taylor and Raimond Gaita, "Integrity," *Proceedings of the Aristotelian Society*, Supplementary Volumes, Vol. 55 (1981) 148.

10. Lynne McFall, "Integrity," *Ethics*, Vol. 98, No. 1 (October 1987) 5–20.

11. *Summa Theologiae*, First Part of the Second Part, Treatise on Virtue, Question 67. See also, Jeffrey Blustein, *Care and Commitment: Taking the Personal Point of View* (Oxford University Press, 1992).

12. This premise is based on the normative statement, "Rabbi Yossi says: Apply yourself to study Torah, for it is not yours by inheritance. Let all your deeds be for the sake of Heaven" (*Mishna Avot* 2:17).

13. "For there is not a righteous man upon earth that does good and does not sin (Ecclesiastes 7:20)."

14. This premise is one that is accepted within the Jewish tradition, as seen by the statement in the Mishna, "Everything is foreseen, yet the freedom of choice is given" (*Mishna Avot* 3:19). Though there has been debate, both within Jewish philosophy and in philosophy more generally about the nature of free will, I accept the general premise that free will exists.

15. For example, see the following literature: Roy F. Baumeister, F. Todd Dianne M. Heatherton, *Losing Control: How and Why People Fail at Self-Regulation* (San Diego: Academic Press, 1994);

Mark Muraven, Roy F. Baumeister, and Dianne M. Tice, "Longitudinal Improvement of Self-Regulation Through Practice: Building Self-Control Strength Through Repeated Exercise," *The Journal of Social Psychology*, Vol. 139, No. 4 (1999) 446–457; M. Muraven and R.F. Baumeister, "Self-Regulation and Depletion of Limited Resources: Does Self-Control Resemble a Muscle?" *Psychological Bulletin*, Vol. 126 (2000) 247–259; Roy F. Baumeister, Kathleen D. Vohs and Dianne M. Tice, "The Strength Model of Self-Control," *Current Directions in Psychological Science*, Vol. 16, No. 6 (December, 2007) 351–355; Michael Inzlicht and Jennifer Gutsell, "Running on Empty: Neural Signals for Self-Control Failure," *Psychological Science*, Vol. 18, No. 11 (November 2007) 933–937; K. D. Vohs, R. F. Baumeister, B. J. Schmeichel, J. M. Twenge, N. M. Nelson, and D. M. Tice, "Making Choices Impairs Subsequent Self-Control: A Limited Resource Account of Decision Making, Self-Regulation, and Active Initiative," *Journal of Personality and Social Psychology*, Vol. 94 (2008) 883–898; Suzanne C. Segerstrom, Jaime K. Hardy, Daniel R. Evans, and Natalie F. Winters, "Pause and Plan: Self-Regulation and the Heart," *How Motivation Affects Cardiovascular Response: Mechanisms and Applications*, eds. Rex A. Wright and H. E. Guido (Washington, DC: American Psychological Association, 2012) 181–198.

16. As opposed to cases of moral dilemma or extreme moral fatigue, such as when Moses struck the rock, see Numbers 20.

17. This premise is based on the normative statement, "Treat His will as if it were your own will, so that He will treat your will as if it were His will. Nullify your will before His will, so that He will nullify the will of others before your will (*Mishna Avot* 2:4)."

18. Isaiah 11:2.

19. Having a metaphysical orientation is important for *Shlemut* for the same reason that meaning is an important component of well-being. As Martin Seligman writes, "Human beings, ineluctably, want meaning and purpose in life. The Meaningful Life consists in belonging to and serving something that you believe is bigger than the self (*Flourish: A Visionary Understanding of Happiness and Well-being*, 12)." Also, having a metaphysical orientation has been shown to reinforce positive lifestyle choices as well as habits despite difficulties that may arise. Though she does not conclude how a person's spiritual orientation is related to better outcomes in

substance abuse recovery, Sarah E. Zemore has found that not only may having a spiritual orientation help prevent the development of substance abuse but there is a role for spirituality in recovery from substance abuse as well. See Sarah E. Zemore, "A Role for Spiritual Change in the Benefits of 12-Step Involvement," *Alcoholism: Clinical and Experimental Research* (2007) 31: 76s–79s.

20. Based on the verse, "For the children of Israel are servants to Me; they are My servants, whom I took out of the land of Egypt. I am the Lord, your God (Lev. 25:55)," Rabbi Yohanan ben Zakkai comments, "For unto me the children of Israel are servants, they are my servants, and not servants of servants" (BT *Kiddushin* 22b).

21. This premise is based on the normative statement, "Rabbi Elazar of Bartosa says: Give Him from His own, for you are your possessions are His." And so David has said, "For everything is from You, and from Your own we have given You" (*Mishna Avot* 3:8).

22. *Mishna Avot* 6:2.

23. This premise is based on the normative statement, "Rabbi Chanina ben Dosa says: Anyone whose fear of sin takes priority over his wisdom, his wisdom will endure; but anyone whose wisdom takes priority over his fear of sin, his wisdom will not endure" (*Mishna Avot* 3:11).

24. BT *Nedarim* 31b. The word *tamim* and the word *shalem* are often seen as synonymous. In fact, Onkelos, a famous convert to Judaism in Tannaitic times (c. 35–120CE), who is attributed as the author of the famous Targum Onkelos, translates the Torah verse, "Be *tamim* with Hashem, your Elohim, (*Devarim* 18:13)" as "Be *shalim*" using a word which is the Aramaic equivalent to *shalem*.

25. Rabbi Judah's explanation is actually found after a slightly different version of Rabbi's statement, which says, "Great is circumcision, for none so ardently busied himself with [God's] precepts as our father Abraham, yet he was called *tamim* only in virtue of having a circumcision, as it is written, 'Walk before me and be *tamim*,' and it is written, 'And I will make my covenant between me and you' (BT *Nedarim* 32a)."

26. The second verse immediately follows the verse about Abraham becoming *tamim*. See BT *Nedarim* 32b.

27. The idea that *Shlemut* cannot be achieved unless the person is bound by belief in a relationship that is greater than he or she has

support from recent research in psychology. For example, Christiano Castelfranchi and Fabio Paglieri have stated that "a goal is not a representation currently and necessarily orienting and guiding an action; instead, it is a representation endowed with this *potential* function, so that it is somehow 'destined' to play this role—but whether or not this role is actually fulfilled depends…on the agent's beliefs ('The role of beliefs in goal dynamics: Prolegomena to a constructive theory of intentions,' 240)." For entertaining examples of how beliefs affect the success of actions and achieving goals, see Charles Duhigg, *The Power of Habit: Why We Do What We Do in Life and Business* (New York: Random House, 2012). Similarly, philosopher Frank Ramsey has provided an apt metaphor to convey the direct relationship between beliefs and actions in saying that beliefs are "maps by which we steer," meaning that beliefs not only describe the world but also serve a function in determining how a person will act in it ("Truth and probability").

28. Psalms 119:1.
29. For one example, see Joseph Raz, *Ethics in the Public Domain: Essays in the Morality of Law and Politics* (Oxford: Clarendon Press, 2001).
30. Maimonides admits that only the Divine Law of the Torah is two-tiered and that all other legal systems pertain solely to the political realm in establishing peace and security. For more information, see MN II:40; Pines, 383–384.
31. For examples of how Maimonides demonstrates the first tier of the law's purpose, see his reasons for what constitutes a proper witness in *Hilkhot Edut* 11:1–5; his reasons for the severity of murder and the social rectifications allowed due to its severity in *Hilkhot Rotseah* 4:8–9 and *Hilkhot Melakhim* 3:10; how the prohibition to bear a grudge is meant to allow for a stable environment, trade, and commerce in *Hilkhot Deot* 7:8. Also, regarding the *Eglah Arufah* (the law of the decapitated calf), Maimonides notes that atonement is mentioned with regard to it (*Hilkhot Rotseah* 10:2), yet in *Moreh Nevukhim* he gives a social reason for the ritual, namely to find the killer. The social benefits of the commandments against prohibited relations and of circumcision are also discussed in *Moreh Nevukhim* III, 49. In *Hilkhot Yesode HaTorah* 4:13, Maimonides calls the commandments a great good that God has allowed for stable liv-

ing. In *Hilkhot Genevah* 7:12, he writes, "Whoever denies the commandment of just measures is considered as if he denied the Exodus from Egypt [by which the Jewish people became a nation], which is the first of God's commandments. Conversely, one who accepts the commandment of just measures is considered as if he acknowledges the Exodus from Egypt, which brought about all of God's commandments."

32. Proverbs 2:2.

33. Bahya ben Joseph ibn Pakuda, Yehudah ibn Tibbon, and Daniel Haberman, *Sefer Torat Hovot HaLevovot* (New York: Feldheim, 1996) 249.

34. See J.B. Scheenwind's *The Invention of Autonomy* (Cambridge: Cambridge University Press, 1998), where he argues that the idea of moral autonomy developed from the seventeenth and eighteenth centuries, when conceptions of morality changed from obedience to self-governance, until the onset of Kant, who was the first to use the idea of autonomy in the sense of giving oneself law (from *auto-* "self" + *nomos* "custom, law").

35. This premise is based on the normative statement, "Rabbi Nehorai said: Exile yourself to a place of Torah, and do not assume that it will come after you, for it is your colleagues who will cause it to remain with you, and do not rely on your own understanding" (*Mishna Avot* 4:18).

36. See, for example, Louis E. Newman, "Law, Virtue and Supererogation in the Halakha: The Problem of 'Lifnim Mishurat Hadin' Reconsidered," *Journal of Jewish Studies*, Vol. 40 (1989).

37. BT *Bava Metsia* 83a.

38. BT *Berakhot* 7a, 20b, 45b; BT *Bava Kama* 99b; BT *Bava Metsia* 24b, 30b; BT *Ketubot* 97a; BT *Avodah Zara* 4b; see also *Mekhilta d'Rabbi Shimon bar Yohai* (Exodus 18:20); *Mekhilta d'Rabbi Ishmael* (*Masekhta d'Amalek, Yitro* 2).

CHAPTER 5

The Law

INTRODUCTION

And what great nation is there, that has statutes and ordinances so righteous as all this law, which I set before you this day?[1]

In this chapter, I will first describe the difference between Aristotle and Maimonides with respect to their views on the role of the law in their theory of ethics. In the next chapter, I will provide a contemporary explanation of how the law may instill practical and theoretical concepts in its adherents. In particular, I will show that the law shapes a person's mental processes and provides both theoretical and practical concepts which a person uses in his or her daily living through two mechanisms, namely (1) by creating social categories through which a person comes to understand the world and (2) by integrating those concepts into a person's understanding of the world through their use in influencing daily behavior and in shaping a person's habits so as to be in line with legal norms.

These two mechanisms that the law utilizes are also found in Maimonides' conception of the law and its relation to theoretical reasoning and understanding. However, the ways in which the two mechanisms are described are different, since the philosophical framework in which I am using them is contemporary and not Aristotelian.

© The Author(s) 2017
I. Bedzow, *Maimonides for Moderns,*
DOI 10.1007/978-3-319-44573-1_5

The Role of the Law According to Aristotle

In those days there was no king in Israel; every man did that which was right in his own eyes.[2]

In order to appreciate my conception of how the law shapes moral and intellectual virtues, as well as how it differs from an Aristotelian or Maimonidean paradigm, I will first provide an outline of how Aristotle and Maimonides conceive the role of the law in social and moral life as well as how it relates to the development of the virtues. I will then provide my conception of the role of the law in a contemporary Jewish virtue ethics.

Aristotle begins his inquiry in the *Nicomachean Ethics* with the assumption that his students have had a proper moral upbringing. His inquiry is meant only to reflect philosophically on that which is already assumed and his intention is to educate those who already possess a proper, albeit unreflective, conception of the good. Aristotle asserts that his lectures will be ineffectual in providing a basis for moral development to those who do not already possess a firm moral grounding. He writes,

> Now each man judges well the things he knows, and of these he is a good judge. And so the man who has been educated in a subject is a good judge of that subject, and the man who has received an all-round education is a good judge in general. Hence a young man is not a proper hearer of lectures on political science; for he is inexperienced in the actions that occur in life, but its discussions start from these and are about these; and, further, since he tends to follow his passions, his study will be vain and unprofitable, because the end aimed at is not knowledge but action.[3]

When Aristotle describes *eudaimonia* as that to which all people aim,[4] he presupposes that "all people" are those who already have been given a good education and therefore have, if not a proper conception of the good, then one that is relatively close to what Aristotle contends is the correct opinion so that they may be convinced by him.[5] Because Aristotle's main audience consists of people who already have been socialized by their upbringing, the effective cause of which Aristotle speaks, which moves a person toward his or her natural *telos*, is not strictly biological; rather, there is interdependence between biology and social influences. Intellectual and moral development depends on the person cultivating his or her social character as a second nature. This sociality, as opposed to that which is strictly biological, is what Aristotle considers part of what is unique to humanity, and it is through a person's second nature that *eudaimonia* can be attained.

According to Aristotle, abiding by the law of the state is a necessary precondition to human development and *eudaimonia*, but it is not the effective cause for it. This is so because humans do not voluntarily choose to obey the law so as to bring them to their final end. It is the choice of pursuing human flourishing, once they are already habituated by the law, which people voluntarily choose. Moreover, the law in essence becomes irrelevant as practical reason develops. Initial obedience to the law is a continuing part of character education that is begun at home, where the political community plays the role, albeit at the level of the state, played by parents at the level of the household. Also, it is the compulsory power of the law, that is, its punishments and penalties, which serve to initiate the process of socialization.[6] Part and parcel of its socializing role, the laws of the state also aim to provide the general societal conditions for individuals to attain *eudaimonia* as individuals. It does not, however, provide it per se, either to the statesman or to its citizens.

Aristotle does admit that because people may at times in their lives falter in using their practical reason, the laws of the state will always be necessary. He writes,

> But it is difficult to get from youth up a right training for excellence if one has not been brought up under right laws; for to live temperately and hardily is not pleasant to most people, especially when they are young. For this reason their nurture and occupations should be fixed by law; for they will not be painful when they have become customary. But it is surely not enough that when they are young they should get the right nurture and attention; since they must, even when they are grown up, practice and be habituated to them, we shall need laws for this as well, and generally speaking to cover the whole life; for most people obey necessity rather than argument, and punishments rather than what is noble.[7]

Maimonides shares Aristotle's contention that the compulsory obedience to the law is not the efficient cause that pushes a person toward his or her final end.[8] An efficient cause is something that motivates a person to act toward the good or toward an ideal to which he or she aspires. Punishment through the law is a means to keep people in check; it serves a restraining function. Though one could argue that an efficient cause is anything that produces a change of motion,[9] it is easy to recognize that there should be a distinction between physical causes and ethical ones, especially since Aristotle already recognizes in his ethics that a person, as a rational being, acts voluntarily and is not just a biological mass that becomes an effect of a prior cause. Therefore, unlike a beast that fears the whip or a leaf that blows in the wind, a rational human being is ethically motivated by his or her rational conception of the good.[10] As to the person who follows the law from fear of punishment, Maimonides writes,

> It is not fitting to serve God in this manner. A person whose service is motivated by these factors is considered one who serves out of fear. He is not on the level of the prophets or of the wise. The only ones who serve God in this manner are common people, women,[11] and minors. They are trained to serve God out of fear until their knowledge increases and they serve out of love.[12]

As it pertains to the ethical development of individuals, the compulsory force of the law at its initial stage for Maimonides, and for all stages for Aristotle, is for the pedagogic purpose of habituation and for maintaining a peaceful and secure social environment so that people can develop their potential. Only when good actions already have begun to shape a person's moral character can voluntary choice—based on practical wisdom for Aristotle and the law for Maimonides—allow for movement toward one's *telos*. Of course, to serve God from love entails that the person has acquired theoretical wisdom and knowledge of the proper way to act, yet, for Maimonides, the law provides both forms of knowledge. Therefore, to appreciate what the motivating impetus is for Maimonides, one must understand it from the perspective of a person who has already accepted the law as obligatory rather than from the perspective of what makes the law obligatory.

If he adopted a strictly Aristotelian framework for his ethics, Maimonides' conception of the law would be limited to being solely a necessary precondition to human ethical development; it would not be a direct means for a person to attain his or her *telos*. However, Maimonides does not adopt a strictly Aristotelian framework. He has a two-tiered conception of law,[13] *which includes the law's ability to promote intellectual and moral development directly.*

Maimonides' Two-Tiered Conception of the Law

But his delight is in the law of Hashem; and in His law does he meditate day and night.[14]

Maimonides presumes that a person can pursue four types of perfections, which he delineates in his last chapter of *Moreh Nevukhim*. The first is perfection as regard to possessing property. Yet he dismisses this perfection as imaginary, since its pursuit will not result in perfection in any sense. The second kind of perfection is physical, and it includes one's constitution and temperaments. Maimonides similarly dismisses this perfection as worthy of primary pursuit since it does not allow for the soul to achieve perfection. The third kind of perfection is moral perfection, which he calls the highest degree of excellence in a person's character. While this type of perfection is worthy of attainment, and most of the commandments are meant to assist in the achievement of this perfection, its pursuit is nevertheless not for its own sake but rather for the highest kind of perfection. Moral perfection is only a means to another end because it is necessarily social by nature, and interpersonal relations allow one to become an instrument for another. While this is not in itself a negative effect, it is not conducive to the ultimate achievement because it is dependent upon factors outside of one's control. Also, when one removes himself from interpersonal relations, a person's moral perfection is of no consequence. The fourth kind of perfection is what Maimonides calls the true perfection of man. It is possession of the highest, intellectual faculties, which allow a person to apprehend true metaphysical opinions. Unlike moral perfection, true human perfection is not dependent on social life and therefore not subject to varying social conventions. Therefore, it is more stable than moral perfection simply by virtue of the fact that it is not dependent on others, neither for its values nor for the ability of its manifestation in action.

Departing from Aristotle, Maimonides explicitly asserts that the law serves a dual purpose, namely, the welfare of the body, that is, facilitating moral perfection, and the welfare of the soul, that is, facilitating intellectual perfection.[15] Welfare of the body does not refer to the physical health of an individual,[16] since this would contradict his dismissal of the second type of perfection which men seek to attain. When the Torah does promote physical health, it is not directly, such as in prescribing only healthy foods and proper balance between work and rest. Rather, the Torah affects a person's health by restraining his or her base desires, such as his or her appetite, so that the person's moral and intellectual constitution has a positive effect on his or her bodily health. Hannah Kasher writes, "Maimonides, on the other hand, does not believe that the digestion of forbidden foods causes a change in the character of the person involved. The basic contribution of the dietary laws to the observant Jew is their very essence as prohibitions, which therefore teach man to curb his base desires."[17] Concern over the welfare of the soul is demonstrated by the fact that through the law a person acquires correct beliefs, each according to his or her capacity. As for the welfare of the body, the law provides a means for proper social living. Social living has two components, even if they are intimately related. First, the law establishes rules for social order. Second, it allows for the acquisition of moral character traits that are useful for social life and political affairs. That the law provides for both is asserted by Maimonides as follows:

> The true Law then, which as we have already made clear is unique—namely, the Law of Moses our Master—has come to bring us both perfections, I mean the welfare of the states of people in their relations with one another through the abolition of reciprocal wrongdoing and through the acquisition of a noble and excellent character.[18] In this way the preservation of the population of the country and their permanent existence in the same order become possible, so that every one of them achieves his first perfection; I mean also the soundness of the beliefs and the giving of the correct opinions through which ultimate perfection is achieved. The letter of the Torah speaks of both perfections and informs us that the end of this Law in its entirety is the achievement of these two perfections.[19]

Similarly, with respect to the *Mishna* which states that the world is sustained by truth, judgment, and peace,[20] Maimonides notes that this means that when a state is upright, the law can also promote the development of moral virtues (peace) and intellectual virtues (truth). As such, both the world and each individual, who is thought to be a "small world," are sustained by the law.

Maimonides' second tier, which serves the higher purpose of providing for the welfare of the soul, is based on his conception of the relationship between the law and theoretical reasoning. For Maimonides, the law relates to theoretical reasoning in that it provides a person with correct beliefs,[21] which must then be fully apprehended through theoretical speculation. Theoretical speculation therefore presupposes the authority of the law in establishing—or at least directing a person to discovering—what is true, yet the law also requires a person to engage in speculation so that he or she can turn accepted beliefs into sincerely held convictions. This point will be discussed further in my examination of theoretical reasoning and intellectual virtue below. Corresponding to his dual purpose of the law, Maimonides also distinguishes between two forms of studying the law, each of which is relegated to a particular welfare. On the one hand, there is the legal study of the law, which is jurisprudence and the understanding of normative precepts in all of their particularities. The philosophical study of the law, [22] on the other hand, is "the science of Law in its true sense. Or rather its purpose is to give indications to a religious man for whom the validity of our Law has become established in his soul and has become actual in his belief—such a man being perfect in his religion and character, and having studied the sciences of the philosophers and come to know what they signify."[23] Isadore Twersky aptly describes the dual role that Maimonides held, based on his two-tiered conception of the law, as follows: "While the jurist generally cares only about the law, the arena of actions and behavior, and considers any preamble or postscript inept and pointless, the philosopher cares primarily about the rational principle and philosophic animus, the moral standard and the intellectual objective, rather than the content of the law and its specific imperatives. Maimonides as jurist and philosopher combined both interests in all his writings."[24] Through the philosophical study of the law, a person engages in theoretical speculation so as to understand the truth of those ideas about the world which the law imparts.[25]

Maimonides maintains the relationship between the law and theoretical speculation throughout his writings. In the introduction to *Moreh Nevukhim*, Maimonides asserts that God wants a person to be perfected (and that societies should be improved) through His laws, yet he admits that perfection by way of fulfilling the commandments can only come after one has adopted certain intellectual beliefs and has understood them through the study of the natural and Divine sciences.[26] Similarly, in the beginning of the *Mishne Torah*, Maimonides writes,

> I maintain that it is not proper for a person to stroll in the *Pardes* unless he has filled his belly with bread and meat. "Bread and meat" refer to the knowledge of what is permitted and what is forbidden, and similar matters concerning other commandments. Even though the Sages referred to these

as "a small matter"—for our Sages said: "'A great matter,' this refers to *Ma'aseh Merkavah*. 'A small matter,' this refers to the debates of Abaye and Rava,"—nevertheless, it is fitting for them to be given precedence, because they settle a person's mind. Also, they are the great good which the Holy One, blessed be He, has granted, [to allow for] stable [living] within this world and the acquisition of the life of the world to come. They can be known in their totality by the great and the small, man or woman, whether [granted] expansive knowledge or limited knowledge.[27]

Yet even though one must first be filled with "meat" in order to philosophize, Maimonides spends the first chapters of the *Mishne Torah*, which precede this comment, discussing philosophical ideas. The reason for doing this is the same as that put forth in *Moreh Nevukhim*, namely, philosophical ideas are provided by the law to set the perspective for learning the law properly, so that a person is efficacious in perfecting himself or herself through performing the commandments and contemplating their details.[28] Complete philosophical investigation, however, is only permitted after the person has become more knowledgeable in the law and habituated in its observance.

It is important to stress that, for Maimonides, the law does not entirely replace the need for theoretical speculation; rather, it only communicates correct ideas in a summary manner. Their understanding through philosophical inquiry will consequently bring ultimate perfection. For example, the law commands that a person believe in God, yet it does not inform a person of what belief entails in all of its complexity and detail.[29] Also, the beliefs that concern the whole of existence, which are validated through theoretical speculation, are only implicitly prescribed in commandments such as to love God.[30] The law is thus necessary to impart proper beliefs, yet it is insufficient as a means to transform those beliefs into knowledge and correct convictions.[31] Only through theoretical speculation can a person come to understand the truth of the law's commanded beliefs. Maimonides writes in the *Moreh Nevukhim*,

> It is through this wisdom, in an unrestricted sense, that the rational matter that we receive from the Law through tradition, is demonstrated. ... The Sages, may their memory be blessed, mention likewise that man is required first to obtain knowledge of the Torah, then to obtain wisdom, then to know what is incumbent upon him with regard to the legal science of the Law—I mean the drawing of inferences concerning what one ought to do. And this should be the order observed: The opinions in question should

first be known as being received through tradition; then they should be demonstrated; then the actions through which one's way of life may be ennobled, should be precisely defined.[32]

In other words, though the law aims at the welfare of the body and of the soul, Maimonides admits that ultimate perfection consists in knowing everything that is within the capacity of a person to know in accordance with his or her ultimate perfection. Moreover, he writes, "It is clear that to this ultimate perfection there do not belong either actions or moral qualities and that it consists only of opinions *toward which speculation has led and that investigation has rendered compulsory.*"[33] The law provides only general opinions and demands further speculation because the law, and the concepts which it conveys, must be applicable to the majority; its success in being understood cannot be dependent on the circumstances of individuals or of the times.[34] Providing general opinions allows for the broadest influence on society, quantitatively if not qualitatively.

Two Examples

Maimonides' contention that theoretical and practical knowledge are provided by the law and that acceptance of certain beliefs is a prerequisite to moral development, which is in turn a prerequisite to intellectual growth, is exemplified in his treatment of the relationship between *hinukh* and *limmud* and in his discussion regarding the proper process for conversion.

Aristotle distinguishes between habituation and training, which allow for the development of the practical intellect, and education, which helps a person develop his theoretical intellect.[35] Maimonides similarly distinguishes between *hinukh* and *limmud*. *Hinukh*, as physical training in how to perform commandments, is given to children who are not yet intellectually mature enough to understand their meaning. Likewise, due to their lack of maturity, children are not obligated to perform commandments outside of their need for training. *Limmud*, on the other hand, is a lifetime obligation to study Torah and Jewish law for its theoretical as well as practical importance.

Even though children must learn how to perform commandments in order to fulfill their legal obligations upon reaching maturity, in order for the observance of commandments to contribute to one's moral and intellectual development, Maimonides asserts that one should first learn about the metaphysical importance of one's actions through studying Torah and

Jewish law. Then one will come to act properly, and proper action will ultimately help a person to engage in deeper theoretical speculation. This charge is apparent in Maimonides' use of the verse, "Hear, O Israel, the *hukkim* and the *mishpatim* which I speak in your ears this day, that you should learn them, and observe to perform them."[36] In explanation of this verse, he writes, "Therefore, you find [regarding] the command in the whole Torah 'you should learn' and afterwards 'to perform them' [because] learning precedes action, since learning will bring [a person] to perform action but action does not bring [a person] to learn, and that is what is stated in the Talmud that learning brings one to action."[37] The type of learning to which Maimonides refers is not technical training in how to perform the commandments. The word to describe that type of learning is *hinukh* and not *limmud*. If Maimonides is referring to the initial learning of how to act, then his explanation of the verse would be superfluous, since it is obvious that learning how to execute the correct physical movements of an action will enable a person to act correctly. Nor can he simply mean that action never leads a person to learn, since he admits elsewhere that *hinukh* and continual habituation helps one to develop the virtues, which will consequently help to develop his or her intellect.[38] This latter notion is further confirmed by Maimonides' explanation of Rabbi Hanina Ben Dosa's maxim in *Mishna Avot*, "Everyone whose fear of sin precedes his wisdom, his wisdom endures, whereas everyone whose wisdom precedes his fear of sin, his wisdom will not endure."[39] Maimonides explains,

> Behold, this matter is also agreed upon by the philosophers: when the habit of [moral] virtues precedes wisdom until it will be a firm trait, and afterwards one were to study wisdom which would stimulate him towards those good qualities, he would increase in delight and love of wisdom and in determination to add to it, since it would bestir him toward what was habituated. However, when evil traits precede, and afterwards one were to study, wisdom would preclude him from what he would desire through habit. Wisdom would be burdensome to him and he would forsake it.[40]

By emphasizing the idea that learning leads to action, therefore, he is asserting that theoretical wisdom relates to practical activity by giving a person the proper perspective and the right motivation for proper action.

Jonathan Jacobs has made the following observation regarding the difference between Aristotle and Maimonides as it pertains to practical wisdom and the law: "For Aristotle, practical wisdom involved a certain kind of knowledge distinct from scientific knowledge, and it was identified as an intellectual virtue because it has its own objects of knowledge. For Maimonides, ethical understanding is integrated into broader wisdom about the created order and God but what is ethically required is given (in ways that need further elaboration through study and experience) by the Law. There is not, in his view, a distinct department of knowledge, its object being of practical wisdom, as there is for Aristotle."[41] Though Aristotle does combine the theoretical and the ethical when he discusses the view of the noble-and-good person, who, through theoretical reflection, finds goodness praiseworthy in and of itself, Sara Broadie distinguishes the good person from the noble-and-good person by saying that the good person misconceives the nature of happiness either because he has no views about the value of virtue or because he just accepts the importance of natural goods at face value; he is, nevertheless, a genuinely good person who does virtuous activity wholeheartedly. The noble-and-good person, on the other hand, is reflective about goodness and finds it praiseworthy in and of itself.[42] Thus, for Aristotle, theoretic activity, as the contemplation of first principles, does not offer practical prescriptions; however, as the means to understand and appreciate how the world works, it provides an end to practical wisdom in conferring the status of nobility to an activity over and above it being considered good. In other words, to act for the sake of the good is a choice in line with the expectation of personal benefits, whether they are natural benefits or external benefits; it is a practical choice stemming from practical wisdom. If one chooses to act for the sake of nobility, on the other hand, it is a choice that comes from the perfection of all of a person's excellences, both practical and theoretic. For Maimonides, because the law is the source of both theoretical and practical knowledge, and because the law obligates a person to accept certain beliefs as well as perform certain actions, he maintains that there is a closer and more direct relationship between theoretical contemplation's influence on moral development and habituation's influence on intellectual development.

Another example of how Maimonides' contention that theoretical speculation must precede proper performance of the commandments is his introduction of an additional requirement for conversion over those which are mentioned in the Talmud. The Talmud states that converts should be taught a few major commandments and some minor commandments, specifically mentioning the commandments of gleanings (*leket*), forgotten sheaves (*shikhehah*), leaving the corners of the field (*peah*), and tithes given to the poor (*maaser ani*). The Talmud also mentions the prohibition to eat forbidden fat (*helev*) and the prohibition to work on Shabbat as examples of what to teach.[43] The Talmudic commentators note that these commandments are meant to inform the potential convert of the differences between the values he or she is abandoning and those being adopted through conversion.[44] Those values can only be inferred through the performance of the commandments.

In addition to the Talmudic examples, Maimonides adds that one should also inform potential converts about certain principles of the Jewish faith, that is, the unity of God, and of the prohibitions against idolatry. The potential convert should also be made aware of the World to Come.[45] His justification for these additions is his contention that only through correct beliefs can proper fulfillment of the commandments be possible. He states this explicitly when he says of the potential convert, "Just as he is informed of the punishment [for disobeying] the commandments; so, too, he is informed about the reward for [their observance]. We tell him that by observing these commandments, he will merit the life of the world to come. *For there is no completely righteous man other than a master of wisdom who observes these commandments and knows them* [my emphasis]."[46]

* * * *

In summary, according to Maimonides, the compulsory nature of the law serves to socialize individuals so that their second nature is open for moral development, yet the law also provides correct beliefs so that moral development is properly oriented and allows for intellectual development for those who further speculate on those beliefs. The only question is—in today's world, how can one explain the way the law does this?

NOTES

1. Deuteronomy 4:8.
2. Judges 17:6.
3. NE 1194b28-1095a5.
4. NE 11095a15–21.
5. Aristotle is not saying that everyone has a sound moral education. Rather, he is saying that only those with a sound moral education recognize that it is to *eudaimonia* that they aspire, and that they are "all the people" who will be edified by his lectures.

6. NE 1180a6–24.
7. NE 1179b32–1180a5.
8. In other words, fear of punishment, whether Divine or otherwise, is not the efficient cause in Maimonides' framework.
9. *Physics* 194b29.
10. This view is in line with the saying of Hillel that a brutish man cannot fear sin and an ignorant man cannot be pious (Avot 2:6).
11. While this should go without saying, Maimonides' adoption of Aristotelian conceptions of women is another place where I depart from his framework.
12. *Hilkhot Teshuva* 10:1. This Halakha, and its relation to Maimonides' fuller definitions of love and fear of God will be discussed below. The point of bringing it here is to emphasize that Maimonides recognizes that the law as a means to habituate actions cannot be the starting point of ethics, but only of socialization, as he completes the passage with "*They are trained to serve God out of fear until their knowledge increases and they serve out of love.*"
13. Maimonides admits that only the Divine Law of the Torah is two-tiered and that all other legal systems pertain solely to the political realm in establishing peace and security. For more information, see MN II:40; Pines, 383–4.
14. Psalms 1:2.
15. Though mentioned explicitly in *Moreh Nevukhim*, Maimonides also refers to this idea in *Mishne Torah, Hilkhot Temura* 4:13, where he writes, "Most of the Torah's laws are nothing other than 'counsels given from distance' from 'He Who is of great counsel' to improve one's character and make one's conduct upright."
16. However, see *Hilkhot Avodat Kokhavim* 11:12.
17. Hannah Kasher, "Well-Being of the Body or Welfare of the Soul: The Maimonidean Explanation of the Dietary Laws," *Moses Maimonides: Physician, Scientist, and Philosopher*, eds. Fred Rosner and Samuel S. Kottek (Northvale: Jason Aronson, 1993) 133.
18. Both "relations with one another through the abolition of reciprocal wrongdoing" and "the acquisition of a noble and excellent character" are part of welfare of the body.
19. MN III:27; Pines, 511.
20. *Mishna Avot* 1:18.
21. Even when Maimonides' contemporaries agreed that there is a relationship between prescribed actions and beliefs, they did not

always agree as to the reasons Maimonides associated with commandments or with how Maimonides derived the reasons for the commandments through his interpretation of the activities associated with them. Not only is this seen by the numerous critiques that exist on the third part of *Moreh Nevukhim* but also critiques of Maimonides' interpretation of Biblical laws are prevalent throughout the rabbinic literature of the Middle Ages. For one example, as it pertains to the symbolic meaning of the Sabbath, see Nahmanides' commentary on Deuteronomy 5:15.

22. In this conception, "philosophy" cannot be seen simply as a school of thought and Maimonides' Jewish philosophy cannot be seen simply as a synthesis of two realms of knowledge into one consistent viewpoint. Rather, "philosophy" has a second meaning, whereby it is defined as a set of tools and methods of argument which are used to articulate concepts. This two-fold conception of "philosophy" is supported by what Maimonides wrote in his *Treatise on Logic* (though the attribution is subject to dispute, as has been discussed by H. Davidson in his article, "The Authenticity of Works Attributed to Maimonides," *Me'ah She'arim: Studies in Medieval Jewish Spiritual Life in Memory of Isadore Twersky* (Jerusalem, 2001) 118–125). There, Maimonides calls the term "philosophy" a homonym, claiming that it can refer either to the sciences in particular or to the use of demonstration in acquiring knowledge. In other words, "philosophy" may mean either the principles and dogmas held by various philosophical schools or the method of studying natural and Divine science.

23. MN Intro, Pines, 5.

24. Isadore Twersky, *Introduction to the Code of Maimonides* (*Mishneh Torah*) (New Haven: Yale University Press, 1980) 359.

25. Maimonides' understanding of the importance of the law as a means to instill correct beliefs is preceded by Saadia Gaon. In *Emunot v'Deot*, to the question of why knowledge was given via prophecy when it could be acquired through proper speculation, he writes, "We say, then, [that] the All-Wise knew that the conclusions reached by means of the art of speculation could be attained only in the course of a certain measure of time. If, therefore, He had referred us for our acquaintance with His religion to that art alone, we would have remained without religious guidance whatever for a while, until the process of reasoning was completed by us so that we

could make use of its conclusions. But many a one of us might never complete the process because of some flaw in his reasoning (Saadia ben Joseph, and Samuel Rosenblatt, *The Book of Beliefs and Opinions* (New Haven: Yale University Press, 1976) 31)."

26. MN Introduction, Pines, 8–9.

27. *Hilkhot Yesode HaTorah* 4:13. Maimonides' literal interpretation of the Talmudic text, which calls *Ma'aseh Merkavah* a great matter and the debates of Abaye and Rava a small matter, so that it serve as a proof-text for the permissibility, or necessity, to study metaphysics, was not readily accepted by the majority of the Talmudic commentators, nor by halakhists who otherwise followed Maimonides' legal analysis deferentially. For example, Rabbi Nissim Gerondi explains that the matter was small for the *Tannaim* but not for everyone and concludes, "Rambam wrote what he wanted, and if only Rambam didn't write it." Rabbi Yom Tov ben Avraham Asevilli writes that the correct understanding is not like Maimonides, and that Rambam will atone for what he wrote. Even Rabbi Yosef Karo, who is known as a defender of Maimonides, writes in *Kessef Mishna* that he disagrees with him. The vituperative responses to Maimonides' interpretation should be seen as a measure of the uniqueness of Maimonides' approach of conflating the higher order of the law and philosophy. See *Kessef Mishna, Hilkhot Yesode HaTorah* 4:13; see also *Shulhan Arukh, Yoreh Deah* 246:4, including the gloss of Rabbi Moshe Isserles.

28. This idea is supported by Nahmanides' description of *Sefer Madda*, of which *Hilkhot Yesode HaTorah* is part. "It is the index to the books of the Rabbi of blessed memory on the Talmud and the introduction to all his compositions." See his Letter to the French Rabbis (Nahmanides and Charles Ber Chavel, *Writings & Discourses*, Vol. 2 (New York: Shilo Pub. House, 1978) 389).

29. The question of how a person can be commanded to believe and if believing something can be voluntary will be discussed in Chap. 4.

30. MN III:28, Pines, 521.

31. See Rabbi Joseph Kafih's letter to Marc Shapiro, where he amends his translation of אעקתאד from אמונה to דעה and rephrases the sentence,

"לפי שראיתי שזה תועלת **באמונה** לפי שאני אספתי...אלא אחר התבוננות וישוב הדעת ועיון **בדעות** נכונות ובלתי נכונות, וסכום מה שצריך **להאמין** מהם ובירורו **בטענות** וראיות..."

to

"לפי שראיתי שזה תועלת **בדעה** לפי שאני אספתי ... אלא אחר התבוננות וישוב
הדעת ועיון **בסברות** נכונות ובלתי נכונות, וסכום מה שצריך **להיות בדעה** מהם
ובירורו **בהוכחות** וראיות..."

Marc Shapiro, *Studies in Maimonides and His Interpreters*
(Scranton: University of Scranton Press, 2008) 26 (Heb. Section).

32. MN III:51, 633–4.
33. MN III:27, Pines, 511, emphasis mine.
34. MN III:34. Maimonides also admits that the Torah was framed for
the Jewish community at a certain point in their historical development. Yet, this further supports the requirement for each individual to search for the underlying meaning behind historically
predicated laws.
35. *Politics* 1338a9–13.
36. Deuteronomy 5:1.
37. Introduction to *Commentary on the Mishna*. Maimonides' view is
based on BT *Kiddushin* 40b.
38. See *Shemonah Perakim*, Chapter 7; *Hilkhot Deot*, Chapters 1 and 5.
39. *Mishna Avot* 3:9.
40. Translation from Moses Maimonides and Arthur David, *The
Commentary to Mishnah Aboth* (New York: Bloch Pub. Co., 1968)
52.
41. See Jonathan Jacobs, *Law, Reason, and Morality in Medieval Jewish
Philosophy* (Oxford: Oxford University Press, 2010) 125.
42. See *Ethics with Aristotle*, 379. This is confirmed by Aristotle's distinction between goodness and nobility-and-goodness, where the
former is chosen for its own sake as good, whereas the latter is
chosen for its own sake as good but it is also chosen because it is
noble (EE 1248b15–25).
43. BT *Yevamot* 47.
44. See the commentaries of *Rashi* and *Ritva*.
45. *Hilkhot Issure Biah* 14:2–4.
46. Ibid.

CHAPTER 6

A Contemporary Explanation of the Law's Construction of Reality

How the Law Constructs Reality

Beloved are Israel that they were given the instrument through which the world was created; greater still [is the demonstration of God's] love that it was made known to them that they were given the instrument through which the world was created.[1]

Though law is often described as the collection of rules which regulate disputes among people in society, by virtue of its effectiveness in regulating disputes, it also provides a means through which people can envision how society should function.[2] Just as language serves as a means of description and as a means to formulate socially meaningful concepts, so too does law, in prescribing the way that people should behave toward one another (its behavioral effect), or in cooperation with one another as a group, help shape a group's vision of the world,[3] since coordinated, social action is imbued with the same type of symbolism as language (its hermeneutic effect).[4]

Neither language nor law, however, has complete control over what determines a people's culture or cognitive schema. Moreover, neither language nor secular legal systems dictate truth or morality; rather, they serve as a means to influence how people think about truth and morality. The difference between Truth (with a capital "T" in the ontological sense) and that which a person claims is true (with a lowercase "t" in the epistemic sense) is a function of how accurate the person's tools of investigation are, that is, the meanings of words attributed to concepts[5] and how the

© The Author(s) 2017
I. Bedzow, *Maimonides for Moderns,*
DOI 10.1007/978-3-319-44573-1_6

laws implement and enforce those concepts,[6] as well as how thorough the person investigates what he or she believes is true through theoretical speculation and in becoming sensitive to how effective practical norms are in implementing those truths.

With respect to secular legal systems, though Joseph Raz claims that the law has supreme authority to interfere with any kind of activity, it does not mean that secular law alone has moral authority. The authority of the law, according to the various schools of legal positivism, is justified either by the power of its author/enforcer or through recognition by its adherents. According to natural law theorists, secular law's authority stems from the logical relationship in which it stands to moral principles. Therefore, particular laws of the state or even a legal system in general, whether seen through positivist or natural law theory perspectives, can impose on its subjects or citizens activities which are immoral according to a theonomous perspective, since people are fallible when it comes to their ability to apply logic or moral reasoning to society. *Moreover, it should be emphasized that secular law does not determine right or wrong, yet it can greatly influence how people think about what is right or wrong if they do not have other influences on their moral reasoning.*

In my view, Jewish law and Noahide law differ from secular law in a way that disallow them from being explained through either a positivist or natural law theory lens. Their adherents are, therefore, less at risk of succumbing to moral relativity and subjectivism than their secular counterparts. The fact that God created a world with a certain normative order, revealed that order to Adam, Noah, and the Jewish people, and commanded them to follow it indicates that the authority of the law is not wholly dependent on naturalistic moral premises alone. On the other hand, the fact that the Noahide law is so general in its explicit demands and that the Torah necessitates an oral dimension whereby particular rulings are supported by hermeneutical/logical principles indicate that authority of the law is dependent on the relationship between God and His servants, such that those who recognize the rules are also those who enforce it and apply it to new situations.[7] Divine law, by virtue of the fact that it represents the Divine will, has the ultimate authority to set moral norms, yet its correct application can only occur when those who uphold it understand the relationship they have to it.[8]

The idea that the Torah projects an ontological order onto reality can be seen in the rabbinic literature through the use of the rabbinic term *Oraita*. *Oraita* is not an Aramaic translation of the word "Torah," if

"Torah" were meant simply as teaching; in that case, the Aramaic translation would be *'ulfana* or *yalfana*. Rather, *Oraita* is linguistically related to the Indo-European word *arta* (cosmic order),[9] regarding which Emile Benveniste writes,

> We have here one of the cardinal notions of the legal world of the Indo-European to say nothing of their religious and moral ideas: this is the concept of "Order" which governs also the orderliness of the universe, the movement of the stars, the regularity of the seasons and the years; and further, the relations of gods and men, and finally the relations of men to one another. Nothing which concerns man or the world falls outside the realm of "Order." It is thus the foundation, both religious and moral, of every society. Without this principle everything would revert to chaos.[10]

The Talmudic Sages describe the Torah in the same fashion. With regard to establishing Order, the Sages state that just as an architect uses blueprints to build a palace, so did God look into the Torah and create the world.[11] With regard to reverting to chaos were it not for the Torah, the Sages state that the entire creation of the world was dependent on the Jews accepting the Torah. If they would not have accepted the Torah, the world would have reverted to its original *tohu va-vohu*, its primordial state.[12]

In saying that the Torah projects an ontological order onto the world, however, I am not saying that there is only one way to describe the world in light of the Torah. From an internal Jewish perspective, the Sages proffer that there are 70 ways to understand the Torah,[13] which indicates that they recognize that concepts in the Torah can survive different paradigms and languages of explanation, and that there can be diversity within a unified people. From an external perspective, the Sages state that every single word that God spoke was split into 70 languages, corresponding to each of the 70 nations of the world.[14] Multi-lingual communication is not primarily for Israel's benefit in gaining a deeper understanding through linguistic comparison; rather, it is to provide a means for universal acceptance. Each nation can hear the Torah in its own language in order to adopt it as part of its national ethos. This notion is supported by the Sages' explanation of the second time the Israelites received the Torah, which occurred during the last weeks of Moses' life and before their entrance into the land of Israel. The verse which introduces Moses' repetition states, "On the other side of the Jordan in the land of Moab, Moses began explaining this

Torah saying."[15] The Sages understand the word "explain" to mean that Moses expounded on the Torah in the 70 languages of the nations of the world.[16] Moreover, after he finished explaining the Torah to the people, the Torah records Moses commanding the people to erect stones, coat them with plaster, and inscribe upon them all the words of this Torah, *well clarified*.[17] Because the word "explain" and "clarified" are linguistically related in Hebrew, the Sages understood that the inscription on the stones was also written in 70 languages.[18] The giving of the Torah by Moses to the Israelites was modeled after the giving of the Torah on Mount Sinai. Translations of the Torah were given for the sake of the nations of the world so as to provide a means for them to learn the lessons the Torah provides. As these two forms of multiplicity attest, while each of the 70 facets or languages may provide a slightly different understanding of the Torah, "these and those are the words of the living God." Moreover, understanding Torah concepts through different paradigms may enrich one's own appreciation of them as well as allow one to discover nuances that can explain more effectively the Torah's intent.[19]

The way in which law influences how people perceive reality is as follows: Law establishes social patterns and behaviors which a person who lives within the legal system takes for granted. The institutions that the law creates to organize social life are also perceived as independent of any individual's subjective understanding of the world. Even though a person may raise "Cartesian doubt" about the societal/social reality that the law establishes, when a person engages in communal life, he or she must accept the way in which society is organized and the categories by which it functions as real in order to live efficaciously.[20] Through the way they behave toward one another, or in cooperation with one another as a social group, people learn to identify with each other and the society in which they live as it is shaped by the law under which they live, since coordinated, social action is imbued with the same type of symbolism as language. Lenn Goodman explains,

> Laws are not symbolic in the first intention. Symbolism is not what they are about. But all laws have symbolic significances, and all express attitudes towards the values they intend. ... Penal laws may seek deterrence or reform, but they also, always, intend a message, express a norm, in uniquely coded symbols reserved for those occasions when vital social standards clearly have been overstepped. Whether or not a punishment effectively deters some future crime, it expresses a societal attitude about specific values.[21]

Furthermore, in creating legal categories through which experience is classified and evaluated (not simply for its own sake but also for the sake of prescribing social norms),[22] people use the objectivity of these categories to describe their experiences to others as well as to understand their own experiences subjectively.

The manner in which law objectifies experiences by setting the parameters according to which one is able to behave in a socially meaningful way is similar to the way in which language objectifies the meaning of communication through the pragmatic parameters which society develops. *Halakha* is not a set of a priori norms nor is it similar to syntactic or even semantic rules. While each *halakha* is important as an expression of the Divine will, individual *halakhot* do not make meaningful sense in the same way as a word or a sentence does. Living a *halakhic* life, on the other hand, does allow a person to understand the Divine will, since he or she can learn how individual expressions of the Divine will fit into a greater communication—or revelation.[23]

This claim, however, must be mitigated by the fact that Jews no longer live solely under the authority of Jewish law, though they may never have lived under the sole authority of Jewish law without any other social or legal influence.[24] Therefore, Jewish law is not the only institutionalized communal system which influences its adherents' reality. Moreover, a person can currently live within a number of legal and social systems which need not cohere with each other. This situation would be similar to one where a person is multi-lingual and can negotiate between the different worldviews which each language expresses. Because, however, legal systems are incompatible with each other as a matter of law, since all legal systems assert supremacy over its adherents, a person living under two legal systems, such as contemporary Jews who are also members of secular states, will find that he or she may have conflicting definitions of a concept, or may imbue incompatible meanings to an idea, by virtue of the influence of two different legal systems on his or her conception of reality.[25]

Just as with Maimonides' theory, I am not claiming that the coercive power of the law causes its adherents to identify with the concepts and norms which it institutionalizes. Though Divine reward and punishment are certainly components of the legal system, they are not constitutive of the law.[26] Jewish law is a product of Divine revelation, where God's will gives authority to the law, yet Divine authority does not cause its norms, concepts, and values to inhere in the minds of those observing it. For Jewish law to provide a worldview to its adherents, there must first be an acceptance on the part of its adherents of the normativity of the law. The Talmudic sages recognize the importance of the Jewish people voluntarily accepting the Torah, as seen in the following passage: "'And they stood under the mount.' Rabbi Avdimi bar Hama bar Hasa said: 'This teaches that the Holy One, blessed be He, overturned the mountain upon them like an [inverted] cask,' and said to them, 'If you accept the Torah, it is well; if not, there shall be your burial.' Rabbi Aha bar Jacob observed: 'This furnishes a strong protest against the Torah [in that they did not voluntarily accept it].' Said Raba, 'Yet even so, they re-accepted it in the days of Ahasuerus, for it is written, '[the Jews] confirmed, and took it upon themselves [etc.]:' [this means that] they confirmed what they had accepted long before.'"[27] Without voluntary commitment, the Sages recognize that the authority of the law would be seriously challenged. Through a person's voluntary commitment to the law, the norms and concepts inherent therein will become factors to be considered in his or her practical and theoretical reasoning. Regarding the institutional facts created by law, Peter Hulsen writes,

> Whereas in the case of physical matter, acceptance as a fact follows on observing a situation, the opposite is the case in relation to institutional facts. Institutional facts are facts, not because they *are* states of affairs, but because they are *generally accepted as* states of affairs. In other words, an institutional fact is a meaning-content which achieves intersubjective existence simply and solely by being generally accepted as such.

Moreover, once a set of institutional facts are accepted as facts, they become the primary tools for interpreting a situation since those categories are deemed as normative and constitutive of social life.[28] Engagement with the law on an individual level becomes an activity of personal development, and laws come into effect as the product of a continual purposive effort[29] on a societal level. Reward and punishment remain as considerations for acting, yet they serve only as "auxiliary partial reasons" for those who have not fully embodied the values and concepts inherent in the law.[30]

The way in which accepting the law's embedded social concepts and theoretical examination (and justification) of those concepts influences a person's view of his or her social world is similar to the way in which accepting and reflecting upon physical laws of nature influences a person's understanding of the physical world around him or her. For example, both Isaac Newton and Albert Einstein proposed a theory of gravity, yet, even though both theories describe what each calls gravity, they do so in very different ways. Moreover, neither theory is completely accurate in describing what occurs in nature, while, at the same time, both theories are correct to some degree. In the same way, different legal systems may describe social life in ways that closely approximate what occurs, yet they may describe social life very differently. Which approximation a person accepts will influence how he or she views the world. Even though one may argue that societal laws prescribe and scientific laws describe, thus making this analogy incorrect, when societal laws are accepted by their adherents in a way that influences how they organize and categorize social life, institutional facts also play a descriptive role in explaining how society functions. This will be further explained in the section which discusses explanatory and normative facts.

John Searle has argued that the acceptance of institutional facts need not be a conscious decision on the part of those who voluntarily participate in the constitutive rules that create such facts. The manner in which this unconscious or semiconscious acceptance occurs is as follows: Human institutions create a "Background," which is a set of non-intentional or preintentional capacities that enable intentional states to function. The Background provides the means for linguistic and perceptual interpretation and understanding and therefore provides a structure for consciousness, since the content of human consciousness is predicated on how the world of which a person is conscious is seen to be ordered. The Background also shapes people's expectations and motivations since human institutions define the relationships between various institutional facts; it, therefore, also disposes people toward certain behaviors. Accordingly, a person may behave a certain way because the structure of societal/social life, as formed by the rules of the community, cause him or her to do so, yet his or her behavior is not the result of following those rules but rather a result of becoming disposed to behaving that way. Searle writes,

> So there are in fact constitutive rules functioning causally, and we do in fact discover those rules in the course of our analysis. But it does not follow that a person is able to function in a society only if he has actually learned and memorized the rules and is following them consciously or unconsciously. Nor does it follow that a person is able to function in society only if he has "internalized" the rules as *rules*. The point is that we should not say that the man who is at home in his society, the man who is *chez lui* in the social institutions of the society, is at home because he has mastered the rules of the society, but rather that the man has developed a set of capacities and

abilities that render him at home in society; and he has developed those abilities because those are the rules of his society.[31]

As a person becomes further habituated through his or her fulfillment of the law, reward and punishment become auxiliary partial reasons because they begin to lose strength as reasons for acting. Therefore, though they may be taken into consideration when reasoning about how to act, acting for the sake of the law *and out of the recognition that the law is a means to understand God's will for humanity* becomes the primary reason to act. The use of the law's power to reward and punish as a safeguard to compliance is similar to Aristotle's notion that the law facilitates habituation when people slip or have lapses in judgment.

Acting for the sake of the law and out of the recognition that the law is a means to understand God's will for humanity is not uncritical observance; rather, it entails fully understanding the law's spirit through theoretical and practical speculation. Therefore, the law's influence on a person's perception of reality is not confined to "common knowledge." Even philosophical inquiry rests on the examination of concepts which are grounded in the way a person acts in the world.[32] Abstract concepts are examined using physical and sensorimotor terms from daily experience,[33] which serve to create conceptual metaphors[34] that allow a person to "grasp"[35] the abstract concepts.[36] Current research in cognitive neuroscience which examines how people grasp and experience abstract concepts through physical experiences has found that the process of abstraction is as follows: People rely on what they already know about a familiar bodily and sensory domain to reason about, interpret, and evaluate a less familiar immaterial domain through the process of "cognitive scaffolding." The cognitive scaffold serves as a means for creating metaphors, which are systematic conceptual mappings from a source domain (the sensorimotor experience) to a superficially dissimilar target domain (the abstract concept).[37] When a person then engages in philosophical inquiry and abstract thought, he or she often uses the social and linguistic, as well as legal, norms which have shaped his or her cognitive schema to explain ideas through metaphor.[38]

Law also contributes to the formation of a group's ontology through the creation of "legal fictions." For example, according to Torah law, there are only two categories of social domains, namely a public domain and a private domain. However, rabbinic law increases the number of categories to four, adding *Karmelit* and *Makom Patur*. A *Karmelit* is not a private domain because it has no walls to demarcate it nor is it a public domain since it does not contain streets or markets that are 16 cubits wide. It is a domain whose category definition is that which is between, and comparable to both, a private and a public domain. A *Makom Patur* is an area, located in a public domain, that is less than four handbreadths (*tefahim*) by four handbreadths and either higher than three handbreadths from the ground or deeper than three handbreadths in the ground. It is a domain whose category definition is that which is smaller than a private domain. These two domains are both legal fictions in the sense that they are only rabbinically mandated. Yet in the reality of social life, these categories are as real as the Torah categories of public and private domains by virtue of the fact that their normativity has been accepted by those who voluntarily follow the rabbinic decree.

Legal fictions, however, are not meant to replace truth; as rabbinic decrees, they are meant to protect a person from the negative consequences of transgressing the norms that are anchored in the truths established by the law.[39] The *Karmelit* and the *Makom Patur* are never considered as Torah-defined categories of social space, even when people act as if they are equally normative as Torah-defined categories. Just as Lon Fuller defines a legal fiction as "either (1) a statement propounded with a complete or partial consciousness of its falsity, or (2) a false statement recognized as having utility,"[40] the rabbinic decree is always recognized as such.

When there is an objective doubt in reality,[41] legal fictions do have more influence on determining what is accepted as truth. For example, Rabbi Asher ben Yehiel writes that when prohibited food is mixed with permitted food in a proportion that legally would render the recognition of the prohibited food nullified, the non-kosher food is transformed into actual kosher food, so that each individual piece is now 100 percent kosher. The state of each piece no longer has anything to do with probabilities. In other words, it is not that the food is only legally permitted as a mixture; rather, each individual piece of food, some of which once had the identity of forbidden food, now has the identity of kosher food.[42]

The importance of the law's ability to create legal fictions in addition to constructing societal concepts and definitions is that theoretical reasoning and (as I will show in the following chapters) practical reasoning is dependent on facts and socially accepted fictions. Moreover, cognitive scaffolding builds not only upon physical facts but also upon societal–legal facts as well. One example of such is Marx's well-known theory of "alienation."[43] Donald Kelley explains,

But the fundamental form of "alienation" was not that Hegelian state of inner isolation that has monopolized the attention of students of Marx. Rather, paralleling Marx's own shift from idealistic to materialistic premises, it was estrangement from property—a problem that was widely discussed by civil lawyers, especially with regard to the *ager publicus*, that original common land of the Romans that so fascinated Marx and that continued to concern him in *Das Kapital*.[44]

Marx's social philosophy of "alienation" was built on his legal training and his dissatisfaction with the legal fictions which determined property rights in Germany. As the example of Marx shows, despite the law's role in creating institutional facts, dissatisfaction can still arise when society, or norms that arise in social groups within society, create conflicting facts or values which challenge other institutional facts. Yet when contradiction between facts is not so great as to challenge the legitimacy of the societal order, the law, both in organizing social categories and in imposing clarity when life is unable to offer it, provides society's members with more than just rules and legal concepts; it also serves as the cognitive foundation for society's worldviews and the philosophical speculations of its members. In determining how to live one's life, a person must consider social facts, socially significant physical facts, legal categories, and prescriptive legal norms. How they relate to each other and how a person responds to them will influence what he or she thinks is possible and proper to do in society.

A word should be said about how people who do not identify with the law should be treated by those who do, as well as how *hiddush*, or creativity, can occur within the four cubits of Jewish law. One's responsibilities toward others is not dependent on whether the other people identify with the law or not (as long as they are not actively against it). Beliefs and moral norms may be learned through social interaction, but they are not contingent upon a person's participation in social life. In fact, a true test of whether one acts from one's identification with those beliefs and norms or whether he or she acts out of a sense of pure reciprocity or self-interest is in whether one performs acts of *hesed* and *tzedaka* in addition to *mishpat* or not. With respect to the possibility for creativity under the law, creativity does not arise *ex nihilo*, since the creative impulse is a creating one and only God creates something from nothing. Rather, as the Sages recognized, the verse "All your children will be students of Hashem and your children will have abundant peace (*shalom*),"[45] should not be read with "your children" but with "your builders."[46] In other words, creativity does not stem from influences wholly outside the law but, on the contrary, it shows that one has an intimacy with one's tradition, like a child has to a parent, so that he or she can build on—yet remain steadfast to—the past in a way that affirms his or her own individuality as well.

EPISTEMIC AND MORAL OBJECTIVITY

Where were you when I laid the foundations of the earth? Declare, if you have the understanding.[47]

In relying on the Torah for the grounding of moral and theoretical truths and in arguing for a theory of truth that is more in line with coherent-ism than foundationalism, I am susceptible to the serious critique of having arbitrary criteria for justification. One may also challenge my view by claiming that such a premise could legitimize any coherent depiction of the world without leaving any possibility for criticism. The latter critique makes my conception of virtue ethics susceptible to being considered relativistic and perspectivalist. The challenge of relativism is that rational debate between, and rational choice among, rival coherent worldviews is impossible. The challenge of perspectivalism is that no worldview can deny the legitimacy of its rivals, since no worldview can offer any other a good reason to reject its premises. Therefore, no worldview can claim to be true; rather, each is a complementary perspective to envision the world.

However, the Torah and the Noahide laws are not simply societal con-structions, equal to any other legal system, they serve as an ontological anchor which opposes the notion of arbitrary justification and restricts the claim that any coherent view is legitimate. Because God mandated the general Noahide laws and the more particular laws of the Torah,[48] they represent objective theoretic and moral truths. This is the position that Maimonides held, since he equated God's will with truth. A contemporary Jewish virtue ethics may also ground itself on this premise theologically, yet to explain it philosophically, one would need a different account than that of Maimonides, since it cannot rely on the Aristotelian metaphysics that Maimonides used. A contemporary philosophical account rests more on being able to explain a person's ability to discover truth than need-ing to demonstrate truth's existence, since the latter is a premise that the majority of philosophers already accept to some degree. A response to these challenges would entail an account of authority and interpretation/translation[49] which can show how normative standards within the tradition allow for continuity while simultaneously allowing for adaptability to new circumstances. While this is the work of another project, I would like to say a few words about translation as it relates to the issue of maintaining objectivity, as it might help to clarify the law's role in the achievement of virtue.

Translation is as much a question of epistemology as it is of language, and it can be seen either as a practice of explanation or as a practice of elimination. With respect to the latter, translation becomes a process of reinterpreting events or concepts in a way that rejects the original schema in which those events or concepts were understood. For example, reductionist theories of religion reinterpret religious experience in a way that invalidates non-reductionist explanations. Translation as a process of explanation, on the other hand, allows for the validation of previous schemata, even if they contradict the new framework.

These two ways of understanding translation can be found in the Sages' discussion over the translation of the Torah into Greek. Regarding writing a translation of Scripture, the Mishna gives two opinions.

> There is no difference between books [of Scripture] and phylacteries and the mezuzah parchments except that the books may be written in any language whereas phylacteries and the mezuzah parchments may only be written in [Hebrew with] Assyrian script. Rabban Shimon ben Gamliel states that even books [of Scripture] they did not permit to be written [in any language] other than in Greek.[50]

Originally the Sages allowed the Bible to be translated into any language; that is, the study of the Bible from foreign language texts was considered legitimate.[51] By the time of Rabban Gamliel, however, the Sages prohibited study from foreign language texts despite its permissibility according to Torah law, except for those texts written in Greek.[52] The Talmud provides two reasons for the Greek exception. The first is based upon an actual incident; the second upon Scriptural justification.

> Rabbi Yehuda said: When our teachers permitted Greek, they permitted it only for a scroll of the Torah. This was on account of the incident in connection with King Ptolemy, as it has been taught: It is related of King Ptolemy that he brought together seventy-two elders and placed them in seventy-two [separate] rooms, without telling them why he had brought them together, and he went in to each one of them and said to him, "Write for me [a Greek

translation of] the Torah of Moses your master." God then prompted each one of them and they all conceived the same idea and wrote for him.[53]

The Sages did not write an exact translation of the Torah for Ptolemy nor did they provide an elucidation based upon the oral tradition. The rabbis made certain changes to the text in order to prevent angering Ptolemy due to misconceptions which would have arisen if the Torah was translated literally. Ptolemy anticipated that the Sages may provide an inaccurate translation if they collaborated and therefore separated them to ensure a correct rendition. A miracle occurred, however, and all the Sages provided the same substitutions in their respective translations. Therefore, even though the Sages relate that when the Torah was translated into Greek in the days of Ptolemy darkness came upon the world for three days,[54] due to the miracle regarding the translation, the Sages permitted that the Torah continue to be written in Greek but prohibited any other language.[55]

The second reason given for the allowance of a Greek translation is based on Noah's blessing to his middle son. After Noah awoke from his drunken stupor and realized what Ham had done to him and how Shem and Yaphet had given him honor, he gave Yaphet the following blessing: "May God extend Yaphet, and he will dwell in the tents of Shem."[56] To understand the rabbinic use of this blessing, it is important to realize that the Greeks are traditionally known to descend from Yaphet and the Israelites from Shem. The Talmud records the supposed reasoning of Rabban Shimon ben Gamliel.

> Rabbi Yohanan further said: What is the reason of Rabban Shimon ben Gamaliel? Scripture says, "God extend Yaphet, and he shall dwell in the tents of Shem." [This means] that the words of Yaphet shall be in the tents of Shem. But why not say [the words of other descendants of Yaphet, such as] Gomer and Magog? Rabbi Hiyya ben Abba replied: The real reason is because it is written, "Let God extend [yaft] Yaphet," implying, let the chief beauty [yafyut] of Yaphet be in the tents of Shem.[57]

The Scriptural support provided by Rabbi Yohanan is meant to explain the reasoning of Rabban Shimon ben Gamliel and to reject Rabbi Yehuda's explanation. However, Rabbi Yohanan must still explain why, if Torah law allows translation in any language, is there a rabbinic decree that prohibits all but Greek. Rabbi Yohanan's use of scriptural support shows that translations had only become problematic after external pressure had forced a division between the written word and its traditional understanding—Yaphet was no longer in the tents of Shem but rather the reverse; therefore, a rabbinic prohibition was needed to reinforce the interpretative community. Use of the verse also demonstrates that Rabbi Yohanan was not justifying the decree outside of the ethos of the Torah.

As the debate between Rabbi Yehuda and Rabbi Yohanan conveys, the success of translation as explanation depends on the cohesion of the community in understanding the ethos of the Torah in practice. In other words, it depends on the existence of an Oral Torah. One way to see this is through the rabbinic explanation of the following verse in Hosea, "Though I wrote for him the major portion of [the precepts of] my law, they were counted a strange thing." The Midrash gives the following account:

> When God revealed Himself at Sinai to give the Torah to Israel, He communicated it to Moses in order: Bible, Mishnah, Talmud, and Haggadah, as it says, "And God spoke all these words." Even the question a pupil asks his teacher God told Moses at that time. After he had learned it from God, He told him to teach it to Israel. Moses said: "Lord of the Universe, shall I write it down for them?" God replied: "I do not wish to give it to them in writing, because I foresee a time when the heathen will have dominion over them and take it away from them, and they will be despised by the idol-worshippers. Only the Bible will I give them in writing; the Mishnah, Talmud, and Haggadah I will give them orally, so that when the idolaters enslave them, they will remain distinct from them."[58]

The purpose of the Oral Torah is to keep the Torah personal and its observers distinct. It speaks of a community with an interpretative tradition that upholds an authoritative reading of the Written Torah. Not every reading can be legitimated and not every reader can rightly claim to be Israel. Only those who live within and as members of the community will be able to understand the Torah properly. Those outside the community, who rely on their own literary methods, cannot access the Torah's true meaning.

The importance of a community that shares a common general perspective is so great that the Sages recognize that the Oral Torah must exist in conjunction with the written one and not subordinate to it. The second time Moses receives the tablets, the verse records the statement, "And the Lord said to Moses, write for yourself these words, for according to (יפ לע, lit. on the mouth of) these words have I established My covenant with you and with Israel."[59] The Sages understand this verse as follows:

> Rabbi Yohanan said: "Write for yourself these words, for according to these words"—i.e. both written and oral law—"I have established My covenant with you." Should you reverse the two, making the oral law into a written one, or vice versa, you will not receive any reward. Why? Because thus I gave it: one a written and the other an oral law. Rabbi Yehudah ben Rabbi Shimon explained the verse: "Write for yourself these words, for according to these words"—the written and the oral law—I have established a covenant with you that you should read them in this way. If you will change them, then know that you are nullifying the covenant. Hence it says, "Write for yourself these words."[60]

Elsewhere, Rabbi Yohanan states regarding this verse, "God made a covenant with Israel only for the sake of that which was transmitted orally," as it says, "For according to these words I have made a covenant with you and with Israel."[61]

By providing a different lens through which to understand the Torah whether that lens is linguistic or philosophical, the process of translation/ interpretation inevitably accepts either the notion of conceptual relativity or the notion of conceptual pluralism. Yet conceptual relativity or pluralism is not moral relativism or perspectivalism. Conceptual relativity accepts the premise that one can have multiple frames of reference which are cognitively equivalent yet which are incompatible when taken at face value. In other words, though the various explanations of a particular phenomenon correspond to one another, they cannot be simply conjoined. Despite any contradiction, however, both descriptions attest to the veracity of the phenomenon and to the translatability from one frame of reference to the other. As a philosophical tool, conceptual relativity allows a philosopher to understand seeming contradictions as a problem of improperly conflating frames of reference rather than of logical inconsistencies. Though the seeming contradiction can now cohere along a tradition's changing schemata, it remains incoherent to discuss each schema relative to another.

Conceptual pluralism, on the other hand, accepts the premise that multiple descriptions can be cognitively equivalent yet may be incompatible when taken at face value. For example, a person can describe the room in which he or she sits in terms of tables and chairs or in terms of atoms and atomic particles. Though the descriptions are different, one description does not contradict the other. Rather, they use different conventions. The tool of conceptual pluralism allows the philosopher to understand seeming contradictions, not as stemming from a conflation of frames of reference but rather as a conflation of descriptive conventions. As such, differences in the understanding of certain theological and philosophical concepts within an overarching religious worldview need not be a cause for factioning; rather they can be understood in terms of using different descriptive conventions.

Acceptance of the notions of conceptual relativity and conceptual pluralism does not, however, imply that the translator must be a relativist or a perspectivalist. Belief in the normativity of the Jewish tradition disallows the acceptance of an explanation that veers too far from that which the tradition can accept. The limits of translation are therefore similar to the limits that reasoning imposes as will be discussed in the section on practical reasoning. Appendix II, which gives a genealogy of the expression *Moshe emet v'Torato emet*, also attempts to show how the tradition might provide a way to think about the truth of the Torah given its transmission over time. As I said in the introduction, but which I want to reiterate here, in recognizing that I am attempting to give Jewish virtue ethics a contemporary language for its expression, I understand that its expression is one of interpretation and must be based in the Jewish tradition's historical ideals, foundational texts, and practices, *and how the people explain and justify their behavior in light of them.*

* * * *

In claiming that the law influences the development of a person's worldview, I therefore advocate a moral realist position yet not a moral naturalist one. Moral naturalists, and many contemporary virtue ethicists are in this camp, argue that moral value is a part of nature, and they therefore propose that moral questions can have objective answers that are grounded in empirical studies.

I may pragmatically accept notions of objectivity and externality in the sense that meaning is independent of a person's sensations, intuitions, and imagination, yet recognize that it is not completely independent of the laws upon which the community can both express and judge them.[62] However, my acceptance of this notion of objectivity is only due to the limits of human comprehension. Oftentimes, we must settle for coherence rather than correspondence in our examination of truth, but the Torah and the Noahide laws nevertheless allow us to rely on the idea that Truth exists and to aspire for correspondence even when we must justify our beliefs through coherence.

Because that which gives human action and moral development meaning should be understood in the context of the biological and psychological qualities of each individual and by how individuals live in their social and cultural world, not only do the different roles that people have influence their worldview but they also shape the different, particular teleologies that people may pursue. The difficulty in basing a theory of ethical development on a single, overarching concept is that, like most monisms, the benefit of concentrating different components into a unified concept so as to provide a general account of a phenomenon in theory comes at the cost of being unable to explain any nuance or to appreciate the richness of a phenomenon in reality due to a lack of diversity of the variables of explanation. As William James wrote, "Whoever claims *absolute* teleological unity, saying that there is one purpose that every detail in the universe subserves, dogmatizes at his own risk."[63] Rather, I believe that while each person may share the same purpose generally, in the sense that one should strive to perform God's will to the best of his or her ability, the unique, general purpose that we all share has no practical meaning for us as individuals until it is complemented with the particularities that are important for each person.

The recognition that having a monistic approach in the study of human beings may forgo the ability of having a deeper understanding on the subject is found not only among philosophers. Clifford Geertz, in *The Interpretation of Cultures*, advocates for a thick description of a human behavior because, he asserts, only through understanding behavior in context can a person understand its meaning. He writes,

> My point, which should be clear ..., is not that there are no generalizations that can be made about man as man, save that he is a most various animal, or that the study of culture has nothing to contribute towards uncovering of such generalizations. My point is that such generalizations are not discovered through a Baconian search for cultural universals, a kind of public-opinion polling of the world's peoples in search of a *consensus gentium* that does not in fact exist, and, further, that the attempt to do so leads to precisely the sort of relativism the whole approach was expressly designed to avoid.[64]

Rather, Geertz argues, a proper anthropological methodology should recognize that human existence is a synthesis of biological, psychological, social, and cultural factors, where each factor contributes to a unitary system of analysis and is not seen as an accretive contribution. Therefore, unity and diversity are maintained in tension, since "human nature" is dependent on the culture in which it is expressed.

My contemporary theory recognizes that "the mind of each [person] is different from that of the other, just as the face of each [person] is different from that of the other,"[65] and that each person is a "small world" in his or her own right. There is a recognition that human beings have many different talents, and that each individual is unique both in the particular details of his or her *telos* and in its pursuit. This is not to say that human beings do not all share a common purpose in the Divine plan; rather, it means that how each person contributes to that purpose is based on his or her uniqueness. The Talmudic Sages already recognized the uniqueness of each individual, as seen in the Mishna which states, "Adam was created alone in the world … to portray the greatness of the Holy One, Blessed be He, since when a person stamps many coins with a single seal, they are all alike. But when the Sovereign of sovereigns, Blessed be He, fashioned all human beings with the seal with which he made the first person, not one of them is like any other."[66] In other words, my view is that humans as a collective are not instruments for some specific use according to a special function, but rather are agents who collectively, yet individually, work to accomplish certain goals.

This idea of the complementarity of humans within a society is not novel for the Jewish tradition. (By complementarity, I mean a situation where no one person can fully accomplish the unitary goal set by society; therefore, people work together to achieve the singular goal. The situation would be a morality equivalent to the political image on Hobbes' cover of his *Leviathan*, which portrays a body formed of a multitude of citizens on which a king's head is on top.) Moreover, the idea of complementarity allows for the recognition of mutual responsibility as well as for the development of humility. Rabbi Shneur Zalman of Liadi explains this idea as follows:

> Our sages instruct us to be humble before every person, because each and every person has qualities and levels that the other does not, and they each need one another. Thus, there is an advantage and quality to each and every person in which he is higher than his friend—and for this, his friend requires him. This can be compared to a body that comprises many parts, from head to foot; even though the feet are at the bottom and the lowest in quality and the head is at the top and the highest, nonetheless in one aspect there

is an advantage and quality to the feet—for the body needs them to walk, and they are what holds up the body and the head. ... The head cannot be considered complete without the feet. Similarly, the entire Jewish people are referred to as one body. Even one who is convinced that he is the head as compared to his friend, cannot be complete without him.[67]

Because each person cannot achieve his or her own moral goals without relying on others, no person can think of himself or herself as outside of the moral community or superior to any other member. Rather, the recognition of others' limitations is also an admission of one's own, leading to one's appreciation of others and humility for oneself. From a macro perspective, many different forms of social and intellectual life, albeit within the societal and social framework provided by Jewish (or Noahide) law, can provide for human flourishing. Differences in how each person aspires to become a servant of God do not contradict a conception of a universal Jewish (and non-Jewish) morality; rather, it reinforces tolerance and diversity within the moral community.

NOTES

1. *Mishna Avot* 3:14.
2. See Joseph Raz, who writes, "But if a society is subjected to a legal system then that system is the most important institutionalized system to which it is subjected. The law provides the general framework within which social life takes place. It is a system for guiding behaviour and for settling disputes which claims supreme authority to interfere with any kind of activity. It also regularly either supports or restricts the creation and practice of other norms in the society. By making these claims the law claims to provide the general framework for the conduct of all aspects of social life and sets itself as the supreme guardian of society (*Practical Reason and Norms*, 154)."
3. See William T. Allen, who writes, "Every general field of law embraces materials from which analysis can unearth the deepest questions that our social life recurringly presents to us. In some fields of law such questions lie near the surface, barely disguised by legal terminology and procedure. Most clearly, this is the case with the field of constitutional law, in which contests between claims of individual autonomy and claims of community are commonplace.

But it is hardly less true of criminal law, with its basic questions of culpability and punishment, or of tort law or contract. Other fields of law—one thinks of the various fields of commercial law, of intellectual property, or of taxation—appear or are more technical, more narrowly 'legal.' In such fields, legal problems may seem less pregnant with potentialities and answers may seem, and thankfully sometimes are, less controversial. It is easy in such fields to lose sight of-indeed it may sometimes be difficult to ever catch a first glimpse of-the contestable philosophical or political presuppositions that lie at their foundations, buried beneath the legal superstructure." William T. Allen, "Contracts and Communities in Corporation Law," *Washington and Lee Law Review*, Vol. 50 (1993) 1395.

4.   See Eric A. Posner, "Symbols, Signals, and Social Norms in Politics and the Law," *The Journal of Legal Studies*, Vol. 27, No. S2 (June 1998) 765–797. For an alternative conception of law in metaphorical rather than symbolic terms, see Moshe Sokol, "Mitzvah as Metaphor," *A People Apart: Chosenness and Ritual in Jewish Philosophical Thought* (Albany: State University of New York Press, 1993) 201–228.

5.   One example which demonstrates how different languages incline their speakers to consider concepts differently pertains to the study of human emotions. In English, an emotion is a mental state that arises spontaneously, rather than through conscious effort, and is accompanied by physiological changes in the person. An emotion is more than just a feeling. A feeling pertains either to a physical or to a mental state; an emotion is a combination of both a mental feeling and a physical change. For example, a person can feel hungry, but he or she cannot have an emotion of hunger. On the other side, though people say that the feeling one gets after eating chocolate is similar to love, anyone who has been in love knows that the emotion of love is incomparable, simply by virtue of the fact the feeling one gets when eating chocolate is missing that particular mental component that one experiences when in love. Human emotion as an objective category is such an intuitive idea in English-speaking countries that it is the focus of analysis in biology, psychology, and in the humanities.

In German, however, there is no indigenous word for emotion. *Gefühl*, its usual translational equivalent, does not have the same connotations as the word "emotion." *Gefühle* is used to describe mental states alone, and *Gemütsbewegung* roughly means "a movement of the mind" and not a combination of mental and physical changes. Contemporary academic German borrowed the word "*Emotion*" from English due to the lack of a German translation of the term. In Russian, *čuvstvo* roughly means feeling in general and *čuvstva* implies mental feelings. Even the French *sentiment* differs from the English "sentiment" in that the French word does not connote emotion whereas the English word does. Though it is considered an objective category in English-speaking cultures, the inability to similarly describe human emotions in other languages supports the idea that concepts and their meanings are influenced by the languages used to denote them. See Anna Wierzbicka's *Emotions Across Languages and Cultures: Diversity and Universals.*

6. For one example, Arthur H. Miller and Vicki L. Hesli write with respect to the meaning of democracy among the elites and the masses in post-Soviet Russia, "In short, democracy can have different meanings with numerous implications for a variety of social values and institutional arrangements. The important question here is: to what extent are these democratic theorists' meanings of democracy reflected, if at all, in the notions of democracy held by citizens living in the societies experiencing transitions from authoritarian rule? Moreover, if democracy is to be 'rule by the people', then we would want to know if the political leaders—those who are actually formulating the institutions and procedures for these newly emerging democracies—have a conception of democracy that is similar to that expressed by the ordinary citizens. If there are major discrepancies between the meanings of democracy expressed by the mass and elite in post-Soviet societies we need to be concerned about the extent to which representation is actually occurring in these countries." See Arthur H. Miller and Vicki L. Hesli, "Conceptions of Democracy Among Mass and Elite in Post-Soviet Societies," *British Journal of Political Science*, Vol. 27, No. 2 (1997): 163–164.

7. In the Talmud, the Sages use the verse, "It [The Torah] is not in heaven, that you should say: 'Who shall go up for us to heaven, and bring it to us, and make us to hear it, that we may do it?'" (Deuteronomy 30:12), as a proof-text to support their authority to make halakhic decisions that seem to be contrary to the law accord-

ing to the Heavenly court. See BT *Bava Metsia* 59b for the most popular example.

8. See the section below regarding epistemic and moral objectivity.

9. *Golden Doves with Silver Dots*, 138.

10. *Indo-European Languages and Society*, 380.

11. *Genesis Rabba* 1:1.

12. BT *Shabbat* 88a. Similarly, Rabbi Judah Loew writes in the first chapter of *Netivot Olam*, "Therefore, the Torah reinforces and supports everything so that the world will continue to be sustained, and all of this is because the Torah is the order (*seder*) for human beings in terms of how they should act and behave. Furthermore, just as the Torah is the order (*seder*) for human beings, so is it the order (*seder*) for the entire world, only that the order (*seder*) for human beings is apparent and explicit...but the order (*seder*) for the world is also found in the Torah since the Torah is nothing but the order (*seder*) for all existence."

13. Numbers Rabbah 13:15.

14. BT *Shabbat* 88b; See also Exodus Rabbah 5:9.

15. Deuteronomy 1:5.

16. Midrash *Tanhuma*, *Devarim*, 2; Genesis Rabbah 49:2.

17. Deuteronomy 27:1–8.

18. BT *Sotah* 32a.

19. The translation by Onkelos was considered by the Sages to be a part of the Oral Torah and not an authorized translation of the Written Torah. The translation of Rabbi Yonatan was similarly considered. However, the Sages began to disapprove of translations when the political environment in Israel changed because of the danger of studying translated texts outside of the pedagogical community as well as due to the possibility of either deliberate mistranslation or improper interpretation. See BT *Megilla* 3a and the explanation of Rabbi Tzvi Hirsch Chajes on BT *Megilla* 3a; BT *Megilla* 8b; Turei Even, *Megilla* 8b; See Hatam Sofer, *Megilla* 8b; BT *Megilla* 9a-b; Genesis Rabba 36:8.

20. Peter L. Berger and Thomas Luckmann, *The Social Construction of Reality*, 23.

21. *God of Abraham*, 204–205.

22. For how this relates to property, see J. David Bleich, "The *Metaphysics* of *Property* Interests in Jewish *Law*: An Analysis of 'Kinyan'," *Tradition*, Vol. 43, No. 2 (2010) 49–67. For how it

relates to the identity of artifacts, see Eli Hirsch, "Identity in the Talmud," *Midwest Studies in Philosophy*, Vol. 23(1999) 166–180.

23. The fact that the Sages recognized that the law is a complete system to be observed and not a collection of laws to follow is demonstrated from the following: "It is Rabbi Meir who said: 'One who is suspected of ignoring one religious law is suspected of disregarding the whole Torah... Our Rabbis taught: 'If one is prepared to accept the obligation of a *haver* except one religious law, we must not receive him as a *haver*. If a Gentile is prepared to accept the Torah except one law, we must not receive him [as an Israelite].'" BT *Behorot* 30.

24. See, for example, *Drashot HaRan, Derasha* 11.

25. See Joseph Raz, *Practical Reason and Norms* (London: Hutchinson, 1975). For an example of a situation where Jewish law conflicts with American law, see Ira Bedzow and Michael Broyde, "The Multifarious Models for Jewish Marriage," *AJS Perspectives*, Spring 2013.

26. This idea that the law's normativity in influencing a worldview (though not the state's power in terms of demanding compliance) is based on a person's commitment to it is similar to that found in Lon Fuller, *The Morality of Law* (New Haven: Yale University Press, 1964). For a comparable view among Jewish legal scholars, Isaac Breuer (1883–1946) writes as follows: "For the law is independent of state coercion. The mark of state coercion does not belong in the definition of justice and of its excellent representative, the law. Law is simply the binding rule of the community which is supported by the will of the whole community. The will of the whole community must keep the law and it must be sufficiently powerful to bend the will of the individual. But the flexibility of the communal will need not manifest itself in *the absolute coercion of the state*, but can also do so in the *compulsive psychic power* to which the individual with his motive-complex succumbs." (Isaac Breuer, *Concepts of Judaism* (New York: Israel Universities Press, 1974) 48).

27. BT *Shabbat* 88a.

28. Peter Hulsen, "Back to Basics: A Theory of the Emergence of Institutional Facts," *Law and Philosophy*, Vol. 17, No. 3 (1998) 284.

29. For an examination of how Jewish jurisprudence uses purposive interpretation, see Michael Broyde and Ira Bedzow, *The Codification of Jewish Law and an Introduction to the Jurisprudence of the Mishna Berura* (Academic Studies Press, 2013).

30. For more information on "auxiliary partial reasons," see Joseph Raz, *Practical Reason and Norms* (London: Hutchinson, 1975) Chapter 5.

31. John Searle, *The Construction of Social Reality*, 147.

32. *Philosophy in the Flesh*, 37.

33. Taking George Lakoff's claim even further, Cheryl Taylor et al. has shown that actual bodily movement (agency) is less important in determining the way a person will evaluate an object than inferential cues to agency (perceived agency). See Cheryl Taylor, Charles G. Lord, and Charles F. Jr. Bond (2009), "Embodiment, Agency, and Attitude Change," *Journal of Personality and Social Psychology*, 97 (6), 946–62.

34. See Owen Barfield's *History in English Words*, where he writes, "When a new thing or a new idea comes into the consciousness of the community, it is described, not by a new word, but by the name of the pre-existing object which most closely resembles it (24)."

    See also James Geary's *I Is an Other: The Secret Life of Metaphor and How It Shapes the Way We See the World*, where he writes, "Metaphorical thinking - our instinct not just for describing but for *comprehending* one thing in terms of another, for equating I with an other - shapes our view of the world, and is essential to how we communicate, learn, discover, and invent (3)."

35. The metaphor of "to grasp" as indicating understanding is found in many languages, such as in English, French, Italian, German, and Polish.

36. The Hebrew term for proverb (*mashal*) demonstrates how metaphor is used to understand abstract or more theoretical ideas through analogy to more concrete or mundane concepts. The word *mashal* is related to the verb *moshel*, which connotes a specific form of ruling. When the verb *moshel* is used in the Bible, it is most often in the context where the ruler is dissimilar to those being ruled. For example, *moshel* is used to describe the political relationship between Israel and the nations, both when the nations rule over Israel and when Israel rules over the nations. It is similarly

used to describe the Emorite Sihon's rule, since his territory was originally part of Moab. Also, the verb is often used to describe God's rule over the world, where its use indicates that God's rule is wholly different than the rule of any human king. The emphasis on this dissimilarity when using the verb *moshel* can be seen from the situation where Gidon refuses the men of Israel after he killed the two Midianite kings. The men of Israel say to Gidon, "Rule over us (*m'shal banu*), you, your son, and your grandson, for you have saved us from the hand of Midian!" To which Gidon replies, "I shall not rule over you (*lo emshol ani bakhem*), nor shall my son rule over you; Hashem shall rule over you (*yimshol bakhem*)." Yet Gidon still serves as their leader.

The verb *moshel* is not only used in a political context. God says that the sun and moon will rule over the day and night. When God distinguishes Adam from Eve based on the different roles they played in eating from the Tree of Knowledge, God says that Adam will rule over Eve, when previously they were considered to be of one flesh. God tells Kayin that he can rule over his evil inclination, informing us that the two inclinations should be considered as two distinct entities whereby the evil inclination is meant to serve the good inclination and not work in partnership. Also, both Eliezer in Abraham's house and Josef in Jacob's house are distinguished from everyone else through the fact that Abraham says that Eliezer rules over his household and through the fact that Josef's brothers suspect that Josef desires to rule over them. According to Jewish law, if a man buys a bondwoman, he does not rule (*moshel*) over her in order to be able to sell her to a strange man. He cannot treat her as an inferior being that is wholly distinct from him, since both are equally servants to God and must follow His law.

Moshel therefore implies a relationship of unlike kinds between a superior and an inferior (whether politically, morally, or religiously), whereby the inferior is meant to serve the superior and the superior is meant to guide the inferior to do so. It is not a relationship of mutual benefit, whereby each side needs the other to fill a lack that each side may have. Nor is it a unification of like kinds for the purpose of more effectively accomplishing shared goals.

When the word *mashal* is used in the Bible, it generally has a few different connotations. It could either be used to introduce a prophecy, such as with Bilaam, Isaiah, and Ezekiel. Or it is used to describe a popular saying, such as "Is Saul also among the prophets?" It is also used in conjunction with words like astonishment and conversation piece when used to describe Israel's fate among the Gentiles. Yet though these connotations are extremely different in terms of who says them, to whom they are said, and in the manner in which they are spoken, they all have a particular commonality. The relationship between the meaning of the words used and the meaning they are meant to symbolize are not equal or of the same category. However, it is only through these words that the recipient of them can get any idea of the knowledge it contains, even if only at the superficial level. For example, the words that the prophets spoke do not convey God's will in its entirety, but it does give its listener enough to begin his or her examination. The question, "Is Saul among the prophets?" has a very easy superficial answer, but the question is really meant to direct a person into thinking about what it means to be among the prophets. Similarly, if they sin, Israel's fate becomes a conversation piece among the Gentiles; their description of the people of Israel, even if it may contain a true historical or sociological account, could never describe what it means to be part of Jewish people. The words of a *mashal* are therefore meant to guide inferior, superficial ideas to provide insight into superior, deeper concepts.

37. John A. Bargh, "What Have We Been Priming All These Years? On the Development, Mechanisms, and Ecology of Nonconscious Social Behavior," *European Journal of Social Psychology*, 36 (2) (2006), 147–68; Mark Johnson, *The Meaning of the Body* (Chicago: University of Chicago Press, 2007); George Lakoff, "The Contemporary Theory of Metaphor," in *Metaphor and Thought*, ed. Andrew Ortony (Cambridge: Cambridge University Press, 1993) 203–51; Mark J. Landau, Brian P. Meier and Lucas A. Keefer, "A Metaphor-Enriched Social Cognition," *Psychological Bulletin*, 136 (6) (2010), 1045–67; Meng Zhang and Xiuping Li, "From Physical Weight to Psychological Significance: The Contribution of Semantic Activations," *Journal of Consumer Research*, 38 (6) (2012), 1063–75; Yangie Gu, Simona Botti and

David Faro, "Turning the Page: The Impact of Choice Closure on Satisfaction," *Journal of Consumer Research*, Vol. 40, August 2013.

38. Though cognitive neuroscientists are empirically observing how this process works, the philosophical pragmatists have suggested this process as a philosophical methodology. See, for example, John Dewey, *Human Nature and Conduct* (New York: Barnes & Noble, Inc., 2008) and William James, *The Sentiment of Rationality* (London: Longmans, Green and Co, 1905).

39. Once the law is recognized as a form of social organization, then the way in which it organizes society will influence what will constitute a social fact. Furthermore, those social facts will be true by virtue of the legal standards that created them.

40. Lon L. Fuller, *Legal Fictions* (Stanford: Stanford University Press, 1967) 9.

41. The difference between a subjective doubt and an objective doubt is that the former is one in which doubt arises due to the lack of awareness of an individual, the latter is when a doubt in the situation could never be avoided. For more information, see *Shakh, Yoreh Deah* 110, *Kuntres ha'Sfeikot*.

42. *Rosh, Hullin* 7:37.

43. Karl Marx, *Economic and Philosophic Manuscripts of 1844* (New York: International Publishers, 1964).

44. Donald R. Kelley, "The Metaphysics of Law: An Essay on the Very Young Marx," *The American Historical Review*, Vol. 83, No. 2 (Apr., 1978) 364.

45. Isaiah 54:13.

46. BT *Berakhot* 64a.

47. Job 38:4.

48. For information on the relationship between Jewish and Noahide law, see Rabbi J. David Bleich, "Mishpat Mavet Bedenai Benai Noach," Jubilee Volume in Honor of Rabbi Joseph D. Soloveitchik 1:193–208 (5754); Rabbi J. David Bleich, "Hasgarat Posh'a Yehudi sheBarach LeEretz Yisrael," Or Hamizrach 35:247–269 (5747); Professor Nahum Rakover, "Jewish Law and the Noahide Obligation to Preserve Social Order," Cardozo L.Rev. 12:1073-xxxx (1991); Professor Nachum Rakover, "Hamishpat Kerech Universali: Dinim Bebnai Noach" 15–57 (5748); Encyclopedia Talmudit, "Ben Noach" 3:348–362; Professor Aaron Lichtenstein, The Seven Laws of Noah (2nd Ed., 1986); Michael Broyde, "The

Obligation of Jews to Seek Observance of Noachide Laws by Gentiles: A Theoretical Review," *Tikkun olam: social responsibility in Jewish thought and law*, Edited by David Shatz, Chaim I. Waxman and Nathan J. Diament (Northvale, N.J. : Jason Aronson, 1997).

49. I combine interpretation and translation because the two are often-times seen as synonymous in the Jewish tradition. For example, the word *l'targem* means to interpret, to explain, as well as to translate. We have already discussed above the Sages understanding the terms "explain" and "well clarified" to mean that Moses' expounded on the Torah in the 70 languages of the nations of the world. The same phenomenon occurs in the time of Ezra. When the Jews returned from exile and Ezra gathered the people to hear the words of the Torah, Scripture relates, "They read in the scroll, in God's Torah, clearly, with the application of wisdom, and they helped [the people] understanding the recitation (Nehemiah 8:8)." The rabbinic understanding of this event is that they read the Written Torah, gave clear understanding through translation, and taught how to punctuate the unpunctuated text (BT Nedarim 37b; Genesis Rabbah 36:8). The translation given, however, was not composed by Ezra for the moment. As the verse in Proverbs relates, "Hear, my child, the instruction of your father, and do not forsake the Torah of your mother (Proverbs 1:8.)," the Aramaic translation is traditionally considered to have been given at Sinai corresponding to the native language of the Israelite matriarchs (Maharsha, Hiddushe Aggadot, Megilla 3a).

50. BT *Megilla* 8b.

51. Turei Even, *Megilla* 8b.

52. See Hatam Sofer, *Megilla* 8b.

53. BT *Megilla* 9a-b.

54. *Tur, Orah Hayyim* 58.

55. See, however, Maimonides, *Hilkhot Tefillin* (1:19), who writes, "Permission was granted to write the Torah scrolls in Greek only. However, the Greek [of which permission was granted] has been forgotten from the world. It has been confused and sunk into oblivion. Therefore, at present, all three sacred articles [phylacteries, mezuzah parchments, and Torah scrolls] must be written in [Hebrew in the] Assyrian script alone."

56. Genesis 9:27.

57. BT *Megilla* 9b. See also Genesis Rabba 36:8.
58. BT Exodus Rabbah 47:1. See also Midrash Tanhuma, VaYera, 5; Ki Tissa 34.
59. Exodus 34:27.
60. Exodus Rabba 47:3.
61. BT *Gittin* 60b.
62. See Gottlob Frege, *The Foundations of Arithmetic: A Logico-Mathematical Enquiry into the Concept of Number* (Evanston: Northwestern University Press, 1980).
63. William James, *Pragmatism and Other Writings* (New York: Penguin Group US, 2000) 64.
64. Clifford Geertz, *The Interpretation of Cultures: Selected Essays* (New York: Basic Books, 1973) 40.
65. BT *Berakhot* 58a.
66. Mishna *Sanhedrin* 4:5.
67. *Likutei Torah, Nitsavim* 42a.

CHAPTER 7

Practical Reason

Practical Reason in Aristotle and Maimonides

Should he reason with unprofitable talk, or with speeches wherewith he can do no good?[1]

By adopting a certain view of practical reason, my contemporary framework for Jewish virtue ethics not only departs from an Aristotelian or Maimonidean framework but also marks the beginning of a divergence from their respective views regarding moral and intellectual virtues. The reason for this divergence is that contemporary philosophy and science no longer accord with medieval positions in biology, psychology, and metaphysics, which underlie Aristotle's and Maimonides' ethics. Because my contemporary vision and theirs significantly part ways at this point, I will first provide a description of Aristotle's and Maimonides' views of practical reason before providing my own.

For Aristotle, the law serves as a tool for social stability and for moral development in the sense that it serves as a means to habituate good actions, yet not in the sense of being a means to actualize one's potential. In Maimonides' conception of Jewish law, on the other hand, the law does promote moral and intellectual development. The difference between the two views is that, for Aristotle, a person reaches perfection through the exercise of his own practical and theoretical reasoning, whereas, for Maimonides, he reaches perfection by internalizing practical and theoretical norms and concepts that are embedded in the law. The consequence of having the law serve as the means through which a person attains

© The Author(s) 2017
I. Bedzow, *Maimonides for Moderns*,
DOI 10.1007/978-3-319-44573-1_7

perfection is that Maimonides has no explicit place for practical reasoning in his theory, whereas for Aristotle practical reasoning is a *sine qua non* for ethical living.[2]

Moreover, for Aristotle, living according to, and for the sake of, obedience to the law by definition cannot constitute an ethical life. For Maimonides, on the other hand, obedience to the law is the pinnacle of the ethical life. According to Aristotle, in obeying the law, a person may act in the proper way, yet he does not develop the intellectual ability to discern the best way to act according to his own reasoning and independent of his obligation to follow the law. Because living well consists of choosing good and noble actions for their own sake, *and for no other reason at all*, excellence cannot be achieved when a person acts out of obedience to the law. He writes:

> As we say that some people who do just acts are not necessarily just, i.e. those who do the acts ordained by the laws either unwillingly or owing to ignorance or for some other reason and not for the sake of the acts themselves (though, to be sure, they do what they should and all the things that a good man ought), so it is, it seems, that in order to be good one must be in a certain state when one does the several acts, i.e. one must do them as a result of choice and for the sake of the acts themselves.[3]

Aristotle similarly writes in *Politics*, "The excellence of the subject [who is under the law] is certainly not [practical] wisdom, but only true opinion."[4] Though Aristotle does recognize the importance of the law, it serves solely a pedagogical role in his ethics and as a means of control and security in his political theory. The person who lives well lives in accord with the law but is not obedient to it, just as those who follow the law live in accord with right reason but not from it. Denial that the law can substitute for personal deliberation in choosing how to act and thus live justly and nobly leads Aristotle to affirm that "it is not possible to be good in the strict sense without practical wisdom, nor practically wise without moral excellence."[5]

Another limitation of the law in instilling moral virtues stems from the fact that it is what Aristotle calls "intelligence without desire."[6] To act from virtue means to act for the right reasons by doing what is virtuous for its own sake. This means that for the virtuous person, the non-rational part of the soul must be in line with his or her rational part or, in other words, that his or her emotions motivate the right action as much as his or her reason justifies it.[7] The law, however, cannot prescribe emotion directly; one can only hope that it is developed through habituation via legislation. Similarly, the determination of motive by the judiciary can only uncover the dispositions individuals already have, and its recommendations for rehabilitation can only influence a person's disposition indirectly in the same way that the law's influence is only indirect. Maimonides, in fact, disagrees with Aristotle on both of these points, as will be shown.

In *Shemonah Perakim*, where he sets the principles for his theory of ethics, beginning with his view of the soul and its role in forming a person's moral disposition, Maimonides writes that the rational part of a person's soul consists of both a theoretical aspect and a practical one. He explains,

> Reason, that faculty peculiar to man, enables him to understand, reflect, acquire knowledge of the sciences, and to discriminate between proper and improper actions. Its functions are partly practical and partly speculative (theoretical), the practical being, in turn, either mechanical or intellectual. By means of the speculative power, man knows things as they really are, and which, by their nature, are not subject to change. These are called the sciences in general. The mechanical power is that by which the arts, such as architecture, agriculture, medicine, and navigation are acquired. The intellectual power is that by which one, when he intends to do an act, reflects upon what he has premeditated, considers the possibility of performing it, and, if he thinks it possible, decides how it should be done.[8]

By assuming that reason enables a person both to acquire knowledge of the sciences *and* to discriminate between proper and improper actions, it would seem that Maimonides presumes that the faculty engages both in theoretical reasoning *as well as* in practical reasoning.

Despite this assumption, many scholars have noted that Maimonides does not in fact ever mention practical reasoning in his philosophy. Furthermore, Raymond Weiss has already noted that practical wisdom is not mentioned as a virtue in any of Maimonides' works: "There is no reference in CM [commentary on the Mishna] to a prophet's use of practical wisdom (*ta'aqqul*) when he temporarily suspends a law; a prophet relies upon 'theorizing' (*naẓar*) and 'syllogistic reasoning' or 'analogy' (*qiyās*) to determine what should be done (CM, Introd.). In the Code, the middle way itself is called the 'measure of wisdom'; H De'ot does not designate practical wisdom as a separate virtue."[9] Joseph Stern writes, "Under reason, Maimonides includes both theoretical and practical powers by which one 'perceives intelligibles, deliberates, acquires the sciences, and distinguishes between base and noble actions' (*EC* 1; see also

GP 1.53, p. 121; 1.72, p. 191). Unlike most of his Arabic counterparts, Maimonides does not posit distinct intellects corresponding to these powers; in particular, he never explicitly refers to a practical intellect."[10] David Shatz has also noted that "whereas Maimonides' philosophic sources saw moral knowledge as a function of 'the practical intellect,' and whereas he [Maimonides] recognizes a practical function of the rational faculty, Maimonides never used the term 'practical intellect' nor the term 'practical rational faculty.'"[11] Howard Kreisel writes, "For all of Maimonides' reticence in discussing the intellect, one is still struck by the fact that not once in any of his writings does he mention the term 'practical intellect' or 'practical rational faculty.' Even when he clearly alludes to this faculty, he fails to mention it explicitly."[12] Charles Raffel adds,

> For Maimonides, Divine Law has consolidated and co-opted most, if not all, of the functions of practical reason at an operative level. While for Aristotle, on an individual basis, 'practical reason issues commands: its end is to tell us what we ought to do and what we ought not to do,' in Maimonides' system, divine commandments and prohibitions embody the divine practical reason. The distinction between Aristotle's fully employed concept of phronesis and Maimonides' recessed view is important in appreciating why the actual operation of personal practical reason is downplayed in Maimonides' account. The extensiveness and expansiveness of the Law's dictates restrict the interplay of phronesis on an individual level.[13]

In a footnote, he continues,

> Maimonides' own reticence on practical reason (*ta'aqqul*) in the Guide is striking. Within the framework of a religious system based on Law, however, the Law seems to take over for moral intelligence at an operative level. In fact, the placement within the Guide of the section on the reasons for the Law, inserted in between the second and third sections of the thematic account on providence, suggests the possibility that the Law, as protector of the health of the body and the mind, displaces phronesis.[14]

The absence of any explicit mention of practical reasoning is compounded by Maimonides' assertion in *Shemonah Perakim* that obedience and disobedience to the law, which would seem to involve deliberation and practical reasoning, is found only in the sentient and appetitive parts of the soul, with the sentient part subservient to the appetitive one. The rational part of a person's soul engages the law only with respect to acquiring true beliefs contained therein. With regard to a person's actions, however, there is no aspect of the rational soul that engages the law. In effect, Maimonides' description of the soul and its association with the law serves as a denial of any role for practical reason to determine the choices a person makes for acting. This is consistent with his delineation of the rational virtues, which he states are theoretical wisdom and intelligence, which are made up of the theoretical intellect, acquired intellect, and excellent comprehension.[15] Also, in his commentary on Mishna*Avot* 5:7, he explains the three intellectual virtues as (1) skillful comprehension so as not to be duped by false arguments, (2) wisdom so as to be able to discuss things according to their proper subject, and (3) the ability to properly prioritize one's learning.

Maimonides' seeming replacement of practical wisdom with the law is demonstrated by the fact that where Aristotle advocates for one to adhere to the mean yet recognizes that such a principle is meaningless without excellent practical reasoning, Maimonides relies on the law to properly habituate people toward the mean by making the choice of right action for them.[16] Maimonides also contends that the law directs all aspects of a person's life, so that a person does not even need to study the political sciences since Divine laws govern human conduct.[17] This demonstrates that the all-encompassing nature of the law precludes a space for practical reasoning, since legal reasoning, or reasoning through the law and about the law governs all realms of human conduct. This is important since Aristotle understands political science and practical wisdom to be the same state of mind, even if their essence is not the same.[18]

What can be seen as a further denial of practical wisdom is Maimonides' use of the expression "Love truth and peace"[19] to refer to the rational virtues of theoretical wisdom and intelligence (truth) and the moral virtues (peace), which give people the ability to follow the law readily. A person following the law does not, therefore, actively choose the mean for himself or herself, but rather he or she acquires dispositions to follow the law, which itself determines the mean.

One may argue that to claim a total absence of practical reasoning in Maimonides' thought would require Maimonides to hold that the law is so explicitly all-encompassing that all one needs to do is to apply it. However, Maimonides' responsa demonstrate that the law must always be adapted to new circumstances, which means that a person would need to use practical reason in order to do so. In response to this claim, it may be helpful to recognize that Maimonides, like Aristotle, distinguishes between types of "practical reasoning" depending on the types of "practical wisdom" upon which one reasons. Therefore, though Maimonides omits the practical intellect from his philosophy, due to role that the law plays in both social and personal development, he does have a concept of equity, and its purpose is to mitigate the difficulties of having a general law.[20] One may say, therefore, in line with the position of David Novak, that Maimonides does contain practical reasoning in his philosophy, though Maimonides does not call it as such due to his reliance on technical categories.[21] Yet while this argument may acknowledge the claim that Maimonides does possess a notion of what we currently call practical reason, and while it does provide explanation regarding the method of reasoning that a person under the law utilizes, I believe it does so at the expense of appreciating other aspects of Maimonides' epistemology and how it relates to his cosmology.

Various theories have been offered to explain this strange absence from Maimonides' ethics. For example, Howard Kreisel suggests that by omitting practical reason from his ethics, Maimonides is emphasizing his contention that only the theoretical intellect is recognized as intellect and that the only function of the rational faculty is theoretical reasoning.[22] Therefore, Maimonides transformed the practical intellect into a capacity of the rational faculty that is corrupted by the body. Human perfection comes from perfection of the theoretical intellect in apprehending the law and perfection of one's appetitive faculty in following it. Political or ethical knowledge thus no longer constitutes a primary part of human perfection, and the practical activity of one who has attained perfection of his intellect is not the same as ethical activity. The practical activity of one who perfects his intellect stems purely from intellectual motivation without any influence from the moral passions, whereas ethical activity is influenced by the moral passions.[23]

David Shatz has a similar theory as Kreisel, in that he distinguishes between the type of morality that a person practices before reaching perfection and that which is a consequence of intellectual perfection. Where the law serves as the guide for propaedeutic morality, consequent morality "results not from *phronesis* but from scientific knowledge."[24] He writes,

> By achieving intellectual perfection, the perfect individual engages in a life of *imitatio Dei* with respect to the Deity's actions. This individual acts toward people as God acts toward the world, that is, exercising the same attributes. For this reason Maimonides spells out what loving-kindness, judgment, and righteousness entail (*GP* 3.53); these are what the intellectually perfect individual practices because of the overflow from the intellect.[25]

As such, they do not come from practical wisdom but rather from one's understanding of the theoretical wisdom of the Torah.

Though Kreisel's and Shatz's theories explain Maimonides' emphasis on theoretical wisdom, it does not deal directly with the absence of mention of practical reason. This absence, I believe, can be partly explained in light of his adoption of Aristotle's epistemology and cosmology. According to Maimonides' (and Aristotle's) epistemology, a person's rational faculty is initially in a state of potential, where it has the capacity to attain knowledge, yet does not in fact possess it. A person's intellect becomes actual by abstracting universal intelligible characteristics from sensible images. When the intellect is completely actualized, and thus becomes the acquired intellect, it possesses all of the forms, and it is constantly engaged in apprehending them. In order for the intellect to be actualized, however, there must be an agent that acts upon it. Maimonides confirms the existence of an Active Intellect that acts upon a person's rational faculty as follows:

> [Its] existence is indicated by the facts that our intellects pass from potentiality to actuality and that the forms of the existents that are subject to generation and corruption are actualized after they have been in their matter only in potentia. Now everything that passes from potentiality to actuality must have necessarily something that causes it to pass and that is outside it. And this cause must belong to the species of that which it causes to pass from potentiality to actuality.[26]

I will not go into the long debate over how Maimonides' epistemology incorporates the imaginative faculty or whether Maimonides adopts Alfarabi's claim that the Active Intellect is a condition for the actualization of the human intellect or Avicenna's position that the Active Intellect is the giver of forms to the human intellect.[27] What is important about Maimonides' epistemology in terms of his position regarding practical reason is the type of knowledge that the Active Intellect imparts. According to both Alfarabi and Avicenna, the Active Intellect only imparts theoretical knowledge unto the human intellect; practical wisdom, and the development of practical reasoning, comes from experience.[28]

Alfarabi defines the theoretical intellect as "the faculty by which we attain, by nature and not by examination or syllogistic reasoning, certain knowledge concerning the necessary, universal premises that are the principles of the sciences."[29] The practical intellect, on the other hand, "is the faculty by which a human being—through much experience in matters and long observation of sense-perceptible things—attains premises by which he is able to seize upon what he ought to prefer or avoid with respect to matters we are to do."[30] Wisdom, that is, the knowledge acquired by the theoretical intellect, is thus for Alfarabi what ascertains the truth of one's *telos*; practical wisdom is what enables a person to surmise how to attain it.[31] Also, when Alfarabi discusses prophecy,[32] he writes that the perfect statesman guides his people either through directly receiving practical wisdom, which is only a translation of theoretical wisdom into practical applications, or through using his own practical reasoning to devise norms which would allow people to attain the goals that theoretical wisdom has shown to be true.[33] Avicenna accepts Alfarabi's distinction between theoretical and practical wisdom and the different ways in which a person acquires them.[34] For Maimonides, however, there is no experience outside of the law; therefore, practical wisdom is replaced with juridical wisdom and practical reasoning with legal reasoning. Moreover, for Maimonides, the theoretical knowledge which the Active Intellect imparts is the wisdom of the Torah, which includes both epistemic and normative knowledge.[35] Therefore, even when a person attains intellectual perfection, his understanding of the world and how one should act within it is rooted in his theoretical understanding of the Torah.

This explanation supports the claims of Raymond Weiss and Howard Kreisel, who have noted that the absence of practical reason in Maimonides' thought is not only a departure from Aristotle but also a departure from Alfarabi's treatment of ethics, as Alfarabi does mention practical wisdom in his *Selected Aphorisms*.[36] One consequence (or reason, depending on what one thinks is the motivation) for Maimonides' departure from Alfarabi in omitting the practical intellect from his philosophy is that Maimonides does not give a legislative role to any of the prophets after Moses. Alfarabi, however, assigns a legislative role to the prophet who has attained perfection.

The absence of practical reason in Maimonides' ethics, and its implications for how to understand the relationship between moral deliberation and obedience to Jewish law, is important for contemporary Jewish ethics, even though contemporary ethics and epistemology have moved away from adopting an Aristotelianmetaphysics or epistemology, because Maimonides' conception of the relationship between Jewish law and ethical development also contradicts Kant's understanding of the essentiality of practical reasoning for ethical decision-making and, thus, impedes Jewish ethics from adopting a Kantian deontology as well.[37] However, even if it can be shown that Maimonides' possessed a notion of practical reason and the practical intellect, one would still need to provide a different account of practical reason which could explain its role as it relates to the law in light of contemporary epistemology. Moreover, given that practical reason is integral to the development of the virtues in Aristotle's ethics, an explanation of practical reason that can do so will also require a re-examination of the nature of the virtues.

In the next section, I will provide an account of practical reasoning that differs from the Aristotelian as well as the Kantian conception of practical reasoning. By introducing a different view of practical reasoning into my conception of contemporary Jewish ethics, I part ways from Maimonides' framework. However, the inclusion of practical reasoning, which includes reasoning about legal facts and norms, allows for a Jewish virtue ethics that can account for the aretological question of how a person can improve his or her intellectual and moral abilities as well as account for the deontological question of how a person can act voluntarily without his or her morality being self-legislated.

AN ALTERNATIVE VIEW OF REASONS AND REASONING

Behold, I waited for your words, I listened for your reasons...[38]

Because my conception of Jewish ethics assumes that Jewish law, and the Jewish tradition which is an outgrowth of the law, creates both norms for action and beliefs for contemplation, similar to Maimonides, Jewish law replaces practical wisdom in an Aristotelian model of ethics, and it replaces the self-legislated moral law in a Kantian ethics. Even though Aristotle and Kant would accept the idea that a deeper understanding of the beliefs contained within the law would involve theoretical reasoning, neither would agree that a deeper understanding of the practical norms contained within the law would involve practical reasoning. Aristotle explains:

> Now understanding is neither the having nor the acquiring of practical wisdom; but as learning is called understanding when it means the exercise of the faculty of knowledge, so "understanding" is applicable to the exercise of the faculty of opinion for the purpose of judging of what someone else says about matters with which practical wisdom is concerned—and of judging soundly; for "well" and "soundly" are the same thing.[39]

Reasoning about how to fulfill the details of a rule would be political reasoning for Aristotle, which he defines as deliberating about a decree in order for it to be carried out in the form of an individual act. For Kant, it would consist of immaturity.[40] Because of this, it is understandable that

Maimonides does not explicitly mention practical reason in his writings, since the Torah, and not practical wisdom, creates norms and obligations. Furthermore, a contemporary description of *Shlemut* cannot include a Kantian view of practical reason, since doing so would undermine the importance of Jewish law.

I nevertheless do believe that a contemporary description of *Shlemut* should include a notion of practical reason. This is not because I disagree with the Maimonidean view that Jewish law creates norms and obligations. Rather, it is because I believe that there is a conception of reasoning that can account for the two-tiered purpose of the Torah, that is, in providing both social norms and theoretical beliefs, and that can account for the goal of serving God as part of an ethical *telos*. Though Kant asserts that morality entails belief in God, this is not the same as saying that morality is grounded in theology. Rather, for Kant, belief in God serves as a means to respond to the antinomy of pure practical reason and not as a claim to metaphysical knowledge. For my conception of Jewish ethics, belief in God is both a metaphysical truth as well as a source of moral motivation.

In order to include practical reason in my description of *Shlemut*, I will define reasoning as "recognizing and responding to reasons." The consequences of adopting this definition are that legal reasoning becomes a subset of practical reasoning and that theoretical and practical reason are much more closely related than other conceptions of reason admit. Both of these consequences differ from the Maimonidean view which treats both sets of relations as very distinct. Another consequence of this view is that one would no longer speak of "reasons for the commandments" but rather one would speak about "reasoning from the commandments." In this section, I will provide a description of this alternative conception of practical reason as recognizing and responding to reasons, as well as some of the consequences that adopting such a description would have. Before discussing practical reason, however, I will begin my analysis with a discussion of what constitutes a reason. When discussing reasoning in this section, I am only examining what may make a reason normative for a person and not what motivates a person to act according to a reason. My discussion regarding what may motivate a person to choose a reason and to respond according to it will be saved for section dedicated to moral motivation. This distinction between *the normativity of reasons* and *the motivation of the person* in responding to them is important because the idea that reasoning is "recognizing and responding to reasons" entails that reasons come with certain normativity to them which is separate from how one is motivated by them, though the two are intimately related.

Moreover, because any full examination of deliberation must account for both the normativity that reasons possess and the motivation of a person who recognizes and responds to various reasons by choosing one of them as a reason to act, this chapter will not discuss how deliberation can serve as an explanatory nexus among different alternatives. Yet, by separating my analysis to a discussion of reasons and to a discussion of how a person reasons, I can analyze (partially) reasons in light of the roles, that is, explanatory or normative, that they serve in reasoning. This analysis, however, is necessarily limited to understanding how reasons can be prioritized theoretically and not in how a person reasons actually. Also, because reasons are necessary but not sufficient for reasoning, a full discussion of how a person engages in moral reasoning must be deferred until one understands the nature of intellectual and moral virtues and their roles in recognizing and responding to reasons. By the time one reads the section on moral motivation, however, all of this should become much clearer.

Explanatory Reasons

In one sense, "a reason" is an explanation; it is a statement that describes why something is the way that it is. As a statement of explanation, however, a reason is also a fact. While the veracity of this fact will be discussed below, at this point it is sufficient to assume that it is accepted as a fact. For example, one could say:

- The reason why a day is (approximately) 24 h is because (approximately) 24 h is the length of time for the earth to make a complete rotation.

Alternatively, one could say:

- It is a fact that (approximately) 24 h is the length of time for the earth to make a complete rotation, and it is a fact that this time period is called a day.

Any statement that provides a reason to explain something can be restated as a fact or a set of facts that describe it. Likewise, when "a reason" serves as an explanation, it is either a fact that describes the relationship between facts or a fact that presupposes other facts within it, and it is oftentimes both. The difference between a reason as a fact that describes the relationship between facts and a reason as a fact that subsumes other facts can also be seen from the example above.

- Twenty-four hours = length of time for earth's rotation = what we call a day (a reason as a fact that describes the relationship between facts)
- Length of time for earth's rotation = the earth rotates around an axis (a reason as a fact that presupposes other facts within it)

Moreover, the facts of which reasons are composed are descriptions of the world relative to our understanding or expression of it. For example, the reason why an apple falls when it separates from the tree branch is because of gravity. However, how the explanation of gravity is understood depends on whether we describe it through Einstein's general theory of relativity or more simply through Newton's law of universal gravitation. Furthermore, it is not the case that those facts which describe relationships between other facts cease to exist when we are not aware of them. Rather, the relationship remains, yet a fact only serves as a reason when a person is aware of it. An explanatory reason would thus have the following definition:

> *An explanatory reason is a fact that describes a relationship between other facts in the world; its existence as a fact does not depend on whether it is perceived and understood by a person, yet the person must perceive the fact and understand it in order to employ it as a reason.*

Reasons are not causes. Causes are typically events that have consequences; reasons are facts that describe the world. A person may give a cause as a reason, such as "the ball moved because another ball hit it." However, the cause of ball's movement is the other ball hitting it; the explanation for why the ball moved is the fact that the other ball hit it. In the first case, there is an event (the other ball hitting it); in the second case, there is a description of an event (that the other ball hit it). This may seem to be a semantic gesture, but it is not. It is a category difference between something that occurs in the world and a person's recognition and response to it.[41] While this distinction may not seem to be a great one with respect to explanatory reasons, it is important with respect to normative reasons, because it allows for a person to perceive a reason for acting and yet still not act accordingly.

Explanatory reasons are not only used to describe and understand the physical world, but also used to explain human behavior as well. To explain human actions, however, explanatory reasons usually must account for a greater number of facts and the complexity in how those facts relate to each other. Those facts will also range from physical facts to social and institutional facts.[42] For example, the sole fact that the day is Saturday may explain to some why people are wearing raincoats when they walk to synagogue rather than holding umbrellas, yet this is so only because those people are also assuming a great number of other facts in their accepting of "it is Saturday" as a reason. The full (or more complete) reason for why the people may be wearing raincoats rather than holding umbrellas is that (1) it is Saturday, (2) it is raining, (3) on Saturday religiously observant Jews do not perform certain activities, (4) one activity which is not to be performed is opening or carrying an umbrella, (5) the people want to go to synagogue, (6) driving is an activity that is not to be performed on Saturday, and (7) they do not want to get wet. All seven facts are part of the reason for wearing raincoats, and many of those facts have other facts subsumed within them as well.

Explanatory reasons are similar to predictions or forecasts, but they are not the same. A prediction or a forecast is a statement of what will occur in the future. When making a prediction or a forecast a person often (though not always) bases his or her statement on inferences drawn from explanations of current or past events. While explanatory facts can also be drawn from inferences of other explanatory facts, the difference between explanatory facts and predictive statements, in terms of the inferences made, is that the former is a deductive contemporaneous extension of an explanation whereas the latter is an inductive extension of an explanation to be applied to a future event. Predictions and forecasts cannot, therefore, explain a future event; they can only provide an educated guess as to what may happen. Even prophecy, which one may call the ultimate prediction since it is not based on human inference but on Divine revelation, is not an infallible explanation of what will occur. For example, Jeremiah tells Hananiah, "The prophet that prophesies about peace, [only] when the word of the prophet shall come to pass, then shall the prophet be known, that Hashem has truly sent him."[43] Yet, if a prophet foretells of doom, his prophecy is not deemed false if it does not come to fruition, as Jonah's prophecy to Nineveh attests. The reason why predictions and forecasts are not explanatory reasons is that reasons are not causes. No matter how well a person or set of circumstances is known, a person's description of events can never include every contingency, and even if it did, free will disallows a necessary causal relationship between the present moment and future actions.[44]

Normative Reasons

In addition to being explanatory, reasons can also be normative. Normative reasons are in some respect also explanatory, since in order for its normativity to be recognized and accepted, reasons must properly explain why a particular behavior is appropriate. Normative reasons, like explanatory reasons, are also composed of facts.[45] Even though the predominant view regarding normative reasons is that they are intentional states such as beliefs and desires, in my view, a normative reason is not an intentional state, yet an intentional state may serve as part of a reason for the person to act. This distinction has two important ramifications for practical reasoning. First, intentional states are no longer internal causes for actions, but rather they are part of internal reasons for acting upon which a person deliberates about whether to respond to them or not. Intentional states are thus different from intentions. Intentional states are the beliefs and desires that a person has and which he or she uses in considering how to act. Intentions to act, which actually guide the action in process, result from deliberation and include more than just intentional states.[46] Also, because normative reasons can be composed of external as well as internal facts, practical reason need not be for the sake of satisfying a desire. The reasons which one accepts may consist of desire-independent facts as well, about which I will explain more below. Second, acting contrary to a reason which consists of intentional states should not be seen as a function of irrationality; rather, it should be considered possibly as a function of bad (or "less than excellent") reasoning or as a function of incorrectly prioritizing reasons. This will be further examined below in the section on bad reasoning versus irrationality and in the section on weakness of will.

While normative reasons contain an explanatory element, they differ from explanatory reasons in two important respects regarding how they serve as reasons. First, explanatory reasons do not provide a reason for a person to act, even when a person is giving an explanatory reason about his or her own actions. Normative reasons, on the other hand, obligate (or serve as a means to motivate)[47] the person who recognizes them to fulfill his or her normative demands. Second, explanatory reasons are oriented toward the present and the past; normative reasons, on the other hand, are future-oriented. A person gives an explanatory reason to describe a previous relationship in the world or a current relationship in the world of which he or she has no active involvement, even if the person had some involvement with the matter previously. Even when a person gives an explanatory reason for why he or she is currently acting, the reason is a description of a previous act, such as making the decision to act. For example, when I was writing these words I did so because I believed that they are correct, or because I had to do a different activity later, or because I had the time to write at that moment. All these reasons given had served as normative reasons before I began to write, yet while writing they served as explanatory reasons in that they explain why I decided to write. If one would want to say that the reasons are continuing to serve a normative function as I continue to write, their role in a normative capacity is always a step ahead of my writing. Their roles as explanatory reasons are either contemporaneous with my writing or backward-looking.

The difference between explanatory reasons and normative reasons can be seen when the explanation for why a person does an action is not the same as the reason why the person was motivated to act or in how he or she justifies acting (which is an explanation). For example:

1. Sara laughed when she heard that she will have a son, because she thought she was too old (explanatory reason).
2. From Sara's perspective, the reason why she laughed was that she thought the juxtaposition of the fact that she was to have a child and the fact that she was too old to have a child was ironic which she saw as a reason to laugh. (From my perspective, it is an explanation of Sara's action. From Sara's perspective before she laughed, the relationship between the two facts were a motivation for acting—normative reason.)
3. Sara actually denied laughing, but if she were to justify it, she could say that she laughed because she, like Abraham, was overcome with emotion for the miracle that was foretold (justification—explanatory reason).

Regarding the second point of the example, while the explanation of Sara's laughing from my perspective includes her motivation, I could only provide it as an explanation after she did in fact laugh. Though it is obvious,

I could not explain her laughing before she actually laughed, but this fact shows an important point, namely that a reason to laugh does not automatically cause her to do so. It could only provide a means to motivate her to do so, yet, even given the reason to act, she still could not have laughed.[48] This shows that normative reasons may serve an explanatory role, when given after the fact, but their explanatory role is different from their normative one.

The force of a normative reason depends on a person recognizing the facts that the normative reason entails, being motivated by those facts to perform the proposed action, and actually performing the action by virtue of the person's recognition of, and motivation by, the facts. Normative reasons must also be able to describe the reality of a situation properly, to explain why the situation contains a normative aspect, and to explain why a particular response is appropriate. A normative reason would thus have the following definition:

> *A normative reason is a fact that describes a relationship between other facts in the world in such a way that the person who recognizes that fact may be motivated to respond in a particular way because of it; its existence as a fact does not depend on whether it is perceived and understood by a person, yet the person must perceive the fact and understand it in order to be motivated by it as a reason.*

Normativity is to some degree a part of the reason itself and somewhat a function of how a person approaches normative facts. It therefore can be the case that a person may recognize that a particular normative fact has a greater or lesser level of normativity than he or she previously considered or than how the fact is objectively considered by the community in which he or she lives.

The normativity of desires and beliefs is readily accepted by philosophers who discuss practical reason; the normativity of external reasons, such as obligations and commitments, on the other hand, is in need of explanation. In my account, external social or institutional facts possess normativity based on the goals that the society that institutes them aims to achieve. Therefore, when a person recognizes those facts, he or she also recognizes the obligations or commitments that they entail.[49] This will be further explained in the next section.

Normative Reasons: External and Desire-Independent

Normative reasons can be internal or external reasons; however, a more accurate way to say this would be that normative reasons may consist of external normative facts as well as internal normative facts. An external normative fact, which may be a physical fact about the world or a social fact such as an obligation or a commitment, exists regardless of whether a person is aware of it or not, and its normativity arises from how different facts relate to each other with a given purpose. Strictly physical facts cannot be normative in the sense of communicating a value judgment, yet they are normative in the sense of establishing expectations for consequences. For example, the fact that objects fall to the ground because of gravity does not have an inherent value judgment associated with it. Yet, the expectation that an object will fall due to gravity can be a factor in determining whether I want to let go of an object or not. Moreover, when physical facts are combined with social or institutional facts in a normative reason, physical facts influence the weight of normativity of the reason by virtue of their relationship to social or institutional facts. For example, the fact that it is raining outside need not become part of a normative reason to wear a raincoat, since a person may want to stay inside. Similarly, the fact that it is Saturday need not become part of a normative reason to wear a raincoat since it may not be raining. However, the facts that it is raining and that it is Saturday do become part of a normative reason to wear a raincoat when they combine with the institutional facts that on Saturday religiously observant Jews do not perform certain activities, that one activity which is not to be performed is opening an umbrella, and that driving is an activity that is not to be performed on Saturday. In this example, the weight of normativity of the institutional facts is dependent on the physical facts of it being Saturday and raining. Also, the normative reason to wear a raincoat is dependent on whether one accepts those social or institutional facts as part of a reason to act. The nature of this acceptance will be discussed shortly below.

An internal normative fact, on the other hand, is usually thought to be the existence of intentional states that a person uses in his or her deliberation. However, when a person recognizes an external fact, the recognition that it may be part of a normative reason also makes it an internal normative fact. The acceptance of the normativity of an external fact creates an intentional state, such as a belief in its normativity and a desire or a sense of obligation to fulfill its demand. By being internalized, a person can use the fact in his or her deliberation. For example, if I borrow a dollar from a person, I may or may not have an internal reason to repay it, but I nevertheless have a reason to do so based on the external social fact that a person must fulfill his or her commitments. Recognition of that fact can thereby become a reason for me to respond appropriately and repay the dollar. If a person does not recognize an external fact, it may still constitute a reason for action in general, yet it will not be seen as a reason for acting by the person who is deliberating on whether or not to act.[50]

Normative reasons, such as keeping a commitment, are not reasons by virtue of a person's higher-order desire to keep all commitments, thereby making the reason to keep a particular commitment a reason for him or her. While it is true that people may have a hierarchy of reasons, one need not explain the reason to keep a particular commitment as being the consequence of having a desire to keep all commitments. To use the example above, the obligation for me to repay the dollar is established once I borrowed it, and it serves as a normative fact regardless of whether or not I have a higher-order desire to accept all commitments. Moreover, the social fact that one must repay a borrowed dollar will be part of a normative reason to repay it even if I did not recognize it. In contrast to the predominant view of practical reason, normative reasons can be external and desire-independent when one looks at reasoning from a "third-person" or evaluative perspective, yet they only become reasons in a person's deliberation over how to respond once he or she recognizes it and accepts it so that it becomes an internal reason. By maintaining this distinction, one can explain how a person could have a reason for keeping a particular commitment, even when he or she does not possess a higher-order desire to keep all commitments. It also can explain how others can understand that a person has a reason to keep a commitment even when the person does not recognize it.

The existence of desire-independent reasons is further supported by how a person relates to society and society's influence on the development of a person's ability to reason. Despite Rawls' philosophical premises, people do not adopt the norms of their social milieu from a position external to the system. Rather, those norms are external constraints that people learn to accept. This is the case regardless of whether one refers to a child who matures in his or her family household or an adult who becomes acculturated into society. In both cases, the commitments that the community establishes as normative are accepted and adopted by its members. Unlike the Aristotelian and Kantian model, where practical reasoning is anarchic in order for reasons to be originated internally, under this conception of practical reasoning, social commitments are often prior to—and a part of—a person's reasoning and not the result of one's decision to accept them by virtue of his or her reasoning. Moreover, social commitments continue to provide reasons even when a person's practical reasoning capabilities are fully developed. Societal institutions do not serve to make a person submit to ethical obligations only to release him or her from them when he or she matures.

What Is Reason(ing)?

If normative reasons are facts about the world which describe the (normative) relationship between reality and the person living in it, then the act of reasoning should be understood as recognizing those facts and responding to them appropriately.[51] Though I will discuss whether rationality is a distinct cognitive faculty in my examination of intellectual and moral virtue and in my section on moral motivation, I want to make one point at present about it as it pertains to practical reason. If reason consists of recognizing and responding to reasons, then rationality is intimately connected to the apprehension of reasons as much as to the evaluation of reasons so as to respond appropriately. Therefore, whether rationality is a distinct cognitive faculty or not, it is dependent on sensory perception and affective states, as well as social and cultural influences over what constitutes a fact and its relation to the world that it describes. Moreover, the dependence of reasoning on these other factors is not as a separate step of gathering reasons to be evaluated but rather it is a part of reasoning itself.

Defining practical reason as recognizing and properly responding to normative reasons necessitates a different set of skills than what we typically think are required for reasoning, since apprehension of external facts is now part of reasoning itself. It also includes an ability to recognize the priorities of values that different facts may have, so as to evaluate different reasons in order to discover which reason has the greatest normative force. When engaging in practical reason, a person cannot deliberate on the situation and the appropriate response as if he or she were an outside observer, since what he or she affirms as reasons is based on his or her relationship to the situation. If a person did try to stand outside of the situation for the purpose of deliberating, his or her reasoning would be incomplete, since the very normativity of reasons depends on how the person relates to the situation.

The relationship between recognizing reasons, the apprehension of external facts, and the society which introduces social and institutional facts is reflected in a person's tendency not to reflect on an idea or belief to which he or she is already firmly committed. Oftentimes, a person's commitment makes an idea or belief a premise from which to deliberate rather than a subject of deliberation. On the other hand, a person will deliberate over his or her beliefs when either experience or another idea or concept by which he or she is confronted contradicts them. Deliberation would then be used to reconcile old beliefs and the new, conflicting information. Thus, it is a change in belief and not belief itself that becomes the impetus for deliberation. This insight applies not only to theoretical speculation, but also in how and why habits are created, which will be discussed below in the section comparing practical and theoretical reason.

The evaluation of reasons so as to respond appropriately is also affected by how one apprehends external facts and the priorities of the society in which he or she lives. A given situation may allow for multiple interpretations, which bear competing, or even conflicting, normative claims. Deliberation would then have to include interpreting one's perception of the situation in a way that best coheres with the person's priorities and beliefs. A person's priorities or beliefs, however, need not be those of society, yet society's priorities will nevertheless be taken into account during deliberation. For example, many times people will accept a proposition or a belief and conduct themselves according to it without actually believing it. They may do so for a number of reasons, such as they may not be fully convinced of the belief or norm, though they may not be dissuaded of it either. By acting according to those beliefs or norms, they achieve a result that only accords with what society establishes as a reason even if they are motivated by a different reason, that is, they act properly but for "the wrong reason." Yet, the "wrong reason" nevertheless must include what is considered to be the "right reason" as a factor, for if the response did not achieve the result desired by themselves or by society, they would not have acted in such a way. Joseph Raz calls acting in this way acting for a non-standard reason, in contrast to acting for a standard reason, which is one that a person follows directly, by which he means that the person has the attitude for performing, and performs the action, for that particular reason.[52] In Jewish parlance, it would be the difference between acting *shelo lishma* and *lishma*.[53]

Ends and Means

Related to the question of whether there can be desire-independent reasons is the question of whether a person can reason about ends as much as he or she can about means.[54] In the conception of practical reason as recognizing and responding to reasons, a person does not have an established end that is innate and teleological which he or she must actualize. Nor is a person's end a response to the antinomy of pure practical reason. Rather, in this conception a person's ethical aspirations are discovered through his or her interactions in the world, whether they be direct, that is, through the teachings of the community, or indirect, that is, by the unconscious adoption of social norms and facts through the person's everyday participation in them.

While this may sound very similar to the process of moral development that Aristotle describes, it differs from Aristotle in two very important respects. First, in my conception of practical reason a person's moral goal is never completely internal even when it is internalized. It is not the case that a person wants to develop his or her potential and thus finds the means to do so. On the contrary, a person's moral goal is based on the relationship he or she has with the world. He or she recognizes reasons to adopt a moral purpose, and through aspiring to fulfill that purpose, the person develops his or her capacity to do so more effectively. The process is the reverse of Aristotle's, since Aristotle proposes that a person desires self-improvement and then acts in the world to attain it. I propose that a person recognizes the commitment to fulfill God's will, then he or she responds with a desire to fulfill God's will by acting a certain way. The consequence of this process is self-improvement.

The second difference between my view and Aristotle's view is that the attainment of one's end does not change the relationship between the person and the norms of the social environment in which he or she resides. For Aristotle, the law is a means for a person to develop proper habits, but its observance is never an end in itself. In my conception, a person may act in accordance with the law for a non-standard reason (and through following the law he or she may develop proper habits), but acting for the sake of the law, that is, acting *lishma*, ultimately is an end in itself, since it represents the end of fulfilling God's will.

Bad Reasoning Versus Irrationality

Because there are two main components of practical reason, one can distinguish between bad reasoning and irrationality. For example, Joseph Raz, who makes a similar distinction as I do, writes, "Good reasoners can be habitually irrational, and, more commonly, perfectly rational people can be bad reasoners. They often make mistakes, but that does not impugn their rationality."[55] Bad reasoning occurs when a person properly recognizes reasons but makes mistakes in his or her deliberation as to how to respond properly. Irrationality occurs when a person cannot recognize reasons.[56] Because reasons contain both internal and external normative facts, irrationality is a social phenomenon as much as it may be a psychological one.

This view of irrationality fits with a conception of mental illness that is found in the Jewish legal tradition. According to many of the Jewish legal codes, a mentally ill person is someone who is unable to comprehend the world around him, even if he can speak coherently with others as if he were lucid. It does not matter if the person has a psychological disorder or a physiological disorder; the codes consider an epileptic while seizing to be in a "mentally-ill" state. While suffering from mental illness, a person is not obligated to keep any of the commandments. Yet, unlike others who are exempt from observing the commandments, one who is mentally ill is not considered to be in a state of duress so as to be exempt, nor does his exemption arise from having a previous conflicting obligation. Rather, the exemption arises from the fact that the person is considered to be outside the normative framework, and therefore, the law does not apply to him. Because the person cannot comprehend the world around him, and thus the consequences of his actions, he cannot be held responsible for them even *de jure* let alone *de facto*. In contrast, a mentally handicapped person is obligated to observe the commandments, because, unlike one who is mentally ill, he is able to understand the world around him, albeit on a superficial level since complexity confuses him more easily than most people.[57] The implications of this legal position is that recognizing reasons, that is, the commitments that one has by virtue of the law, is an essential part of what it means to be rational. If a person cannot recognize reasons to act due to circumstances outside of his control, then it would be unfair to hold him accountable to them. If a person can, but does not, recognize reasons to act, even at the most superficial level, then he is held accountable for them.

This view of mental illness also supports the social nature of rationality, by which I mean that some reasons to be recognized are socially constructed and external to a person's reasoning such that others can recognize them. According to the Jewish legal codes, diagnosing mental illness is not done simply by observing a person's symptoms. Rather, symptoms are analyzed with respect to the broader context of a person's life. Only when a person's behavior cannot be given a rational explanation by others does it suggest mental illness. When, however, a rational interpretation can be given to explain why a person acts in a seemingly irrational way, the person would not be considered mentally ill.[58] From the perspective of moral development, this latter point is exceptionally important, even if it seems like a platitude, since it means that many antisocial behaviors are not in fact indications of irrationality. They may be the result of bad reasoning which turned into bad habits, yet the person who acts in such a manner can still recognize other reasons for acting.

The idea that irrationality is an inability to recognize reasons is found in a responsum of Rabbi Moshe Feinstein, where he discusses a case where a person seems to be completely normal except for the fact that he believes himself to be the Messiah. The person would climb trees in order to give speeches to the people below, and he would walk around naked claiming to emulate the first human being. Rabbi Feinstein distinguishes between being capable to comprehend the purpose and worldview embedded within Jewish law and being capable to conduct oneself in a greater society, whereby the person engages in trade and has social responsibilities. Because the person who claims to be the Messiah is unable to comprehend the mores and values of Jewish law, not that he does not believe in them or accept them but rather that he cannot even understand them enough to be able to accept or reject them, he is exempt from its obligations by virtue of being mentally ill. On the other hand, with respect to living in the greater society, his transactions would be effective since he can understand social norms as any other sane person. In this sense, he is both sane and insane, depending on the standard by which his behavior is judged.[59]

Practical and Theoretical Reason

Because practical reason is recognizing and responding to reasons, theoretical reasoning must be a component of practical reasoning and can be shown to have a very similar process to it. With regard to being a component of practical reasoning, normative reasons consist of both explanatory and normative facts; therefore, the normativity of a reason is dependent on understanding explanatory facts correctly.[60] With regard to the process of theoretical reasoning, knowledge occurs through the recognition of explanatory facts, deliberation to determine the facts' veracity, and then properly responding by either believing them to be true or not.[61] There are two additional ways in which practical and theoretical reasoning are similar in process, namely that in both types of reasoning a person has the ability to accept a fact while not fully believing it, and that both processes are inert in the sense that they are motivated by a sense of relieving a con-tradiction or tension.

In both practical and theoretical reasoning, a person can accept a fact without believing it and then use it in his or her deliberation. With regard to practical reason, the case would be when a person accepts a normative reason and acts upon it for the sake of achieving something other than that for which the normative reason is a reason, that is, he uses the normative reason as a non-standard reason, or *shelo lishma*. With regard to theoretical reason, a person can accept an explanatory fact and allow it to be part of his theoretical reasoning (and practical reasoning, when used for explain-ing a situation), yet he or she still may not be fully persuaded or dissuaded of its veracity. This occurs more often than we think, and many times theo-retical reasoning based on an accepted but not believed premise allows for that premise to be appreciated more fully and ultimately believed after further speculation. The distinction between accepting a premise and fully believing a premise also explains Maimonides' distinction between the command to believe in God and his contention that knowing God is the ultimate goal of human perfection.[62] Rabbi Meir Leibush ben Jehiel Michel Wisser (Malbim) explains Maimonides' change of language from the term "believe" in God, which he uses in *Sefer HaMitzvot* to the term "know" in *Hilkhot Yesode HaTorah*, as follows:

> In his code Rambam deliberately changed the wording from "believe" to "know." He wished to stress the intellectual basis of this precept. ... But these two commandments—the existence and oneness of the Divinity is attained by the direct exercise of men's intellectual faculties. The Lord implanted these concepts in him from birth. They are innate ideas. A man has only to look into his own soul to discover them just as he develops all the rest of his faculties. There was no need to receive them from Moses as an act of faith. They were therefore imparted directly by God who fashioned man's soul. The precept [therefore] consists of making every effort to clarify our knowledge of this, in accordance with the text (Job 12:9): "Who cannot fail to discover that the hand of the Lord is behind all this."[63]

Regardless of his epistemological assumptions, Rabbi Meir recognizes that the commandment to believe in God is really a commandment to accept the theoretical fact of God's existence so that future theoretical and practical reasoning employ that fact as part of a normative reason to know God more clearly and to act according to His will. The goal to know God, on the other hand, is to transform one's acceptance of a belief into personal knowledge, which takes effort and will, and the process of doing so has the consequence of refining one's intellectual virtues.[64] Similarly, Don Isaac Abravanel writes in *Rosh Amanah*,

> Now Maimonides did not count as a positive commandment the form of the belief and its truth, but, rather, knowledge of those things which bring one to acquire beliefs. Therefore he wrote in the first chapter of the *Sefer ha-Madda*, in explaining the first foundation, which is about belief in the necessity of God's existence, that 'to acknowledge this truth is an affirmative precept.' Maimonides did not say that belief in this truth is an affirmative precept, for he did not relate the commandment to belief but to knowing those things which bring one to belief.[65]

Also, Howard Kreisel has pointed out in support of this distinction between accepting correct opinions as beliefs and understanding them intellectually that the commandment to know (*leida*) that there is a Primary Being who brought the world into existence, as laid out in *Hilkhot Yesode HaTorah* 1:1, does not imply detailed scientific knowledge but rather the acceptance of correct opinion.[66]

The difference, however, between practical and theoretical reasoning in this regard is that with respect to practical reason, a person may conclude and be fully committed to a certain action, yet still not perform it. With regard to theoretical reason, on the other hand, the gap between reasoning about the facts one has accepted and concluding one's deliberation with turning those accepted facts into firmly held knowledge is much smaller. This difference is based on the fact that there is a wide range of actions that a person can choose to perform as a response to a situation, and all of them have normative reasons that can motivate the person. Therefore, normative reasons to act one way over another can conflict. When there is a conflict, the person is not fully motivated to perform just one of the choices of actions, and he or she must overcome that gap between deliberation and action in order to perform what ultimately will be chosen as the most appropriate act. Joseph Raz explains, "We could distinguish two elements in a claim that something is an adequate reason for an action: (1) it is a sufficient reason in that it makes the action it is a reason for intelligible, (2) given that it is not defeated by (wholly or partly) conflicting reasons, it is an adequate reason for the action, for conforming to it is not wrong or unreasonable or irrational."[67] An example of a how conflicting normative reasons can result in a gap between reasoning and acting is when Elijah says to the Israelites, "How long will you waver between two opinions? If Hashem is God, follow Him; but if Baal, follow him."[68] The Israelites had normative reasons to follow Hashem and to follow Baal. Of course, we would say that the reason(s) to follow Baal was either incorrect or non-standard and should have thus been defeated by the reason(s) to follow Hashem, yet for the Israelites, the conflicting reasons motivated them equally. Therefore, they could not overcome the gap between reasoning and acting, leaving them to waver between the two opinions. Oftentimes, the gap is closed, not through further deliberation, since conflicting reasons have rational justification, but through the weight that habits give to the priority of those reasons. For example, William James writes:

> Our passional nature not only lawfully may, but must, decide an option between propositions, whenever it is a genuine option that cannot by its nature be decided on intellectual grounds; for to say, under such circumstances, "Do not decide, but leave the question open," is itself a passional decision—just like deciding yes or no—and is attended with the same risk of losing the truth.[69]

With respect to theoretical reasoning, the choices available are to conclude the fact is either true or false. Once deliberation concludes about a fact's veracity (though it may take a lifetime to do so), there are no other options from which to choose how to respond but to know the fact as true.

The example of Elijah's admonition to the Israelites shows that there is an intimate relationship between theoretical and practical reasoning, both in process and in how they work together in securing knowledge and habits. The normative reasons to follow Hashem or Baal contain explanatory facts, and therefore include theoretical reasoning as part of the deliberation, yet the culmination of deliberation was not simply a matter of belief but rather was primarily to act, even though action was predicated on holding, at least to some degree, certain beliefs. Elijah in effect says, "If you accept the explanatory fact that Hashem is God, then you are committed to the normative fact that you must follow Him." From the perspective of developing *Shlemut*, because a person's ethical aspiration is to fulfill God's will fully, theoretical beliefs have normative weight. For example, the Talmudic Sages state, that if a person's study does not lead to action, the person is like one who has no God,[70] since his or her study remains sterile and without effect on his or her life. Moreover, because reasoning in general is a process of recognizing and responding to reasons, whether they be end-reasons or means-reasons, even one who does not have the aspiration to fulfill God's will still aspires for some end, and the recognition of that end is only demonstrated when one appropriately responds to it in action.

Another similarity between practical and theoretical reason is that with respect to both types of reasoning, a person deliberates only when a situation arises which necessitates it. Normative and explanatory facts are usually taken as givens until they seem to contradict other facts that a person recognizes. When there is no contradiction, people act on normative reasons based on previous experience and habits, and they stick to their beliefs without constantly needing to justify them. When a person recognizes a contradiction, he or she will be motivated to reconcile contradictory facts or prioritize normative reasons so that his or her worldview is coherent and his or her behavior is in line with the values and beliefs that he or she holds. Charles S. Peirce describes the process as follows:

> Doubt is an uneasy and dissatisfied state from which we struggle to free ourselves and pass into a state of belief; while the latter [i.e. the state of belief] is a calm and satisfactory state which we do not wish to avoid, or to change to a belief in anything else. On the contrary, we cling tenaciously, not merely to believing, but to believing just what we do believe.[71]

As long as one's beliefs accord to his or her general habits—whether they be habits of perception, desire, or action—they will be maintained without reflection. If, however, there arises a disharmony between a person's beliefs and his or her habits, then doubt will arise, which incurs the need for inquiry until it is resolved. Just as with James' "sentiment of rationality," for Peirce, theoretical speculation does not begin *in abstracto*, but it only puts into greater focus the picture the person already sees.

This type of deliberation does not occur only in philosophical speculation, it also occurs in scientific experimentation as well. For example, Imre Lakatos writes, "Scientists have thick skins. They normally do not abandon a theory merely because facts contradict it. They normally either invent some rescue hypothesis to explain what they then call a mere anomaly or, if they cannot explain the anomaly, they ignore it, and direct their attention to other problems."[72] Similarly, Paul Thagard argues that even though scientists are oftentimes not tenacious dogmatically, they deem it ineffectual to reject a theory that works, albeit insufficiently, unless a better alternative has already been developed to replace it.[73] Therefore, scientists will attempt to salvage a theory by accommodating, or ignoring, anomalies until they have a better framework to account for them comprehensively. Hilary Putnam puts it even more strongly,

> Apparently any fantasy—the fantasy of doing science using only deductive logic (Popper), the fantasy of vindicating induction deductively (Reichenbach), the fantasy of reducing science to a simple sampling algorithm (Carnap), the fantasy of selecting theories given mysteriously available set of 'true observation conditionals,' or, alternatively, 'settling for psychology' (both Quine)—is regarded as preferable to rethinking the whole dogma (the last dogma of empiricism?) that facts are objective and values are subjective and "never the twain shall meet.[74]

The Economist has repeated this as a criticism of scientific experimentation, writing how the complacency of modern scientists has led them to doing too much trusting and not enough verifying, which is a detriment to the whole of science and of humanity.[75]

What is interesting about these examples is that they show that theoretical knowledge is grounded in a system of rules that create an institutional framework through which facts are understood and deemed true. That means that both practical and theoretical reasoning include institutional facts, which include within them normative values. Moreover, explanatory facts and normative facts are not held apart during deliberation; the veracity of an explanatory fact may be gauged by how it would affect a normative fact in the same way that a normative reason is dependent on the explanatory facts being true.

Practical and Legal Reasoning

Despite the differences in their respective descriptions of practical reason, both Aristotle and Kant distinguish between practical reason and legal reasoning. Practical reason, according to both Aristotle and Kant, is a wholly internal process whereby a person deliberates on how to achieve a given end properly. When a person deliberates about his or her action in light of an external (legal) system, the person may be demonstrating political reasoning according to Aristotle or succumbing to the heteronomy of choice according to Kant. He or she would not be exercising practical reason and, therefore, would not be acting morally or with virtue. Because the Aristotelian conception of practical reason disallows the law from playing a role in moral deliberation, Maimonides does not have an explicit place for practical reasoning in his moral philosophy, yet he does utilize legal reasoning, that is, reasoning about the law or about how to act given the law. Similarly, a Kantian conception of practical reason would leave no role for the law with respect to moral reasoning or to establishing moral obligations in a Jewish deontology, though perhaps it could still serve a pedagogical function.

When, however, practical reason is understood as a process of recognizing and responding properly to reasons, then the law no longer need be excluded from moral deliberation or practical reason. When reasoning consists of recognizing external and internal facts, legal reasoning becomes a subset of practical reasoning, whereby legal facts as well as other social and institutional facts are recognized. Moreover, because the law has such a strong influence in shaping the social world of its adherents, from the perspective of a person living in society and making decisions as to how to conduct his or her daily behavior, legal reasoning and practical reason are the same.

While I have conflated legal reasoning and practical reason to be the same process of recognizing and responding to reasons, one should nevertheless distinguish between two forms of normative reasoning (which refer to both legal and practical reasoning), namely that of reasoning for the purpose of establishing objective normative reasons and reasoning for the purpose of acting. For example, when a jurist makes (or discerns) the law in theory or for others, he establishes reasons for acting that are contingent on whether or not the situation arises for such reasons to become normative and on whether they are recognized and accepted by the person in that situation. Similarly, when a person deliberates on a hypothetical case or studies Jewish law for the sole purpose of learning about the law, he or she may be learning normative facts regarding how to act, yet they do not become reasons for acting until they are relevant to a particular situation in which the person must respond appropriately. This type of legal or practical reasoning is similar to theoretical reasoning, since the proper response reached through deliberation is either the acceptance of a normative fact or the transformation of that acceptance into a deeper knowledge of that fact. The difference, however, between this type of reasoning and theoretical reason is that the primary purpose is to understand and appreciate normative facts about the world rather than explanatory facts, even though explanatory facts are included in normative reasons and often have normative implications as well.

On the other hand, when a person receives a judgment from a jurist, the legal decision does not become a normative reason *for the person* until he or she recognizes it as such, though it make be *an objective normative fact* if society accepts the decision as law. In contrast to Kant, who would call such acceptance of another's legal decision subjection to the heteronomy of choice, in accepting the jurist's decision, the person voluntarily makes the external normative reason an internal one. Similarly, when a person reasons about how to act from his or her own knowledge of the law, the person deliberates from previously accepted reasons so as to apply normative facts to those explanatory facts which describe the situation.

Legal reasons are different from other normative reasons, however, in an important respect. It is not only that legal reasons have a greater normative force than competing normative reasons, but also the source and quality of their normativity are different as well. The normativity of other normative reasons stems from the values (and other motivating components) which the reasons entail or include as part of the reason. Legal reasons also include values (and motivating components), yet its normativity is independent of those values (and motivating components).[76] In other words, a rule is a reason to act regardless of one's decision for acting or the value of acting in such a way. Moreover, the normativity of legal reasons is such that it not only serves to promote a particular action, but it also serves as a reason not to perform other actions that are contrary to the rule. In other words, when a person is faced with two competing reasons, each of which provides a reason to respond to a situation in a different way, if one of those reasons is a legal reason, then the evaluation of which competing reason should take priority is not based on the relative force of their respective normative facts. The legal reason provides grounds for dismissing the other, competing reasons. This gap between the normativity of legal reasons and the evaluative normative facts that they contain may lead to difficulties in a person's deliberation regarding the appropriate response to a situation.

Weakness of Will and Moral Dilemmas

Another consequence of conceiving reasoning as recognizing and responding to reasons is that "weakness of will" and moral dilemmas become problems of rationality and not necessarily problems of character or execution exclusively. When a person suffers from "weakness of will," it is not the case that the person has decided on the right course of action and then fails to act accordingly; rather, he or she is not fully committed to the moral course of action upon which he or she has seemed to decide through rational deliberation. As is the case when a person has a moral dilemma, the person recognizes either that there is more than one way to organize the various reasons that he or she perceives to exist or that there is more than one way to respond to the reasons that he or she perceives to exist. When there are numerous ways to recognize reasons or to evaluate their relative priorities in order to respond, one of the four consequences may occur:

1. Alternative responses are equally valued on an objective scale—the person is faced with a moral dilemma.
2. A hierarchy between responses cannot be readily determined—the person is faced with a moral dilemma.
3. Society provides an objective standard by which to prioritize different responses, yet the person nevertheless prioritizes them differently based on his or her own subjective measure—the person suffers from a "weakness of will." In truth, however, it would be more accurate to say, to borrow an expression from the Talmudic Sages, that he or she suffers from a failure to make one's own will align with God's will,[77] since the person responds to the situation based on reasons and does not act contrary to "Reason."
4. When alternative responses are equally valued on an objective scale, yet there is a hierarchy in a person's subjective scale (based on other normative reasons that the person has), and the person chooses to respond in a way that is subjectively inferior to other options available—the person reasons badly (or less than excellently), since the choice made is not the optimal one, yet he or she does not suffer from a "weakness of will," since the choice made was not contrary to any societally preferred response.

In assuming a difference between an objective standard and a subjective standard by which to prioritize reasons, I am relying on John Searle's distinction between ontological objectivity and subjectivity, and epistemological objectivity and subjectivity. Examples of that which has ontological objectivity would be physical objects; that which is ontologically subjective would be a personal experience such as pain. That which is epistemically objective is a fact about the world whose truth is ascertainable without reference to the attitudes or feelings of those who observe or communicate the fact. That which is epistemically subjective is a statement whose truth cannot be determined without reference to the attitudes of those who communicate them.

	Ontologically objective	*Ontologically subjective*
Epistemologically objective	Physical objects	Facts
Epistemologically subjective	Physical sensations	Opinions

Making this distinction has two major ramifications. First, it distinguishes between what occurs in the world and a person's observation or understanding of what occurs in the world. In other words, there is a distinction between causes and reasons. Second, ontological subjectivity does not necessarily imply epistemic subjectivity. Those facts about the world that a society has created, namely institutional facts, are ontologically subjective, since their recognition as a fact is dependent on a person's consciousness, yet they are epistemologically objective, since their collective recognition by society allows for their ascertainment as true to be independent of the attitude of anyone in society in particular. For example, the fact that two people are married is an ontologically subjective fact, since it is dependent on the recognition of a societally instituted relationship. That we can know that two people are married, however, is epistemologically objective, since its truth does not depend on the opinions of anyone in particular.[78] Similarly, external and desire-independent normative facts are those facts which are epistemologically objective, and internal normative facts are those normative facts that are epistemologically subjective.

As it pertains to "weakness of will" or to moral dilemmas, an objective standard for evaluating normative reasons is that hierarchy of priorities that society has instituted such that its "truth," in terms of it being the correct measure of priority, is not based on how any one individual feels about it. A subjective standard for evaluating reasons, on the other hand, would be a prioritization of reasons that is based on personal opinion and not on societal acceptance.

Because practical reasoning includes responding to reasons, how a person ultimately reasons can only be determined by the response itself. Therefore, "weakness of will" cannot be deemed a failure to act according to what a person has decided as the proper response. For example, a person may have a certain conviction to act in a particular way, yet if he or she ultimately acts in a different manner, then he or she has ultimately reasoned to act contrary to what he or she concluded in a prior (unfinished) deliberation.[79] It is not the case that the person acted without intention or was induced to act contrary to his or her own reasoning.[80]

Also, "weakness of will" can occur either through bad (or less than excellent) reasoning, by which I mean incorrectly evaluating reasons, or through ignorance, by which I mean failing to apprehend that certain facts should be deemed as reasons. When used in the latter sense, there is recognition that a person does not possess a fully mature capability to engage in practical reason. Part of the process of moral development is the strengthening of a person's capability to engage in practical reasoning more effectively. At a certain point, however, a person's inability to recognize reasons is no longer a consequence of "weakness of will," but rather is a consequence of irrationality. Again, it is not the case that all people who act with no regard for objective normative reasons should be considered irrational. For example, a sociopath can recognize normative reasons, and even uses them as non-standard reasons in his or her deliberation as to how to respond to a situation. Rationality should not be considered in terms of understanding a person's rationale for acting but in whether the person can recognize normative reasons for acting or not.

In drawing a parallel between "weakness of will" and ineffectual practical reason, I am not relying on Kant's view of the will in that when reason fully determines the will, the will in essence is nothing but practical reason.[81] Kant can conflate the will with practical reason because he already possesses a concept of causality in his concept of a will. Therefore, the concept of a pure will is a concept of causality with freedom, meaning that the will is automatically motivated by the rules imposed by pure practical reason. In my account of reasoning, on the other hand, the will is separate from practical reasoning, yet a person's will relates to his or her ability to reason by providing the focus and the means to recognize reasons, to deliberate on them, and ultimately to respond to them. To use an analogy, in my conception, the will is like propeller and rudder of a boat, which gives power and direction to the boat's course, and the boat is the ability to engage in practical reason. The water is the realm of facts and reasons to be "navigated." The power of the propeller may run out and need to be recharged, and the rudder may lose alignment and may need to be realigned, but when they are set properly, and the boat itself is properly configured so as to move swiftly in the water, then the boat will move as it is supposed to move. Notice that both the boat, that is, the capabilities necessary to reason properly, and the propeller and rudder, that is, the will, still need a person, that is, a soul, to manipulate them. Similarly, in my conception of *Shlemut*, the will is a meta-virtue (capability) which controls the intellectual and moral virtues (capabilities), but it is not equated with the person. This separation between a person's will and practical reason reinforces the idea stated above that the common meaning of the term "weakness of will" is inappropriate in my conception of reasoning, since the person does not suffer from having a will that is too weak to carry out reason's demands but rather he or she suffers from having a will that allows for choosing reasons that are contrary to God's will.

Avera Lishma *(Sinning with Proper Intention)*

The difference between objective and subjective measures to prioritize reasons and the difference between the normativity of legal reasons vis-à-vis other normative reasons allow for one to understand the Talmudic principle, *avera lishma*. *Avera lishma* results from a moral dilemma, whereby the law has established a hierarchy of proper responses to a situation, yet the values embedded within the normative facts which the law encompasses give rise to a normative reason to act in a manner that is contrary to the law. On the one hand, the person has a reason to follow the law, yet, on the other hand, the person seems to have an equally valid reason to follow his or her perception of the values the law (usually) embodies and thus transgress the law. This is not a situation where the person is unaware of the societally accepted, objective reasons for acting, nor is it a situation where the person puts his or her own subjective reasons above objective ones. Rather, it is a case where the person can sincerely claim to be upholding the objective standard, yet the objective standard in this particular case is ambiguous or produces incommensurate reasons.

The Talmud gives two cases of *avera lishma*.[82] The first is that of Tamar, who pretended to be a harlot in order to deceive her father-in-law, Judah, into sleeping with her.[83] In this example, however, Judah ultimately recognizes that Tamar was more righteous that he, since he incorrectly withheld his son Shelah from her as a husband. Nahmanides explains:

> Here too the meaning is, "She is more righteous than I, for she acted righteously and I am the one who sinned against her by not giving her my son Shelah." The purport of the statement is that Shelah was the brother-in-law, [hence he was the first designated to marry her], and if he did not wish to take her as his wife, his father is next in line to act as the redeemer, as I have explained above when I discussed the law of marrying a childless brother's widow [*yibbum*].[84]

The Talmud uses the case of Tamar as an example of *avera lishma* to show that the transgression itself, namely committing adultery due to the fact that she was "engaged" to Shelah, was due to Judah's transgression. He promised his son to her yet kept him from marrying her. Her situation was not in her control. Despite institutional restraints, when she deceived Judah, her motives were *lishma* and not based on personal interest. Nevertheless, she still committed a transgression.

The second example used in the Talmud is that of Yael, the wife of Hever the Kenite, who slept with the general, Sisera.[85] In this example of *avera lishma*, the transgression is not predicated on the erroneous actions of someone else which directly affects Yael's situation. Rather, Yael voluntarily chose to put herself in the situation. Her intention was *lishma*, however, since her relations with Sisera were meant to weaken him so as to defeat him.[86] Despite her transgression, Yael is praised for her actions,[87] because she sought of her own accord to help the nation of Israel in its war against Yavin, the king of Hazor. Even though her people were at peace with Yavin,[88] she nevertheless acted to help Israel through the means by which she was able rather than sit and refrain from assisting.

The Talmud ultimately equates performing an *avera lishma* with performing a commandment *shelo lishma* (with an incorrect intention). Equating an *avera lishma* to performing a command *shelo lishma*, however, does not condone transgressing God's commandments. On the contrary, it emphasizes the ineffectiveness of acting according to the law but not for the sake of it. This can be seen by virtue of the fact that the entire Talmudic discussion of *avera lishma* is grounded in explaining the verse, "For the ways of Hashem are right, and the righteous do walk in them; but willful sinners (*poshe'im*) do stumble therein."[89] Both the righteous and willful sinners may perform the same action, whether it is in accordance with the law or not. Yet, for the righteous, the motivation for acting allows them ultimately to live as God directs them. The motivation of willful sinners, on the other hand, disallows the achievement of *Shlemut*, even when they act according to the law. Of course, righteousness and sinfulness are not measured by a single act, or even by the summation of actions alone. Rather, righteousness and sinfulness are determined by how a person's actions shape his or her general life over time. Therefore, a single act, whether one that is proper but with the wrong intention or one that is improper but with the right intention, are equivalent when taken alone but very different when considered in light of the totality of the person's way of life.

Biblical Example

To support the idea that rationality as attending to reasons can be part of a Jewish ethics, I will show how this process of reasoning can be used to explain the story of Adam and Eve and the exchange with the serpent over eating from the Tree of Knowledge of Good and Evil. In this explanation of the exchange, many of the normative reasons consist of external facts about the world, which Eve or Adam either correctly recognize or not and to which either they correctly respond or they do not.

Initially the serpent questions Eve as to why she cannot eat from the Tree of Knowledge of Good and Evil. The serpent uses the following reason:

1. God said, "You shall not eat of every tree in the garden," which implies that she cannot eat from the Tree of Knowledge of Good and Evil as well.

   *Implied reasons are subsumed within the more general reason, since inferences, as deductive logical conclusions, are just further descriptions of relations between other facts.

Eve answers that she cannot eat from the Tree for the following *incorrect* reason:

1 .God said, "You shall not eat from it, and you shall not touch it, lest you will die."

   *The reason is incorrect because it includes normative facts that are not true.

Because God did not tell Eve this statement directly, she must have heard it from Adam and only afterwards could have recognized this statement as a reason to be considered. Either Adam or Eve added to God's statement, "and you shall not touch it."[90] The additional reason not to touch the Tree comes from the belief that it will further safeguard the original command, yet the reason itself is external. Its externality is obvious if Adam created the reason. If Eve created the reason, it would still be partly external since she must recognize its normative force vis-à-vis the situation. Her internal desire not to touch the tree was not a reason independent of all outside factors. As we will see, her subsequent actions demonstrate that the reason not to touch the tree was distinct from her desire not to touch the tree, since it was weighed in the same way as the other normative facts during her deliberations.

Eve *incorrectly* recognizes the reason to consist of the fact that

1. If she eats from the Tree or if she touches it, then she will die.

Her understanding of the fact that God said the statement is that God was making her aware of the natural consequences of eating from the Tree, that is, that it was poisonous for example. She does not recognize the *correct* reason as consisting of two facts, namely:

1. God said, "You shall not eat from it."
2. If she eats from it, then she will die.

The first normative fact is a proscription, while the second fact explains the consequences of transgressing the proscription.

When Eve saw that the fact—if she touches the Tree, then she will die—was false,[91] then she *incorrectly* thought that the entire reason for not eating from the Tree was false. Therefore, she now had the following reason to eat from the tree:

1. The fact, "if she eats from the Tree or if she touches it, then she will die," is false, which implies that the fruit was good to eat.
2. The serpent told her that if she eats it, her eyes will be open.
3. The serpent told her that if she eats it, she will be like God, knowing good and bad.
4. She desires to have her eyes opened and to know good and bad.

* With respect to the first reason above, "good to eat" does not mean that she thought it was good in the moral sense, only that the fruit was good to eat in that eating it would not kill her. To proffer otherwise would be contradictory to the story, since Eve was only able to know good and evil after eating from the Tree, not beforehand. A different, but not unrelated, way to explain it is that the Bible states earlier that God caused to sprout from the ground "every tree that was pleasing to the sight and good for food" and also "the Tree of Life" as well as "the Tree of Knowledge of Good and Evil."[92] When Eve saw that the Tree would not harm her, she uses similar expressions, namely that she saw that the Tree was "good for eating" and a "delight to the eyes" (as well as "desirable for comprehension").[93] Because the Tree did not harm her, Eve thought that it was similar to all the other trees of the garden, of which she was permitted to eat, only that this Tree was also "pleasing according to her reasoning" to eat it as well.

She did not recognize the normative fact:

1. God said, "You shall not eat from the Tree."

While the latter fact is still a normative reason for her regardless of her recognition of it, because she did not recognize it, she did not consider it in her deliberating. Eve recognized the second and third statements when the serpent told them to her. Her desire became part of her reason to eat when she recognized its normative force and used it in her deliberations as to whether she should eat from the Tree. Only after she ate from the Tree did she recognize that God's statement, 'You shall not eat from the Tree,' was a normative fact to be recognized as a reason. In other words, only after she ate from the Tree did she know that God's commands are reasons to act by virtue of His command. As such, in eating from the Tree, she learned how to think and act morally. She gained knowledge of good and evil.

What is most interesting about the serpent's statement is that it describes moral knowledge in the same way as I have been describing practical reason. "Opening one's eyes" refers to an ability to perceive facts as reasons. When the serpent says that she will be like God, the term used is *Elohim*, which is the name that is used to denote judging and evaluating circumstances. Therefore, to "know good and bad," one must have one's eyes open to reasons as well as have the ability to judge them so as to know whether one's actions are proper or not.[94]

After Adam and Eve ate from the Tree, the Bible states that they recognized that they were naked. From this recognition, they reasoned that they should clothe themselves. Before they ate from the Tree, the Bible states that Adam and his wife were naked, but they were not ashamed. The difference between these two passages is not the existence of the normative reason to clothe oneself when one is naked. Rather, the difference between the passages is that before they ate, they did not recognize this reason, and after they ate, when their eyes were open to moral facts, they did.

After Adam and Eve ate the fruit, they hid from God. When asked why they hid, Adam gives the following explanatory reasons:

1. He heard God's voice in the garden.
2. He was afraid.

The reason he was afraid was because:

3. He was naked.

Being naked is not an obvious reason to be afraid; however, Adam's fear is based on the same reason as the shame Adam and Eve felt while alone. The reason for being ashamed was that it was a response to the recognition that being naked is inappropriate when among equals and thus serves as a motivation to be clothed. The reason for being afraid is that it is a response to the recognition that being naked is inappropriate when in the presence of a superior.

While this conception of reasoning is not Maimonidean, it is consistent with Maimonides' understanding of what had occurred in the Garden of Eden. According to Maimonides, Adam was originally created with intellectual perfection, so that he could acquire truths such as "the heavens are spherical," as well as distinguish between the truth and the falsity. Due to his innocence, however, he did not possess the faculty to assess moral truths, since they are only apparent truths based on social convention. In other words, Adam was able to recognize and respond to explanatory reasons, but not normative reasons. After Adam ate from the Tree of Knowledge of Good and Evil, he was punished and lost part of his intellectual faculty. Yet he gained the moral ability to recognize and respond to normative reasons.[95] According to Maimonides, the idea of one's eyes opening connotes receiving new sources of knowledge.[96] As such, he provides a very similar explanation for what made them afraid. He writes, "*And the eyes of both of them were opened, and they knew that they were naked.* It is not said, *And the eyes of both of them were opened, and they saw.* For what was seen previously was exactly that which was seen afterwards. There was no membrane over the eye that was now removed, but rather he entered upon another state in which he considered as bad things that he had not seen in that light before."[97]

Reasoning from the Commandments and Not Reasons for the Commandments

Accepting the act of reasoning as recognizing and responding to reasons rather than providing reasons for one's desired actions has a further consequence in terms of examining the reasons of the commandments. Maimonides[98] dedicated a great part of his writings to explaining the reasons for the commandments.[99] Don Seeman describes his motivation for discovering reasons for the commandments as follows: "Maimonides' primary interest in the *Guide* is neither apologetic nor inspirational; like Alfarabi and other political philosophers, he seeks rather to demonstrate the prudence and wisdom—even the cunning—of the Divine legislator."[100] Because the commandments are acts of the Divine will, in that God decreed the commandments, and because they are a product of Divine wisdom (and not arbitrary edicts), there must be an identifiable reason that can explain them.

Yet, the practice of endeavoring to provide reasons for the commandments, and the belief that commandments must have reasons, even if one does not (yet) know them,[101] face two major points of opposition. First, there are those who argue that the normative value of the commandments is in the fact that God commanded them, and any search for a different source of normativity would detract from the power of God's decree.[102] This is another way to argue for a strict Divine command morality, yet as we have seen above, by developing a synthesis between Divine command morality and virtue ethics, Maimonides avoids the trap that Socrates set for Euthyphro. Maimonides answers this challenge by conflating God's reason for the command with the rationality of the command, so that by fulfilling a command out of a rational acceptance of it one also acts because God decreed it.

Maimonides' ability to conflate reason with God's will is based on his understanding of the objectivity of truth and its relationship with revelation. For Maimonides, knowledge achieved through philosophical reasoning and through religious reflection are the same, since there is only one objective and absolute standard of truth. As discussed above, the justifiability of Maimonides' explanation, however, is no longer tenable in contemporary philosophy and theology, since it is based on Aristotelianphysics and metaphysics.

Second, Maimonides holds as a premise the idea that the command-ments should not be arbitrary,[103] yet some commandments, or rather particular aspects of commandments, do not have a reason according to Maimonides. For example, with regard to why certain sacrifices are of one animal and some are of another, he writes, "Those who imagine that a cause may be found for suchlike things are as far from truth as those who imagine that the generalities of a commandment are not designed with a view to some utility."[104] Maimonides is not bothered by the arbitrariness of such details since the lack of a reason for these particularities is due to there being no differentiating principle through which to make a reasoned decision.[105] In such cases, any choice would be arbitrary.[106] Arbitrariness, even with respect to these details, however, has been rejected by other rabbinic figures in a way that is relevant to my analysis of practical reason vis-à-vis the law. Nahmanides argues that our lack of knowledge of the rea-sons for certain Torah laws is due only to our own inability to comprehend them and not because God arbitrarily imposed commandments.[107] Rabbi Samson Raphael Hirsch condemns Maimonides' assumption, saying that "he disregards their details—those very details which, together, give the complete picture of the *mitzvah* and which, predominantly are the subject of the *Torah she-B'al Peh*, the Oral Law."[108] He proposes that investigation into the reasons for the commandments, in all their details, should rest on the methodological premise that one must begin one's research by accept-ing the Torah's commandments in their entirety as given facts.

Together Nahmanides' and Rabbi Hirsch's challenges provide for a strong contemporary critique. If the law is the only source providing Divinely commanded beliefs and norms to its adherents, and one cannot inquire into God's reasons, since "My thoughts are not your thoughts, nor are your ways My ways, says the Lord,"[109] then there is no inde-pendent measure to judge the veracity of those beliefs or the validity of the reasons for the commandments. Any reason that one can give to explain a commandment will be influenced by the person's engagement with it in a context that allows it to make sense within his or her world-view. Therefore, rather than searching for reasons for the command-ments, it would be more efficacious to consider the beliefs and norms that the Torah provides through the commandments to be external facts that a person incorporates into his or her own rational thinking. Under this conception, one would philosophize from the law and not about the law. Commandments would have normative and symbolic force, through which meaning would derive. Reasons for acting and thinking about the world would stem from investigating the commandments; it would no longer be the case that acting and thinking about the world would provide reasons for the commandments.

By claiming that one cannot find reasons for the commandments but rather must reason from the commandments, I am not advocating for a dogmatic religion in the sense of requiring a creedal litmus test. Knowledge and belief may be consequences of engagement with the Torah and its commandments, yet ignorance or lack of engagement is not a cause for exclusion from the Jewish people. In this, I may also be breaking from Maimonides, if Menachem Keller's understanding of his view, that adherence to a strictly defined set of dogmas is what makes a person part of the Jewish community, is correct.[110] In my conception of Jewish virtue ethics, one's responsibilities to the members of one's community are not contingent upon intellectual conformity, as long as diversity and pluralism do not threaten the community itself. I also disagree with Kellner that a contemporary Maimonidean must conceive of Judaism as a religion based upon systematic theology, in which doctrinal orthodoxy is primary.[111] As I have shown a number of times in this book and will continue to do so, intellectual apprehension and proper action are intimately related, both in terms of how one understands theological concepts and in how one puts those ideas into practice by fulfilling the commandments.

NOTES

1. Job 15:3.
2. Aristotle writes, "Again, the function of man is achieved only in accordance with practical wisdom as well as with moral excellence; for excellence makes the aim right, and practical wisdom the things leading to it" (NE 1144a7–9).
3. NE 1144a14–20.
4. *Politics* 1277b28.
5. NE 1144b30–3.
6. Nancy Sherman, *The Fabric of Character* (Oxford: Clarendon Press, 1989) 14.
7. Ibid. 27.
8. *Shemonah Perakim*, Chapter one. Translation from Abraham Cohen, *The Teaching of Maimonides* (London: Routledge, 1927) 245.

9. Raymond Weiss, *Maimonides' Ethics: The Encounter of Philosophic and Religious Morality* (Chicago: University of Chicago Press, 1991), 31–2n20.

10. Joseph Stern, "Maimonides' Epistemology," *The Cambridge Companion to Maimonides*, ed. Kenneth Seeskin (Cambridge: Cambridge University Press, 2005) 108.

11. David Shatz, "Maimonides' Moral Theory," *The Cambridge Companion to Maimonides*, ed. Kenneth Seeskin (Cambridge: Cambridge University Press, 2005) 169.

12. Howard Kreisel, *Maimonides' Political Thought: Studies in Ethics, Law, and the Human Ideal*, 1999 63.

13. Charles Raffel, "Maimonides' Theory of Providence," *AJS Review*, Vol. 12, No. 1 (Spring, 1987), 62.

14. Ibid. 100.

15. *Shemonah Perakim*, Chapter 2.

16. *Shemonah Perakim*, Chapter 4.

17. *Maimonides' Treatise on Logic: Critically Ed. On the Basis of Mss. And Early Ed. And Transl. Into English*, 63.

   Miriam Galston explains that Maimonides claimed that political science became superfluous after the revelation of the law while theoretical science did not. She writes, "Far from replacing scientific philosophy, the law in fact reaches its completion through scientific philosophy, which turns the axiomatic and summary opinions into precise and reasoned conclusions." See Miriam Galston, "The Purpose of the Law According to Maimonides," *The Jewish Quarterly Review*, New Series, Vol. 69, No. 1 (July, 1978), 46). Also, see what Maimonides writes regarding, "The Law of the Lord is perfect" in *Shemonah Perakim*, Chapter four and MN II:39.

18. See NE 1141b23.

19. Zekharia 8:19.

20. There has been great debate over whether Maimonides endorses or rejects Aristotle's concept of equity in what he writes in *Moreh Nevukhim* III:34, yet Hanina Ben-Menahem has shown that the discussion in MN III:34 does not deal with the question of equity, since the chapter is about the theoretical and legislative purpose of the law and not the practical and judicial aspect of its application. According to Ben-Menahem, the point of the chapter is to justify the generality of the law, in contrast to Aristotle, who sees law's

generality as a detriment. The difference of perspective between Aristotle and Maimonides is based on the two-tiered system of Divine law. Nevertheless, in his other writings, most substantially in his responsa, Maimonides implements equity to justly apply the law to particular situations. For more information, see Hanina Ben-Menahem, "Reconsidering the 'Guide for the Perplexed' III:34," *Journal of Law and Religion*, Vol. 17, No. 1/2 (2002) 19–48.

21. David Novak has argued that Maimonides assigns vast importance to practical reason through his view of rabbinic legislation vis-à-vis Torah law. After discussing rabbinic law in general, he writes, "One can thus conclude that for Maimonides, practical reason governs the lives of the Jewish people except where there is a specific law of the Torah, and even that can be temporarily repealed if that same practical reason determines that there is here and now what might be called a 'teleological emergency,' which calls for radical action on the part of the authorities without delay" (David Novak, *Natural Law in Judaism* [New York: Cambridge University Press, 1998] 109).

Novak uses the following passage to show that for Maimonides the study of Jewish law is an ethical exercise which cultivates practical reason: "A person is obligated to divide his time for learning into three parts: one third for Scripture; one third for the Oral Torah; and one third for understanding and discerning the end of the matter from its beginning. He should derive one thing from another, compare one thing to another, and understand by means of the methods through which the Torah is interpreted until he knows the root of these methods; how he can derive what is forbidden and what is permitted from these things he has learned from revealed tradition" (Talmud Torah 1:1; quoted by Novak in *Natural Law in Judaism*, 100). The three forms of ratiocination— (1) discerning the end of the matter from its beginning, (2) deriving one thing from another, and (3) comparing one thing to another—correspond to what Novak calls making a teleological inference, deduction, and analogy, respectively. By attributing the first method to accepting the premise that law serves a *telos*, the latter two methods aid in developing a person's practical reason in a way that allows him or her to achieve it. Novak is either using a different definition for practical reason than the Aristotelian defini-

PRACTICAL REASON 193

tion which Maimonides would have used, or he is conflating
Aristotle's, and Maimonides', notions of political wisdom and
practical wisdom.

22. Kreisel, *Maimonides' Political Thought: Studies in Ethics, Law, and the Human Ideal* (1999) 63–92.
23. See Howard Kreisel, "The Practical Intellect in the Philosophy of Maimonides," *HUCA 59* (1988) 189–215.
24. "Maimonides' Moral Theory," 187.
25. Ibid. 186.
26. MN II:4, 257.
27. For a discussion regarding the latter debate, see Joseph Stern, "Maimonides' Epistemology."
28. For an in-depth analysis of the Active Intellect in the philosophies of Alfarabi and Avicenna, see Herbert A Davidson, *Alfarabi, Avicenna, and Averroes on Intellect: Their Cosmologies, Theories of the Active Intellect, and Theories of Human Intellect* (New York: Oxford University Press, 1992).
29. Aphorism 34, Fārābī and Charles E. Butterworth, *Alfarabi, the Political Writings: Selected Aphorisms and Other Texts* (Ithaca: Cornell University Press, 2001) 29.
30. Aphorism 38, ibid. 31. Also, see his *Epistle on the Intellect (Risala fi'l-'aql)*, where he writes that the Active Intellect does not provide the principles of practical reason.
31. Aphorism 53, ibid. 35.
32. Alfarabi's, Avicenna's, and Maimonides's epistemology is intimately related to their prophetologies.
33. In *The Perfect State*, Alfarabi describes two types of prophecy. The first type of prophecy occurs solely through a person's faculty of imagination. In order to understand this phenomenon, one must know that, according to Alfarabi, acquisition of knowledge occurs when the Active Intellect imprints intelligibles upon a human's rational faculty, or material intellect, which correspond to the sensibles that are apprehended by his faculty of sense and stored by his faculty of imagination. As such, the faculty of imagination serves the subordinate role of preserving and manipulating ideas so that they may be subject to rational deliberation. The faculty of imagination, however, also has the additional ability to imitate the imprints it preserves which originate in the rational faculty. Given the fact that intelligibles emanate from the Active Intellect, the

imaginative faculty's ability to imitate them implies that the Active Intellect may also act upon this faculty as well. The most common example occurs when a person dreams. When dreaming occurs in waking life, Alfarabi considers it to be a force of divination. The prophet, by contrast, is the one whose faculty of imagination can receive Divine content not indirectly through dreams but directly from the Active Intellect. He writes:

> It is not impossible, then, that when a man's faculty of representation [imagination] reaches its utmost perfection he will receive in his waking life from the Active Intellect present and future particulars of their imitations in the form of sensibles, and receive the imitations of the transcendent intelligibles and the other glorious existents and see them. This man will obtain through the particulars which he receives 'prophecy' (supernatural awareness) of present and future events, and through the intelligibles which he receives prophecy of things divine (225). [Though the translation of Alfarabi's work used for this analysis employs the term 'faculty of representation,' it is analogous to the term, 'faculty of imagination,' that used in the discussion of the other philosophers.]

Because this form of prophecy has no relation to the perfection of a person's rational faculty, to experience this form of prophecy one need not attain ultimate perfection. Moreover, the ability to prophesy may be a temporary circumstance, dependent upon a person's ability to maintain a proper temperament and preserve his faculty of imagination.

Alfarabi's second description of prophecy, which he designates as Divine Revelation, pertains to the one who has attained perfection of both his rational and imaginative faculties, and "has become actually intellect and actually being thought (intelligized)" (241). In short, he has attained human perfection. Prophecy, in this case, occurs when God's emanation to the Active Intellect is transmitted first to the prophet's perfected rational faculty and then to his perfected imaginative faculty. By virtue of its reception by his rational faculty, he is a philosopher; reception by his imaginative faculty makes him a visionary prophet. His ability to lead people toward the attainment of felicity based upon his knowledge and ability to communicate in a manner that people are persuaded to obey his rule makes him worthy to be the sovereign. In his *Book of Religion*, Alfarabi explains how the sovereign is able to establish a virtuous community based on the content of Divine Revelation. The ruler may either receive a determined set of prescribed acts and opinions, or he may determine what is proper by means of the faculty he acquires through revelation, or both.

In his *Political Regime*, Alfarabi gives a different account of prophecy as Divine Revelation by defining it as the emanation that proceeds from the Active Intellect to the passive intellect through the mediation of the acquired intellect. No mention is made of the imaginative faculty. Alfarabi also asserts that the one who receives Divine Revelation should be made the ruler of the community and has the ability to institute new laws or to change previous laws if he believes it is necessary. With respect to the two accounts mentioned in the *Book of Religion* regarding the establishment of a virtuous community based on Divine Revelation, Alfarabi's statement in the *Political Regime* seems to imply that the application of the content of the ruler's revelation to the practical purpose of improving the city's welfare, and not direct revelation of prescribed acts, is what he holds to be the primary way in which religion is established. If that is the case, then emanation to the imaginative faculty would be relevant only in the case of perfecting the ruler's ability to translate philosophical knowledge into practical social norms. Yet if his imaginative faculty is already perfected, which is the case, the additional benefit of emanation, since it does not provide content not already received, cannot be significant.

See Abu Nasr Farabi and Richard Walzer, *Al-Farabi on the Perfect State: A Revised Text with Introduction, Translation, and Commentary* (Oxford: Clarendon Press, 1985); Abu Nasr Farabi and Charles E. Butterworth, *Alfarabi, the Political Writings: Selected Aphorisms and Other Texts* (Ithaca: Cornell University Press, 2001); and Ralph Lerner and Muhsin Mahdi, *Medieval Political Philosophy: A Sourcebook* (New York: Free Press of Glencoe, 1963).

34. Avicenna also recognizes two levels of prophecy. Like Alfarabi, Avicenna describes the lower level of prophecy as the reception of intelligibles from the Active Intellect by the imaginative faculty. The knowledge communicated through emanation of the Active Intellect to the imaginative faculty is in a symbolic, analogous form, and a perfected rational faculty is not required for its apprehension as such. To understand the universal principles behind the figurative content, however, requires exegesis, and the accuracy of

interpretation depends upon the aptitude of a person's rational faculty. Avicenna's ultimate level of prophecy is experienced by the one who has reached perfection of both his rational and imaginative faculties. Echoing Alfarabi, he describes those who attain this level of prophecy as follows: "The best of people is the one whose soul is perfected [by becoming] an intellect in act and who attains the morals that constitute practical virtues. The best of [the latter] is the one ready [to attain] the rank of prophethood" (*The Metaphysics of the Healing: A Parallel English-Arabic Text*, 359). Yet unlike his predecessor, Avicenna does not allow for the possibility that Divine emanation goes to the imaginative faculty in his higher level of prophecy. Therefore, the higher-level prophet does not receive both theoretical and practical knowledge; rather, the prophet, through the use of his own practical reason, must create a system of laws and religious doctrines meant to assist the populace in attaining its *telos*.

See Avicenna and F. Rahman, *Avicenna's Psychology* (London: Oxford University Press, 1952); and Avicenna, and Michael E. Marmura, *The Metaphysics of the Healing: A Parallel English-Arabic Text* (Provo: Brigham Young University Press, 2004).

35. With respect to prophecy, Maimonides writes, "Know that the true reality and quiddity of prophecy consist in its being an overflow overflowing from God, may He be cherished and honored, through the intermediation of the Active Intellect, toward the rational faculty in the first place and thereafter toward the imaginative faculty" (MNII:36, 369). Yet, unlike the prophets of Alfarabi and Avicenna, Maimonides' prophets do not need practical wisdom in order to translate theoretical truths into practical norms, since the Torah has already provided those norms.

36. See Raymond Weiss, *Maimonides' Ethics*, 30; and Howard Kreisel, "The Practical Intellect in the Philosophy of Maimonides," 191.

37. Kant not only rejects the idea that the Divine will can be the foundation of ethics, but also submits the Divine will to the authority of the morallaw. Though God is essential to morality, Kant argues that God does not impose the moral law on humankind by virtue of His authority. Rather, humankind is equal to God as co-legislators of the moral law, and both are equally obligated by the moral law. Moreover, the validity of the moral system is in its self-legislation and not in its content alone.

Kant has a second reason to reject theological ethics, which is based on the formal structure of his moral theory. As stated above, the ends toward which the will applies the moral law must be given *a priori* in order for the will to be determined by pure practical reason and not by any empirical factor. If an end precedes or grounds the determination of the will, then the will is no longer determined by pure practical reason but rather is determined by the motivations of that empirical end. This creates the following paradox: "the concept of good and evil is not defined prior to the moral law, to which, it would seem, the former would have to serve as its foundation; rather the concept of good and evil must be defined after and by means of the law" (*Critique of Practical Reason*, 65). Therefore, morality cannot be grounded in an external conception of God and religious notions of good and evil (Ibid. 42).

38. Job 32:11.
39. NE 1143a11–16.
40. Kant writes, "*Immaturity* is the inability to use one's own understanding without the guidance of another. This immaturity is *self-incurred* if its cause is not lack of understanding, but lack of resolution and courage to use it without the guidance of another" ("What is Enlightenment?" *Kant's Political Writings* (Cambridge: Cambridge University Press, 1970) 54).
41. John Searle calls reasons "factitive" so that they include propositional intentional states or propositionally structured entities such as obligations, commitments, requirements, and needs. Calling reasons "factitive entities" allows for false beliefs to serve as reasons; it also allows for semantic maneuvering to be avoided while still defining reasons as propositional and relational. See *Rationality in Action*, 103–126.
42. For a detailed account of what constitutes a social and institutional fact, see Chap. 2.
43. Jeremiah 28:9.
44. Therefore, the Bible states that when Hagar placed Ishmael a bowshot away God heard Ishmael's voice "where he is (*ba'asher hu sham*)," meaning that He did not judge Ishmael for future actions but only as he was at the time. See Genesis 21:17 and BT *Rosh Hashana* 17b.

45. Joseph Raz defines a normative reason as follows: "A normative reason is a fact which, when one acts for it, gives a point or a purpose to one's actions, and the action is undertaken for the sake or in pursuit of that point or purpose. Reasons, and this is the common view among writers on the subject, have a dual role here. They are both normative and explanatory." See Constantine Sandis, *New Essays on the Explanation of Action* (New York: Palgrave Macmillan, 2009) 184.

46. A comparison between the etymology of intention and *kavana* (Hebrew for intention) can highlight the difference in what I call intentional states and intention. Intention (which, for this sense, applies to intentional states, such as beliefs and desires) is a stretching (*tendere)* of something toward (*in-*) something else. *Kavana* (כוונה) is a preparing (כ-ו-ן) for something. As such, *kavana* (intention) is the mental state that concludes with action, whereas intention(al states) is a mental state that may lead to continued thinking about a matter.

    In *Halakhic Man, Authentic Jew*, I explain intention as follows: "In other words, in order to perform a religious deed, a person must first understand the world so as to manipulate it for the purpose of the deed and evaluate whether it is worth performing the deed. Only then will he perform it. It is not that intention itself is the cognitive data upon which religious thought is based. Rather, intention demonstrates that the intending actor possesses the requisite religious cognitive data to comprehend and evaluate his actions in light of a religious *telos*" (125).

47. This will be further explained in the section on moral motivation.

48. See Genesis 18.

49. John Searle writes, "The reason does not derive from the institution, rather the institution provides the framework, the structure, within which one creates the reason. The reason derives from the fact that the agent binds her will through a free and voluntary act" (*Rationality in Action*, 204).

50. John Searle writes, "A perfectly rational agent might act rationally on a rationally justified belief that turned out to be false, and a fact in the world might be a compelling reason for an agent to act even in cases where the agent had no knowledge of the fact in question, or had knowledge of it but refused to recognize it as a reason" (*Rationality in Action*, 116). An example of a case where a fact

might be a compelling reason for an agent to act even when the agent had no knowledge of the fact in question would be when a doctor prescribes a drug without knowing that the patient is allergic to it. The fact that the person is allergic to the drug is a reason not to give it to him or her, but it is not part of the doctor's deliberation in whether to give the drug or not, since the doctor was not aware of that fact.

51. For others who understand reasoning as recognizing and responding to reasons in one way or another, see Charles Larmore in *The Autonomy of Morality* (New York: Cambridge University Press, 2008) who describes reasons as follows: "Reasons, too, belong to the fabric of reality. They are not, to be sure, some sort of independent entities, hovering alongside the more down-to-earth things we see and feel. Reasons consist in a certain *relation*—the relation of *counting in favor of*—that features the natural world, the physical and psychological facts that make it up, bear to our possibilities of thought and action. Yet relations of this sort also constitute facts—*normative facts* having to do with what we ought to believe or do, and normative facts also figure in this world, now understood more broadly as the totality of what exists" (128). Also, see Joseph Raz in *Engaging Reason* (New York: Oxford University Press, 1999) and *From Normativityto Responsibility* (New York: Oxford University Press, 2011), who writes, "…Reason is our general capacity to recognize and respond to reasons. There are other capacities that also do that. But Reason is the universal capacity to recognize reasons, one that in principle enables us to recognize any reason that applies to us, and to respond to it appropriately" (*From Normativity to Responsibility*, 86). In *Engaging Reason*, he writes, "Practical reasoning, reasoning about what is to be done, has two aspects. It is concerned to establish how things are and how—given that that is how they are—one is to act (50)," and "The core idea is that rationality is the ability to realize the normative significance of the normative features of the world, and the ability to respond accordingly" (68).

52. *From Normativityto Responsibility*, 40.

53. See Nahmanides, who writes, "It is known that whoever performs a commandment but does not understand it has not fulfilled it perfectly (*b'Shlemut*)" (*Kitve Ramban* I (Jerusalem: Mosad Harav Kook, 1963) 151).

According to Rabbi Yosef Albo, the performance of a command consists of two components, namely the physical action itself and the intention of the actor in fulfilling the command. *Shlemut* is not achieved when a person performs the commandments alone; rather, it comes when the person's will is properly oriented to perform the commandments. In other words, when a person performs an action from a conviction that is "autonomous" or otherwise outside of the societal framework which the law institutionalizes, even though it may be legal, it is done *shelo lishma* (not for the sake of the law). On the other hand, when the law, along with the concepts and values that it imparts, is the source of motivation, the resulting action will be done *lishma* (for the sake of the law). Rabbi Albo contends that this is the case even if the action may not be strictly legal. He demonstrates this point through the passage in the Talmud which states, "A transgression performed *lishma* is better than a command performed *shelo lishma*" (BT *Nazir* 23b and elsewhere). (Though the Talmudic discussion which ensues changes the expression to "[A transgression performed *lishma* is] as good as a command performed *shelo lishma*.") Rabbi Albo understands from this that acting in accordance with a commandment is subordinate to the intention that the actor has when acting. "For this reason," Rabbi Albo writes, "I say that when the Torah component surrounds the *mishpatim* [the social laws of the Torah], it is fitting to give *Shlemut* to the soul more than when social justice [*ha-helek ha-mishpati*] is grounded in civil/social ethics" (*Sefer ha-Ikkarim, Maamar Shlishi, Perek* 28). Though in both cases of *lishma* and *shelo lishma* the act may be legal, only in the former is the manner in which the person acts a means to achieve *Shlemut*.

Basing his delineation of the different ways to perform a commandment on various sources in the Talmud, Rabbi Moshe Hayyim Luzzatto (*Mesilat Yesharim, Perek* 16) gives the following description: To perform a commandment *shelo lishma* is to have impure intentions, yet there are different types of impure intentions that a person can have. The worst type of intention to perform a commandment is in order to deceive people or to gain honor or wealth. This type of intention is so base that it even transforms the action itself, which is done in accordance with the law, into something contemptible. Regarding a person who acts through this type of performance, Rabbi Luzzatto applies the Talmudic passage (JT *Berakhot* 1:5), "It were better had he been smothered by his placenta." A lesser form of *shelo lishma* is to perform a commandment for the sake of reward. Though not contemptible, and though it is considered legal, the act is not moral. Moreover, according to Rabbi Luzzatto, to act from this form of *shelo lishma* is only acceptable on account of the hope that through acting *shelo lishma*, a person will eventually learn to act *lishma* (based on BT *Pesahim* 50b). If someone performs a commandment *lishma*, but also has other motives for acting, even if the *lishma* motive outweighs the other motives, the act is not purely moral. As an example of this, Rabbi Luzzatto uses the Talmudic case of Rabbi Hanina ben Teradion's daughter, who after overhearing some men comment on the grace of her stride, immediately sought, due to this praise, to display even more grace (BT *Avodah Zarah* 18a). An act done truly *lishma* is one that is done only with purity of intention.

54. According to both Aristotelian and Kantian conceptions of practical reason, the end about which a person reasons is not subject to reason itself. Practical reason is only about the means to achieve a certain goal. According to Aristotle, moral choice is a result of deliberation; however, it is not a desired end that is chosen but rather that which contributes to attaining that end (NE 1113a3–5). The end itself is the object of a person's wishes, which is the apparent good as each person sees it according to the disposition of his or her character (NE 1113a31–34). Aristotle writes, "Again, the function of man is achieved only in accordance with practical wisdom as well as with moral excellence; for excellence makes the aim right, and practical wisdom the things leading to it" (NE 1144a7–9). This does not mean that choice consists of two separate and distinct components, that is, that of the end and that of the means to the end. The two components work together so that reason does have an effect on what is desired; however, its affect plays a subordinate role of justifying what is desired and not in giving a reason to desire it (EE 1227b36–7). Aristotle uses the same concave-convex metaphor to refer the two parts of deliberate desire as he uses to talk about the soul (NE 1102a31). For this reason, Aristotle claims that, with regard to choices, it is possible for the aim to be right but the means that contribute to the aim to be wrong or vice versa, which would make the choice, as one uni-

fied act, incorrect. In other words, choices consist not only in what is chosen but also in how and why it is chosen. Moreover, Aristotle has already stated that the appetitive part of the soul is subservient to the intellectual part; therefore, though moral excellence determines the end, it must do so in a way that relates to reason. For this reason, Aristotle writes, "[F]or with the presence of the one quality, practical wisdom, will be given all the excellences" (NE 1145a1–2).

The fact that a person's picture of his or her apparent end is dependent on his or her character contradicts the "Grand End" view of Aristotle's theory of practical wisdom. According to this view, a choice based on practical wisdom is one that has a true picture of the grand end for a person and the correct means in which to realize it with respect to the particular choice at hand. However, deliberation is oftentimes, if not always, concerned with particular ends, which, though they may be means to a grand end deliberation, regards the particular. Moreover, practical wisdom is gained through experience, which implies that the correct view of the end is also gained through experience; it is not the case that only deliberation of the means to the end improves from youth to old age. For a detailed critique of the "Grand End" view, see Sara Broadie's *Ethics with Aristotle*, 198–202.

Similarly, Kant considers practical reason to be a faculty that is strictly involved with procedure. The will is not focused on a substantive goal but rather on maintaining a consistent means to apply a rational principle to moral life, that is, conformity to the moral law, since the moral law is a product of pure practical reason.

55. *Engaging Reason*, 71.
56. Raz writes, "Our rationality expresses itself not only in our deliberation and reasoning, nor in any other specific act or activity, but more widely in the way we function, in so far as that functioning is, or should be, responsive to reasons" (*Engaging Reason*, 71).
57. *Hoshen Mishpat* 35.
58. *Igrot Moshe EhE* 1:120.
59. Ibid.
60. Raz writes, "Theoretical reason is that branch of practical reason that concerns reasons for accepting, recognizing, believing, and asserting propositions" (*Rationality in Action*, 120).

In truth, Kant does not distinguish between theoretical reason and practical reason, but rather calls them two different aspects of the same faculty. He writes, "If the critique of a pure practical reason is to be complete, it must be possible at the same time to show its identity with the speculative reason in a common principle, for it can ultimately be only one and the same reason which has to be distinguished merely in it application" (*Fundamental Principles*, 7).

61. Raz writes, "In fact reason affects our choice of ends and the desires we have just as much as it affects our deliberations and our beliefs. We cannot have a desire except for a reason. Once that is allowed, the motivation for the division of rationality into two distinct capacities disappears. There is no reason for thinking that the capacities which enable us to discern and respond to reasons for desires are different from those which enable us to discern and respond to reasons for belief" (*Engaging Reason*, 73).

62. See footnote 403.

63. Malbim, Commentary on Exodus 20:2, translation taken from Nehama Leibowitz and Aryeh Newman, *Studies in Shemot (Exodus)* (Jerusalem: Dept. for Torah Education and Culture in the Diaspora, 1996) 305.

64. The difference between accepting belief and knowing is demonstrated in the Hasidic literature by the following story about Rabbi Levi Yitzhak of Berditchev: Inspired by what he had heard about the nascent Hassidic movement and its teachings, Rabbi Levi Yitzhak of Berditchev went to the city of Mezeritch to study under the Maggid (Rabbi Dov Ber of Mezeritch). After several months he returned home, and his father-in-law, upset that he left home for so long, asked him "What did you learn in Mezeritch?" "I learned that God exists," Rabbi Levi Yitzhak answered. Clearly upset, his father-in-law retorted, "Even the servant girl knows that!" Yet Rabbi Levi Yitzhak explained, "She proclaims her belief. I know."

65. Isaac Abravanel and Menachem Marc Kellner, *Principles of Faith = Rosh Amanah* (East Brunswick: Associated University Presses, 1982) 155.

66. Howard Kreisel, "Intellectual Perfection and the Role of the Law," *From Ancient Israel to Modern Judaism: Intellect in Quest of Understanding*, Vol. 3 (Atlanta: Georgia Scholars Press 1989) 39.

67. *Engaging Reason*, 97.

68. I Kings 18:21.

69. "The Will to Believe," *William James: Writings 1902–1910*, 464.
70. BT *Avoda Zara* 17b.
71. Charles S. Peirce, *The Essential Peirce: Selected Philosophical Writings, Volume 1* (Bloomington: Indiana University Press, 1992) 114.
72. Imre Lakatos, "Science and Pseudoscience," *Philosophy of Science: The Central Issues*, ed. Martin Curd and J.A. Cover (New York: W.W. Norton, 1998) 23.
73. Paul Thagard, "Why Astrology is a Pseudoscience," *Philosophy of Science: The Central Issues*, eds. Martin Curd and J. A. Cover (New York: W.W. Norton, 1998) 31.
74. Hilary Putnam, *The Collapse of the Fact/Value Dichotomy* (Cambridge: Harvard University Press, 2002), 145.
75. "How science goes wrong," *The Economist*, October 19, 2013, http://www.economist.com/news/leaders/21588069-scientific-research-has-changed-world-now-it-needs-change-itself-how-science-goes-wrong/print
76. Joseph Raz calls this the "opaqueness of rules," since a complete statement of the reason to follow a rule need not include any evaluative statement regarding the appropriateness of the action. See *Between Authority and Interpretation*, 205.
77. *Avot* 2:4.
78. See *Rationality in Action*, 54–56.
79. Raz writes, "The possibility of akrasia depends on the fact that belief that a practical reason is defeated by a better conflicting reason is consistent with belief that it serves a concern that the better reason does not, and that can motivate one to follow it" (*From Normativityto Responsibility*, 42).
80. John Searle writes, "For many of the actions that we do have a reason, there are reasons for not doing that action but doing something else instead. Sometimes we act on those reasons and not on our original intention. The solution to the problem of *akrasia* is as simple as that: we almost never have just one choice open to us. Regardless of a particular resolve, other options continue to be attractive" (*Rationality in Action*, 233–234).
81. See *Critique of Practical Reason*, 57.
82. BT *Horayot* 10b; BT *Nazir* 23b.
83. Genesis 38.

84. Nahmanides, Genesis 38:26. Translation from Nahmanides and Charles Ber Chavel, *Commentary on the Torah: Genesis* (New York: Shilo Pub. House, 1971) 476.

85. Judges 4. The Talmud and the Biblical commentators interpret the verse, "At her feet he knelt, he fell, he lay. At her feet he knelt, he fell; where he knelt there he fell, vanquished" (Judges 5:27), to mean that Sisera had relations with Yael seven times before she killed him.

86. See Rashi, BT *Horayot* 10b; BT *Nazir* 23b.

87. "Curse Meroz," said the angel of Hashem, "Curse! Cursed are its inhabitants, for they failed to come to aid [the nation of] Hashem against the mighty." Blessed by women is Yael, wife of Heber the Kenite; by the women in the tent she will be blessed (Judges 5:23–24).

88. Judges 4:17.

89. Hosea 14:10.

90. The Talmudic Sages offer that the proscription not to touch the tree was authored by Adam so as to make a fence around the original command. Rashi, on the other hand, comments that Eve added the extra proscription herself.

91. This is not explicit in the Biblical text, yet it is taken for granted by the Sages that such was the case.

92. Genesis 2:9.

93. Genesis 3:6.

94. Compare Genesis 3:5 and Genesis 3:7.

95. *Guide for the Perplexed* I:2.

96. He compares this passage with "God opened her eyes" (Genesis 21:19), "Then shall the eyes of the blind be opened" (Isaiah 38:8), and "Which have eyes to see, and see not" (Ezek. 12: 2). He also compares it to "Open ears, he hears not" (Ibid. 40:20).

97. *Guide for the Perplexed* I:2, Pines, 25.

98. That Maimonides endeavored to give reasons for the commandments is obvious from reading the third section of the *Moreh Nevukhim*, yet he also argued that even the *hukkim*, which are traditionally seen as arational commandments, had reasons and that one should endeavor to discover them. See MN III:26 and MN III:31, where he argues that even the *hukkim* will show the nations that the commandments were given with wisdom and understanding. Maimonides' discussion of the reasons for various

commandments is not limited to the *Moreh Nevukhim*, he oftentimes emphasizes the need to discover the reasons for commandments in the *Mishne Torah* as well. Regarding the reasons for the *hukkim*, see *Hilkhot Temurah* 4:13. Regarding reasons for the *mishpatim*, see *Hilkhot Me'ilah* 8:8. See also *Hilkhot Mikva'ot* 11:12, *Hilkhot Shehita* 4: 16.

99. Maimonides was not the only one to give reasons for the commandments. Other medieval Jewish thinkers to do so were Saadia Gaon, Rabbi Bahya ibn Pakuda, Rabbi Abraham Ibn Ezra, Rabbi Abraham Ibn Daud, and Rabbi Judah haLevi.

100. Don Seeman, "Reasons for the Commandments as Contemplative Practice in Maimonides," *The Jewish Quarterly Review*, Vol. 103, No. 3 (Summer 2013) 321–322.

101. As for the reason why the reasons are not easily or generally known, Maimonides writes in his *Sefer HaMitzvot* (negative commandment 365) as follows: "The reasons for these commandments, 'He must not have too many horses,' 'He must not have too many wives,' and 'He must not accumulate very much silver and gold,' are given in Scripture. Since their reason was known it became possible to nullify them, as is well known from the case of Solomon, [who nullified them] in spite of his exalted level of knowledge and wisdom, and his being, '*Yedidyah*' [the beloved of God]. Our Sages said that this is a lesson to people that if God would reveal the reasons for all the commandments, they would find ways to disobey them. If even one who was so great and perfect [i.e. Solomon] could make the mistake of thinking that he could do the forbidden act and avoid the underlying reason for the prohibition, how much more so the more weak-minded masses. Certainly [if they knew the reasons for the commandments] they would disregard them by saying, 'this was prohibited,' or 'this was commanded only for such-and-such a reason. I can avoid the reason for which the commandment was given and ignore [the command itself].' In such a way, the entire Torah could be nullified. G-d therefore concealed their rationale. There is not a single commandment, however, that does not have a reason and purpose. The majority of these causes and reasons, though, cannot be grasped or understood by the masses. But regarding them all the

Prophet says, 'The commandments of God are straight, they make the heart rejoice.'"

102. See, for example, Rabbi Yaakov ben Asher, *Arba'ah Turim, Yoreh Deah*, 181, and Rabbi Yehiel Michael Epstein, *Arukh HaShulhan, Yoreh Deah* 240:2–3.

103. Though in *Shemonah Perakim*Maimonides writes that the *hukkim* are laws that are meant to instill a sense of obedience rather than impart wisdom, Lenn Goodman has argued that Maimonides did not mean that the *hukkim* were arbitrary and meant solely to instill obedience. Rather, because Maimonides believes that rationality is subsequent to the establishment of the law, his explanation of Rabbi Shimon ben Gamliel's statement is meant to emphasize the difference between those laws which have reasons that are readily perceived (*mishpatim*) and those laws which demand that a person first acquiesce to their authority before understanding their rationale (*hukkim*). Yet, whether a commandment is readily perceived or not, its meaning is provided within the context of the law and not outside of it. Therefore, ease of comprehension may result either because a commandment has a counterpart in another legal system under which the person lives or because comprehension of the reason for a command is relative to a person's engagement with it. See Lenn E. Goodman, "Rational Law/Ritual Law," *A People Apart: Chosenness and Ritual in Jewish Philosophical Thought*, ed. Daniel H. Frank (Albany: State University of New York Press, 1993) 147–150.

104. MN III:26, Pines, 509.

105. Arthur Hyman, "A Note on Maimonides' Classification of Law," *Proceedings of the American Academy for Jewish Research*, Vol. 46/47, Jubilee Volume (1928–29/1978–79), 343.

106. Maimonides' rationale for arbitrary choice in the realm of law corresponds to what Aristotle writes in the *Nicomachean Ethics* about legal justice, "that which is originally indifferent, but when it has been laid down is not indifferent, e.g. that a prisoner's ransom shall be a mina, or that a goat and not two sheep shall be sacrificed, and again all the laws that are passed for particular cases…" (NE 1134b20–22).

107. Nahmanides, Deuteronomy 22:6.

108. Samson Raphael Hirsch and Joseph Elias, *The Nineteen Letters* (New York: Feldheim Publishers, 1995), 271.
109. Isaiah 55:8.
110. Kellner, *Must a Jew Believe Anything?*, 7.
111. Kellner, *Must a Jew Believe Anything?*, 65.

CHAPTER 8

The Virtues

DEFINITION OF "VIRTUES"

...in whom was no blemish, but fair to look on, and smart in all wisdom, and knowledgeable in knowledge, and discerning in thought, and has the ability to stand in the king's palace...[1]

The relationship between practical reason and the virtues is an integral part of Aristotle's ethics. For Aristotle, "It is not possible to be good in the strict sense without practical wisdom, nor practically wise without moral excellence."[2] I agree with Aristotle that practical reasoning and the development of the virtues are intimately related. However, I conceive the way in which the two relate as being fundamentally different than in Aristotle's view. Furthermore, due to the differences in our respective conceptions of biology, psychology, and epistemology, our definitions for what constitutes a virtue and the relationship between intellectual and moral virtue are not the same. Aristotle defines virtue generally as

> a habit or trained faculty of choice, the characteristic of which lies in moderation or observance of the mean relatively to the persons concerned, as determined by reason, i.e. by the reason by which the prudent man would determine it. And it is a moderation, firstly, inasmuch as it comes in the middle or mean between two vices, one on the side of excess, the other on the side of defect; and, secondly, inasmuch as, while these vices fall short of or exceed the due measure in feeling and in action, it finds and chooses the mean, middling, or moderate amount.[3]

© The Author(s) 2017
I. Bedzow, *Maimonides for Moderns,*
DOI 10.1007/978-3-319-44573-1_8

In my theory of contemporary Jewish virtue ethics, a virtue is an acquired, active, persisting tendency (disposition, trait[4]) to act reliably toward accomplishing a certain goal and having certain reasons to do so, in a way that informs a person's identity,[5] which is developed through habituation within a community, and by which the person becomes more intelligent in the nuances of acting, requires less effort to act, and yet still aspires to improve through continual performance.[6]

By calling virtue an acquired, active disposition, I seek to avoid the assumption that it is simply a matter of a person's temperament, talents, or natural capacities. Rather, a virtue develops through a successful shaping of one's capabilities for the purpose of accomplishing a specific goal more effectively. The difficulty with conceiving of virtue as a natural capacity is that, though there may be room for development, it is necessarily limited. For example, to use an analogy between virtue and one's ability to see, one can only see as far as one's visual acuity allows; one cannot get better vision through practicing to see.[7] Moreover, a person can use his or her visual acuity for any number of reasons and to accomplish any number of goals, yet a virtue is developed to accomplish a specific goal. Of course, the virtues have a biological component, due to the fact that human beings are biological, yet, just as there is more to humanity than its biology, there is more to the virtues than being natural capacities. Similarly, virtues are different from personality traits, since the latter do not fulfill the entire definition.[8]

Aristotle differentiated between moral virtues, which he saw as character traits, and intellectual virtues, which he thought were cognitive capacities.[9] In my conception of virtue, both intellectual virtues and moral virtues are character virtues. The similarity between intellectual and moral virtues is based on the premise that both a person's search for knowledge and his or her behavior should be motivated by the person's goal(s). As I will discuss further, intellectual virtues are not solely "states by virtue of which the soul possesses truth by way of affirmation or denial,"[10] as Aristotle describes them. They also include how the knower relates to knowledge in terms of shaping his or her worldview and how that knowledge manifests in action. By presuming that intellectual virtues are character traits, I am also presuming that the process of thinking, which could mean either accepting beliefs or transforming beliefs into knowledge, is similar to acting. I am making the distinction between accepting beliefs and transforming beliefs into knowledge because certain beliefs, such as those gained through perception, seem to be passive and involuntary, while other beliefs, such as those that are commanded by Jewish law, seem not to be completely voluntary by virtue of being commanded (though one can choose not to accept them). Nevertheless, the transforming of accepted beliefs into knowledge can still be a voluntary active process. This view will be defended below.[11]

Likewise, a virtue is persisting if it informs the success of a person's actions in achieving his or her goal(s) even in cases where there is outside pressure or if the person has not had the opportunity to act according to that tendency for a long time. The Talmud provides an example of a Sage who did not have a persisting intellectual virtue, and in the end, he lost his ability to study Torah. Rabbi Elazar ben Arak visited Perugia, which was famous for its wine but not for its scholarship. He was attracted to the place and decided to stay, and as a result, his learning vanished. When he returned to the study hall, he arose to read from the Torah. Though he wished to read, "*Hahodesh hazeh lakhem* (This month shall be to you),"[12] he read "*haharesh hayah libbam* (Their hearts were silent)."[13] Because of this story, the Sages voiced the maxim, "Be exiled to a place of Torah, and do not say that it [the Torah] will follow you, for your companions will establish it in your possession; and do not rely on your own understanding,"[14] in order to emphasize the need for continual reinforcement and immersion in a community for the virtues (in this case an intellectual one) to persist.

A virtue is a reliable disposition in that a person with such a virtue is expected to respond to a given situation and across different situations in a consistent manner. This claim will be further discussed when I review the situationist challenge to global character traits, yet in order to anticipate some of the issues involved, I want to define what I mean by "situation." While situationists primarily conceive of a situation as an objective set of circumstances that is independent of the person who is confronted by it,[15] I also consider the cognitive and affective states of the person as part of what defines a situation, since these states will influence how the person understands the meaning of the situation and how he or she will compare it to other situations.[16] A person's cognitive and affective states are not completely subjective, however, since the organization of concepts and the methods of interpreting experiences are embedded within the objective facts that constitute a person's worldview and the goal(s) that a person aspires to achieve.[17]

Walter Mischel and Yuichi Shoda, for example, have argued that features of situations activate cognitive and affective reactions, which are based on a person's prior experience with those features. The features of situations, however, are not only external circumstances, but also how a person has thought, planned, fantasized, and imagined the situation, as well as the emotional states that they invoke. "Thus," they write, "what constitutes a situation in part depends on the perceiver's constructs and subjective maps, that is, on the acquired meaning of situational features for that person, rather than being denned exclusively by the observing scientist."[18] Therefore, what may be seen by an outside observer as inconsistency in responding to similar situations may in fact be the result of the person differentiating between two situations. Similarly, consistency across seemingly different situations may in fact be the result of the person giving a similar meaning to the two situations.[19]

Not all tendencies to act a certain way relate to a person's self-identity. For example, I do not think that my habit of having a cup of coffee in the morning says anything about who I am as a person. For a "tendency to act a certain way" to be considered a virtue, the person must perceive that disposition as an integral part of his or her identity. It must relate to his or her core commitments, aspirations, and ideals.[20]

The virtues do not impel a person to act automatically; they are not moral reflexes. Rather, through use, they continue to shape a person's identity and reinforce his or her orientation to the world, so that he or she becomes more intelligent through continual performance with respect to improving his or her knowledge of how to respond to situations by improving his or her proper conception of events and circumstances and the skills needed to respond. An example of the expectation that a person becomes more intelligent through continual performance is the Halakha that states that in a situation where a person is in a life-threatening situation the wise person is expected not to hesitate in transgressing the Shabbat laws so as to save him or her. The wise person should know immediately how to respond and should not have to deliberate as to whether, or in what ways, one may transgress the Shabbat laws.[21]

The virtues are also not innate; rather, they are acquired through habituation, which consists of education and training. The need for their acquisition is demonstrated by the fact that children are not obligated to perform commandments until they reach a certain level of maturity; before that time, they are given the opportunity to learn how to act through training and to understand why to act through education. Because the virtues include more than a tendency to act by rote, habituation must consist of more than the repetition of actions and the memorization of rules. Rather, habituation must be an integrative moral training that consists of preparation, performance, and appraisal of one's performance so as to be able to understand why one behaves a certain way and how such behavior allows for the achievement or hindrance of one's goals. By discussing with one's parents and teachers about what one should do in a given situation, by having discussions with them about what one has done and its consequences, and by implementing what one has learned by those discussions in the future, a person becomes habituated into moral living. This process of learning how to act and understanding why one should act in a certain way parallels the two levels of Torah learning that was discussed earlier, namely the jurisprudential study of Torah and the philosophical study of Torah. With respect to habituation, however, the primary focus is not substantive but procedural. Where engaging in theoretical and practical speculation is for the purpose of knowing epistemic and normative facts, education and training consists of learning how to think about theoretical and moral questions. Through such a practice, people will become better able to determine the right course of action and execute it properly, thus becoming more reliable in achieving success.

For the purpose of accomplishing one's goal and having the proper reasons to do so, virtue also has the following components: orientation,[22] attention, perception, emotion, motivation, and the ability to act. I will discuss moral motivation later; here I want to give some background to what I mean by orientation, attention, and perception.

Maimonides alludes to the necessity of a proper orientation for the proper development of virtue when he contrasts the righteousness of Rabbi Akiva with wickedness of the apostate, Elisha ben Abuya, or Aher, both of whom entered the *Pardes*.[23] Before entering the *Pardes*, Elisha ben Abuya believed in the notion of Divine reward and punishment, yet afterward he abandoned this belief. Because he could not harmonize the new beliefs that he acquired from his experience in the *Pardes* with his old beliefs and with what he perceived around him, he became mentally distraught, and in the end, he behaved contrary to societal norms in order to demonstrate his opposing views in practice. Though he was a brilliant scholar whose exegetical skills were excellent, because he was not virtuous, he ended up as an apostate. Rabbi Akiva, on the other hand, entered the *Pardes* in peace (*shalom*) and exited in peace (*shalom*). The difference between the two men is that the orientation of Elisha ben Abuya was self-directed, and thus his motivation for personal development was to achieve human excellence for its own sake; it was not for the sake of Heaven.[24] Rabbi Akiva's goal, on the other hand, was to serve God, and his orientation toward that goal remained consistent. Thus, he was able to continue to adhere to the tradition by which he lived and to remain *shalem*.[25] As discussed in my examination of what should be a person's *telos*, the proper orientation is to be directed toward the goal of living by one's faith (*emunah*); this orientation also relates to the reliability of the virtues, since faith and reliance are intimately related.

By attention, I mean the active self-urging to sustain focus.[26] It is a direct willing to attend to something that is not necessarily to one's desire to attend.[27] Maintaining attention is meant to shape and/or strengthen a person's desires actively. An example in Jewish practice of actively directing attention is the reciting of blessings before performing a ritual. When people recite blessings before performing ritual acts, they accomplish three things. They make themselves aware of what they are doing; they make themselves aware of why they are doing it; and they draw attention to the underlying focus which gives their actions meaning.

By perception, I do not mean recognition of what objectively occurs. Any given situation may allow for multiple descriptions, which bear competing, or even conflicting, claims. Moreover, emphasizing different details will highlight different considerations for how to relate to a particular scenario. Perception is the ability to understand different nuances between one situation and another and between the needs of one person and another. It is a skill of recognizing the particular while still having a hold on commonalities. A great example of the importance of perception is a statement by Rabbi Kalonymus Kalman Shapira who writes, "People encounter issues that appear to be contradictory, simply because they have only viewed the subject's external manifestations, and failed to penetrate its inner reality. Had they delved into the heart of the issue, they would have seen that there is really no contradiction at all; there are no questions, no answers—rather, it is all one integrated issue that branches off in different directions."[28] Perception is a skill that is developed not only through direct experience but also through vicarious experiences that one has while studying Torah and Talmud. The Jewish tradition recognizes the necessity of narratives as a means to learn how to apply general rules to concrete situations by the structure of the Bible itself. In his first comment on the Bible, Rabbi Shlomo Yitzhaki writes that if the Torah were solely a book of law, then it should have begun with the first commandment, which is mentioned in Exodus 12:1. The Torah includes the entire book of Genesis and the beginning of Exodus to ground the laws in an underlying worldview. Similarly, Rabbi David Kimhi writes that the story between

Abraham, Sarah, and Hagar was specifically written so that people will learn to acquire good traits and refrain from bad ones through examples.

Martha Nussbaum also argues that moral education requires narrative to be effective. A primary way in which Nussbaum conceives that people can develop their practical reasoning is through reading literature in addition to reading moral philosophy. While philosophy may provide factual knowledge and skills in logic, literature provides the means to develop a creative imagination, by which Nussbaum means "the ability to think what it might be like to be in the shoes of a person different from oneself, to be an intelligent reader of that person's story, and to understand the emotions and wishes and desires that someone so placed might have."[29] Moreover, reading narratives, such as those in the Bible, allows people to develop their moral perception, since narratives provide readers with vicarious situations different from those which they may have in their everyday lives as well as by introducing them to the nuances contained in the moral dilemmas that the characters encounter.

Intellectual Virtue

That the wise man may hear, and increase in learning[30]

One challenge to the conception of epistemological virtues as acquired character traits is the fact that people may hold certain true beliefs without having acquired a level of intellectual virtue.[31] Those who give this critique use, as an example, the fact that perceptual beliefs can be attained even by the youngest of children. In response to this critique, one should recognize that movements of the mind, just as of the body,[32] are not like a switch in that there is either a deliberate act or there is not. On the contrary, there is a spectrum. One can be either totally passive, active in a way that still does not produce an action, or active in a way that does produce an action. While some bodily activity may produce a given consequence with little or no expertise or motivation to do so, such activity should not be compared to a motivated, intentional action.[33] If the analogy from belief to action is apt, then beliefs held despite the lack of a motivated, intentional process of transforming them into knowledge cannot be compared to those beliefs that do need such a process to become knowledge. In other words, some beliefs take less effort than others to know, yet that does not negate the fact that accepting beliefs and turning them into knowledge does not take any effort at all. The relationship between a person's intellectual virtue and the possession of beliefs is explained by Jason Baehr as follows:

> [I]ntellectual virtues do not bear primarily on the domain of belief—to possess or exercise the traits in question is not primarily a matter of believing or forming beliefs in any particular way. This is not to say that intellectual virtues never have any bearing of this kind, for it does seem possible to believe something in an intellectually virtuous way or to believe something "out of" intellectual virtue. Nonetheless, we have seen that intellectual virtues, like moral virtues, bear principally on rational activity. This is evident in their central bearing on the process of inquiry, which involves activities like reading, interpreting, judging, assessing, reflecting, listening, and communicating. Belief, on the other hand, is best understood as a product of inquiry, and thus as a kind of indirect or mediate (though by no means accidental) result of the operation of intellectual virtues and vices.[34]

Moreover, because, as I will show below, wisdom entails that knowledge is put into practice, it is not enough to say that a child believes the same idea as an adult without also considering how that belief influences the decisions of the child and the adult.

An example that demonstrates the preference of knowledge gained through effort over that of passive acceptance of belief is Rabbi Yitzhak Hutner's explanation of the Talmudic expression that a sage has primacy over a prophet (*hakham adif m'navi*).[35] According to Rabbi Hutner, the information that a prophet receives is through direct communication; therefore, once communication has stopped so has the prophet's access to the information. The prophet's acquisition of knowledge, therefore, is both passive and limited, since it is dependent on an external cause. The sage, on the other hand, is able to gain knowledge even when communication is not open and direct, since he can engage in acquiring knowledge through his own independent resources. The sage thus has primacy over the prophet in two interdependent ways. He is able to be closer to God by virtue of having a deeper intellectual understanding of God's will, since he knows more than just what is openly revealed, and his closeness, which is based on his deeper intellectual understanding, is due to the fact that he actively engages in God's knowledge, further demonstrating a stronger and more intimate relationship in practice. In other words, the primacy of knowledge actively gained through intellectual virtue over that which is passively obtained corresponds to primacy of the sage over the prophet.[36]

Rabbi Hutner's explanation of the phrase "a sage has primacy over a prophet" also accords with the following passage in the Jerusalem Talmud:

> The words of the scribes are more beloved than the words of Torah ... to what can they be compared? To a king who sent two emissaries to a certain province. Concerning one of them he wrote, 'If he does not show you my seal and signet, do not believe him.' But concerning the other he wrote, 'Even though he does not show you my seal and signet, believe him.' Thus, in the case of a prophet it is written, 'and he gives you a sign or wonder,'[37] but here [regarding a scribe] it says, according to the instructions they give you.'[38]

The knowledge of the Sage is more reliable than the prophet, since the manner in which he acquired it is more intrinsic to his own capabilities and effort. The reliability of the prophet's knowledge, on the other hand, is dependent on an external sign, just as its acquisition is dependent on an external cause.

The Relationship Between Intellectual and Moral Virtues

Intellectual virtue affects the perception of reasons, how one evaluates reasons, and how one responds after evaluating. However, because affect influences one's perception of reasons,[39] one's ability to evaluate reasons properly,[40] and the manner in which one responds, the line between intellectual virtues and moral virtues cannot be seen as sharply distinct. Moreover, it is well established that the Maimonidean Jewish tradition assumes that most, if not all, actions necessitate a belief component,[41] and that most, if not all, beliefs necessitate a culmination in action,[42] which further blurs the lines between action and thought. I would therefore contend that intellectual and moral virtues are engaged during theoretical and practical speculation as well as when one interacts with others and the world around him or her. Just as the difference between theoretical and practical reasoning was minimized in the previous chapter, so here is the difference between the intellectual and moral virtues minimized. This conception of virtue has the benefit not only of harmonizing the Cartesian mind/body divide, but it also allows for a sense of wholeness, where all aspects of a person, his or her theoretical understanding, practical reasoning, emotions, dispositions, and actions, are all unified and synchronized—which is my definition for *Shlemut*. Moreover, it has the benefit of conceiving the unity of the virtues in terms of wholeheartedness and not as a summation of a number of individual virtues.

Among contemporary virtue theorists, Linda Zagzebski argues that intellectual virtues are a subset of moral virtues, yet intellectual virtues differ from moral virtues in that they have cognitive contact with reality. Nevertheless, contends Zagzebski, neither type of virtues functions independently of the other. For her, "Epistemic evaluation just is a form of moral evaluation."[43] Zagzebski's view is similar to Rabbi Samson Raphael Hirsch. He writes:

> In Judaism, the highest moral perfection of conduct is the purpose of intellectual edification, and it is only such perfection that gives value to intellectual development. In the Jewish conception of the holiness of life, genius is not license for nonobservance of the laws of morality; on the contrary, supreme morality is the test of supreme intellect, and only in it and by it are the nobility and purity of the intellect demonstrated and proven.[44]

According to Rabbi Hirsch, how a person acts reflects the depth of his or her knowledge. When a person says that he or she knows what the right thing to do is, but feels no emotional response to the situation and is not motivated to act accordingly, he or she actually demonstrates (moral) ignorance, since his or her posture toward the proclaimed belief shows a closer affiliation with a conflicting belief than with the one verbalized.

Julia Driver, on the other hand, distinguishes intellectual from moral virtue by arguing that intellectual virtues produce epistemic goods for oneself and that moral virtues contribute to the well-being of others.[45] This is similar both to Aristotle's and Maimonides' conceptions of the difference between intellectual and moral virtues. I would disagree with this distinction, since I contend that intellectual virtue is not oriented solely to acquire knowledge for oneself. With respect to one's intention for acquiring knowledge, the Mishna records Rabbi Ishmael the son of Rabbi Yossi's statement, "One who learns Torah in order to teach, is given the opportunity to learn and teach. One who learns in order to do, is given the opportunity to learn, teach, observe and do."[46] In both sentences, the point is that learning should be other-focused. In fact, if a person's study does not lead to action, the Sages say that the person is like one who has no God,[47] which implies that the knowledge was not gained through intellectual virtue since it was not motivated toward one's ultimate goal. Similarly, Maimonides writes that study and teaching are two components of the same commandment.[48]

In the next two sections, I will respond to the critiques that contemporary philosophers make to argue against the existence of intellectual and moral virtues, namely that the acquisition of belief is not voluntary and that there are no such things as global character traits, respectively.

Intellectual Virtue and the Challenge of Contemporary Epistemology

Who is as the wise man? And who knows the interpretation of a thing?[49]

One difficulty that any contemporary aretology must confront is the prominent position found in contemporary epistemology that the acquisition of belief is not voluntary[50] whereas actions are, or at least can be. Even those who rely on a Humean account of the virtues to provide a basis for a contemporary virtue ethics that avoids Aristotelian notions of causation must confront Hume's distinction between actions and beliefs. To explain, David Hume defines the will as "the internal impression we feel and are conscious of, when we knowingly give rise to any new motion of our body, or new perception of our mind."[51] Though he denies the ability to discover ultimate causes, common knowledge can assume that actions are caused by the will. Hume also admits that the human will is free, since it has the power to determine whether a person acts or not.[52] Thus, he argues that human actions are voluntary. Beliefs, on the other hand, are involuntarily acquired, since they are formed by external causes. According to Hume, beliefs occur when external percepts impress ideas upon the mind with a certain force and vivacity; they are, in fact, simply a vivid and intense conception of an idea which has been impressed upon the mind with a certain force.[53] Beliefs may therefore correlate with particular habits, but, as Hume would readily acknowledge, it cannot be shown that having such habits induces those beliefs.[54]

Acceptance of the notion that beliefs cannot be voluntarily acquired implies that possessing certain beliefs cannot be a legal obligation. This idea is readily apparent in the writings of the ascribed father of modern Jewish thought, Moses Mendelssohn, a contemporary of David Hume. In his book, *Jerusalem*, Mendelssohn denies the ability for law to assist a person in truth's discovery. With regard to legal inducement, he writes, "Laws do not alter convictions; arbitrary punishments and rewards produce no principles, refine no morals. Fear and hope are no criteria of truth.

Knowledge, reasoning, and persuasion alone can bring forth principles which, with the help of *authority* and *example*, can pass into *morals*."[55] Mendelssohn's contention that laws cannot induce belief is similarly found in the writings of another contemporary, John Locke. In his *Letter Concerning Toleration*, Locke writes:

> And upon this ground I affirm, that the Magistrate's Power extends not to the establishing of any Articles of Faith, or Forms of Worship, by the force of his Laws. For Laws are of no force at all without Penalties, and Penalties in this case are absolutely impertinent; because they are not proper to convince the mind. Neither the Profession of any Articles of Faith, nor the Conformity to any outward Form of Worship (as has already been said) can be available to the Salvation of Souls, unless the truth of the one, and the acceptableness of the other unto God, be thoroughly believed by those that so profess and practice. But Penalties are no ways capable to produce such belief.[56]

It is not the authority of the law that teaches belief. Authority lies with the philosopher who, through his independent reasoning, has attained true knowledge of the world, and in acting according to those true principles becomes an example of moral and intellectual excellence.[57]

The question of whether the process of acquiring beliefs is voluntary or not, however, does not originate in the modern period. It has a place in medieval philosophy as well and was even the basis of one of the challenges to Maimonides' ethical system, namely his contention that belief in the existence of God is a commandment.[58] I do not intend to review the entire debate over whether belief or knowledge of God is a commandment; rather, I only intend to discuss that which is directly related to the question of whether beliefs can be voluntarily acquired or not. However, in order to provide some background to the debate, there are three major positions regarding whether belief in the existence of God is a commandment. The first category consists of those who consider belief in the existence of God to be a commandment, and this is the position of Maimonides and Nahmanides, though Nahmanides can be seen to amalgamate the three positions.[59] The second category consists of those who do not consider belief in the existence of God to be a commandment, but they do contend that it is a commandment to believe in a particular relationship between God and the Jewish people or between God and the world. For example, Rabbi Moshe ben Rabbi Jacob of Coucy (Semag) writes that the first positive commandment is to believe that the One who gave the Torah on Mount Sinai through Moses is Hashem our Elohim who took the Jews out of Egypt. This does not assume that belief in God is a commandment only that the God in which one believes is the One who gave the Torah. Rabbi Nissin Gerondi holds a similar view. Similarly, Rabbi Yitzhak ben Rabbi Yose (Semak) writes that the first commandment is to believe that the One who created the world is the One who controls it. This also does not assume that belief in God is a commandment; rather, it demands that the God in which one believes is not the God of philosophy but rather One that has Divine providence. Rabbi Yosef Albo holds a similar view. The third category consists of those who do not consider belief in the existence of God to be a commandment at all. Rabbi Hasdai Crescas and Don Isaac Abravanel argue for this position.[60] For example, Rabbi Hasdai Crescas challenges Maimonides' contention, claiming that belief in the existence of God could not be a commandment for the following reason. He writes:

> It is already shown by those who investigate the meaning of the word "commandment" and its implication, that it only applies to things to which will and choice pertain. Surely, if belief in the existence of God is not something to which will and choice pertain, then one must not apply the term "commandment" to it.[61]

God cannot command that one believe anything; rather, only actions can be commanded. Beliefs, however, are necessary to understand properly why one is commanded and how one relates to the Commander.[62]

Another difficulty with Maimonides' assertion that there is a commandment to believe in the existence of God is that in Maimonides' Aristotelian framework, thinking has a passive component that necessitates an external entity for the person to acquire knowledge. For Aristotle, the thinking part of the soul is capable of receiving intelligible forms, yet it cannot actualize knowledge by itself. Only the Active Intellect can turn the potential knowledge that the human mind possesses into actual knowledge. For Maimonides, the Active Intellect is the lowest of the celestial spheres. One may respond that the command to believe in God, according to Maimonides, may be to prepare oneself actively to be able to join with the Active Intellect so that one can come to belief. Yet, this response is only relevant if we were to accept the Aristotelian cosmology upon which Maimonides' aretological ethics is based. Since, however, we have already admitted that contemporary epistemology, even in Jewish philosophy, no longer accepts Aristotle's epistemological framework, we must still attempt to construct a Jewish aretology that conceives of belief, or at least its transformation into knowledge, as a voluntary endeavor.

Even if belief in God is not commanded as Maimonides' claims, the question of whether the process of acquiring beliefs is voluntary or not and how it can help to construct a conception of intellectual virtue is still relevant. Regardless of its strictly juridical force, the Torah still teaches that God exists and is One and that He provides for all creatures.[63] Whether these beliefs are explanatory facts or normative facts, by virtue of one's goal to serve God with love, they affect a person's view of the world, since they must find coherence with all the other facts on which a person relies.

The debate over whether the acquisition of belief is voluntary or not seems to revolve around three questions. First, is voluntariness dependent on the existence of choice, or is free choice and free will distinguishable? In other words, is there a difference between choosing and being voluntary? Second, is thinking similar to acting? Third, can there be a helpful distinction between belief and knowledge as it pertains to these questions?[64] If it is possible to show that there is a distinction between voluntariness and free choice and to show that there is similarity between the process of thinking and of acting, then belief can be shown to be voluntary. If, on the other hand, all that I can demonstrate is that there is a difference between belief and knowledge, then I can at least show that transforming belief into knowledge is an active process which necessitates intellectual virtue. This last question may be dependent on whether there is a distinction between types of beliefs just as there are distinctions between types of actions. For example, just as there are involuntary acts, such as reflexes and movements in the autonomic nervous system, there could be involuntary perceptual or memory beliefs. Also, just as there are voluntary actions, such as those that occur after moral deliberation, there are voluntary beliefs, such as those that occur after intellectual deliberation. A Jewish aretaic epistemology could then focus on the types of beliefs that demand intellectual deliberation, just as a Jewish aretaic ethics would focus on actions that result from moral deliberation.

Voluntariness and Choice

A dominant position in contemporary analytic philosophy is the idea that actions are considered voluntary when the actor could have acted otherwise; the actor had a choice whether to act or not. Thinking that one acts freely is not enough to prove that he or she is in fact acting voluntarily.[65] For example, A.J. Ayer rejects the position of some philosophers that freedom consists in being conscious of necessity, claiming that it perverts the normal usage of the word freedom. He writes, "For suppose that I am compelled by another to do something 'against my will.' In that case, as the word 'freedom' is ordinarily used, I should not be said to be acting freely: and the fact that I am fully aware of the constraint to which I am subjected makes no difference to the matter. I do not become free by becoming conscious that I am not."[66] Similarly, a person who is compelled by a strong tendency, such as kleptomania, could not be said to be acting freely, since he or she has no choice in whether to steal or not. Ayer does, however, admit that certain actions can be said to be freely performed, namely where there is a possibility of choice that is not subject to overriding tendencies and that are not compelled by another person.[67] Therefore, providing a naturalist causal explanation for an action does not entail that the act was not free,[68] and he assumes that the range of freely performed actions are those that are internally chosen without overriding constraint. Roderick Chisholm calls this internal choosing an instance of immanent causation, rather than transeunt causation, since human agency causes certain events to happen without any external cause for that agency.[69]

Harry Frankfurt, on the other hand, argues that some acts should be considered voluntary even when a person cannot choose otherwise. According to Frankfurt, humans are not unique in their ability to make choices or to act on motives or desires. Rather, what is exceptional about humans is their ability to evaluate and self-reflect on their desires and choices. Human will is not that which pulls a person to act willy-nilly, since people have conflicting motivations due to having numerous desires concurrently. Therefore, the will must be seen as that which moves a person to perform an action voluntarily.[70] Based on this framework, freedom of choice is neither a sufficient nor a necessary condition for an action to be considered voluntary. For example, if a person performs an action that he desires to perform, and performs it because he desires to perform it, and his motivating will to perform it was the will that he desired, then the person acts voluntarily. The question of whether there are alternate possibilities to act is not a direct part of the equation. Rather, it is subsumed within the question whether the person's motivating will is the will that he desired, so that if he wanted to do something yet was not given the possibility and therefore chose to do what was available despite his motivating will then his action was involuntary.[71] I would temper this claim somewhat, however, and say that because the person chose an alternative and performed an action, then he or she did act voluntarily to some extent. As such, one can conceive of volition as a function of the options available and the motivation of the actor.

Frankfurt uses his theory to challenge the "principle of alternate possibilities" that is commonly held in contemporary analytic philosophy. The principle of alternate possibilities is the assumption that a person is only morally responsible, that is, he or she acts voluntarily, if it were possible to have acted otherwise. The principle further assumes that coercion disallows voluntary action. As a counterexample, Frankfurt offers a case where a person is coerced to perform an act that he had already committed himself to performing. If the person acts based on his commitment and not due to coercion, then, according to Frankfurt, he acted willingly and thus voluntarily. It is therefore possible that a coerced act can still be voluntary, since the existence of alternate options is not essential to voluntariness. Rather, what is necessary is the person's identification with the action performed.[72]

The Jewish legal tradition also recognizes that willingness need not require the existence of alternate possibilities, yet it draws a different line between coerced and voluntary action than Frankfurt does, since Frankfurt only demands that the person identifies with the action performed while the Jewish legal tradition holds that an individual's willingness should also be considered in light of his or her social obligations. For example, the Talmud records the ruling that a person can be compelled to sell something that he previously committed voluntarily to sell, and it would not be considered a sale under duress. The Talmud extends this principle to validate compelling a person to offer a sacrifice that he previously vowed to give. The Talmud then applies this principle to allow coercing a husband to give his wife a divorce, even though coerced divorces are usually not considered valid. The justification for these rulings is the idea that in each of the cases the coerced person benefits from the coercion.[73] The Tosafists provide an economic reason for why the case of divorce is analogous to that of a sale: in the sale there is an exchange of goods and through the divorce the man is no longer obligated to provide for his wife.[74] Others, however, understand the benefit in terms of facilitating voluntary action. The person is provided with a means to carry out what he has demonstrated he wants to do. With regard to a coerced divorce, the demonstration of desire is based on being a member of a community and accepting the social obligations that the community demands. In the words of Maimonides:

> Why is this deed of divorce not void? ... Because the concept of being compelled against one's will applies only when speaking about a person who is being compelled and forced to do something that the law does not obligate him to do. ... If, however, a person's evil inclination presses him to negate a command or to commit a transgression, and he was beaten until he performed the action he was obligated to perform, or he dissociated himself from the forbidden action, he is not considered to have been forced against his will. On the contrary, it is he himself, in his evil inclination, who was forcing [him to transgress]. With regard to this person who [outwardly] refuses to divorce [his wife]—he wants to be part of the Jewish people, and he wants to perform all the commands and eschew all the transgressions; it is only his evil inclination that presses him. Therefore, he is beaten until his [evil] inclination has been weakened, and he consents [to the divorce], he is considered to have performed the divorce willfully.[75]

This is similar to the case mentioned by Frankfurt, where a person has conflicting first-order desires, which weaken his second-order desire to adhere to the law. Only, in the case of divorce, the court provides the means by which the person can make his weakened second-order desire his volition. Maimonides' view has resonance with that of Jean Jacques Rousseau, who writes that for the social compact to be effective, whoever refuses to obey the general will shall be compelled to do so by the whole body politic. He explains that this means nothing less than that the person will be forced to be free.[76] From the Talmudic exchange, however, one learns that for an action to be considered as willing, despite the presence of coercion, two things are required. First, there must be a recognizable indication that the person acts willingly. Second, there must a reason for why the person would act willingly, such as receiving a benefit from the action.[77]

The contemporary debate in analytic philosophy, and its Jewish counterpart, seems to be an extension of the debate in medieval philosophy over the primacy of *liberum arbitrium* versus *libertas* or, in modern parlance, the difference between negative liberty and positive liberty.[78] If acquiring a belief, or transforming it into knowledge, is a similar process as acting, then one could rely on the notions of *libertas* and of positive liberty to show that it is voluntary. Relying on *libertas* and positive liberty, one could say that even if beliefs are considered as coerced, in the sense that they are given to a person when percepts are passively turned into concepts and as memories are formed, then at least the process of turning them into knowledge through identifying with them and securing them as part of one's worldview would nevertheless be voluntary. The process would also allow for the development of intellectual virtues that help a person reinforce and strengthen those beliefs.[79] Therefore, as to the question of whether voluntariness is dependent on the availability of choice, we can answer that for the development of virtue, it need not be. Moreover, from the theological premise that every generation accepted the Torah at Sinai, coercion to abide by the law may still result, in Rousseau's sense, in a freely willed act for the sake of the development of virtue.

The Similarity Between Thinking and Acting

The distinction made in contemporary epistemology between thinking and acting rests on the assumption that beliefs and actions are not comparable. For example, Jonathan Kvanvig writes, "This idea of there being a 'deed' of true believing, of the truth of one's believing being 'attributable to the agent as his or her own doing,' raises precisely the problem we have been discussing. Beliefs are not actions and thus are not creditable or attributable to the agent in the way actions are."[80] Linda Zagzebski, on the other hand, has noted that even though knowing is currently construed as a state rather than as an act, Aristotle and medieval Aristotelians referred to the "act of knowing" and not the state of knowing. She offers that the reason for this change in how knowing is conceived is either because, today, perceptual knowledge is the paradigm example or because the concept of agency has narrowed.[81]

Among contemporary virtue epistemologists, however, there is a strong assumption that the process of turning beliefs into knowledge is similar to performing actions willingly, at least in the way that Frankfurt defines the term willingly. For example, Ernest Sosa calls belief an intellectual performance whose aim is truth, and he contends that for a belief to be considered as knowledge, it must be accurate (true), adroit (showing epistemic competence), and apt (resulting from epistemic competence and not a matter of luck). Moreover, to be uniquely human knowledge, it must be reflective in the sense that the person must aptly believe the belief to be apt and can thus defend it against skeptical doubt.[82] Sosa also defines reflective knowledge to be when "one's judgment or belief manifests not only such direct response to the fact known but also understanding of its place in a wider whole that includes one's belief and knowledge of it and how these come about."[83] Based on his conception of reflective knowledge, Sosa defines intellectual virtue as a faculty relative to the person's environment that has an inner nature which allows the person, given the circumstances and the topic, to very likely attain truth and avoid error.[84]

John Greco defines virtue as a reliable ability to achieve something[85] or as a kind of success from ability.[86] Intellectual virtue, then, would be the ability to achieve knowledge. Greco, however, uses a different theory of reliabilism from Sosa to ground his theory of virtue. For Sosa, the basis for cognitive virtue is the inner nature of the cognitive subject. Greco, on the other hand, demands that the person also be subject to epistemic standards to which he or she must conform. These external constraints assist in anchoring the person's inner cognitive faculty so that it does not attain inner knowledge that has no relation to an external truth. Under this framework, knowledge is virtuous both subjectively (internally), as it is based on a person's cognitive ability, and objectively (externally), since it is a subjective belief reliably attained in conformance to epistemic standards. For Greco, these standards, however, are not normative etiological cognitive rules as in deontological epistemology;[87] rather, they are the standards, which may even be empirically determined, that allow one to recognize what constitutes virtuous intellectual activity.[88]

To explain their theories, both Sosa and Greco use analogies to action, such as archery and baseball.[89] The use of action analogies shows that we intuit that the process of acting and the process of thinking is relatively similar so that examples from one realm can shed light on the other, and based on how we think and talk about mental processes, the similarity seems to be correct. Though one may want to maintain an analytic distinction between the mind and the body to allow for the primacy of one over the other, we do not speak about the mind and the body using wholly different terminologies to explain how each one operates. Moreover, recognition of the harmony, even if one does not want to accept it as a unity, of the mind and the body allows for the construction of a holistic contemporary aretology, where epistemological and physical behavior are two sides of one coin.[90]

Though he is not self-described as a virtue epistemology, Alvin Plantinga has a similar theory which he calls proper functionalism. According to Plantinga, a belief is warranted if (a) it has been produced by cognitive faculties that are working properly, (b) the cognitive environment is sufficient to make a person's cognitive faculties work properly, (c) the part of the design plan that governs the production of that belief is aimed at the production of true beliefs, and (d) the design plan is a good one in that there is a high statistical probability that a belief produced under these conditions will be true.[91] In other words, true, warranted belief is based on the reliable success of a properly functioning cognitive faculty that is designed to aim toward truth. Ernest Sosa has noted that his account of a reliabilist virtue epistemology is similar to Plantinga's theory of proper functionalism in that both agree that internalism is insufficient to account for knowledge and that knowledge demands that certain faculties operate in a way that is truth conducive. Their disagreement, he acknowledges, is in what constitutes proper functioning.[92] Plantinga acknowledges that he and Sosa may agree as to their respective epistemologies, yet their difference in fact lies in their respective underlying metaphysics, since Plantinga presupposes a religious metaphysics while Sosa does not.[93]

Linda Zagzebski relies directly on Harry Frankfurt's argument against the principle of alternate possibilities to show that even if knowledge is conceived in a way that disallows counterfactuals, knowledge can still be depicted as the result of agent causation rather than of event causation.[94] Like Frankfurt's analysis in the realm of action, Zagzebski argues that agency, and not alternate possibility, is central to whether a person can be considered to have acquired a belief. Causal processes that take away agency, therefore, also take away a person's knowledge, even if he or she still possesses a certain belief, just as for Frankfurt it takes away moral responsibility. An epistemic agent, for Zagzebski, "is one who reliably reaches her epistemic end and who reaches her epistemic end because of *her*, not by chance or because of something outside of her."[95] Despite her disagreement with Ernest Sosa as to what constitutes a virtue,[96] her description of how knowledge is acquired is very similar.

In the Jewish tradition, two modern Jewish thinkers, who came from different religious factions, each upheld the idea that there is similarity between thoughts, speech, and action in a way that allows for belief acquisition to be an agent-centered performance. Rabbi Hayyim of Volozhin, in *Nefesh HaHayyim*, writes that thought, speech, and action are controlled by three aspects of a person's soul, the *nefesh*, the *ruah*, and the *neshama*, respectively, and they are expressions of a person, which he or she should attempt to perfect.[97] Also, in a manner similar to some of the virtue epistemologists mentioned above, he compares mental faculties to faculties of the body. For example, he writes, "The eye represents thought, for 'eyesight is dependent on mental faculties' (*Avoda Zara* 28b). The spirit (*ruah*) represents speech, for the *Targum* of 'Man became a living being (*ruah*)' (Bereshis 2:7) is 'Man became a speaking (*ruah*) creature.' The soul (*nefesh*) represents action, as in 'the soul (*nefesh*) which will do' (*Bemidbar* 15:30)."[98] He contends further that the depth, or success, of a person's thinking depends on his or her ability[99] and effort.[100] In one passage he explains the process of thinking as follows: When a person's thoughts join to a particular matter, then the thought of the matter is obtained by the thinking person. It is an active process, yet the motivating source of action is hidden from the person, since it is rooted in his *neshama*. To support this description, Rabbi Hayyim uses the verse, "the breath (*nishmat*) of *Shaddai* gives them understanding,"[101] as an analogy to this process. The *neshama* which was breathed into the nostrils of the first man[102] is the essential aspect which gives humans life and their motivation for thinking. Yet it is also unable to be fully comprehended by humans since it is part of God, who is beyond the realm of human understanding.[103] Because the source of motivation is hidden, one may think that the thinking process is passive or imposed on the person from without; to correct this misconception, Rabbi Hayyim continually reminds his readers that the source of motivation is internal and the process is active and dependent on personal ability and effort.

In a similar, but not the same, manner, Rabbi Shneur Zalman of Liadi calls thought, speech, and action garments of the soul, which actively express the soul's will. He also describes thinking as the active process of grasping concepts.[104] Because the Hasidic dynasty which he founded is based on his understanding of the importance of a person's mental faculties, I will quote his definitions for wisdom, understanding, and knowledge, which clearly allow for a virtue epistemology. He writes:

> The intellect of the rational soul, which is the faculty that conceives any thing, is given the appellation of *chochmah* [wisdom]—כ"ח מ"ה—the "potentiality" of "what is." When one brings forth this power from the potential into the actual, that is, when [a person] cogitates with his intellect in order to understand a thing truly and profoundly as it evolves from the concept which he has conceived in his intellect, this is called *binah* [understanding] … *Da'at* [knowledge], the etymology of which is to be found in the verse: "And Adam knew (*yada*) Eve," implies attachment and union. That is, one binds his mind with a very firm and strong bond to, and firmly fixes his thought on, the greatness of the blessed *En Sof* [the Infinite], without diverting his mind [from Him]. For even one who is wise and understanding of the greatness of the blessed *En Sof* will not—unless he binds his knowledge and fixes his thought with firmness and perseverance—produce

in his soul true love and fear, but only vain fancies. Therefore *da'at is* the basis of the *middot* [emotional faculties/virtues] and the source of their vitality.[105]

The relationship between the active process of thinking and one's motivation to think is best exemplified in Rabbi Shneur Zalman reconciliation of the Talmudic exhortation, "Be righteous and be not wicked; and even if the whole world tells you that you are righteous, regard yourself as if you were wicked,"[106] with the Mishnaic statement, "And be not wicked in your own estimation."[107] He writes that most people are unable to subdue their base desires completely and might at times have conflicts in motivation. Yet, even those who are not completely righteous can still remove themselves from evil by controlling their thoughts, speech, and actions. The type of person who can do that is called a *Beinoni* (intermediate person who is between righteous and wicked). Such a person uses his or her free will to choose in actual practice to "turn away from evil and do good," since he or she thinks, speaks, and/or acts contrary to his or her initial motivation. Through this practice, Rabbi Shneur Zalman notes, a person is able to serve God with love.[108] Rabbi Shneur Zalman thus relegates free will and choice to the control over a person's thoughts, speech, and actions while leaving the base motivations of a person (not to mention any biological and environmental influences that might determine his or her makeup) outside of his or her control.[109] Therefore, as to the question of whether thinking is similar to acting, we can rely on the explanations of these two great rabbinic figures, as well as the literature in contemporary virtue epistemology, to provide a firm basis that it can be construed as such.

The Difference Between Belief and Knowledge

The notion in contemporary epistemology that knowledge is justified true belief is a consequence of the approach which holds that truth and knowledge are valued by their propositional content without any relation to the believer and his or her social milieu. A knowledgeable person, according to many contemporary epistemologists, is a person who possesses many true, justified beliefs, regardless of whether those beliefs influence his or her daily life. Even among certain reliabilist virtue epistemologists, knowledge is a possession that is no different from beliefs. Linda Zagzebski quips about reliabilism as follows: "The aim is to have as many true beliefs as possible while paying the price of as few false beliefs as can be managed."[110] This type of knowledgeable person is not same as the wise person typically conveyed by the Jewish tradition, because the Jewish tradition does distinguish between accepting beliefs, which is similar to the contemporary metaphor of possessing them, and knowing truth, which means that the beliefs have been internalized and integrated into a person's worldview and reasoning.

In previous chapters, I have already discussed the nature of belief/faith (*emunah*) as it relates to truth (*emet*). Here, I will discuss the nature of knowledge and understanding as it relates to wisdom. Knowledge (*da'at*) in Hebrew is a relational term. Used with respect to abstract ideas as well as with people or events, it conveys that a person has a familiarity with the object known. In one respect it is a passive receipt, since familiarity is something given through contact with an object or person. Yet, in another respect, it is active, since familiarity demands that the person exert himself or herself to receive and increase it. In the Bible, understanding (*bina/tevunah*) is also a relational word, yet in a different way than knowledge (*da'at*). Knowledge is a relationship between a person and something external to a person; understanding is when a person sees a relationship between two things external to him or her. A person must know each thing before he or she can understanding how they relate to each other. As such, understanding is an expansion of knowledge. This description of understanding is similar to that of Jonathan Kvanvig and of Wayne Riggs. Kvanvig describes it as follows: "Understanding requires the grasping to explanatory and other coherence-making relationships in a large and comprehensive body of information. One can know many unrelated pieces of information, but understanding is achieved only when informational items are pieced together by the subject in question."[111] Similarly, Riggs writes, "Understanding has a multitude of appropriate objects, among them complicated machines, people, subject disciplines, mathematical proofs, and so on. Understanding something like this requires a deep appreciation, grasp, or awareness of how its parts fit together, what role each one plays in the context of the whole, and of the role it plays in the larger scheme of things."[112] Contrary to the notion of knowledge in contemporary epistemology, where the veracity of the belief proposition is independent of the person and the effort to possess knowledge is an effort of acquisition, the veracity of knowledge (*da'at*) and understanding (*bina/tevunah*) according to my definitions is dependent on the relationship between the person and that which he or she knows, and the effort to possess knowledge and understanding is the effort of deepening that relationship.

As seen through how it is used in the Bible, wisdom (*Hokhmah*), another concept that is not typically found in contemporary epistemology is an orientated perceptual schema which allows a person to take his or her knowledge and apply it correctly to a dynamic reality.[113] When the Hebrew word for wisdom is used in a verb phrase, it is always expressed in the *kal* verbal form,[114] which indicates that the acquisition and practice of wisdom is an active process. To draw meaning from syntactical constraints, to be wise it is not enough to consider passively the possible relations between cause and effect. This is so because to believe a conception of reality as true rather than as simply possible demands that one actively engage in the conception so that the idea is reinforced by one's sentiment and actions. Based on this, Rabbi Samson Raphael Hirsch defines a wise person (*hakham*) as follows:

> A *Hakham* is one who takes in all that is in front of him. He recognizes things for what they are and for what they should be. Both—the nature of things and their intended purpose—are given; man need not create them. The truest *Hakham* is one who learns the nature and the purpose from the One Who assigned things their nature and purpose.[115]

Where wisdom (*Hokhmah*) is using one's knowledge in a way that corresponds to one's goals, intelligence (*sekhel*) is the ability to grasp ideas and concepts.[116] The increase of one's intelligence would be a result of one's faculties. How a person turns his or her intelligence into wisdom is a result of his or her virtues.

A Talmudic example can demonstrate the accuracy of this definition. Alexander of Macedon asked the Sages ten questions, one of which was "Who is called wise?" To this question, the Sages replied, "Who is wise? He who can perceive consequences."[117] The Sages' answer regarding who is considered wise is also Rabbi Shimon's answer to Rabbi Yohanan ben Zakkai's question of which is the proper path that a person should walk.[118] To have wisdom, the knowledge a person acquires must be organized according to a particular orientation that allows for a coherent focus toward a goal. One's schema must also allow for the prioritization of information according to how effective it is in maintaining that focus. In terms of perceiving consequences, a wise person not only must have a refined sense of perception, but must also possess the proper hermeneutical tools in order to make correct inferences. It is not a knowledge that one can own; it is a relation to the world that one has. Intelligence (*sekhel*), on the other hand, can be increased and developed like a skill, since it is the ability to grasp ideas and concepts. One can be intelligent without being able to apply his or her knowledge to the world. Through wisdom, there is a direct relationship between epistemology and ethics. Therefore, even if one were to challenge the notion that the acquisition of beliefs is neither voluntary nor comparable to acting—though the previous sections are meant to affirm those claims—nevertheless, the manner in which one understands those beliefs and acts upon them would still necessitate a voluntary process, which the person can aspire to improve so as to achieve his or her goals. This alone provides a place for intellectual virtue.

SITUATIONISM VERSUS DISPOSITIONISM

> *It is the glory of God to conceal a thing; but the glory of kings is to search out a matter.*[119]

After defending intellectual virtue against the challenges put forth by contemporary epistemology, I will now defend the notion of moral virtue against challenges put forth in contemporary philosophy and psychology. A major challenge to the existence of global character traits is the claim that the situation in which a person finds himself or herself is a greater indication of behavior than the character that he or she has developed. This view is called "situationism" because it claims that the situation, rather than the person's character, best predicts and explains how someone will act in a given circumstance. While this claim has been relatively resolved in psychology,[120] it still has a strong following in philosophy. Situationist philosophers primarily support their position through the findings of experiments such as the Milgram shock experiments,[121] the Good Samaritan study,[122] and the Stanford Prison Experiment.[123]

In philosophical circles, the two most prominent challengers to virtue ethics based on these experiments are Gilbert Harman and John Doris. Harman defines character traits as long-term, stable, and broad dispositions, and habits to act a certain way, both of which help to explain some of the things that a person does.[124] The fact that they are broad means they influence behavior across a wide range of circumstances.[125] Based on the results of these experiments, Harman claims that there is no empirical basis for the existence of character traits,[126] since these experiments empirically contradict the expectations that one would have for behavior if global character traits actually existed. Therefore, he argues, when we do use the notion of character to explain behavior, we commit attribution error.[127]

John Doris' challenge against the existence of global character traits rests on the explanatory and predictive aspects that such traits are meant to possess. According to Doris, the possession of global character traits should manifest consistent behavior across circumstances. Therefore, one should be able to explain a person's behavior if he or she recognized that the person possesses certain traits. Also, one who has this knowledge should be able to predict the person's behavior as well. The above experiments, however, disconfirm both expectations, and have thus disproved the existence of global character traits.[128] Doris does, however, argue that a person may possess local traits.

Some have responded that in denying the existence of global character traits, Harman and Doris have presupposed that people either fully possess certain traits or they do not possess them at all.[129] Moreover, they assume that most people are thought to fully possess certain traits. These assumptions ignore the idea that improving one's character is a lifelong process, and even when virtues are almost fully possessed they are never secure. There is always a possibility for failure. "For there is not a righteous man on earth, that does good and sins not."[130] Christian Miller has summarized this point eloquently:

> For it has rarely been part of the view [of virtue ethicists] that possession of a virtue is an all or nothing phenomenon; rather, it comes in degrees. In addition, acquiring a particular virtue is typically thought to be a very gradual process full of numerous setbacks. The life of progression to full virtue is one of continuous struggle in overcoming character defects and external obstacles. For the Plato of the *Republic*, true virtue can be achieved through participation in a long and demanding educational process out of which very few ever emerge successfully. Similarly for Aristotle, the virtues are traits that must be habituated in children and positively reinforced in adults over extended periods of time.[131]

The results of these experiments do not, therefore, disconfirm the existence of character traits; rather, they affirm that most people have not achieved full attainment of the virtues.

Another response to the situationist challenge is to amend Aristotle's theory of virtue in a way that supports Maimonides' theory. Aristotle argues for the unity of the virtues. If a person has one of them, then he or she has them all, and if a person possesses practical wisdom (*phronesis*), then he or she possesses all of the virtues as well. The unity of the virtues is a necessary component of the notion of virtues as excellences; a person cannot develop toward actualizing his or her potential without developing all aspects of his or her potential. Two corollaries derive from the unity of the virtues, namely the principle that true virtue cannot lead a person astray and the principle that the virtues are self-sufficient. Maimonides' theory of the virtues, on the other hand, does not accept the unity of the virtues, nor does it accept that the virtues alone are sufficient to live a moral life. For Maimonides, even the one who has perfected his or her nature must evaluate his or her actions continually for fear that he or she may incline toward an extreme.[132]

Similar to Maimonides' theory in not fully accepting an Aristotelian conception of the unity of the virtues, Neera Badhwar has argued that though the virtues are related to each other, they are not unified across all domains. Rather, she advocates for a limited unity of virtues, where virtues are united within domains, but not necessarily across them.[133] Badhwar's limited unity of the virtues also accepts that practical wisdom is necessary for virtue, yet it conceives of practical wisdom differently from Aristotle, since she claims that it is possible to possess practical wisdom in some areas of life but not in others.[134] A limited unity of the virtues and a disunity of practical wisdom thus allow for virtue ethics to speak of character, yet it admits that certain situations may have greater influence on behavior than others, especially in those areas where a person is not experienced.

Among psychologists there is a general consensus that having a theory of character traits and recognizing the challenge of situationism are not completely contradictory. Rather, a person's behavior in a given situation is a function of his or her character and the situation at hand.[135] In terms of how much influence either character or a situation has over behavior, it may be possible to see the two as being on the same spectrum, albeit at different ends. The less firmly one possesses the virtues, the more influenced by a situation a person will be,[136] and the more one possesses the virtues, the less influence a situation will have on a person. This does not mean that behavior is not, or should not be, contextually relevant for a situation; rather, it means that the person will choose the right response based on his or her virtuous disposition and not solely, or primarily, due to external pressure, whether it be conscious pressure or otherwise. Moreover, in terms of developing certain character traits, there are psychologists, such as Daniel Heller, Wei Elaine Perunovic, and Daniel Reichman, who propose that personality traits develop through the way situations influence behavior and experience, and therefore, social roles, and the situations they entail, can have strong effect on how a person's personality will develop.[137]

Given that behavior is affected by one's character and the situation in which one finds oneself, and if one accepts that the virtues are not unified and seldom fully developed except in the case of those rare fully moral individuals, the deleterious influence of a situation on moral behavior (and, in the long term, moral development) should be mitigated. While avoidance of morally questionable situations may allow for a person to escape the harm they may cause to one's moral development, it will certainly not guarantee positive moral growth. In my conception of Jewish ethics, the study and practice of Jewish law serves to "create" situations that have within them a distinctive organization of both the components of the situation and the psychological features of the person in the situation. Therefore, as a person learns and gains experience so as to understand that organization better, he or she will improve in responding appropriately. Intellectual engagement and experience will strengthen the relationship between character traits and behavior, since different situations will continually be seen to fit into an organizational structure, thereby mitigating the variability of situations and the situationist critique. In the section, "The 'Affect' of Love," I will provide an example of how Maimonides posits that the law is meant to influence a person's sentiments.

This view of the virtues, which is Maimonidean in the sense that it denies the necessary unity of the virtues and, thus, requires the law to direct a person in living a moral life, allows for a more efficacious view of moral improvement than Aristotle's (or those who uphold situationism and deny any ability for moral improvement). In his discussion of voluntariness and responsibility, Aristotle remarks that people who have become unjust and self-indulgent on their own accord are nevertheless voluntarily unjust and self-indulgent, even if they can no longer change their character.[138] The reason is because the person's voluntary choices led him or her to become this way. For Aristotle, the inability to change is not only due to the person's disposition; it is also a product of the improper development of practical wisdom. As Sara Broadie explains:

> Now if the vicious person comes to hate himself and his modes of practical
> acceptance, it does not follow that he knows in a practical way how else to

be or even how to begin to change. At the moments of choice and action he has no other moves to make, and no other ways of seeing and classifying his particular circumstances, than those which express the detested character.[139]

For Aristotle, a person's character is only plastic during the formative years of development. After a person has become habituated to a certain disposition, he or she will benefit or suffer from the consequences of a rigid, inflexible character.

On the other hand, Maimonides asserts that even if a person is wicked his whole life, he could still repent at the end of it and thus atone for all his transgressions.[140] Unlike in Aristotle's framework, in Maimonides' a person can still recognize another way to be, since correct action is not based on the development of practical wisdom but rather on the law.[141] Jonathan Jacobs explains:

> This is where the difference between the Maimonidean conception of the law and the Aristotelian conception of practical wisdom is particularly important. The Law includes strategies of repentance in a way that practical wisdom does not. That is, for Maimonides, one does not need personal resources of wisdom in order to find a way to restore one's soul. Such resources are given in the Law. In that sense, the individual, even a very bad one, is never altogether without guidance, and also need not rely solely on his or her own judgment of who is an example to emulate or learn from.[142]

Using an analogy between ethics and medicine, Alexander Broadie explains the difference as follows: "Maimonides' perspective is that of a doctor interested in restorative medicine, whereas Aristotle's perspective is that of a doctor interested in preventative medicine."[143] The reason for this difference in orientation is that for Maimonides the ethical mean is God's way,[144] and a person is already commanded to act according to the mean and thus be habituated in it.[145] Only when people stray from God's law do they suffer from excess or deficiency, and it is at that time that they would go to the wise person who, as a healer of the soul,[146] teaches them to return to the proper path.[147] Aristotle also uses a doctor analogy, yet never in the sense of restoring moral health, but rather only with respect to teaching people how to live a healthy life.[148] Because, for Aristotle, the mean is neither explicit nor as readily perceived as is the law, the ethical doctor must convey what to do solely based on his judgment of the particulars of each case so as to find the mean and maintain a lifestyle according to it.[149] One can therefore lose one's way on the path of moral development more easily and more permanently according to Aristotle's theory than for Maimonides.

NOTES

1. Daniel 1:4.
2. NE 1144b30-3.
3. Nicomachean Ethics 2.6.15.
4. I will use these three words interchangeably without making any significant or practical distinction between them. Rather, they will all have a connotation that relates to character.
5. Because virtue, both intellectual and moral, relates to a person's character, I am a proponent of "virtue responsibilism" rather than "virtue reliabilism," the latter of which conceives of virtue as a faculty. With respect to virtue epistemology, those in the "virtue responsibilism" camp are Jonathan Kvanvig, James Montmarquet, Linda Zagzebski, and Christopher Hookway. Those in the "virtue reliabilism" camp are John Greco, Alvin Goldman, and Ernest Sosa.
6. Though one may argue that the same definition could be used to define vice, the difference lies in the goals a person has and his or her reasons for having them. As such, a person could have the proper goals, yet not have the capabilities to be fully virtuous, or he or she can have excellent capabilities, yet uses them for fulfilling improper goals and thereby is vicious. As stated a few times already, this definition of vice and virtue is not relativistic since goals are external (albeit internalized) and grounded in the moral objectivity of the Divine will.
7. In order to make the analogy, I am assuming that there are no "glasses" or "contact lenses" or "laser surgery" for the virtues.
8. Jason Baehr lays out the differences between intellectual virtues and faculties, talents, temperaments, and skills, yet his distinctions apply to moral virtues as well. Faculties, talents, temperaments, and skills differ from virtues since the former fail to bear on the character of the person vis-à-vis his or her goal(s). Faculties, talents, and temperaments are natural, whereas skills and virtues are acquired. Faculties and talents can operate independent of personal agency, whereas virtues cannot. Temperaments are psychological, yet they do not have the same cognitive or orientation requirement

as does virtue. Skills do not have the same type of motivation and aspiration as does virtue. See *The Inquiring Mind*, 32.

9. EE 1220a5-13. For an insightful elucidation of Aristotle's distinction between intellectual and moral virtues, see Linda Zagzebski's *Virtues of the Mind*.

10. NE 139b15-16.

11. The idea that intellectual virtues are character traits is shared by Jason Baehr, who writes, "[I]nquiry has a robustly active dimension. It involves observing, imagining, reading, interpreting, reflecting, analyzing, assessing, formulating, and articulating. Success in these activities is hardly guaranteed by the possession of sharp vision, sensitive hearing, or an impeccable memory. Rather, it requires an exercise of certain intellectual character traits. It can require, for instance, that one engage in *attentive* observation, *thoughtful* or *open-minded* imagination, *patient* reflection, *careful* and *thorough* analysis, or *fair-minded* interpretation and assessment. As this suggests, inquiry makes substantial personal demands on inquirers. It demands an exercise of a range of 'intellectual character virtues'" (*The Inquiring Mind*, 1).

12. Exodus 12:2.

13. Each Hebrew word differs only by one letter from the original, and the mistaken letter bears some resemblance to the original letter.

14. BT Shabbat 147b.

15. For example, within the psychological literature upon which philosophical situationism is based, studies have tried to show that the helpfulness of people is correlated to weather, noise level, familiarity with the person to be helped, and whether the location is urban or rural, without any reference to the internal states of the person who is being helpful or not. For a few examples, see Cunningham, Michael R. "Weather, Mood, and Helping Behavior: Quasi Experiments with the Sunshine Samaritan." *Journal of Personality and Social Psychology*, Vol. 37, No. 11 (1979) 1947; Mathews, Kenneth E., and Lance K. Canon. "Environmental Noise Level as a Determinant of Helping Behavior." *Journal of Personality and Social* Psychology, Vol. 32, No. 4 (1975) 571; Shaffer, David R., Mary Rogle, and Clyde Hendrlck. "Intervention in the Library: The Effect of Increased Responsibility on Bystanders' Willingness to Prevent a Theft." *Journal of Applied Social Psychology*, Vol. 5, No. 4 (1975) 303–319; Gelfand, Donna M., et al. "Who Reports

shoplifters? A Field-Experimental Study." *Journal of Personality and Social Psychology*, Vol. 25, No. 2 (1973) 276.

16. Within the last ten years there has been a strong push in social psychology to re-examine the concept of a situation so as to find a universally acceptable taxonomy. See, for example, Reis, Harry T. "Reinvigorating the Concept of Situation in Social Psychology." *Personality and Social Psychology Review*, Vol. 12, No. 4 (2008) 311–329; Wagerman, Seth A., and David C. Funder. "Personality Psychology of Situations." Corr, Philip J., and Gerald Matthews, eds. *The Cambridge Handbook of Personality Psychology* (Cambridge University Press, 2009); Swann, William B., and Conor Seyle. "Personality Psychology's Comeback and Its Emerging Symbiosis with Social Psychology." *Personality and Social Psychology Bulletin*, Vol. 31, No. 2 (2005) 155–165.

17. Kristjan Kristjansson shows, through his examination of the different approaches to individuating experiences, "that people (and dictionaries!) understand the essence of situations to lie in affordances of human goals" (*Virtues and Vices in Positive Psychology*, 145).

18. Mischel, Walter, and Yuichi Shoda. "A Cognitive-Affective System Theory of Personality: Reconceptualizing Situations, Dispositions, Dynamics, and Invariance in Personality Structure." *Psychological Review*, Vol. 102, No. 2 (1995) 252. They continue later in the article, "The theory's most basic assumption, namely that the personality system is not made up of a set of isolated tendencies, factors, or components, but consists of a psychologically meaningful organization of relationships among cognitions and affects (Table 1, Figure 4), has clear implications for the study of personality: The relationships among the person's important encodings, beliefs, and expectations (e.g., about the self), the enduring goals pursued, the key strategies used, and the affects experienced, all in relation to relevant features of situations, become the terrain the personologist needs to map. The ultimate goal becomes to articulate the psychological structure that under- lies this organization within the personality system. The development of models to capture this organization becomes the theoretical challenge in the research agenda in particular content domains" (259).

19. A philosopher who relies on Mischel and Shoda to provide a theory if virtue as social intelligence is Nancy E. Snow. See her *Virtue as Social Intelligence: An Empirically Grounded Theory*.
20. For an informative analysis of what constitutes a "self," see Kristjan Kristjansson, *The Self and its Emotions*.
21. *Hilkhot Shabbat* 2:3.
22. Among those contemporary virtue theorists who also include orientation as a component of virtue is Jason Baehr, who writes, "My proposal, then, is that an intellectual virtue is a character trait that contributes to its possessor's personal intellectual worth on account of its involving a positive psychological orientation toward epistemic goals" (*The Inquiring Mind*, 102). See also Robert Adams in *A Theory of Virtue*, and Thomas Hurka in *Virtue, Vice, and Value* who discuss the requirement of being positively oriented with respect to moral virtue.
23. MN I:32. The Pardes has traditionally been understood as a mystical experience or as an intense metaphysical contemplation.
24. JT *Hagiga* 2:1.
25. For one example of Rabbi Akiva's view of the necessity to adhere to tradition, see BT *Berakhot* 61b, where he states that if it is dangerous to study Torah because of the Roman decree against it, neglecting it would be even worse, since Torah is one's life and the length of one's days. For another, see BT *Menahot* 29b, where Rabbi Akiva expounds many laws from Scripture and attributes them to Moses who received them at Sinai.
26. This should be distinguished from passive attention, which is the result of coming into contact with something one finds interesting. It is a product of prior association and attraction.
27. This notion of attention is the opposite of Simon Weil's. Simon Weil describes attention as a negative effort. Though deliberate and voluntary, it is not active in the sense that a person directly attends to something. As she describes it, "Attention consists of suspending our thought, leaving it detached, empty, and ready to be penetrated by the object; it means holding in our minds, within reach of this thought, but on a lower level and not in contact with it, the diverse knowledge we have acquired which we are forced to make use of. Our thought should be in relation to all particular and already formulated thoughts, as a man on a mountain who, as he looks forward, sees also below him, without actually looking at

them, a great many forests and plains. Above all our thought should be empty, waiting, not seeking anything, but ready to receive in its naked truth the object that is to penetrate it" (Simone Weil, *Waiting for God* (New York: Putnam, 1951) 62). Weil's view of attention is based on her emphasis on passivity and self-sacrifice. Through removing any notion of self that a person may have, Weil argues, he or she allows for the other to become manifest in his or her mind.

28. *Chovas HaTalmidim*, 209. Similarly, he writes, "The heartache that you feel and the consistency of your searching are dependent upon the way you look at things. Let's take the example of a rich person who lost his fortune. If he continues to view himself as a wealthy man, and he tells himself, 'I'm really a rich person!' then his thoughts will revolve around the fact that he's really supposed to be rich. He will constantly wonder: Why do other rich people have so much? What happened to all my ample and luxurious possessions? In this case, his state of affairs weighs very heavily on his heart, and he will never cease to look for ways in which he might be able, with God's help, to return to his former lifestyle. If he stops looking at himself as a rich person who lost his fortune, however, and starts viewing himself as a pauper like all the others, he will no longer continue to obsessively look for ways to reverse his situation. True, he will wish that he win the lottery or fall upon a fortune in some other way, but these wishes will remain just that— wishes and imagination. He won't, however, suffer heartache as a result, and he won't look for more than dry bread in a nice, warm basement" (Ibid. 235-7).

29. Martha Nussbaum, *Creating Capabilities: The Human Development Approach* (Cambridge: Harvard University Press, 2011) 95–96.

30. Proverbs 1:5.

31. The opposing critique against those who conceive of virtue as a function is that there are certain beliefs that a person can have whether or not he or she intellectually functions well. Linda Zagzebski gives as a pithy comparison that a delicious espresso produced by a well-functioning machine is just as delicious as one that came from a poorly, albeit working, machine.

32. I would not normally make such a stark distinction between the mind and the body, and only do so here to make the point clear even for those who do adopt this distinction.

33. For examples of this difference as it relates ritual slaughter and immersion in a mikveh, see Ira Bedzow, *Halakhic Man, Authentic Jew*, 128–129.

34. *The Inquiring Mind*, 208.

35. BT *Bava Batra* 12a.

36. See Yitzhak Hutner, *Pahad Yitzhak: Hanukah* (Brooklyn: Gur Aryeh Institute for Advanced Jewish Scholarship, 2003) 65–68.

37. Deuteronomy 13:1.

38. BT *Avoda Zara* 2:4.

39. For a few resources on this topic, see Niedenthal, Paula M., and Shinobu Ed Kitayama. *The Heart's Eye: Emotional Influences in Perception and Attention* (Academic Press, 1994); Jonathan R. Zadra and Gerald L. Clore, "Emotion and Perception: The Role of Affective Information," *Wiley Interdisciplinary Reviews: Cognitive Science*, Vol. 2, No. 6 (2011) 676–685; and Phelps, Elizabeth A., Sam Ling, and Marisa Carrasco. "Emotion Facilitates Perception and Potentiates the Perceptual Benefits of Attention", *Psychological Science*, Vol. 17, No. 4 (2006) 292–299.

40. For a few resources on this topic, see Damasio, Antonio. *Descartes' Error: Emotion, Reason, and the Human Brain* (Penguin, 2005); LeDoux, Joseph. *The Emotional Brain: The Mysterious Underpinnings of Emotional Life* (Simon and Schuster, 1998); and Panksepp, Jaak. *Affective Neuroscience: The Foundations of Human and Animal Emotions* (Oxford University Press, 1998).

41. For an in-depth analysis of the debate over whether action does in fact necessitate a belief component or not, please see "Rabbi Soloveitchik: Halakha as the Foundation of a Weltanschauung," in Ira Bedzow, *Halakhic Man, Authentic Jew*. For a discussion of those who disagree with the Maimonidean claim that belief is primary or necessary, see Menachem Kellner's *Must a Jew Believe Anything?*

See Kalonymus Kalman Shapira who writes, "Action without thought is ineffective, as is pure thought without the appropriate physical actions. (Kalmish E Kalonimus and Aharon Sorski, *Chovas Hatalmidim (The Students' Obligation) and Sheloshah Ma'amarim (Three Discourses)*" (Jerusalem: Feldheim, 2011, 421).

See also Rabbi Hayyim of Volozhin who writes, "And even if it's certain that regarding commandments too, the primary requirement for them is the act of doing, and the additional intention and purity of thought is not required for fulfilling [the commandment] in any way, as was explained above at the end of Gate 1 with certainty (with God's help), even so, he should join holiness and purity of thought to the primary act of doing, to arouse and cause even greater rectifications in the worlds than there would have been if the commandment was performed without attachment and holiness of thought." *Nefesh HaHayyim Shaar* 4, *Perek* 3; translation taken from Hayyim of Volozhin and Eliezer Lipa (Leonard) Moskowitz, *The Soul of Life: The Complete Neffesh Ha-chayyim* (Teaneck: New Davar Publications, 2012), 396.

42. This is supported by the following Talmudic passages:

> A favorite saying of Raba was: The goal of wisdom is repentance and good deeds, so that a man should not study Torah and Mishna and then despise his father and mother and teacher and his superior in wisdom and rank, as it says, "The fear of Hashem is the beginning of wisdom, a good understanding have all they that do thereafter." It does not say, "that do," but "that do thereafter" (BT *Berakhot* 17a)

> Rabbi Yosi said: Whosoever says that he has no [desire to study the] Torah, has no [reward for the study of the] Torah. Is not this obvious?—But [this must be the meaning]: Whosoever says that he has only [an interest in the study of the] Torah has only [reward for the study of the] Torah. This, however, is also obvious!—But [the meaning really is] that he has no [reward] even [for the study of the] Torah. What is the reason?—Rav Papa replied: Scripture said, "That you may learn them and observe to do them, whosoever is [engaged] in observance is [also regarded as engaged] in study, but whosoever is not [engaged] in observance is not [regarded as engaged] in study" (BT *Yevamot* 109b).

43. *Virtues of the Mind*, 256.

44. Samson Raphael Hirsch and Daniel Haberman, *The Hirsch Chumash: Shemos* (New York: Feldheim, 2000), 714.

45. "The Conflation of Moral and Epistemic Virtue," *Moral and Epistemic Virtues*, 114.

46. *Avot* 4:5.

47. BT *Avoda Zara* 17b.

48. *Sefer HaMitzvot*, positive commandment 11.

49. Ecclesiastes 8:1.

50. One strong proponent of the involuntary nature of belief is Richard Swinburne. In his book, *The Evolution of the Soul*, he writes, "Belief is a passive state; believing is a state in which you are, it is not a matter of you doing something. And it is an involuntary state, a state where you find yourself and which you cannot change at will" (Richard Swinburne, *The Evolution of the Soul* (Oxford: Clarendon Press, 1986) 126).

51. David Hume, *A Treatise of Human Nature* (New York: Barnes & Noble, Inc., 2005) 306.

52. David Hume, L.A. Selby-Bigge, and P.H. Nidditch, *Enquiries Concerning Human Understanding and Concerning the Principles of Morals*, 3d ed. (Oxford: Clarendon Press, 1975) 95.

53. David Hume, *A Treatise of Human Nature*, 79–85. See also what he writes in the Appendix, "Belief consists merely in a certain feeling or sentiment; in something that depends not on the will, but must arise from certain determinate causes and principles of which we are not masters" (624).

54. Not every modern philosopher held that the acquisition of belief was involuntary. For example, in the Fourth Meditation, Descartes contends that the will is unlimited and can affirm or deny any proposition, thus supporting the voluntary nature of belief. However, even though there were (and are) philosophers who contend that belief acquisition is voluntary, it is not (yet) the dominant position in contemporary epistemology.

55. Moses Mendelssohn and Allan Arkush, *Jerusalem, or, on Religious Power and Judaism* (Hanover: Published for Brandeis University Press by University Press of New England, 1983), 43.

56. John Locke, *A Letter Concerning Toleration* (Indianapolis: Hackett Publishing Company, 1983), 27. See, however, Locke's *Essay Concerning Human Understanding*, Book 2, Chapter 21, where he distinguishes between two types of thinking. Thinking as the power to receive ideas or thoughts from an external source is a passive power, yet thinking as the power to bring into view ideas at will, and to compare them, is an active power.

57. Locke's views on the inefficacy of the law to induce belief, however, were not universally held. Jonas Proast, an English High Church Anglican clergyman, challenged Locke's claim and argued that though coercion may not directly cause a change in a person's beliefs, it may nevertheless indirectly inculcate beliefs or at least

make a person receptive to them. Though secular contract theorists have sided with John Locke's view of the relationship between law and religion, John Witte and Thomas Arthur have shown that the Anglo-American doctrine regarding the purposes of criminal law and punishment developed analogously to Protestant theological doctrines regarding the pedagogical function of law in enhancing spiritual development. See John Witte and Thomas C. Arthur, "The Three Uses of the Law: A Protestant Source of the Purposes of Criminal Punishment?" *Journal of Law and Religion*, Vol. 10, No. 2(1994).

58. Maimonides writes that belief in the existence of God is a Torah commandment in his *Sefer HaMitzvot* (Positive Commandment #1), in *Hilkhot Yesode HaTorah* (1:6), in his commentary on the Mishna, and in the *Moreh Nevukhim* (II:33). Note, however, that in the *Sefer HaMitzvot* Maimonides uses the term "believe" yet in *Hilkhot Yesode HaTorah* he uses the term "know."

59. See his commentary on Exodus 20:2.

60. See Abravanel's commentary on Exodus 20:2; see also chapter 18 of *Rosh Amanah*. For more information on this debate, see Menachem Kellner, "Maimonides, Crescas, and Abravanel on Exod. 20: 2. A Medieval Jewish Exegetical Dispute," *The Jewish Quarterly Review*, Vol. 69, No. 3 (1979) 129–157; and the introduction to his translation of *Rosh Amanah* (*Principles of Faith: Rosh Amanah* (Fairleigh Dickenson University Press, 1982)).

61. Hasdai Crescas, Preface to *Or HaShem*, trans. Shlomo Fisher (Jerusalem, 1990) found at http://www.daat.ac.il/daat/vl/tohen.asp?id=153. Rabbi Crescas gives two other reasons for why belief in the existence of God could not be a commandment. One of them is based on a different exegetical methodology from that used by Maimonides. The other is that commandments are relational, meaning that a command cannot be imagined without a known commander. Therefore, when one puts forth belief in the existence of God as a commandment, he presupposes belief in the existence of God before knowing the command to believe in the existence of God, which is circular. Also, if he puts forth belief in the existence of God before the commandment to believe, it would necessitate that the commandment to believe in the existence of God be without purpose, since it is already done. Rabbi Crescas does not deny that belief in God is the foundation of observing the

Torah, since the Torah and its commandments must have come from an Author and a Commander. However, belief in the existence of God is prior to the acceptance of the commandments.

62. Rabbi Crescas' distinction between beliefs and actions with respect to will and choice is a bit more complicated, since he affirms determinism in a way that still allows for some form of free will. In a word, Rabbi Crescas contends that human actions are contingent per se, yet with respect to the causes that brought them about they are necessary. Free will exists by virtue of the fact that humans are ignorant of the causes by which they are affected. See Meyer Waxman, "The Philosophy of Don Hasdai Crescas: Chapter V," *The Jewish Quarterly Review*, New Series, Vol. 10, No. 1 (July 1919) 25–47.

63. Kellner, 22.

64. This question relates to the contemporary issue in epistemology regarding the value of knowledge over belief and epistemic evaluation. See Christopher Hookway, "Cognitive Virtues and Epistemic Evaluations," *International Journal of Philosophical Studies*, Vol. 2, No. 2, 211–227.

65. A.J. Ayer, "Freedom and Necessity," *Free Will*, ed. Gary Watson (New York: Oxford University Press, 1982) 15. Similarly, Roderick Chisholm argues that a person is responsible for an act, in that it was done voluntarily, if it was in his or her power to perform it; however, he contends that the power to perform entails a power not to have performed the act. Therefore, the existence of an external, or even internal, cause for which the person is not responsible yet which caused the deed to occur precludes the act from being considered voluntary (Roderick Chisholm, "Human Freedom and the Self," *Free Will*, 25). Peter Van Inwagen also notes that it is generally agreed that free will should be understood in terms of the power or ability of a person to act otherwise, or at least the belief that the agent could have acted otherwise. (See Peter Van Inwagen, "The Incompatibility of Free Will and Determinism," *Free Will*, 46–58.)

66. A.J. Ayer, "Freedom and Necessity," *Free Will*, 19. In the matter of human compulsion, Ayer contends that it need not be the case that another physically moves a person so that he or she does an action. It is enough for the other person to indirectly compel him or her. For example, he writes that if a man points a pistol at a person's

head, though the choice to disobey may be present, it may still be compulsion, especially if no reasonable person would choose to disobey. As we will see below, this contradicts the Jewish legal perspective of the relationship between freedom of action and constraint by indirect compulsion.

67. A.J. Ayer, "Freedom and Necessity," *Free Will*, 22.

68. Ayer justifies this contention by adopting Hume's theory that what we think of as causation is really only logical necessity or correlation, but is not in fact the case that one event is ultimately a cause for another.

69. Roderick Chisholm, "Human Freedom and the Self," *Free Will*, 28, 32. In making this claim, Chisholm distinguishes between a Hobbesian approach to human action and a Kantian approach. In a Hobbesian approach, if one knows what a person's beliefs and desires are, and how strong they are, and one knows the situation in which the person is and to what he or she is subjected, then one can logically deduce what the person will do. In a Kantian approach, on the other hand, and this is the approach that Chisholm adopts, there is no logical or necessary causal connection between wanting and doing. The Hobbesian approach is similar to the assumptions that Harman and Doris have for challenging the existence of global character traits, as will be discussed below.

70. In Frankfurt's language, the will is that which turns a second-order desire, which is a desire to desire a certain action, into a second-order volition. See Harry Frankfurt, "Freedom of the Will and the Concept of a Person," *Free Will*, 84.

Frankfurt admits that it is possible to have second-order desires without having second-order volitions. He calls such a person a "wanton" since he or she does not care about his or her will. This type of person completely abandons any consideration of the desirability of his or her desires and pursues whatever inclination is strongest at the moment. To distinguish a wanton from a person who wills, Frankfurt uses the example of an unwilling addict who hates his addiction versus an addict who does not care. The unwilling addict has conflicting first-order desires, and a second-order desire of desiring not to take drugs, which he wants to constitute as his will. Because, when taking the drug, the unwilling addict acts contrary to his second-order desire, Frankfurt contends that his will is not free. Yet his lack of free will is different from the wanton addict, since, as he is led solely by his first-order desires, he does not have a will which he desires nor a desire to have a different will. The case of the unwilling addict can be considered similar to Ayer's kleptomaniac. This analysis begs the question of whether the desire to make a second-order desire a volition is in fact a third-order desire, thus allowing for the possibility of an infinite regress. Frankfurt recognizes this possibility, yet counters that common sense ultimately provides a limit. Also, the class of wantons is broader than a class of addicts, since it also includes animals and very young children, who only have first-order desires.

71. Gary Watson has a similar notion of freedom in that he argues that actions are unfree when a person is unable to get what he or she wants most, and that the inability is due to his or her own will. Therefore, it is not the choice of actions which provides the possibility of freedom, but rather whether one's desires and one's values are the same. If there is a source of motivation that is independent of a person's set of values, then he or she may be motivated to act contrary to what he or she deems worth doing. See Gary Watson, "Free Agency," *Free Will*, 96–110.

72. See Harry Frankfurt, "Alternate Possibilities and Moral Responsibility," *Journal of Philosophy*, Vol. LXVI, No. 23 (December 4, 1969).

73. BT *Bava Batra* 47b-48a. See BT *Yevamot* 106a; BT *Arakhin* 21a; BT *Rosh HaShana* 6a. See also BT *Kiddushin* 50a, where it discusses explicitly that the person must state that he is willing and cannot only stipulate it mentally, since mental affirmations are not recognized to reveal intent unless there is a strong presumption that the person acts on an internal will (Rabbi Hananel).

74. BT *Bava Batra* 48a, s.v. *ileima miha d'tanya*.

75. *Hilkhot Gerushin* 2:20. For this reason, coercion by the court must be required by the law and according to the law; otherwise, it will be seen as simple compulsion.

76. Book Four, Chapter Seven of the *Social Contract*.

77. Due to the second reason, a coerced present, just as an unauthorized coerced divorce, would not be considered effectuated. See *Shulhan Arukh, Hoshen Mishpat* 205:2.

78. See Isaiah Berlin, *Four Essays on Liberty* (London: Oxford University Press, 1969), and Charles Taylor, "What's Wrong with Negative Liberty," *Law and Morality: Readings in Legal Philosophy*, eds.

David Dyzenhaus, Moreau S. Reibetanz, and Arthur Ripstein (Toronto: University of Toronto Press, 2007) 359–368.

79. This depiction of belief acquisition as voluntary is based on a motivational virtue epistemology. Motivational theories deny that belief is caused by the evidence to which one is confronted; rather, the causal route is by way of intellectual virtues. However, virtue theories can also be reductive in the sense that the content of belief is still justified on its own accord, and thus they still have a causal component, yet they also allow for intellectual virtues to contribute to the proper understanding of justification. Jonathan Kvanvig provides a good explanation of the different types of virtue epistemology in his book, *Intellectual Virtues and the Life of the Mind*.

80. Jonathan Kvanvig, *The Value of Knowledge and the Pursuit of Understanding*, 96.

81. See Linda Zagzebski, "Must Knowers be Agents?" *Virtue Epistemology: Essays on Epistemic Virtue and Responsibility*, eds. Abrol Fairweather and Linda Zagzebski (New York: Oxford University Press, 2001) 144.

82. Ernest Sosa, *A Virtue Epistemology* (Oxford: Oxford University Press, 2007) 22–24.

83. Ernest Sosa, "Reliabilism and Intellectual Virtue," *Knowledge in Perspective* (Cambridge: Cambridge University Press, 1991) 246. Sosa's view has the benefit of conceiving beliefs as a form of action or performance, yet his concept of virtue is that a virtue is a faculty or a function rather than the excellence of a faculty or a function. It is closer to Plato's view, as found in *Gorgias* and *Republic*, of virtue as *techne*, than it is of Aristotle's view of virtue as *arête*.

84. Ernest Sosa, "Intellectual Virtue in Perspective," *Knowledge in Perspective* (Cambridge: Cambridge University Press, 1991) 284–289.

85. John Greco, "Virtues and Vices of Virtue Epistemology," *Epistemology: An Anthology*, eds. Matthew McGrath, Ernest Sosa, and Jaegwon Kim Matthew (Blackwell Publishing, 2008) 454.

86. John Greco, *Achieving Knowledge* (Cambridge: Cambridge University Press, 2009) 3.

87. A normative etiological cognitive rule in deontological epistemology would be the epistemological equivalent of Kant's moral imperative. It is a rule that is the motivating cause for the person's thinking.

88. John Greco, *Achieving Knowledge*, 42–46. For my theory of Jewish ethics, those standards would be found in Jewish law and the Jewish tradition.
89. Another theorist who discusses belief in language that is usually reserved for action and uses analogies to sports is Wayne Riggs; see his "Reliability and the Value of Knowledge," *Philosophy and Phenomenological Research*, Vol. 64 (January 2002).
90. This idea is based on the following Talmudic passage: Antoninus said to Rabbi: The body and the soul can both free themselves from judgment. Thus, the body can plead: The soul has sinned, [the proof being] that from the day it left me I lie like a dumb stone in the grave [powerless to do aught]. Whilst the soul can say: The body has sinned, [the proof being] that from the day I departed from it I fly about in the air like a bird [and commit no sin]. He [Rabbi] replied: I will tell thee a parable. To what may this be compared? To a human king who owned a beautiful orchard which contained splendid figs. Now, he appointed two watchmen therein, one lame and the other blind. [One day] the lame man said to the blind, "I see beautiful figs in the orchard. Come and take me upon thy shoulder, that we may procure and eat them." So the lame bestrode the blind, procured and ate them. Some time after, the owner of the orchard came and inquired of them, "Where are those beautiful figs?" The lame man replied, "Have I then feet to walk with?" The blind man replied, "Have I then eyes to see with?" What did he do? He placed the lame upon the blind and judged them together. So will the Holy One, blessed be He, bring the soul, [re]place it in the body, and judge them together, as it is written, "He shall call to the heavens from above, and to the earth, that he may judge his people": "He shall call to the heavens from above"—this refers to the soul; "and to the earth, that he may judge his people"—to the body (BT *Sanhedrin* 91a-b).
91. Alvin Plantinga, *Warrant and Proper Function* (Oxford: Oxford University Press, 1993) 194.
92. Ernest Sosa, "Proper Functioning and Virtue Epistemology," *Warrant in Contemporary Epistemology: Essays in Honor of Plantinga's Theory of Knowledge*, eds. Alvin Plantinga and Jonathan L. Kvanvig (Lanham: Rowman & Littlefield Publishers, 1996) 268.

93. Alvin Plantinga, "Respondeo," *Warrant in Contemporary Epistemology: Essays in Honor of Plantinga's Theory of Knowledge,* eds. Alvin Plantinga and Jonathan L. Kvanvig (Lanham: Rowman & Littlefield Publishers, 1996) 368.

94. This notion of agency is similar to Christine Korsgaard's interpretation of autonomy as reflective endorsement. See her *Sources of Normativity* (Cambridge: Cambridge University Press, 1996).

95. Linda Zagzebski, "Must Knowers Be Agents?" *Virtue Epistemology: Essays on Epistemic Virtue and Responsibility,* eds. Abrol Fairweather and Linda Zagzebski (Oxford: Oxford University Press, 2001) 155.

96. Ernest Sosa considers virtue a faculty, while Linda Zagzebski considers it the excellence of a faculty.

97. *Nefesh HaHayyim, Shaar* 1, *Perek* 15, 17; *Shaar* 2, *Perek* 16, and other places.

98. Hayyim Volozhiner and Chanoch Levi, *Ruach Chayim: Rav Chaim Volozhiner's Classic Commentary on Pirke Avos* (Southfield, MI: Targum, 2002) 254. See also, *Nefesh HaHayyim, Shaar* 1, *Perek* 14 for another use of the eye analogy.

99. *Nefesh HaHayyim, Sha'ar* 4, *Perek* 28.

100. Ibid. *Shaar* 4, *Perek* 24.

101. Job 32:8.

102. Genesis 2:7.

103. *Nefesh HaHayyim, Shaar* 2, *Perek* 17.

104. Shneur Zalman of Liadi, Nissan Mindel, Nissen Mangel, Zalman I. Posner, and Jacob I. Schochet, *Likuṭe Amarim: Tanya* (London: "Kehot" Publication Society by the Soncino Press, 1973) 17.

105. Ibid. 11.

106. BT *Nidda* 30b.

107. *MishnaAvot* 2:13.

108. Yet there is one caveat, "For in order to change his habitual nature, he must arouse the love of God by means of meditation in his mind on the greatness of God, in order to gain mastery over the nature that is in the left part [of the heart] which is full of blood of the animal soul (*nefesh behemit*) originating in the *kelipah,* whence comes his nature. This is a perfect service for a *benoni.* Or, he must awaken the hidden love in his heart to control, through it, the nature that is in the left part, for this, too, is called service— the waging of war against his nature and inclination, by means of

exciting the love that is hidden in his heart" (*Liḵuṭe Amarim: Tanya*, 65-6).

109. Rabbi Shneur Zalman's understanding of free will and choice, and the meaning of righteousness and wickedness, can be reconciled with Maimonides' statements in *Hilkhot Teshuva* by claiming that Maimonides refers to situations of Divine judgment and not the essence of a person (see *Liḵuṭe Amarim: Tanya*, Chapter 1).

110. Linda T. Zagzebski, *Virtues of the Mind: An Inquiry into the Nature of Virtue and the Ethical Foundations of Knowledge* (New York: Cambridge University Press, 1996) 26.

111. *The Value of Knowledge and the Pursuit of Understanding* (Cambridge: Cambridge University Press, 2003) 193.

112. "Understanding 'Virtue' and the Virtue of Understanding," *Intellectual Virtue: Perspectives from Ethics and Epistemology*, eds. Michael DePaul and Linda Zagzebski (New York: Oxford University Press, 2003) 217.

113. See Zagzebski who writes that "wisdom is an epistemic value qualitatively different from the piling up of beliefs that have the property of justification, warrant, or certainty. Wisdom is neither a matter of the properties of propositional beliefs, nor is it a matter of the relations among such beliefs; it is a matter of grasping the whole of reality" (*Virtues of the Mind*, 50).

114. Verbs in the *kal*, or *pa'al*, form are in the active voice, and can be either transitive or intransitive.

115. Samson Raphael Hirsch, *The Hirsch Chumash: Bereshis* (New York: Feldheim, 2000) 760.

116. Ibid. 99–100, 643.

117. BT *Tamid* 32a.

118. *Mishna Avot* 2:13. It is fitting that Rabbi Shimon is the one to have repeated this definition, since he was known as a person who feared sin. Also, this answer is different than Ben Zoma's answer to the question, yet I believe that the Sages' answer is a better definition for who is wise than Ben Zoma's. The reason is as follows:

With respect to the question, "Who is called wise?" Ben Zoma answers "He who learns from all people," and as support, he cites the verse, "From all my teachers I have grown intelligent." The difficulty in understanding this proof text is twofold. First, there are verses in the Bible that use the word for "wisdom" and that give the same message of learning from others. For example:

- "The way of a fool is straight in his own eyes; but he that is wise hearkens unto counsel" (Proverbs 12:15).
- "Hear instruction, and be wise, and refuse it not" (Proverbs 8:30).
- "When the scorner is punished, the thoughtless is made wise; and when the wise is instructed, he receives "knowledge" (Proverbs 21:11).

The second difficulty with Ben Zoma's choice of proof text is that there are many verses in the Bible which provide a description of what constitutes as wise man, such as "The wise in heart is called a man of discernment; and the sweetness of the lips increases learning" (Proverbs 16:21). There are also many verses in the Bible which give suggestion as to how one can acquire wisdom. In fact, the verse that immediately precedes the one that Ben Zoma cites does just that! "Your commandments make me wiser than my enemies: for they are ever with me" (Psalms 119:98). Therefore, it seems that Ben Zoma conflates intelligence and wisdom, contrary to the view of the Sages.

119. Proverbs 25:2.
120. In psychology, the situation-disposition debate started with Walter Mischel's book, *Personality and Assessment*, which challenged the assumption that there were general consistencies in a person's behavior. Mischel's book sparked an incredible literature over whether the situation or a person's character determines behavior. However, the contemporary consensus is that behavior is a function of both personality and situation.
121. In the Milgram shock experiments, people were told to give electric shocks to another person at progressively higher voltages. The experiment was designed to determine to what extent people will obey orders even when they believe that doing so would hurt another person and/or be immoral. It was originally expected that only a small fraction of subjects would give a shock of maximum voltage to another person, yet, contrary to predictions, the experiments showed that over half of the subjects gave, albeit uncomfortably, another person a shock of maximum voltage. See Stanley Milgram, *Obedience to Authority: An Experimental View* (Harper Perennial Modern Classics, 2009).
122. In the Good Samaritan study, seminary students thought they were participating in a study on religious education. They would

begin the "study" in one building and were then told to go to another so as to continue. The experimenters would vary the degree of urgency to get to the second building, either by telling them that they were already late or that they still had a few minutes to get there. They would also vary the tasks the students had to perform when they got there. Some students were asked to prepare a talk about seminary jobs; others were asked to give a sermon about the story of the Good Samaritan. On the way to the second building, the seminary students would see a man slumped in an alleyway. The study showed that the amount of time which the person had to get to the second building influenced whether he or she stopped, while the content of the talk had very little influence. See John M. Darley and C. Daniel Batson, "From Jerusalem to Jericho: A study of Situational and Dispositional Variables in Helping Behavior," *Journal of Personality and Social Psychology*, Vol. 27, 100–108.

123. The Stanford prison experiment was designed to test the psychological effects of becoming either a prisoner or a prison guard. Though the experiment was supposed to last two weeks, it had to be cut short since the participants exceeded any expectation in conforming to their respective roles. Student guards enforced authoritarian measures and even subjected some of the prisoners to psychological torture. Many of the student prisoners passively accepted psychological abuse and readily harassed other prisoners at the behest of the guards. See Philip G. Zimbardo, *Stanford Prison Experiment* (Stanford University, 1971).

124. Gilbert Harman, "Moral Psychology Meets Social Psychology," *Proceedings of the Aristotelian Society*, Vol. XCIX (1999) 316–318.

125. This is to be distinguished from local character traits, which influence behavior when in a narrowly defined set of circumstances. The difference between the global and local character trait of honesty would be if one were always honest versus one who is always honest with his or her family.

126. Harman, "Moral Psychology Meets Social Psychology," 316.

127. In explaining the Milgram experiment, Harman argues that one cannot attribute a character flaw to those people who administered the dangerous shock, since too many people gave the shock to another person. Rather, because most people do not have the disposition to hurt others, it must be that the situation, and not

people's character, prompted them to act (See Harman, "Moral Psychology Meets Social Psychology," 322). Harman drew the same conclusion from the Good Samaritan study. One would have expected seminarians speaking on the story of the Good Samaritan to act like one, as its moral would have been on their minds, yet only the urgency of the situation had any effect on the person's behavior. Because people commit attribution errors in explaining people's behavior, these experiments, Harman contends, show that the belief in the existence of character traits rests on nothing but a fallacy.

128. John Doris, "Persons, Situations, and Virtue Ethics," *Nous*, Vol. 32, No. 4 (2002) 505–510.

129. See Joel Kupperman, "The Indispensability of Character," *Philosophy*, Vol. 76, 239–250, who writes that Harman makes two fundamental flaws in his argument, he assumes that a character trait is either perfect or non-existent, and he assumes that there is only one correct response or action for every virtuous person in a given situation.

130. Ecclesiastes 7:20.

131. Christian Miller, "Social Psychology and Virtue Ethics," *The Journal of Ethics*, Vol. 7, No. 4 (2003) 378.

132. "Similarly, the perfect man needs to inspect his moral habits continually, weigh his actions, and reflect upon the state of his soul every single day. Whenever he sees his soul inclining towards one of the extremes, he should rush to cure it and not let the evil state become established by the repetition of a bad action." *Shemona Perakim*, Chapter Four; translation from Moses Maimonides, Raymond L. Weiss, and Charles E. Butterworth, *Ethical Writings of Maimonides* (New York: Dover Publications, 1983) 73.

133. Neera K. Badhwar, "The Limited Unity of Virtue." *Noús*, Vol. 30, No. 3 (1996) 307. This is not the same as local character traits, for which Doris advocates, since it refers to the combination of traits and not individual traits, yet it is not so far away from a theory of localized dispositions.

134. The reason for Badhwar's disagreement with Aristotle is that, for Aristotle, practical wisdom requires knowledge of particulars and not only of universals, yet, Badhwar argues, no one can have the amount of experience that Aristotle requires so that his or her practical wisdom can envisage the unity of a person's whole life in

all its particulars. Most people have experience in a few areas, or even if they have experience in many areas, their lack of what is required by Aristotle makes practical wisdom impossible. Therefore, it would be more productive to construct a modified conception of practical wisdom, which allows for its disunity but also for its existence. See Neera K. Badhwar, "The Limited Unity of Virtue," 315.

135. David C. Funder, "Persons, Behaviors and Situations: An Agenda for Personality Psychology in the Postwar Era," *Journal of Research in Personality*, Vol. 43 (2009), 120–126. Two theories that conceptualize the relationship between personality and situation in a way that allows for general traits are "Cognitive-Affective Processing System (CAPS)" and "The Density Distributions Approach." According to CAPS, behavior is determined by stable "if-then" relationships. As long as the if-then relationship is constant, then so will behavior be consistent. When the relationship changes, such as in a different situation, then behavior will change as well. According to The Density Distributions Approach, traits entail a range of responses and not a particular response. Therefore, variability in behavior across situations may still be within a consistent range. See Mischel, Walter, and Yuichi Shoda. "A Cognitive-Affective System Theory of Personality: Reconceptualizing Situations, Dispositions, Dynamics, and Invariance in Personality Structure." *Psychological Review*, Vol. 102, No. 2 (1995) 246; and Fleeson, William. "Toward a Structure-and Process-Integrated View of Personality: Traits as Density Distributions of States", *Journal of Personality and Social Psychology*, Vol. 80, No. 6 (2001) 1011.

136. This statement itself needs further study, since how a person responds to a situation depends on how he or she interprets it. What features of the situation are considered relevant, how different aspects of a situation relate to each other, and which impulses in the person the situation affects all depend on how a person focuses his or her attention, the dispositional traits he or she already possesses and in what degree, and how the situation is considered in light of past situations and views of the future. Therefore, it can never be that the situation alone influences behavior, though situations like the Milgram shock experiments and the Good

Samaritan study may reveal how strong a person's virtuous character must be so as to behave properly.

137. See "The Future of Person–Situation Integration in the Interface Between Traits and Goals: A Bottom-Up Framework," *Journal of Research in Personality*, Vol. 43, No. 2 (April 2009), 171–178.

138. NE1114a20-22.

139. Sara Broadie, *Ethics with Aristotle*, 161.

140. *Hilkhot Teshuva* 1:3.

141. "It is manifest that repentance also belongs to this class, I mean to the opinions without the belief in which the existence of individuals professing a law cannot be well ordered. For an individual cannot but sin and err, either through ignorance—by professing an opinion or a moral quality that is not preferable in truth—or else because he is overcome by desire or anger. If then the individual believed that this fracture can never be remedied, he would persist in his error and sometimes perhaps disobey even more because of the fact that no stratagem remains at his disposal. If, however, he believes in repentance, he can correct himself and return to a better and more perfect state than the one he was in before he sinned. For this reason there are many actions that are meant to establish this correct and very useful opinion, I mean the confessions, the sacrifices in expiation of negligence and also of certain sins committed intentionally, and the fasts. The general characteristic of repentance from any sin consists in one's being divested of it. And this is the purpose of this opinion. Thus the utility of all these things become manifest" (MNIII:36; Pines, 540).

142. Jonathan Jacobs, "Plasticity and Perfection: Maimonides and Aristotle on Character," *Religious Studies*, Vol. 3, No. 4 (December 1997) 499.

143. Broadie does not intend to imply that Aristotle did not have a model of restorative medicine as part of his ethics, only that it played a minor role, whereas for Maimonides it played a major role while the model of preventative medicine played a minor one. See Alexander Broadie, "Medical Categories in Maimonidean Ethics," *Moses Maimonides: Physician, Scientist, and Philosopher*, eds. Fred Rosner and Samuel Kottek (Northvale: Jason Aronson, Inc., 1993) 119.

144. *Hilkhot Deot* 1:5.

145. *Hilkhot Deot* 1:7.

146. Maimonides uses an explicit analogy comparing the physically ill to the morally ill, and he often discusses the case where someone has slid from a virtuous state to a vicious state. See Alexander Broadie, "Medical Categories in Maimonidean Ethics," *MosesMaimonides: Physician, Scientist, and Philosopher*, eds. Fred Rosner and Samuel S. Kottek (Northvale: Jason Aronson, 1993) 125–126.

147. *Hilkhot Deot* 2:1. See also MN III:49; Pines 605, 612.

148. NE 1097a11-13; NE 1102a21; NE 1105b14-16; NE 1114a16; NE 1174b25-6; NE 1180b33. For an explicit recognition of both aspects of the medicine analogy applied to God and His commandments, see Rashi's comment of the verse, "And He said, 'If you hearken to the voice of Hashem, your God, and you do what is proper in His eyes, and you listen closely to His commandments and observe all His statutes, all the sicknesses that I have visited upon Egypt I will not visit upon you, for I, Hashem, heal you (are your physician)" (Exodus 15:26). Rashi comments, "And if I do bring [sickness upon you], it is as if it has not been brought, 'for I, Hashem, heal you.' This is its midrashic interpretation. According to its simple meaning, [we explain:] 'for I, Hashem, am your Physician' and [I] teach you the Torah and the commandments in order that you be saved from them [illnesses], like this physician who says to a person, 'Do not eat things that will cause you to relapse into the grip of illness.' This [warning] refers to listening closely to the commandments, and so [Scripture] says: 'It shall be healing for your navel. (Prov. 3:8).'"

149. As Alexander Broadie notes, "For Aristotle, the doctrine of the mean enables him to provide a conceptual framework within which he can present a program of upbringing for the young. They are to be trained to be good citizens, and mistakes dare not be made in the training, for the outcome of the training is *hexis*, a character trait which is so fixed as to be hardly alterable. In Aristotle's view, the acquisition of a virtuous character, as of a vicious one, is the acquisition of a second nature, an abiding state. This is not to say that, for Aristotle, a person cannot lose his virtuous state or rise above his previously vicious one. It is to stress the degree of fixedness of the state acquired by the initial training. For Maimonides, on the other hand, conceptualizing virtue as a mean implies a perspective from which virtue presents itself as achievable by therapeutic methods" ("Medical Categories in Maimonidean Ethics," 125).

CHAPTER 9

Moral Motivation and *Shlemut*

RECOGNITION OF NON-VIRTUOUS REASONS

Should he reason with unprofitable talk, or with speeches wherewith he can do no good?[1]

Up to this point, we have discussed how practical reasoning enables a person to recognize and respond to reasons. We have also discussed how the virtues play an essential part in the process of recognizing reasons and evaluating which reasons should be accepted as normative. However, we have not yet explained how, after recognizing a reason to act and accepting its normativity, a person becomes motivated to act upon it. We must also explain how motivation influences deliberation. In this chapter I will first discuss whether the virtuous person can recognize non-virtuous reasons, whether a virtuous person's reasons for acting are intrinsic or extrinsic, and whether his or her motivation is internal or external. I will then explain the difference between a continent person and one who has attained *Shlemut*.

John McDowell argues that a virtuous person does not have temptation; his or her perception of a situation disallows competing motivations. In other words, the virtuous person does not recognize reasons to act non-virtuously.[2] If that were the case, however, the virtuous person would not be able to empathize with others who act in a non-virtuous manner, or with those who sin, so as to be able to rebuke them. Similarly, a virtuous person could not serve as a judge of a community, since he would not see the non-virtuous as rational. With respect to the need for empathy in

© The Author(s) 2017
I. Bedzow, *Maimonides for Moderns*,
DOI 10.1007/978-3-319-44573-1_9

order to rebuke a person, though it is a commandment to rebuke one's fellow if and when he sees his fellow sinning or going down the wrong path,[3] the obligation to rebuke is contingent on the person's ability to do so effectively.[4] If a person is able to understand the sinner's reasoning and motivation, so that he can rebuke him in a way that will persuade him of the error of his ways and will lead him to repent, then one must do so. However, as is succinctly put by Rabbi Yehiel Michael Epstein, "Just as a person has an obligation to say something that can be heard, so does he have an obligation to not say something that won't, as it states [in Proverbs 9:8,] 'Reprove not a scorner, lest he hate you; [reprove a wise man, and he will love you.]'"[5] The virtuous person must be able to see the sinner's reasons to act as reasons, and as Rabbi Epstein notes, the sinner must be able to see why his reasons for acting were incorrect for rebuke to be effective. With respect to dispensing judgment, if a scholar states that he has a plausible reason to exonerate a person who is on trial, he joins the Sanhedrin.[6] The scholar, however, is not a simple rabbinical student, since in order to be qualified to be a judge, one must possess the highest level of righteousness, and he must have wisdom and understanding in both Torah and secular matters.[7] Nevertheless, this virtuous person can understand reasons for the defendant's questionable actions so as to exonerate him. Of course, the scholar may be incorrect in terms of the reasons he offers to show that the defendant's actions are non-culpable, and it still may be concluded that the person committed a transgression. Yet the appointment of the scholar to the Sanhedrin demonstrates that the virtuous person can recognize a range of reasons to act, even if he cannot accept them as reasons *for him* to act or because they are not sufficiently dispositive all things considered. Unlike McDowell's virtuous person, one who has attained *Shlemut* recognizes alternative reasons for acting, but he or she prioritizes them in such a way as to be motivated to respond according to the alternative which most closely aligns with his or her goals and the appropriate methods to attain them.[8] This is not to say that the virtuous person must recognize other reasons; it only means that he or she can.

In recognizing reasons for the sinner's actions, the rebuker and the judge consider the sinner to be rational, yet to be a bad reasoner. If it were the case that the virtuous person could not recognize the sinner's reasons for acting, then he or she could not hold him or her accountable for them. The sinner would be seen as irrational and thus outside the realm of halakhic jurisdiction.

Furthermore, in being able to recognize alternatives that are contrary to the law, the virtuous person is always at risk of being tempted to sin when his or her will is weak, thus affecting the person's capacity to reason and to be motivated by proper reasons, "For there is not a righteous man upon earth that does good and sins not."[9] However, this risk is mitigated by the fact that the motivation to perform an action is not based simply on a function of the number of alternatives a person recognizes. Each alternative recognized has a level of normativity associated with it, and the person has a corresponding level of motivation to pursue it, which is based on his or her evaluation of the alternative's reasonableness.[10]

Intrinsic or Extrinsic Reasons

I turned about, and applied my heart to know and to search out, and to seek wisdom and the reason of things…[11]

We have seen above that normativity lies in reasons. Now, we will examine how motivation lies in the reasoner and in how he or she relates to those reasons. Julia Annas is one of many virtue theorists who have argued that a person's motivation to perform moral acts is intrinsic, which implies that the activity is experienced as being its own end. In fact, this idea has its roots in Aristotle's conception of *eudaimonia*, which is sought for its own sake and not for the sake of something else. She also contends that while engaging in the activity, the person is not conscious of his or her self, but rather is in a state of "flow."[12] Annas discounts the idea that virtuous people act for the sake of fulfilling an obligation or to effect good consequences with the following argument: In the case of a brave person who saves another, it would not be virtuous if he or she were to respond to another's needs because he or she resolved to perform it or because he or she wanted to be the type of person who responds bravely. If that were the case, then the virtuous person thinks about others only through his or her own aims and objectives, which she contends is an unacceptable way to conceive of virtue.[13] On the contrary, Annas argues, "Someone who is, as we say, truly or really brave, the mature brave person, will respond to the other person's need for rescue without having to work out what a brave person would do, or what would be a brave action here."[14] In her conception, the brave person responds directly in a similar way as someone who has developed a practical skill responds when the situation calls for that skill to be put to action.

In making this argument, Annas seems to be conflating two issues, namely the knowledge of how to respond properly and one's intention for responding. In knowing how to respond, the virtuous person acts immediately, without thinking about how to act, whether it is an obligation to do so, or if he or she even wants to act in such a manner. If a person responds in action, then it is a given that the person knows that he or she should act and that he or she wants to do so as well. What makes an act stem from virtue, on the other hand, is in having the proper answer to the question, "Am I acting because it is a commandment and because I want to fulfill God's will or not?"[15] To use Annas' example, to act from virtue requires not only that a person has the ability and disposition to act bravely (knowing how to act) but one must also be brave for the right reasons (intention). As discussed in the section on reasoning, the right reason does not only include the belief that the action is appropriate for the situation; it must also include the normative fact that God's will demands it. Motivation, therefore, cannot be, as Annas contends, the feeling that a particular action is enjoyable;[16] one must be motivated to act as a servant of God. For example, with respect to learning Torah, Rabbi Ovadia Yosef writes that one who learns (Torah in fulfillment of a command) and is happy (*sameach*) in his learning fulfills the commandment to learn Torah *lishma*. If, however, a person learns for his own pleasure (*oneg*),[17] it is considered *shelo lishma*.[18] This is not to say that the person must overcome inclinations to act to the contrary; rather, it only means that he or she must respond to the correct reasons for action, whether he or she recognizes reasons to the contrary or not. Though Annas is correct in saying that "it is the mark of the mature virtuous person that her actions are not motivated by thoughts that are routed through thoughts of the self,"[19] that does not mean that her actions are not motivated by reasons that include more than an evaluation of one's pleasure in engaging in the activity. Lorraine Besser-Jones remarks:

> We must thus acknowledge that the distinctive mark of the mature virtuous person—that which she cannot be considered virtuous without—is not the interest, enjoyment or pleasure that she takes in the exercise of virtue, and that there is no meaningful purpose to be had by idealizing her experience to include this facet. Instead, we ought to understand her in terms of her commitment to virtue.[20]

In a slightly different manner from the way than Besser-Jones describes it, I would say that in conceiving of virtue in terms of commitment, one must distinguish between virtues and values. Values are the priorities that a tradition imparts to its adherents; virtues, on the other hand, are the capabilities that the adherents develop so that those values can be adopted and can be reflected in their behavior. Values, which are embedded within normative reasons and their recognition, are a source of motivation for acting; virtues provide the ability to recognize and respond to reasons and their values appropriately.

One could imagine, however, that Annas' conceptualization of virtuous activity as "flow" could aptly apply to how a virtuous person continues to engage in an activity, rather than in describing how he or she is motivated to become engaged in an activity. For example, there is a principle in Jewish law that one who is engaged in performing a commandment is exempt from performing other commandments during that time.[21] The reason for this exemption is that when a person is engrossed in performing a commandment, interrupting one's engagement to pursue another command will detract from one's focus and ability to fulfill the demands of the first. Therefore, in order to allow for the proper performance of the task at hand, one is exempt from considering other demands so that he or she can reach a state of "flow" in attending to the present concern.[22] Another way to look at Annas' conceptualization is as follows: Ola Svenson identifies four different types of decisions. The first type consists of those decisions that include repeated, automatic responses, habits, and those decisions which have no direct reference to values or goals. Those decisions are not reflexes; they are decisions about which a person previously deliberated vis-à-vis certain goals, yet the choices have become more natural and the deliberation more unselfconscious due to his or her experiences.[23] Annas' description of the virtuous person's intrinsic motivation to act could actually be a case where the person's motivation has become an unselfconscious, continuing reliance on previous decisions.[24]

A difficulty that one finds in discussing motivation vis-à-vis goals is that oftentimes both words are defined in terms of an ideal state. For example, Ken Gilhooly and Evridiki Fioratou accept as given that goals are internal representations of internal states and that motives are considerations that excite a person to reach that state.[25] With these conceptions of goals and motivation, intrinsic motivation is seen to be more important in creative problem solving, and extrinsic motivation is at best enabling and at worst detrimental to achieving one's goals.[26] From the perspective of a contemporary Jewish virtue ethics, however, goals are not states to be achieved; rather, they are value-laden activities that are performed with excellence. Moreover, unlike those activities that exemplify states of "flow," such as mountain climbing or playing chess, the activities that constitute one's moral goals are both interpersonal and theonomic.[27] Therefore, there always exists an extrinsic motivation, since one's goals have a focus toward that which is outside of oneself. Creative problem solving may be fun, but when used to solve a moral difficulty the motivation to exercise it stems from a recognized moral need and a goal of trying to fill that need, all of which is seen through the lens of fulfilling God's will. Under this conception of goals and motivation, extrinsic motivation is primary, and intrinsic motivation is secondary.[28]

INTERNAL OR EXTERNAL MORAL MOTIVATION[29]

Here I am...[30]

While motivation may be engendered through the recognition of external values, motivation itself relies on more than just simple recognition. A central issue[31] with which debates regarding moral motivation must contend is whether a Humean theory of motivation is correct or not.[32] According to David Hume, belief is insufficient to motivate action; motivation always requires an additional desire or conative state. Therefore, moral judgments actually express a person's pre-existing desires or motivations rather than originating in his or her beliefs.[33] Those who reject this premise contend that moral motivation need not depend on the existence of a previous desire.[34] Anti-Humeans differ as to whether belief alone is sufficient to motivate directly or whether those beliefs produce desires which then motivate the person in conjunction with those beliefs. Regardless of which process occurs, anti-Humeans acknowledge that a failure to be motivated is a cognitive rather than simply a conative issue.

Related to the issue of whether beliefs or desires motivate action is whether moral judgments motivate necessarily or only contingently.[35] Motivational judgment internalism (anti-Humean) posits that there is a necessary connection between a person's judgment of a fact and the motivation that his or her judgment elicits.[36] Motivational judgment externalism (Humean), on the other hand, denies the existence of a necessary connection between moral judgment and motivation. It posits that having a reason to do an action implies that a person is able to be motivated to do it, yet that motivation stems from the person's desire to do so and not from the judgment itself.[37] If a person is not motivated to act by a certain reason, then the reason cannot be a reason for him or her.[38] In other words, any connection is purely contingent.[39]

Many motivational internalists, as well as externalists, accept Hume's division between beliefs and desires, as well as the primary distinction between the two in terms of their respective "directions of fit." Mark Platts describes the difference as follows:

> Beliefs aim at the true, and their being true is their fitting the world; falsity is a decisive failing in a belief, and false beliefs should be discarded; beliefs should be changed to fit with the world, not vice versa. Desires aim at realisation, and their realisation is the world fitting with them; the fact that the indicative content of a desire is not realised in the world is not yet a failing in the desire, and not yet any reason to discard the desire; the world, crudely, should be changed to fit with our desires, not vice versa.[40]

Beliefs aim to fit the world (mind-to-world direction of fit), and desires aim to change it (world-to-mind direction of fit). Therefore, in explaining how people who share the same beliefs are not always motivated in the same way, Humeans argue that people have different desires which reflect their different motivations. Anti-Humeans, on the other hand, argue that while beliefs primarily have a thetic (mind-to-world) direction of fit, moral beliefs can also have a telic (world-to-mind) direction of fit. They therefore answer the difficulty in a different way:[41] When people with shared beliefs are not similarly motivated, they may have other beliefs in conflict which cause them to prioritize those shared beliefs differently.[42] Some have challenged this internalist view, despite accepting the idea that moral facts have a telic component, by arguing that the dominant direction of fit is responsible for a belief's function; therefore, because beliefs are primarily thetic, they are motivationally inert.[43]

While I contend that those who sincerely evaluate a situation and decide which action would be the proper response are also motivated to respond accordingly, I do not advocate simply for motivational judgment internalism. Nor do I support the notion that people have separate conative motives to act on their judgments, as is proffered by motivational judgment externalists. Both camps separate cognitive and affective processes, yet current research in psychology strongly indicates that these processes are more interdependent than either Humeans or anti-Humeans assume. Emotions influence cognition; cognitive processes influence the arousal of emotions; and the combination of the two provide a means to recognize reasons for acting and the motivation to act.[44]

Emotions affect cognition directly through a person's use of affective heuristics and indirectly through influencing how one's cognitive abilities will be engaged.[45] In addition to the cognitive heuristics of imaginability, memorability, and similarity, which assist people in making judgments,[46] people use affective heuristics whereby they consider the positive and negative feelings consciously or unconsciously associated with the mental representations of the task at hand in making their decisions.[47] Emotions can also function more directly as heuristics for guiding or stopping one's search for information[48] and for the kind of information for which a person searches.[49] This would blur the lines between intellectual virtue and moral virtue.

Emotions affect cognition indirectly through influencing a person's ability to focus attention.[50] Affective reactions also influence how a person organizes and categorizes social experiences, to the point where totally different situations can find commonality by the sole fact that they elicit similar emotional responses.[51] Furthermore, not only do one's immediate emotions influence cognition, future expected emotions also play a role in decision-making by being part of the goal for the deliberative process. Many models of decision-making assume that people try to predict the emotional consequences of their decisions and take their predictions into consideration when deliberating.[52]

From the other direction, cognitive processes influence emotions directly through one's evaluation of circumstances. According to the appraisal theory of emotion,[53] the way a person interprets and explains his or her circumstances will cause him or her to have an emotional response based on that appraisal.[54] Richard Lazarus, who built on Magda Arnold's concept of appraisal to become one of the most influential proponents of appraisal theory, argues that emotions disclose a relationship between a person and his or her environment, which includes the person's assessment of how relevant the situation is to his or her goals. Emotions, therefore, must include a cognitive component, which consists of the person's appraisal of the situation.[55] Lazarus also identifies two methods of appraisal which affect emotions. Primary appraisal is directed at establishing the significance or meaning of an event. Secondary appraisal is directed at assessing one's ability to cope with its consequences. Though a person appraises a situation in order to discover the meaning it should have in light of his or her goals and his or her attainment, the person will experience an emotion that corresponds to his or her cognitive interpretation. Although appraisal theorists acknowledge that many emotional phenomena cannot be explained through evaluating the significance of a situation, such as those that relate to memory associations and emotional reactions to music,[56] the theory has not been discredited by these examples, and psychologists admit that more complicated appraisals may occur in these situations.[57]

Many psychologists also recognize the existence of recursive processes between cognition and emotion, especially when memories are introduced into the evaluation of a situation.[58] For example, affect priming preferentially inclines a person to retrieve certain information from memory which will then influence deliberation.[59] Also, reasoning about one's emotional reactions will influence future appraisals of similar circumstances.

For the purpose of conceiving the relationship between emotion and cognition as it pertains both to reasoning and motivation, the fact that virtues entail commitment implies that the normative weight of a reason is not measured in terms of detached reasoning but in how a reason relates to the person's level of commitment to the values he or she has inhered. Yet, commitment depends on both cognitive and affective components, though the two are not in fact so starkly distinct.[60] Therefore, when a person evaluates alternative reasons, he or she does not consider the rationality of each in light of purely epistemic judgments (internalist view), nor does the person measure each alternative by how it relates to his or her desires (externalist view). Rather, the process of reasoning and becoming motivated to act is as follows: A person will perceive and interpret a situation through the lens of his or her worldview, which includes—and is influenced by—commitments and desires. Through this perception and appraisal, the person will recognize and evaluate potential reasons to which he or she has both a cognitive and affective connection in varying degrees based on those commitments and desires. The person will choose the reason to act which has the greatest normative force and will be motivated to act through his or her appreciation of that normativity. *I am thus distinguishing between the authority of a reason, which is based on the legitimacy of the facts that exist; the level of normativity of a reason, which is based on the values embedded within those facts; the level of normativity of a reason for a particular person, which is based on his or her recognition and evaluation of those facts; and the level of motivation of a person who recognizes those facts, which is based on the virtues that the person has developed.* For the fully virtuous person who has attained *Shlemut*, the level of normativity of a reason in general and *for him or her* will be the same, and his or her level of motivation will correspond to the recognition of the reason's normativity.

For those who have not attained such a level of virtue, there may exist a disconnect between the normativity of a reason, his or her recognition of it, and his or her motivation to act on it.

Gerd Gigerenzer gives a good example of how motivational reasoning includes both cognitive and affective components working together interdependently for the purpose of committing to a relationship: Imagine *Homo economicus* trying to find a woman to marry. He would have to find out all the possible options and all the possible consequences of marrying each one. He would have to do tons of research to avoid subjective probabilities, and after many years of research he would probably find out that his final choice had already married another person who did not do these computations, but rather just fell in love with her. Alternatively, in searching for a mate, one could have an aspiration level. Once this aspiration is met, as long as it is not too high, the person will find a partner. Yet to avoid exchanging one's wife for a different one (based on one's "rational" criteria), emotions give him the ability to develop commitment. Gigerenzer concludes, "Here we see one function of emotions. Love, whether it is romantic love or love for our children, helps most of us to create a commitment necessary to make us stay with and take care of our spouses and families. Emotions can perform functions that are similar to those that cognitive building blocks of heuristics perform."[61] Emotions, like love, do not confirm one's "rational" choice of a spouse; they influence one's choice and reinforce one's commitment to her. So too in any case of moral decision-making,[62] one's rational response to a situation is both cognitive and affective.

Similarly, the relationship between cognitive and motivational heuristics supports the idea that reasoning and becoming motivated to respond to reasons are two parts of the same process. In fact Dan Zakay and Dida Fleisig state, "Both types of heuristics are actually similar in terms of process. The distinction between the two types is sensible only when the motivation to utilize them and the degree of motivational gain associated with their outcomes are considered."[63] Motivational heuristics are those that enable a person to make a judgment in circumstances where he or she does not have all the information, yet they also help to assure a certain outcome will result from one's deliberation.[64] Given our discussion of the similarity between theoretical and practical reasoning, motivational heuristics would seem to be used regularly, even in situations where one may think that only cognitive heuristics would be present, such as cases where the goal is the attainment of knowledge without directly consequent action, since a person's theoretical as well as practical reasoning is oriented according to his or her virtues.

THE "AFFECT" OF LOVE[65]

Forsake her not, and she will preserve you; love her, and she will keep you.[66]

Though I just mentioned that moral decision-making is shaped by a person's commitments, and I used love as an example of what constitutes the development of a commitment, one may ask, "To what relationship is the moral person committed?" Commitment to one's beliefs does not constitute a relationship, since beliefs are instrumental to theoretical and practical knowledge, which in turn is valued according to how it is used. Also, one could agree with Julia Annas that a virtuous person should not relate to another through his or her own objectives, yet Annas understands moral motivation as related to the activity, which is difficult to understand in terms of love deepening a commitment to a relationship. In my conception of Jewish virtue ethics, the love that influences moral decision-making is directed outward in two directions; it is one's love for God and one's love for his or her fellow. Yet, though from the perspective of the direction of affect they are two different relationships of love; from the perspective of their influence on a person's actions, they are two sides of the same coin.

The Jewish tradition recognizes that the relationship that one should have with another should not be mediated through one's personal aims and objectives. Even though the Torah commands that a person love one's neighbor like oneself,[67] the self-referring language was never meant to imply that one relate to another self-referringly.[68] The following Talmudic discussion about which is a greater principle of the Torah regarding how one should view his fellow underscores this point:

> Ben Azzai said: "This is the book of the descendants of Adam" is a great principle of the Torah. Rabbi Akiva said: "But you shall love your neighbor as yourself" is an even greater principle; hence you must not say, "Since I have been put to shame, let my neighbor be put to shame." Rabbi Tanhuma said: If you do so, know whom you put to shame, [for] "in the likeness of God made He him."[69]

Ben Azzai emphasizes the inherent equality of all men as descendants of one father; however, he focuses on mankind in the abstract, making his principle vulnerable to those who attempt to do great things on behalf of mankind while at the same time hurting individuals. Rabbi Akiva emphasizes that each person is an individual, yet his principle, too, is not without criticism, since it allows for a subjective evaluation of others based on one's self-esteem. Rabbi Tanhuma's re-reading of Ben Azzai's proof text[70] incorporates the demand for objectivity into Rabbi Akiva's intended meaning. One should love his neighbor as he should love himself, yet even if he does not love himself, he should still love his neighbor since he is created in God's likeness.

In addition to the Torah's commandment to relate to others through a commitment of love, the Torah also demands that one's actions, even those that are interpersonal, be grounded in and motivated by one's love for God. In the *Mishne Torah*, Maimonides writes that serving God out of love means to occupy oneself in Torah and commandments and to walk in the paths of wisdom, yet, at the same time, to be bound up in love with God until he is obsessed and lovesick, never diverting from this focus.[71]

Despite the fact that they are two independent commandments, their influences on a person's behavior overlap. For example, in his *Book of Commandments*, Maimonides writes that the command to love God includes promoting the service of God to others as a demonstration of one's love for other people, thus making one's own theological awareness a part of his or her interpersonal concerns.[72] Yet he also writes that the obligation to imitate God's ways actually stems from the command to love one's neighbor, thus making the way one interacts with others a demonstration of his or her theological awareness.[73] From these two statements, one can infer that a person's love of God and his love for his fellow are intimately related. Motivation for acting always includes two components—recognition of God's will and recognition of a person's needs (whether the person is another or oneself depends on the situation and its demands). To return to Rabbi Tanhuma's resolution of the debate between Rabbi Akiva and Ben Azzai, there is no practical difference between loving a neighbor for himself or herself as one loves oneself and loving him or her as a creation of God, since one should recognize both.

Furthermore, the commitment to fulfill these commandments is strengthened through a person's internalizing the values they impart. Maimonides writes that even though knowledge of God should be a person's primary goal, it becomes the motivation to imitate His ways by performing acts of *hesed, mishpat,* and *tzedaka.* Maimonides explains, "The object of the above passage is therefore to declare, that the perfection, in which man can truly glory, is attained by him when he has acquired—as far as this is possible for man—the knowledge of God, the knowledge of His Providence, and of the manner in which it influences His creatures in their production and continued existence. Having acquired this knowledge he will then be determined always to seek loving-kindness, judgment, and righteousness, and thus to imitate the ways of God."[74] Simply to fulfill the commandments to love one's neighbor and to love God and to fulfill them out of moral and intellectual perfection demand the same behaviors. The difference between the two is in internalizing a love for—and commitment to—one's neighbor that is based on a grand theologico-social framework.[75]

Even though it is commanded, love, whether it is for God or for one's fellow, serves as a part of one's reasoning and motivation because it becomes part of a person's disposition through education and training. While other deontologies, such as that of Kant, cannot conceive of a command or an obligation to love,[76] the Jewish tradition does recognize the command to love as being directed toward shaping one's disposition. For example, the author of *Sefer HaHinukh* defines the commandment to love another Jew as having compassion for him, regarding both his physical and his financial needs, just as a person would have compassion for his own self and his own needs.[77] Also, in the introduction to his book, *Duties of the Heart*, Rabbi Bahya ibn Pakuda writes:

> When it became clear to me that, according to the dictates of reason the [duties of the heart] should obligatory, I said to myself, "Perhaps they are not mentioned in the Torah, and that is why no one has ever written a book about them to familiarize us with the subject and reveal its principles." But when I searched for them in the Torah, I found them mentioned many times, for example. … Love your neighbor like yourself.[78]

Similarly, in the "Gate of Mercy" of *The Ways of the Tzaddikim* the author introduces the trait of mercy as one of the thirteen attributes of God, and then instructs his readers to do everything that they can to cultivate this character trait as part of the command to love one's neighbor as himself. Rabbenu Nissim also discusses how the command to love one's neighbor as himself is directed toward developing a proper disposition whose foundation is in one's heart.[79] Moreover, Maimonides writes in the introduction to his *Book of Commandments*: "Know that all the commandments of the Torah and its admonitions deal with four matters: ideas, actions, dispositions, and words. ... Similarly we are commanded to behave with certain dispositions such as being commanded to have pity and mercy and to be charitable and benevolent, as it says 'And you shall love your neighbor as yourself,' and we are warned against being hateful, vengeful, bearing grudges, and seeking blood, as well as other such evil dispositions."[80] By continually interacting with others through God's commandments, a child develops an affinity to the people with whom he interacts and with the values that his community instills in him. As the child reaches the age of maturity, he starts to identify with the social norms of the community and is able to understand the consequences of his actions. Yet he is not yet mature enough to comprehend fully what it means to commit oneself wholeheartedly to God and to relationship with others. By the age of 20, at which point the person becomes liable for his actions by Heavenly decree and not only by societal Jewish courts, a person's character has had the time, if properly habituated, to develop fully a love for God and one's neighbor, which will properly influence his reasoning and motivation.

CONTINENCE AND *SHLEMUT*

...if only they will observe to do according to all that I have commanded them, and according to all the law that My servant Moses commanded them...[81]

In the section discussing legal reasons, I wrote that legal reasons are unique because the source and quality of their normativity is different from that of other normative reasons. While legal reasons include values and motivating components, their normativity is independent of them. A rule is a reason to act regardless of one's motivations for acting or the value of acting in such a way. Because of this dual nature of normativity, acting for the sake of the law can mean two things. It can mean either that the person understands that the law is an exclusionary reason to act, or it can mean that the person, in addition to acknowledging that the law is an exclusionary reason, also understands the values and reasons within the law and is motivated by them as well.

Both the continent person and the one who has attained *Shlemut* act according to the law and for the sake of the law. The difference between the two is that, for the continent person, the law serves as an exclusionary reason for acting. For the person who has attained *Shlemut,* on the other hand, recognition of both the normativity of the law *and the values inherent to the law* motivates the person's actions. Therefore, the service of the one who attains *Shlemut* is done without any latent conflict in motivation; he or she serves God with *simcha*.

Simcha is popularly translated as happiness, but, unlike the word *oneg* (happiness) which connotes a sense of self-indulgence, *simcha* should not be understood in the hedonic sense.[82] For example, Rabbi Samson Raphael Hirsch defines *simcha* as follows, "the feeling of steady and constant spiritual and moral 'growth,' the continuous growth of all that is truly human in us, a blissful joy of life that is not subject to change in any manner by the outward circumstances which life may bring."[83] I would be wary to use the phrase "all that is truly human in us," since it may be interpreted in an essential manner, thus equating the innate value of a person's essence to the value a person gives to the world through his or her actions. Therefore, I would (slightly) adapt Rabbi Hirsch's definition as follows: *Simcha is the visceral contentment that one has when he or she understands the importance of his or her actions, both in their global, interpersonal dimension and in their intimate, theonomic dimension, which reinforces one's behavior and strengthens the relationship one has with God and his or her fellow human beings.* This definition of *simcha* aligns with the way the word is used in the halakhic literature[84] as well as with how the Psalmist uses the term in his call to serve God with *simcha*.

According to Maimonides, *simcha* does not consist of temporary periods of elation, nor does it involve frivolity. In fact, levity is discouraged since it may lead to lewdness.[85] Rather, *simcha* is a constant good-natured temperament of magnanimity and patience. In interpersonal interactions, the one who has *simcha* receives everyone with a friendly countenance.[86] In terms of evaluating his or her personal situation, the person has an optimistic outlook, where life is interpreted in the best possible light—he or she is satisfied with whatever is his or her lot,[87] and even suffering is accepted as an opportunity to improve, which turns personal grief into joy.[88] Through *simcha*, not only will a person direct all of his or her attention to the goal of knowing God and fulfilling His commandments,[89] in turn, God may assist in deepening his or her spiritual consciousness, as is demonstrated by the fact that prophecy cannot rest upon a person when he is sad or languid, but only when he has *simcha*.[90]

While we have already discussed other aspects of how the law habituates one's thinking and acting so as to attain *Shlemut*, with regard to showing a person how to act and respond in ways that is not only *lishma* but also with *simcha*, the law emphasizes the development of gratitude. For example, a person should recite a blessing on hearing good news as well as on hearing bad news. When hearing favorable tidings, he or she should recite the blessing: "Blessed are You, Hashem, our God, King of the universe, who is good and does good." On hearing bad tidings, he or she should recite the blessing: "Blessed are You ... the true Judge."[91] These blessings are intended to make a person recognize that God has provided the benefit, so that he or she appreciates God's concern and does not think that he or she was the sole cause of the good effect. Similarly, when bad things occur, he or she should not think that they are arbitrary or unfair; rather, there is a bigger picture that one may not understand.[92] This idea is supported by the fact that Maimonides writes that the obligation to make a blessing on bad tidings is implied by the verse, "And you shall love Hashem, your God ... with all your might." "All of one's might" means that we are commanded to acknowledge and praise God with *simcha* even at times of difficulty. Moreover, the Talmud records a position that criticizes having different blessings as a demonstration that we do not understand that everything that God does is for good.

> "And Hashem shall be King over all the earth; in that day shall Hashem be One, and His name One."[93] – Is He then not One now? Said Rabbi Aha bar Hanina, "Not like this world is the future world. In this world, for good tidings one says, 'He is good, and He does good,' while for evil tidings he says, 'Blessed be the true Judge.' In the future world it shall be only 'He is good and He does good.'"[94]

Our acceptance of bad tidings rather than understanding the good that is meant by them is a failure on our part to recognize or to rely on (in the sense of *emunah*) the belief that our relationship with God has as a consequence our own self-improvement. Therefore, even bad tidings should be seen as ultimately positive in the teleological sense.[95]

A person is also obligated to have *simcha* during the holidays, which serve as regular reminders of God's taking the Jewish people from Egypt. Yet this obligation is not simply a matter of enjoying the day.[96] To fulfill one's own obligation of *simcha*, one gives to others. To children, one gives sweets. Husbands buy attractive clothes and jewelry for their wives, according to their financial capacity.[97] While eating meat and drinking wine is part of the commandment to have *simcha*, for there is no happiness without partaking of meat or wine, this as well is not simply gustatory delight. The meat is in remembrance of the *Korban Hagiga* and other peace offerings, which are voluntary offerings of thanksgiving that are sacrificed to

God on the holiday.[98] Wine establishes the holiday meal, since one makes *Kiddush* on wine before the meal begins. Therefore, having wine means people having an established meal together rather than eating alone. The communal aspect of eating is further demonstrated by the demand to feed converts, orphans, widows, and others who are destitute and poor. One who locks the gates of his courtyard without feeding the poor and the embittered is not rejoicing as commanded, but rather is "rejoicing with his gut." Maimonides calls the latter type of happiness a disgrace, and to such a person the following verse is applied: "Their sacrifices will be like the bread of mourners, all that partake thereof shall become impure, for they kept their bread for themselves alone."[99]

The festive spirit of the holiday is meant to invoke feelings of gratitude and praise. To reinforce the association between *simcha* and gratitude, the Sages decreed that people recite *Hallel* on all holidays,[100] except for Rosh Hashana and Yom Kippur, since the latter are days of repentance, awe, and fear, and are not days of extra celebration. Though one does not recite *Hallel* on Purim, the reading of the Book of Esther is considered to be its replacement, since hearing the story of Purim should invoke recognition of God's salvation and gratitude to Him.[101] For the same reason why Rabbi Aha bar Hanina says that we will no longer say "Blessed be the true Judge" in the future, it is forbidden to fast or recite eulogies on a holiday,[102] since the focus should be on God's obvious bestowal of goodness and not on feelings of loss. Through the obligatory stopping from our everyday life to recognize the Exodus of Egypt and to demonstrate our gratitude through giving to others without expectation of return, the Torah provides regular intervals to introduce or reinforce a perspective which can allow one to serve God with *simcha*.

While Jewish law shows how to develop gratitude through choreographing action, the Psalmist explains how to do so through his poetry. In Psalm 100,[103] he writes, "*A Psalm of thanksgiving (todah): Shout to Hashem, all the earth.*" The word *todah* signifies both recognition of something and acknowledgment of the consequences of that thing. For example in the *modim* blessing of the *Amida*, it first states, "We recognize that You are Hashem (*modim anakhnu lakh she-…*)," and it then continues with "We give thanks and speak of Your praise regarding… (*nodeh lekha u'n'saper tehilatecha al…*)," where "recognize" and "give thanks" are different conjugations of the same word. The psalm thus begins from the standpoint of being aware of one's relationship with God, the obligations that it entails, and a wholehearted acceptance of the demands of that relationship. Only through the lens of appreciation and gratitude can service of God ever be with *simcha*. Otherwise one is unable to orient his or her perception of reality to a cognitive schema that can appreciate this relationship in terms of the norms it demands and the values it imparts. "*Serve Hashem with simcha; come before His presence with singing (renana).*" This type of singing is not formal or established in its content (as is a *shir*), nor is it harmonious (like a *zemer*). It is a quick voicing of exaltation, and it is usually concerning one's appreciation of God's strength.[104] This form of singing is often juxtaposed with the type of shouting (*hariyu*) of which the Psalmist speaks in the first verse,[105] which implies that the shouting is also a visceral exclamation rather than a formal sounding.[106] In both verses the Psalmist is stating that *simcha* often manifests in spontaneous expressions of gratitude, whether it is directed outwardly to benefit all of the earth or inwardly to oneself as an experience of emotion which corresponds to the person's appraisal of his or her actions (similar to "whistling while you work").

The Psalmist now explains how one can serve God with *simcha*. "*Know that Hashem is God; He has made us, and we are His (written as "and we have not [made us]"), [we are] His people and the flock of His pasture.*" To reach a level whereby one can serve God with *simcha*, one must first recognize that Hashem is God. This is not knowledge strictly in the propositional sense; one must also know that God made us and thus has sole authority to determine how we are to live. We did not make ourselves, and thus, we do not have authority to determine our own moral structure or to take credit for our well-being.[107] Just as a shepherd controls the travels of his flock, so does God determine His people's social values and norms. Though we have already seen how knowledge is a relational term, it is worth citing the words of the prophet, Jeremiah, who exclaims quite passionately how knowing that Hashem is God leads to actions. He states, "Thus says Hashem, 'Let not the wise man glory in his wisdom, neither let the mighty man glory in his might, let not the rich man glory in his riches. But let him that glories glory in this, that he understands and knows Me—that I am Hashem who exercises mercy, justice, and righteousness, in the earth; for in these things I delight,' says Hashem."[108] "*Enter into His gates with thanksgiving (todah), and into His courts with praise (tehila); give thanks (hodu) to Him, and bless His name.*" *Simcha* is reinforced not only through habituation of actions and inhering beliefs so that one fully identifies with them. A necessary part of reinforcement is continually expressing gratitude,[109] yet, again, before one can enter the courtyard, one must go through the gates. Just as recognition precedes deliberation and response, acknowledgment of God precedes thanksgiving and praise. Moreover, praising God consists of blessing His name. Blessing God in this case is not simply granting that God is the source of blessing for humanity. To bless God is to declare one's devotion to the fulfillment of God's will. Rabbi Hirsch explains, "*Berakha* (blessing) expresses in words what *Avoda* (service) expresses in deeds. What makes *tefilla* (prayer) an acceptable substitute for *korban* (sacrifice) (*tefilla bamakom korban*) is not the *bakashot* (supplications) of the *Shemona Esrei*, but the *berakhot* (blessings) that conclude them. For when we say *barukh*, we vow to devote all our energies and resources to God's service—as *lehem isha laShem* (food of a burnt offering to God), to sustain and perpetuate the holy."[110] "Give thanks (*hodu*) to Him, and bless His name" thus reflects "Come before His presence with singing (*renana*)" and "Shout to Hashem, all the earth," respectively, in that one's identification with God's will and one's avowal to fulfill it will result both in personal exaltation and the desire to spread the knowledge of God's will in public.

The Psalmist concludes with a general declaration stating for what one should be grateful. "*For Hashem is good; His mercy endures forever; and His faithfulness (emunah) to all generations.*" Hashem is good, and thus serving God is meant to benefit those who do so, even if the benefit is not the reason for one's service. God's mercy extends forever so that a person has an opportunity to repent if his or her service falters, and more generally, there is always opportunity for continual improvement. Finally, one can rely on His faithfulness in every generation, which provides encouragement to live by one's faith.

With gratitude the *eved Hashem* (servant of God) serves with love and becomes the righteous who lives by his or her faith (*emunah*). God's will, as dictated by the Torah, not only provides theoretical and practical concepts which instill in him or her a worldview and teach him or her the proper ways to act, the values embedded within the law become his or her values, and the person's commitment to those values make them become part of his or her identity. Through experience and habituation, the servant's intellectual and moral virtues improve, making success in reaching one's goals easier. Moreover, as with many loving relationships, through continual engagement, the love that grows for God and for one's fellow causes the person's responses to situations to seem more spontaneous, and his or her growing, loving gratitude allows for the person to continue experiencing *simcha* from all of his or her actions.

If followed as instructed, and one does not veer to the right or to the left,[111] the teleological journey of life has a good and straight path (*derekh tova v'hayeshara*):[112] Through serving God, one will attain *Shlemut* and be able to serve God with *simcha*.

> *It is not incumbent upon you to finish the task, but neither are you free to absolve yourself from it. If you have learned much Torah, you will be greatly rewarded, and your employer is trustworthy (ne'eman) to give you the reward of your labors. And know, that the reward of the righteous is in the World to Come.*[113]
>
>   *Light is sown for the righteous, and gladness for the upright in heart.*
>   *Rejoice (simchu) in Hashem, you righteous;*
>   *and give thanks (hodu) to His holy name.*[114]

NOTES

1. Job 15:3.
2. "Are Moral Requirements Hypothetical Imperatives," *Mind, Value, and Reality* (Cambridge: Harvard University Press, 1998) 77–94.
3. Leviticus 19:17.
4. *Sefer HaMitzvot*, Commandment 239.
5. *Arukh HaShulhan, Orakh Hayyim* 156:9.
6. *Hilkhot Sanhedrin* 10:8.
7. *Hilkhot Sanhedrin* 2:1–7.
8. As discussed in the section about reasons and reasoning, those goals are based on God's will and the person's understanding of how to fulfill it, given his or her capabilities and the context of the situation.
9. Ecclesiastes 7:20.
10. See Jeffrey Seidman's "Two sides of 'Silencing,'" who distinguishes between rational silencing, that is, not recognizing non-virtuous actions, and motivational silencing, that is, not being tempted by non-virtuous actions (*The Philosophical Quarterly*, Vol. 55, No. 218 (January 2005) 68–77).
11. Ecclesiastes 7:25.
12. Julia Annas, "The Phenomenology of Virtue," *Phenomenology and the Cognitive Sciences*, Vol. 7, No. 1 (2008) 29. The idea of "flow" was conceptualized by Mihaly Csikszentmihalyi. See his *Flow: The*

Psychology of Optimal Experience (New York: Harper & Row, 1990).

13. "The Phenomenology of Virtue," 22.
14. Ibid. 24.
15. It will be shown below that this question includes whether one intends to help the person sincerely; it is not a question of whether God or the person takes precedence. Rather, it is assumed that it is God's will that a person love God *and* his or her fellow.
16. Op. cit. 28.
17. The importance of the difference between *simcha* and *oneg* will be discussed below.
18. *Yalkut Yosef, siman* 1.
19. "The Phenomenology of Virtue," 30.
20. Lorraine Besser-Jones, "The motivational state of the virtuous agent," *Philosophical psychology* 25.1 (2012): 104.
21. BT *Sukkah* 25a.
22. See Rashi, BT *Sukka* 26a s.v. *holkhim.*
23. In level-2 decisions, there is a stereotypical and static mapping of alternatives, and the person decides based on an attractiveness to one or a few attributes of a particular option. Level-3 decisions use trade-offs between the attractiveness of aspects of different attributes and transform attributes into new ones. In level-4 decisions, the decision-maker encounters a new and unfamiliar problem in which alternatives have to be elicited or created. Parts of decision-making processes at this level include problem-solving.
24. See Ola Svenson, "Differentiation and Consolidation Theory of Human Decision Making: A Frame of Reference for the Study of Pre- and Post-decision Processes," *Acta Psychologica*, Vol. 80, No. 1 (1992) 143–168.
25. K.J. Gilhooly and E. Fioratou, "Motivation, Goals, Thinking and Problem Solving," *Cognition and Motivation: Forging an Interdisciplinary Perspective*, ed. Shulamit Kreitler (Cambridge: Cambridge University Press, 2013) 273.
26. Ibid. 285.
27. By theonomic, I mean that the goals are governed by God.
28. Of course, certain forms of extrinsic motivation are superior to others. For example, Rabbi Bahya ibn Pakuda differentiates between two types of fear and three types of love of God. Fear of God may consist of either fear of punishment and/or trials or it

may stem from the recognition of God's exaltedness. Love of God may consist of loving for the goodness that is bestowed, loving because of the forgiving of one's sins, or loving out of recognition of God's greatness. See *Hovot HaLevovot, Sha'ar Ahava*.

29. Moral motivation is a component of the more general phenomenon of *normative motivation*.

30. Genesis 22:1.

31. There is a second, equally important debate in the topic of moral motivation regarding the nature of moral claims. Non-cognitivists argue that there are no such things as moral facts or moral properties. Moral statements, therefore, do not make truth claims or state the beliefs of a person; rather they express non-cognitive attitudes, similar to statements of desire or approval. Cognitivists, on the other hand, argue that moral statements do express beliefs and make truth claims. Because I contend that social and institutional facts can be normative, I place myself in the cognitivist camp. Therefore, I will not discuss theories of motivation as they relate to non-cognitivism, and I will only look at the internalism-externalism debate from within the cognitivist camp.

32. Michael Smith argues that the Humean claim that motivation has its source in the presence of a relevant desire and means-end belief can be justified by the following claims: (1) Having a motivating reason is, inter alia, having a goal, (2) having a goal is being in a state with which the world must fit, and (3) being in a state with which the world must fit is desiring. Phillip Petit, on the other hand, counters that Smith's argument in support of a Humean theory of motivation is too simple. He argues that both Humeans and anti-Humeans agree that motivating reasons involve desires; where they disagree is whether motivation always is based solely on desire or whether reason can lead to having a desire. See Michael Smith, "The Humean Theory of Motivation," *Mind*, New Series, Vol. 96, No. 381 (January 1987) 36–61; Phillip Pettit, "Humeans, Anti-Humeans, and Motivation," *Mind*, New Series, Vol. 96, No. 384 (October 1987) 530–533.

33. Those desires may or may not be moral. Different desires can move an individual to do what he or she judges to be the right act to do, such as to be well regarded by friends and neighbors, to advance one's own interests, or to promote the welfare of others.

34. Those who hold this premise in one way or another are Thomas Nagel, John McDowell, Mark Platts, David McNaughton, Jonathan Dancy, Thomas Scanlon, and Russ Shafer-Landau.

See Thomas Nagel, *The Possibility of Altruism* (Oxford: Oxford University Press, 1970); John McDowell, "Virtue and Reason," *Monist*, Vol. 62 (1979) 331–350; Mark Platts, "Moral Reality and the End of Desire," *Reference, Truth, and Reality*, ed. Mark Platts (London: Routledge and Kegan Paul, 1980); David McNaughton, *Moral Vision: An Introduction to Ethics* (Oxford: Basil Blackwell, 1988); Jonathan Dancy, *Moral Reasons* (Oxford: Basil Blackwell, 1993); Thomas Scanlon, *What We Owe to Each Other* (Cambridge: Harvard University Press, 1998)' and Russ Shafer-Landau, *Moral Realism: A Defence* (Oxford: Clarendon Press, 2003).

35. Though I will not discuss it, there is another form of internalism that is different from the one I will discuss. *Existence internalism* (anti-Humean) is the position which posits that there exists a necessary connection between a (moral) fact having a certain normative status and a person's motivation to act according to that fact. A person's motivation is wholly dependent on recognizing the fact itself and does not depend on the desire or disposition of the individual.

J.L. Mackie attributes this view to Plato. See his *Ethics: Inventing Right and Wrong* (New York: Penguin, 1977). For a broad overview of the different types of internalism, see Stephen Darwall, "Internalism and Agency," *Philosophical Perspectives*, Vol. 6, No., Ethics (1992), 155–174.

36. Non-cognitivists, like those in the emotivist camp, have also supported motivational judgment internalism by arguing that judging an action as right expresses an approval for that action without demanding that the judgment convey a truth-value.

37. W. David Falk, "'Ought' and Motivation," *Proceedings of the Aristotelian Society*, Vol. 48 (The Aristotelian Society; Blackwell Publishing, 1947) 492–510; Sigrun Svavarsdottir, "Moral Cognitivism and Motivation," *The Philosophical Review*, Vol. 108, No. 2 (April 1999) 161–219.

38. Bernard Williams, "Internal and External Reasons," *Moral Luck* (Cambridge: Cambridge University Press, 1981).

39. Shafer-Landau is a motivational externalist but he is not a Humean; he argues that moral beliefs are intrinsically motivating but only contingently since they may fail to motivate under conditions of extreme exhaustion, serious depression, or overwhelming contrary impulses (Shafer-Landau, *Moral Realism: A Defence*, 147–148).

40. Mark B. Platts, *Ways of Meaning: An Introduction to a Philosophy of Language* (London: Routledge & K. Paul, 1979) 256–257.

41. McNaughton, *Moral Vision*, Chapter 7; Margaret Olivia Little, "Virtue as Knowledge: Objections from the Philosophy of Mind," *Nous*, Vol. 31 (1997) 59–79.

42. Shafer-Landau, *Moral Realism: A Defence*, 129–130.

43. Hilla Jacobson-Horowitz, "Motivational Cognitivism and the Argument from Direction of Fit," *Philosophical Studies: An International Journal for Philosophy in the Analytic Tradition*, Vol. 127, No. 3 (February 2006) 561–580.

44. Ola Svenson has shown how difficult it is to differentiate between cognitive and emotional motives in deliberation. See Ola Svenson, "Values, Affect, and Processes in Human Decision Making: A Differentiation and Consolidation Theory Perspective," *Emerging Perspectives on Judgment and Decision Research*, eds. Sandra L. Schneider and James Shanteau (Cambridge: Cambridge University Press, 2003) 287–326.

45. Heuristics are simplifying rules of thumb that a person uses to make judgments when faced with uncertainty or incomplete or ambiguous information. See Dan Zakay and Dida Fleisig, "Motivation and Heuristic Thinking," *Motivation and Cognition*, 291.

46. Dan Kahneman, "A Perspective on Judgment and Choice: Mapping Bounded Rationality," *American Psychologist*, Vol. 58 (2003) 697–720.

47. Paul Slovic, Melissa Finucane, Ellen Peters, and Donald G. MacGregor, "The Affect Heuristic," *Heuristics and Biases: The Psychology of Intuitive Judgment*, eds. Thomas Gilovich, Dale Griffin, and Dan Kahneman (Cambridge: Cambridge University Press, 2002) 397–420; Paul Slovic, et al. "The Affect Heuristic," *European Journal of Operational Research*, Vol. 177, No. 3 (2007) 1333–1352.

48. Gerd Gigerenzer and Peter M. Todd, "Fast and Frugal Heuristics: The Adaptive Toolbox," *Simple Heuristics That Make Us Smart* (1999).

49. Alice M. Isen, "Positive Affect and Decision making," *Handbook of Emotions*, eds. M. Lewis and J.M. Havieland (London: Guilford Press, 2004) 417–435; Mary Francis Luce, James Bettman and John W. Payne, "Choice Processing in Emotionally Difficult Decisions," *Journal of Experimental Psychology: Learning, Memory and Cognition*, Vol. 23 (1997) 384–405.

   This reminds me of what the quotation I brought from Charles S. Peirce earlier: "Doubt is an uneasy and dissatisfied state from which we struggle to free ourselves and pass into a state of belief; while the latter [i.e. the state of belief] is a calm and satisfactory state which we do not wish to avoid, or to change to a belief in anything else." Charles S. Peirce, *The Essential Peirce: Selected Philosophical Writings, Volume 1* (Bloomington: Indiana University Press, 1992) 114.

50. Phillip L. Ackerman, "Personality and Cognition," *Cognition and Motivation*, 69.

51. Paula Niedenthal and Jaiman Halberstadt, "Grounding Categories in Emotional Response," *Feeling and Thinking: The Role of Affect in Social Cognition*, ed. Joseph P Forgas (New York: Cambridge University Press, 2000) 357–386.

52. George Lowenstein and Jennifer S. Lerner, "The Role of Affect in Decision Making," *Handbook of Affective Sciences*, 620.

53. The appraisal theory of emotion is not the only theory of emotion to which people ascribe. The categorical theory of emotion proposes the presence of six basic, distinct, and universal emotions, namely happiness, anger, sadness, surprise, disgust, and fear. The dimensional theory of emotion, on the other hand, proposes fundamental dimensions that constitute emotional spaces.

   For information on the category theory of emotion, see Paul Ekman, "Argument for Basic Emotions," *Cognition and Emotion*, Vol. 6, No. 3–4 (1992) 169–200; Paul Ekman and Wallace V. Friesen, "Constants Across Cultures in the Face and Emotion," *Journal of Personality and Social Psychology*, Vol. 17, No. 2(1971): 124–129; Paul Ekman, E. Richard Sorenson, and Wallace V. Friesen, "Pan-cultural Elements in Facial Displays of Emotion," *Science*, Vol. 164, No. 3875 (1969) 86–88; Phillip Johnson-Laird and Keith Oatley, "Basic Emotions, Rationality, and Folk Theory," *Cognition & Emotion*, Vol. 6, No. 3–4 (1992) 201–223; Silvan Tomkins and Robert McCarter, "What and Where Are the Primary Affects? Some Evidence for a Theory," *Perceptual and Motor Skills*, Vol. 18, No. 1 (1964) 119–158.

For information on the dimensional theory of emotion, see James A. Russell, Maria Lewicka, and Toomas Niit, "A Cross-cultural Study of a Circumplex Model of Affect," *Journal of Personality and Social Psychology*, Vol. 57, No. 5 (1989) 848; James A. Russell, and Merry Bullock, "Multidimensional Scaling of Emotional Facial Expressions: Similarity from Preschoolers to Adults," *Journal of Personality and Social Psychology*, Vol. 48, No. 5 (1985) 1290–1298; Harold Schlosberg, "Three Dimensions of Emotion," *Psychological Review*, Vol. 61, No. 2 (1954) 81–88.

54. Magda B. Arnold, *Emotion and Personality* (New York: Columbia University Press, 1960); Klaus R. Scherer, Angela Schorr, and Tom Johnstone, *Appraisal Processes in Emotion: Theory, Methods, Research* (Oxford: Oxford University Press, 2001).

55. Richard S. Lazarus, "Progress on a Cognitive-Motivational-Relational Theory of Emotion," *American Psychologist*, Vol. 46, No. 8 (1991) 819–834.

56. Phoebe C. Ellsworth, "Sense, Culture, and Sensibility," *Emotion and Culture: Empirical Studies of Mutual Influence*, eds. Hazel R Markus and Shinobu Kitayama (Washington, DC: American Psychological Association, 1994) 23–50.

57. Klaus Scherer, "Introduction: Cognitive Components of Emotion," *Handbook of Affective Sciences*, 564.

58. Marc D. Lewis, "Self-organising Cognitive Appraisals," *Cognition & Emotion*, Vol. 10 No. 1 (1996) 1–26; Dacher Keltner, Phoebe C. Ellsworth, and Kari Edwards, "Beyond Simple Pessimism: Effects of Sadness and Anger on Social Perception," *Journal of Personality and Social Psychology*, Vol. 64, No. 5 (1993) 740.

59. Priming is the process where a given stimulus activates mental pathways, thereby enhancing the ability to process subsequent stimuli related to the priming stimulus in some way. For the relationship between affect priming and affect infusion, see Joseph P. Forgas, "Mood and Judgment: The Affect Infusion Model (AIM)," *Psychological Bulletin*, Vol. 117, No. 1 (1995) 39–66. Affect infusion occurs when affects exert a subconscious influence

on the way people think, form judgments, and behave in social situations.

60. For two examples supporting this claim, see Ximena B. Arriaga and Christopher R. Agnew, "Being Committed: Affective, Cognitive, and Conative Components of Relationship Commitment," *Personality and Social Psychology Bulletin*, Vol. 27, No. 9 (2001) 1190–1203; and Devon Johnson and Kent Grayson, "Cognitive and Affective Trust in Service Relationships," *Journal of Business Research*, Vol. 58, No. 4 (2005) 500–507.

61. Gerd Gigerenzer, "Smart Heuristics," *Thinking: The New Science of Decision-Making, Problem-Solving, and Prediction*, ed. John Brockman (New York: Harper Perennial, 2013) 50.

62. A Jewish man is obligated to marry because (a) "It is not good that the man should be alone; I will make him a helpmate for him, (Gen. 2:18)" and (b) so that he may fulfill the command to procreate, which is impossible to do without a woman. See *Tur, Shulhan Arukh, Even HaEzer* 1.

63. Dan Zakay and Dida Fleisig, "Motivation and Heuristic Thinking," *Motivation and Cognition*, 296.

64. Ibid. 301.

65. I am giving the word "affect" a double *entrendre* to mean either the experience of feeling or emotion and/or to have an influence on or to effect a change in something.

66. Proverbs 4:6.

67. Leviticus 19:18.

68. For one example of interpreting the verse away from aspiring toward self-fulfillment, see Nahmanides, who writes, "And you should love your neighbor as yourself—This is an expression by way of overstatement, for a human heart is not able to accept a command to love one's neighbor as oneself. Moreover, Rabbi Akiva has already come and taught, 'Your life takes precedence over the life of your fellow-being.' Rather, the commandment of the Torah means that you are to love one's fellow-being in all matters, as one loves all good for oneself…Therefore Scripture commanded that this degrading jealousy should not exist in his heart, but instead a person should love to do abundance of good for his fellow-being as he does for himself, and he should place no limitations upon his love for him. It is for this reason that it is said of Jonathan's [love for David], that he loved him as he loved his own

soul, because Jonathan had removed [altogether] the attribute of jealousy from his heart, and he said [to David] that he shall be king over Israel, etc." (Nahmanides, Leviticus 19:18).

69. *Midrash Rabbah* Genesis 24:7; see also *Sifra, Kedoshim* 4:12.
70. Rabbi Tanhuma's proof text is a continuation of Ben Azzai's.
71. *Hilkhot Teshuva* 10:2–3.
72. Positive Command Three.
73. Introduction, Book of Commandments, *Shoresh* 2.
74. MN III:54
75. There is debate as to whether Maimonides believed that intellectual perfection entailed social action or engagement solely in intellectual endeavors; I refer the reader to the relevant sections as well as their footnotes, for greater discussion on this topic.
76. Because he believes that a person cannot love another person on command, Kant interprets this commandment as referring to practical love rather than inclination. To love one's neighbor with practical love means that a person should endeavor to perform his duties toward another gladly, not that he should actually be disposed to act gladly for another since then the command would negate itself. Because, as Kant writes, man can never be free of self-love, "it is necessary to base the disposition of the creature's maxims on moral constraint and not on ready willingness, i.e., to base it on respect which demands obedience to the law even though the creature does not like to do it, and not on love, which apprehends no inward reluctance of the will to obey the law (*Critique of Practical Reason*, 87)." In effect, Kant's translation of the Golden Rule, that one should love his neighbor as oneself, would be that one should endeavor to curb his or her reluctance to obey the moral law and fulfill his or her duties as they manifest in particular cases as one relates with other people.
77. Commandment 243.
78. Bahya ibn Pakuda, Sefer Hovot HaLevovot / Duties of the Heart, trans. Moses Hyamson (Jerusalem: Feldheim Publishers, 1970) 13–15.
79. *Derashot HaRan, Derasha* 5.
80. Introduction, Book of Commandments, Shoresh 9.
81. II Kings 21:8.

82. For one example, in *Midrash Tehillim* it states in reference to the verse, "Serve Hashem in *simcha*": "But it says [elsewhere], 'Serve Hashem in fear (*yirah*).' If there is yirah, how can there be *simcha*, and if there is *simcha*, how can there be *yirah*? Rabbi Aivo states, 'When you stand to pray, your heart should be happy (*sameach*) that you are serving God, who is unlike any other in the world'" (Midrash Tehillim 100:2). Similarly, the students of Rabbenu Yonah write, "Even though regarding human [authority], *yirah* and *simcha* are contradictory, since at the time a person fears (*pahad*) another he stands recoiled in worry, regarding the Holy One, blessed be He, this is not so. On the contrary, when a person meditates on His greatness and is in fear before Him, he will become happy (*yisamach*) and be joyful (*yagil*) in this fear, since it will serve as a means to motivate him to perform the commandments. He will be overjoyed (*sas*) and happy (*sameach*) in its fulfillment, for he knows his reward is with Him and his actions before Him. On this type of happiness (*simcha*), we find one verse that states, 'Serve Hashem with *yirah*,' and another that states, 'Serve Hashem with *simcha*,' meaning, 'Serve Hashem with *yirah*, and with this *yirah* you will be *sameach* and joyful" (Commentary on BT *Berakhot* 30b).

83. Samson Raphael Hirsch, *The Psalms* (Jerusalem: Feldheim Publishers, 1991) 195.

84. In referring to what *simcha* connotes according to Jewish law, the legal corpus I will use for this examination is Maimonides' *Mishne Torah*. The reason why I decided to use the *Mishne Torah*, as opposed to the *Shulhan Arukh* or other legal works, is twofold. Maimonides' juridical principle is to rule according to what he perceives as legally correct. He does not take a consensus approach, as does the *Shulhan Arukh*, which decides matters primarily based upon majority rule. Also, Maimonides upholds the belief in the unity of Jewish thought and Jewish law; therefore, his *Mishne Torah* already includes philosophical abstractions within its practical prescriptions, thus making the analysis easier.

85. *Hilkhot Deot* 2:7.

86. Ibid. 1:4.

87. Ibid. 2:7.

88. Ibid. 2:3.

89. Ibid. 3:2.

90. *Hilkhot Yesode HaTorah* 7:4.
91. *Hilkhot Berakhot* 10:3.
92. This discussion lends itself to a much greater discussion of theodicy. This is not the place to discuss it. The intention here is in emphasizing the psychological benefits of having a perspective that allows for reinforcing the theonomic relationship and not the metaphysical cause and effect of that relationship.
93. Zekharia 14:9.
94. BT *Pesahim* 50a.
95. It may be very hard to understand the benefit of bad tidings, which the Book of Job demonstrates clearly, yet the difficulty to understand does not negate the demand to accept one's circumstances and to act in the best way given those circumstances. For example, Rabbi Akiva was known to uphold the view that "Whatever the All-Merciful does is for good." See BT *Berakhot* 60b–61a and BT *Moed Kattan* 21b.

    Also, the Talmud recounts that when Rabbi Akiva was being taken out for his execution by the Roman government it was time to say the evening *Shema*. As the executioners combed his flesh with iron combs, he began to recite the *Shema*. His students said to him, "Our teacher, even to this point?" He responded, "All my days I have been troubled by this verse, 'with all your soul,' [which I interpret,] 'even if He takes your soul.' I said, 'When shall I have the opportunity of fulfilling this? Now that I have the opportunity shall I not fulfill it?'" (BT *Berakhot* 61b). Rabbi Akiva's students could not understand how he could maintain perspective, because they saw the circumstances of Rabbi Akiva's situation as a challenge in that they presented an opposing message than the *Shema*. The *Shema* mentions the bounty that Jews will receive if they keep the commandments, yet Rabbi Akiva is being executed. Rabbi Akiva, on the other hand, did not see a challenge, but rather an opportunity. For him, there was no conflict; God provided, even in such a dire circumstance, the possibility for further understanding and commitment. His positive perspective is grounded by his belief that he is beloved by God; therefore, he interprets God's providence in a way that continuously demonstrates that he is loved.
96. That would be *oneg*. For example, Maimonides writes, "What is meant by [Shabbat] *oneg*? This refers to our Sages' statement that a person must prepare a particularly sumptuous dish and a pleas-

antly flavored beverage for the Sabbath. All of this must be done within the context of a person's financial status" (*Hilkhot Shabbat* 30:7). Regarding eating and drinking in the context of *simchat yom tov*, he writes, "Although eating and drinking on the holidays are included in the positive commandment [to rejoice], one should not devote the entire day to food and drink. The following is the desired practice: In the morning, the entire people should get up and attend the synagogues and the houses of study where they pray and read a portion of the Torah pertaining to the holiday. Afterwards, they should return home and eat. Then they should go to the house of study, where they read [from the Written Law] and review [the Oral Law] until noon. After noon, they should recite the afternoon service and return home to eat and drink for the remainder of the day until nightfall" (*Hilkhot Yom Tov* 6:19).

97. *Hilkhot Yom Tov* 6:18.
98. *Hilkhot Hagiga* 1:1.
99. *Hilkhot Yom Tov* 6:18.
100. *Hallel* is a Jewish prayer which is a recitation from Psalms 113–118. Its recitation used for praise and thanksgiving on Jewish holidays.
101. *Hilkhot Megilla v'Hanukah* 3:6.
102. *Hilkhot Yom Tov* 6:17.
103. The Sages attribute this psalm to Moses, see BT *Bava Batra* 14b. This psalm is said as part of the morning service every morning, except for Shabbat, holidays, and the days preceding Passover and Yom Kippur. It may therefore be seen as a means to habituate its ideas into daily practice.
104. Psalms 59:17; 81:2; 95:1.
105. Psalms 59:17; 81:2; 95:1.
106. Regarding the singing, see Psalms 84:3, which states, "My heart and flesh sing (*yeranenu*) to the living God." Regarding the type of shouting, see Joshua 6, regarding the people's shouting before attacking Jericho.
107. For a point of reference, see Deuteronomy 8:11–17, which states, "Beware lest you forget the Hashem your God, by not keeping His commandments, and His ordinances, and His statutes, which I command you this day. For when you have eaten and are satisfied, and have built good houses, and dwelt therein; and when your herds and your flocks multiply, and your silver and your gold is multiplied, and all that thou have is multiplied; then your heart will

be lifted up, and you may forget Hashem your God, who brought you forth out of the land of Egypt, out of the house of bondage… and you may say in your heart: 'My power and the might of my hand has gotten me this wealth.'"

108. Jeremiah 9:22–23.
109. There has been a lot of empirical research on how gratitude increases well-being. For a few examples, see Robert A. Emmons and Michael E. McCullough, "Counting Blessings Versus Burdens: An Experimental Investigation of Gratitude and Subjective Well-being in Daily Life," *Journal of Personality and Social Psychology,* 84.2 (2003): 377; Philip C. Watkins, et al., "Gratitude and Happiness: Development of a Measure of Gratitude, and Relationships with Subjective Well-being," *Social Behavior and Personality: An International Journal,* 31.5 (2003): 431–451; Jeffrey J. Froh, William J. Sefick, and Robert A. Emmons, "Counting Blessings in Early Adolescents: An Experimental Study of Gratitude and Subjective Well-being," *Journal of School Psychology,* 46.2 (2008): 213–233; Loren Toussaint and Philip Friedman, "Forgiveness, Gratitude, and Well-being: The Mediating Role of Affect and Beliefs," *Journal of Happiness Studies,* 10.6 (2009): 635–654.
110. Samson Raphael, Hirsch, *The Hirsch Chumash: Sefer Bereshis,* trans. Daniel Haberman (Jerusalem: Feldheim, 2000): 250.
111. Deuteronomy 17:11.
112. I Samuel 12:23.
113. *Avot* 2:16
114. Psalms 97:11–12.

APPENDIX I: *LIFNIM MISHURAT HADIN*

Jewish scholars, who argue for the existence of a Jewish ethic independent of Jewish law, often use the concept of *lifnim mishurat hadin* to support the assertion that supererogation in Jewish ethics stems from a sense of ethical autonomy. I will show that "supererogation" in this sense is an incorrect translation.[1] Through examining the relevant Talmudic passages which discuss the concept of *lifnim mishurat hadin*, I hope to show that the concept is more akin to voluntary obedience to the spirit of the law than to a notion of ethical autonomy. As in the case of a person who has attained *Shlemut* and is serving God with *simcha*, acting *lifnim mishurat hadin* is a demonstration that the person, in addition to acknowledging that the law is an exclusionary reason, also understands and is motivated by the values within the normative reasons that the law embodies. The person will therefore act in a way that is "more" than just legally required while acting according to the ethos that the law imparts. The acceptance of principles and concepts embedded within the law thus allows for the manifestation of the ethical within the legal. This understanding of *lifnim mishurat hadin* supports the view that the law can shape a person's beliefs, since, even when he or she acts "supererogatorily," it is the law that provides the beliefs which motivate such action. This view is in line with Rabbi Lichtenstein's understanding of *lifnim mishurat hadin*, which for him is an aspect of Halakha and not a morality of aspiration that is superimposed upon the law.[2] For Rabbi Lichtenstein, because the Halakha demands that

© The Author(s) 2017
I. Bedzow, *Maimonides for Moderns*,
DOI 10.1007/978-3-319-44573-1

people attempt to transcend their minimum obligations, supererogation is, at times, obligated by the Halakha itself. Yet the obligation of supererogation has a higher bar for justification, in that there must be clear legal support for it and not solely a vague moral demand. Moreover, as shown through the Talmudic cases below, the one who acts *lifnim mishurat hadin* oftentimes takes a position that shows concern for the individual with whom the person is concerned over the societal norms by which the two regularly interact. As such, *lifnim mishurat hadin* is more closely aligned with acting through righteousness (*tzedaka*) than strictly through justice (*mishpat*).

TALMUDIC SOURCES

Lifnim mishurat hadin is used only in a few places in the Talmud, yet it is mentioned both in legal contexts and in theological contexts. I will primarily focus on the legal cases, though we will touch upon the theological ones as well.

Case I There was a certain woman who showed a *denar* to Rabbi Hiyya and he told her that it was good. Later she again came to him and said to him, "I afterwards showed it [to others] and they said to me that it was bad, and in fact I could not use it." He therefore said to Rav [Abba Arikka], "Go forth and change it for a good one and write down in my register that this was a bad business." But why [should he be different from] Danko and Issur[3] who would be exempt because they needed no instruction?[4] Surely, Rabbi Hiyya also needed no instruction?—Rabbi Hiyya acted *lifnim mishurat hadin*.[5]

When one examines this passage within the greater Talmudic discussion in which it is placed, it seems more accurate to understand Rabbi Hiyya's actions as being grounded in his embodying the spirit of the law, rather than in autonomous ethical reasoning or simply in legal obedience.[6]

Immediately preceding the account with Rabbi Hiyya, the Talmud gives two contradictory *braitot*[7] regarding the situation where a *denar* was shown to a money changer and he declared it to be good, but it was subsequently found to be a "bad," that is, no longer valid, coin.

It was stated: If a *denar* was shown to a money changer [and he recommended it as good] but it was subsequently found to be bad, in one *braita* it was taught that if he was an expert he would be exempt but if [he was] an amateur he would be liable, whereas in another *braita* it was taught that whether he was an expert or an amateur he would be liable.

To resolve the contradictory *braitot*, Rabbi Papa states that the first *braita* refers to a case of an expert such as Danko and Issur, who made a mistake regarding a new stamp at the time when the coin had just [for the first time] come from the mint. Therefore, his error is not due to his expertise (or lack thereof) but rather to a situation beyond his control. In all other cases, however, both the expert and the amateur would be liable.

Preceding this discussion is a discussion directly related to it[8] regarding the disagreement between Rabbi Meir and the Sages over whether an expert slaughterer who made a mistake and rendered an animal unfit was obligated to pay the animal's owner for damages. Shmuel, in the name of Rabbi Meir, argues that he would be liable to pay, whether he was commissioned to slaughter the animal for a fee or if he did it gratis. The Sages, on the other hand, rule that an expert would be exempt if he slaughtered the animal for free and liable if he slaughtered it for hire. For the Sages, the difference between acting gratis and for hire is that in the former case one does not assume responsibility for damages whereas if done for hire then one does. The responsibility for error comes from his responsibility for the animal and not from the reliability of one's slaughtering. An amateur, on the other hand, would be liable in all cases, since his proficiency would not allow one to consider an error to be outside of the slaughterer's control. He is therefore considered to be negligent in all cases of error.

This disagreement between Rabbi Meir and the Sages, however, is only a particular instance of a more fundamental disagreement between them. Rabbi Meir holds that one is liable for any damage, whether it is a consequence of direct action or due to negligence, while the Sages hold that, in the case of negligence, no action can be instituted in the civil courts to redress the wrong, though the person would be liable according to Divine justice. What this means, according to the Sages, is that the law admits that there is liability in a case of negligence, yet it recognizes that restitution cannot be imposed by the court system. The relationship between the two discussions is that, though the expert is not directly responsible, there is nonetheless also an element of negligence in his behavior.

The direct relationship between the story of Rabbi Hiyya and the disagreement between Rabbi Meir and the Sages regarding the obligation to compensate for loss is supported by the exchange between Rabbi Shimon ben Lakish and Rabbi Elazar, which is recorded immediately after the story about Rabbi Hiyya. Rabbi Shimon ben Lakish showed a *denar* to Rabbi Elazar, who told him that it was good. Rabbi Shimon ben Lakish then said to him, "You see that I rely upon you," to which Rabbi Elazar replied, "Suppose you do rely on me, what of it? Do you think that if it is found bad I would have to exchange it for a good one? Did not you yourself state that it was only Rabbi Meir who adjudicates liability in an action for damage done indirectly (as would be the case in negligence), which apparently means that it was only Rabbi Meir who maintained thus whereas we do not hold in accordance with his view?" Rabbi Shimon ben Lakish, however, replies, "No; Rabbi Meir maintained so and we hold with him." This means that, according to Rabbi Shimon ben Lakish, even an expert money changer would be liable for damages according to the law.

In light of the greater Talmudic discussion, Rabbi Hiyya's actions, as being *lifnim mishurat hadin*, can be understood in two ways. Either Rabbi Hiyya acted according to what he saw was the law, which he held was in accordance with the position of Rabbi Meir, and thus the term *lifnim mishurat hadin* means that he acted according to a more stringent minority legal opinion (i.e. within the line of that which is legally permissible) even though the law usually accords with the majority. Alternatively, Rabbi Hiyya acted according to the opinion of the Sages, yet in order to remove himself from the potential of Divine judgment due to his negligence, he acted *lifnim mishurat hadin* and paid the damages, even though he was not obligated to do so by a civil court. In other words, he understood the normative values embedded within the law, and he was motivated in acting according to them even though it demanded that he do more than what was legally required.

Case II Rabbi Ishmael beRebbi Yossi was walking on a road when he met a man carrying a load of sticks. The latter put them down, rested, and then said to him, "Help me to pick them up." "What are they worth?" [Rabbi Ishmael] inquired. "Half a zuz," was the answer. So [Rabbi Ishmael] gave him the half zuz and declared them ownerless.[9] Thereupon [the carrier] re-acquired them. [Rabbi Ishmael] gave him another half zuz and again declared them ownerless. Seeing that he was again about to re-acquire them, he said to him, "I have declared them ownerless for all but you."[10] Yet was not Rabbi Ishmael beRebbi Yossi an elder for whom it was undignified [to help one to take up a load]?—He acted *lifnim mishurat hadin.*[11]

The greater Talmudic discussion in which this account is placed provides context to see how Rabbi Ishmael embodies the spirit of the law through his understanding the norms and concepts that the law means to impart even in circumstances where the law cannot enforce them. As such, he is not acting "supererogatorily," but rather he is fulfilling the law's demands in the ideal manner. Immediately preceding the account of Rabbi Ishmael, the Talmud records the Sages' inquiry.

> [If a distinguished elder finds an object in a field and the owner of the object lives in a town, and] it would be his practice [i.e. it would not contradict his dignity] to return such an object in a field [since few people would see him], but it would not be his practice to return it in the town, what would be the law [should he return the object or not]?

The Talmud records that the question remained unanswered. The Talmud then records general parameters to an elder's exemption from the Torah commandment to help a person pick up another's load that has fallen from his animal. If he would load and unload the bundle himself, he must also help his friend load and unload the bundle. The juxtaposition of the Sages' discussions of the two commandments, that is, to return a lost object and to help load and unload another's animal, demonstrates that the Sages understand that the two commands are related in terms of the details of their obligations and the exemptions of an elder. Therefore, the actions of Rabbi Ishmael should been seen in light of the doubt raised by the Sages regarding finding an object in a field as well as in light of the general limits of an elder's exemption regarding his personal evaluation of the fallen object.

Rabbi Ishmael was in doubt as to whether he was in a place where there were only few people around so that he should consider the situation as if he were in a field (since the man called him of all people, one could guess such was the case), and he was in doubt as to whether he would pick up the sticks himself. Depending on how he considered the circumstances or the personal value of the sticks were he to own them, any action he would then take could be either a fulfillment of a Divine command, a transgression, or even a denigration of the Torah's honor (as embodied in his status as an elder). For example, if he would pick up the sticks if they were his, but he does not help, he would transgress the prohibition, "You shall certainly help him."[12] If he would not pick them up if they were his, but he nevertheless does help, he would disgrace the honor that he has acquired through his Torah scholarship. Because of the ambiguity that the situation creates in terms of how to respond, and in order to act in a way that would remove him from legal doubt and potential transgression, Rabbi Ishmael changed the circumstances of the scenario. He bought the sticks in order to remove the potential obligation of having to help lift them. By doing so, he can more effectively and more confidently adhere to the Torah values he has adopted and respond in a way that achieves the law's and its exemption's purposes. His actions are within the bounds of the law (*lifnim mishurat hadin*), but not legally mandatory.

Case III   Rav Yehuda once followed Mar Shmuel into a street of wholemeal vendors, and he asked him: What if one found here a purse? [Mar Shmuel] answered: It would belong to the finder. What if an Israelite came and indicated an identification mark? [Mar Shmuel] answered: He would have to return it. Both? [Mar Shmuel] answered: [He should act] *lifnim mishurat hadin*. Thus the father of Shmuel found some asses in a desert, and he returned them to their owner after a year of 12 months[13]: [he went] *lifnim mishurat hadin*.

Rava once followed Rabbi Nahman into a street of skinners—some say into a street of scholars—and he asked him: What if one found here a purse? [Rabbi Nahman] answered: It would belong to the finder. What if an Israelite came and indicated its identification mark? [Rabbi Nahman] answered: It would [still] belong to the finder. But that one keeps protesting! It is as if one protested against his house collapsing or against his ship sinking in the sea.[14]

Both cases are found within a broader Talmudic discussion regarding the requirement to return lost objects. Specifically, the issue of the broader Talmudic passage is as follows: A person is permitted to keep a lost object that he finds in a place where crowds are commonplace, since it is assumed that the owner has despaired of the object's return, yet there is a question as to whether this applies regardless of the demographic makeup of the crowd or whether it applies only in a locale where the majority of the people are heathens, but not where the majority are Israelites.[15]

The street of the wholemeal vendors and the street of skinners are places where the majority of the people found are heathens.[16] Therefore, it can be presumed that the original owner despaired of the object when he realized he lost it. Rabbi Nahman upholds the presumption that the Israelite despaired of the purse. He, therefore, does not believe that the person who later comes to claim it actually hoped to find it (and thus did not despair of it). He disregards the person's claim, since it is so far-fetched that he could have maintained such hope to find his lost item. Like protesting against one's house collapsing or against one's ship sinking in the sea, protesting in this situation would be to no avail. The finder is thus the legitimate owner.

Shmuel, on the other hand, recognizes the legality of the presumption, yet he does not allow it to override a normative fact. He believes that the person who lost the object would not lie and say that he did not despair of it, even though it is common that one would do so in such a situation.[17] Shmuel, therefore, rules that a person should not rely on what is permissible by legal presumption but, instead, should act to fulfill the commandment of returning lost objects in a way that demonstrates appreciation of the values inherent therein.[18]

The case about Shmuel's father should be understood as an actual demonstration of Shmuel's argument. Shmuel's father acted *lifnim mishurat hadin* because he returned the animals, even though he was only obligated legally to give the person their monetary equivalent. The legal obligation to give only the monetary equivalent is based on the premise that it may be too expensive to keep the animals; therefore, one is permitted to sell them. Though Shmuel's father had a right of ownership over the animals since he could have bought them for their monetary value, the original owner still had a (weaker) right of ownership, just as the person whose lost object had distinguishing marks. Shmuel's father, therefore, fulfilled the command to return lost objects in the literal sense, rather than rely on a legal permissibility.[19]

Case IV The question was raised: If a man sold [a plot of land] but [on concluding the sale] he was no longer in need of money, may his sale be withdrawn or not?[20] Come and hear: There was a certain man who sold a plot of land to Rav Papa because he was in need of money to buy some oxen, and, as eventually he did not need it, Rav Papa actually returned the land to him! [This is no proof since] Rav Papa may have acted *lifnim mishurat hadin*.

Come and hear: There was once a famine at Nehardea when all the people sold their mansions,[21] but when eventually wheat arrived Rabbi Nahman told them: The law is that the mansions must be returned to their original owners![22]

There the sales were made in error since it eventually became known that the ship was waiting in the bays. If that is so, how [can we explain] what Rami bar Samuel said to Rabbi Nahman, "If [you rule] thus you will cause them trouble in the future," [whereupon] he replied, "Is famine a daily occurrence?" and to which the former retorted, "Yes, a famine at Nehardea is indeed a common occurrence."

And the law is that if a man sold [a plot of land] and [on concluding the sale] was no longer in need of money the sale may be withdrawn.[23]

Though Rav Papa is said to have acted *lifnim mishurat hadin*, the conclusion of the Talmudic discussion states that Rav Papa actually acted according to the law.[24] The question, then, is why the Talmud originally described Rav Papa's actions as *lifnim mishurat hadin*, even though the description is subsequently rejected.

With respect to sales that are predicated on a condition, and that condition is not made explicit at the time of the sale, there is a question as to how one needs to consider an implied condition. Is its consideration based on the fact that a large number of people also have that condition as part of their transactions, or is it based on the fact that a large number of people know that the individual in question has that condition in mind?

In the case of Rav Papa, the presumption[25] that there were specific reasons for the sale was based only on the intentions of one person. In the second case, the presumption was based on the intentions of a large group of people. Under the assumption that the strength of a presumption is based on the number of people who intend it, Rav Papa would be acting within his rights to possess the land. If the strength of a presumption is not based on the number of people having a certain intention but rather on the fact that an individual's intention is well known, the sale would be void and Rav Papa would be obligated to return the land. Therefore, to avoid the possibility of transgressing the law, he returned the land.

Ultimately, however, the Talmud ruled that consideration is based on how well an individual's intentions are known; therefore, Rav Papa's decision was not *lifnim mishurat hadin*, it was legally obligatory. This case demonstrates that acting *lifnim mishurat hadin* is to act in a way that most ideally promotes the values inherent in the law, since it shows that later generations may recognize that such action is in fact the only way to abide by it.[26]

THE PROOF-TEXT FOR *LIFNIM MISHURAT HADIN*

The Talmudic source for the demand that one act *lifnim mishurat hadin* is based on the verse, "And you shall teach them the statutes (*hukkim*) and the laws (*torot*, sing. Torah), and you shall show them the way they must walk therein, and the work that they shall do."[27] The Talmud parses the verse in the following manner: "Rabbi Yosef learned: *and you shall show them*—this refers to their house of life; *the way*—that means the practice of loving-kindness (*hesed*); *they must walk*—to visit the sick; *therein*—to burial; *and the work*—the strict law (*din*); *that they shall do*—*lifnim mishurat hadin*."[28] Rabbi Shlomo Itzhaki (Rashi) interprets the phrase, "their house of life" to mean that one should teach them a trade so that they can support themselves.[29] Rashi's understanding of the phrase is based on the statement of Rabbi Ishmael that one must teach his son a trade—"But does not Rabbi Ishmael teach, 'Choose life!' [which means that one must teach his son] a trade!"[30] The verse that Rabbi Ishmael cites describes a life which is more than just mere existence. "I call heaven and earth to witness against you this day, that I have set before you life and death, the blessing and the curse; therefore choose life, that you may live, you and your seed; to love Hashem your God, to hearken to His voice, and to cleave to Him; for that is your life, and the length of your days; that you may dwell in the land which Hashem swore to your fathers, to Abraham, to Isaac, and to Jacob, to give them."[31] The verse implies that the choice of life is the choice to love God, obey the commandments, and live a life that is shaped by a Torah worldview. No matter how much Torah a person learns, however, if he is unable to support himself, he will be unable to choose life. This is supported by Rabbi Yehudah's statement that one who does not teach his son a craft teaches him to be a thief.[32] Therefore, after the Torah verse above already states, "And you shall teach them the statutes (*hukkim*) and the laws (*torot*, sing. Torah)," it is only natural that the next imperative would be to teach people a trade to support themselves. This is supported by the fact that *hukkim* are those rules which are meant to provide a person with an orientation through their adherence, since the rationality of their obligation is not readily apparent. *Torot*, on the other hand, are those concepts that one must accept and subsequently adopt through understanding them. The Sages thus infer that the verse teaches that it is not enough to act and think as explicitly required; one must develop proper judgment and understanding in order to implement the values of the law in daily practice.

The Talmud questions the explanations for "the way they must walk therein," saying that visiting the sick and burial are already part of doing acts of loving-kindness (*hesed*). The Talmud responds to say that these two are explicitly mentioned, since one should perform them even when it comes at a personal expense. This explanation fits with the general verse, in that "the way" is the dominant expression and "they must walk therein" supports it in the sense that not only must you show them the way but also there will be times you must show them to walk therein even when they do not understand why. Those times are when it is difficult to do acts of loving-kindness (*hesed*) of one's own accord without seeming reciprocity. This also fits with the definition of *hesed* given above, which is that *hesed* is given to a person who can never (or is assumed never to be able to) return that *hesed* in the future.[33]

The same construct applies to the latter part of the verse and the Sages' explanation of it. Not only must you show them "the work," but when they are unwilling of their own accord to do the work or they do not recognize that they should do the work based on their understanding of the law, you must show them "that they shall do" it, that is, that such action is in fact demanded by the law or by the values that the law embodies. This means that *lifnim mishurat hadin* is a part of the law (*din*), just as visiting the sick and burial are part of acts of loving-kindness (*hesed*). To act *lifnim mishurat hadin* would be to act in accord with the greater vision of the law, even when it is seemingly not in one's immediate or obvious best interest to do so. This fits with the definitions of *mishpat* and *tzedaka* given above, where *mishpat* is related to a clear understanding of reciprocity, and *tzedaka* relates to giving to another with whom one lives interdependently, so that the person might be able to return that *tzedaka* one day in the future, making reciprocity an implied premise of social life but not a presumption upon which obligation rests.

This understanding of *lifnim mishurat hadin* gives clarity to the statement of Rabbi Yohanan, "Jerusalem was destroyed because the people based their judgments on Torah law, but they did not act *lifnim mishurat hadin*."[34] The Tosafists remark that the Talmud elsewhere gives *sinat hinam* (baseless hatred) as the reason for the destruction of Jerusalem,[35] yet they resolve the difficulty by saying that the two together caused it.[36] By associating the strict application of the law to *sinat hinam*, the Tosafists recognize that *lifnim mishurat hadin* occurs when people see each other for who he or she is and not as a consequence of how the law regulates interaction.[37] Like acts of loving-kindness (*hesed*), *lifnim mishurat hadin* is an extension of the command to love one's neighbor as oneself by incorporating *tzedaka* into *mishpat*. It demands that one lives *within the lines of the law* (*lifnim mishurat hadin*) so as to respect the people whom the law brings together.[38] The Torah projects an order onto the world and imparts social norms and concepts to it, yet only so that the person who serves God with *simcha* can improve the world and the lives of those people who inhabit it by embodying those norms that the law imparts.[39]

POSTSCRIPT: NAHMANIDES' AND MAIMONIDES' CONCEPTIONS OF *LIFNIM MISHURAT HADIN*

The classification of *lifnim mishurat hadin* as voluntary obedience to the spirit of the law fits the explanations of Nahmanides' and Maimonides' conceptions of *lifnim mishurat hadin*, even though they fundamentally disagree with each other regarding the meaning of the concept and even if they do not agree explicitly with my definition either.

Nahmanides' view of *lifnim mishurat hadin* is conveyed in his comment on the Biblical verse, "You shall do what is right and good in the eyes of Hashem, so that it will be good for you, and you shall come and take possession of the good land that Hashem swore to your forefathers."[40] He writes that after the Torah states that one keep God's statues and testimonies, it commands the Jews also to act in accordance with the principles laid out by the explicit commands, even in a situation where there is no explicit commandment to follow. The purpose of this general command is to recognize that the law cannot explicitly cover all aspects of a person's conduct. Therefore, it gives an "elastic clause" which gives authority to the Torah to regulate conduct not explicitly mentioned. In order to do this, however, one must develop practical reason through experience as well as receptivity to the values and concepts that the Torah imparts.

Maimonides' view, on the other hand, is often understood to be that *lifnim mishurat hadin* is an act of piety that is in no way required. However, when one examines his use of the term throughout his writings, it seems to reflect something more than simply piety for piety's sake. Rather, it seems to reflect a tool that one uses to bolster his or her identification with Torah values so as to better align one's reasoning with Torah norms and concepts. In *Shemonah Perakaim*, Maimonides writes that the pious, in order to prevent their disposition from slipping to the wrong side of the mean, would incline themselves toward the more proper extreme as a precaution. They would remain *lifnim mishurat hadin*, yet only as a means to treat themselves from a spiritual or moral malady, and not because they thought it was the ideal. Only when the ignorant saw these people acting *lifnim mishurat hadin*, without knowing their intention for doing so, did they begin to copy them, thinking that it was a pious or virtuous ideal.[41]

In *Hilkhot Yesode HaTorah* 5:11, Maimonides gives criteria for when a scholar should act *lifnim mishurat hadin*.

> There are other deeds which are also included in [the category of] the desecration of [God's] name, if performed by a person of great Torah stature who is renowned for his piety—i.e., deeds which, although they are not transgressions, [will cause] people to speak disparagingly of him. This also constitutes the desecration of [God's] name. ... Everything depends on the stature of the sage, with respect to the extent he must be careful to go *lifnim mishurat hadin*. [The converse is] also [true] ... to the extent that all praise him, love him, and find his deeds attractive—such a person sanctifies [God's] name. The verse, "And He said to me: 'Israel, you are My servant, in whom I will be glorified,'" refers to him.

From this Halakha, one can infer two different aspects of *lifnim mishurat hadin*. The Sage acts supererogatively, yet not because he thinks it is correct to do so. Rather, whether he should act *lifnim mishurat hadin* or not depends on how others around him will interpret his actions! Moreover, the others who interpret his actions are not meant to see them as representing a moral ideal outside of the law so as to copy them. Rather, they are supposed to praise the person, as a servant and representative of God. Acting *lifnim mishurat hadin*, therefore, is not a piety of acting as one knows is right, but rather a piety of acting so as to sanctify God.

In *Hilkhot Deot* 1:5, Maimonides provides a similar explanation of *lifnim mishurat hadin* as he does in *Shemonah Perakim*. He writes,

> A person who carefully [examines] his [behavior], and therefore deviates slightly from the mean to either side is called pious. What is implied? One who shuns pride and turns to the other extreme and carries himself lowly is called pious. This is the quality of piety. However, if he separates himself [from pride] only to the extent that he reaches the mean and displays humility, he is called wise. This is the quality of wisdom. The same applies with regard to other character traits. The pious of the early generations would bend their temperaments from the intermediate path toward [either of] the two extremes. For some traits they would veer toward the final extreme, for others, toward the first extreme. This is referred to as *lifnim mishurat hadin*. [Yet] we are commanded to walk in these intermediate paths—and they are good and straight paths—as [Deuteronomy 28:9] states: "And you shall walk in His ways."

In acting with piety, one avoids walking in what Maimonides calls the good and straight paths, which, as he describes in the following Halakha, are paths of graciousness, mercy, holiness, righteousness, justice, and perfection, to name a few. Therefore, it is difficult to assume that the pious person is living on a higher spiritual level than the wise person who acts as commanded and does so completely. Moreover, from a teleological perspective, because piety is mentioned before wisdom in this Halakha, it would seem that wisdom is the ideal and that piety is a means to achieve it. Therefore, according to this Halakha, one should understand acting *lifnim mishurat hadin* as a means to train one's disposition to fully embody the principles and values inherent within *din*, just as acting through piety is moving to an extreme in order to enable a wise person to embody the mean more perfectly.

Appendix II: A Genealogy of the Expression *Moshe emet v' Torato emet*

The expression *Moshe emet v' Torato emet* (Moses is true and his Torah is true) is a familiar one, and it is often said with the intent to provide either praise to the Torah or encouragement to those who uphold it. Oftentimes when it is written, it is used as an exclamatory reinforcement to affirm that the opinion set forth is the absolutely correct one. Yet its usage in common parlance does not fully convey the depth of its meaning. For while it is true that the expression *Moshe emet v' Torato emet* means that both Moses and his Torah are true, the import and gravity of their truth is lost when the expression is meant only to support a point already made or believed.

In this appendix, I will primarily examine the connotations the expression conveys as it is found in the Talmud, yet I will also show, through a few examples, how its connotation has stayed constant through the Middle Ages to the Modern period. My reason for providing only a few examples is that, though many have used the phrase, few explain its meaning beyond that which is meant in common parlance.

Moshe emet v' Torato emet uses the term *emet* in two distinct ways. Even in the case of *Moshe v' Torato emet*, the word *emet* is used polysemously. *Moshe emet* is meant to signify that the interpretation of the Torah which is being asserted is the correct one. The meaning which is proposed claims authority by its affiliation to Moses' authority. *Emet* in this case means truth in the sense of reliable, trustworthy. *Torat emet* is meant to

© The Author(s) 2017   307
I. Bedzow, *Maimonides for Moderns*,
DOI 10.1007/978-3-319-44573-1

signify that the content and the directives of the Torah should be understood as being the correct way to live; it is an expression that asserts that the experience or reality created by observing the Torah is the best one. *Emet* in this case means truth in the sense of being the proper or most suitable for a purpose. These two implications of *Moshe emet v' Torato emet* oscillate in terms of which has primacy, throughout history and depending on the argument put forth. For example, when the Torah is compared to other religions and philosophical systems, *Torato emet* is often emphasized. On the other hand, when one interpretation of the Torah is being defended against other interpretations, *Moshe emet* is usually underscored.

In the Talmud, the expression "*Moshe v' Torato emet*" is attributed to the men of Korah; in fact, the entire expression that they exclaim is, "Moses and his law are truth and we are liars (*bada'in*)."[42] The expression is telling for two reasons. First, Moses' truth is juxtaposed with their lies, meaning that from one it is possible to clarify the understanding of the other. Second, the men of Korah use the word *bada'in* rather than *shakranim*. This difference is more than just semantic, since the difference between *badai* and *sheker* has more to do with how and why something is false than just the fact that the content of the statement is not true. Therefore, *emet* should be taken as the opposite of *badai* rather than *sheker*.

Sheker is a lie in the sense that the statement is false yet has the possibility of being true, so that the statement is not one made in vain. In terms of considering whether a statement is *sheker* or not, the statement as a whole is considered in light of what can be gained by its verity and by the intentions of the one who made it. For example, if, at the time of a person's death, he says that he has sons or that he has no brothers so that he thereby exempts his wife from *yibbum*,[43] his statement is considered in relation to what it can achieve. If it cannot achieve anything,[44] then the statement is considered either as true or as having the presumption of being true. The reason for this is that we assume that people think, "why should I lie" if there is no benefit in doing so.[45] This idea is the basis for the legal concept of *migo* which is the principle that if one could have given a better excuse than the one given, we believe the one given.[46]

The Talmud gives a fuller description of the meaning of *sheker* in distinguishing a false oath from an oath made in vain. If a person swears to have eaten, but has not in fact done so, it is a false oath. An oath made in vain, on the other hand, is when one swears about that which is contrary to known facts, such as if one swears that a man is a woman or that a rock is a piece of gold.[47] Speaking in way that is obviously untrue is not even considered to be *sheker*; it is, rather, a waste of words. Falsity, as *sheker*, must have the potential to be true, yet it in fact lacks any truth to it. Similar is the difference between false witnesses and conspiring witness. False witnesses give testimony that is not true, but it is the testimony itself that is under scrutiny. Conspiring witnesses also give testimony that is not true, but it is not the testimony that is directly suspect. Rather, suspicion rests on whether the witnesses could have even known the content of their testimony. Also, a *shakran* is someone who says things that are completely untrue.[48] Moreover, because of the lack of any truth, a false statement cannot be maintained, as Rabbi Yohanan said in the name of Rabbi Meir, "Any piece of slander, which has not some truth in the beginning, will not endure in the end."[49]

Badai, on the other hand, is a lie in the sense that the statement misrepresents the truth. For example, the Talmud provides a conversation between the Satan and Abraham on his way to sacrifice Isaac. At first, the Satan attempts to make Abraham stumble, not by telling him *sheker* but rather by making observations and asking him questions which, though not completely false, are meant to undermine the truth of his mission. Unsuccessful, the Satan finally reports to Abraham a truth, that he will sacrifice a lamb and not his son, yet even still Abraham dismisses him. The reason for Abraham's dismissal of the Satan is that "it is the penalty of a liar (*badai*), that should he even tell the truth, he is not heeded."[50] Notice how the expression uses the term *badai* and not *shakran*. Because the Satan mixed truth with falsity, and thus misrepresented the truth, the content of his words became suspect so that even the part that was true could not bear witness to itself.

The Talmud also cites Rabbi Yehudah as saying that one who translates a verse from the Torah literally, rather than using the authorized translation of Onkelos, is a liar (*badai*), since he misrepresents the meaning of the verse.[51] Similarly, Tractate *Derekh Eretz* records the statement, "Let your tongue acquire the habit of saying, 'I do not know,' lest you be led to speaking falsehoods (*itbade vetea'ahez*)."[52] The meaning of this advice is that it is better to say that one does not know something, than to give a half-truth based on partial knowledge. The Talmud suggests this advice even when a person knows the truth, yet the truth may be interpreted falsely by others. To answer why Moses said, "Thus says Hashem, 'About midnight will I go out into the midst of Egypt'"[53] even though Moses knew that this would occur exactly at midnight, the Sages say that Moses thought that Pharaoh's astrologers might make a mistake in their calculations and would then say that Moses was a liar.[54] Therefore, in order to avoid any misinterpretation of Moses' proclamation, which would result in a denigration of God's miracle, Moses spoke inexactly so as to allow for greater clarity with respect to the bigger picture.

Badain are, therefore, those who misrepresent the truth in a way that denigrates its message and its author. Their lies may seem, on a superficial level, to be true, or a rational challenge to what is deemed true, yet once recognized as lies, no longer does even the truth that may be within them have weight. This definition is in line with what Korah and his men said which made them admit that they were liars (*badain*). The Bible states that Korah and his men rebelled against Moses. They protested that he and Aharon appropriated too much power for themselves given that the entire congregation is holy.[55] Korah did not speak a falsehood by saying that the entire congregation is holy; even before this incident the Torah calls the Jewish people holy a number of times.[56] Yet Korah misrepresented the meaning of that holiness. According to the *Midrash Tanhuma*, in saying that the entire congregation is holy, Korah meant that each individual in the entire congregation received the Torah; therefore, it is in the power of each individual to fulfill it. By usurping the authority to provide its proper explanation, and in appointing people to certain functions, Moses and Aharon appropriated power which was not theirs.[57] The Midrash further explains that the more explicit challenges that Korah raised were not direct falsehoods either; rather, in a similar way to the Talmudic account of the Satan's attempt to dissuade Abraham, Korah asked questions on the details of general commands in order to reveal seeming inconsistencies in Moses' teachings.[58] He did not speak outright falsity as in *sheker*; instead, he mixed truth with skepticism in a misleading way (*badai*) so as to undermine the authority of Moses.

If the type of lies (*badain*) that are juxtaposed with the truth (*emet*) of Moses and his Torah are those that add confusion and skepticism and which leave a person without knowledge of how one should act, then the truth (*emet*) of Moses and his Torah must be in the clarity and surety of the proper way to live. Before discussing Moses' truth specifically, this definition already corresponds to the description of *Torat emet* as found in the Bible. For example, after chastising the people, and especially the Kohanim, for disrespecting God by sacrificing unfit animals on the altar, Malachi reminds the tribe of Levi, in which the Kohanim are included, that God made a covenant with Aharon so that his line will always be the one serving in the Temple. The reason Aharon received this covenant, in the words of Malachi, was "for the sake of the fear which he feared Me, for he was in awe of my Name. The teaching of truth (*Torat emet*) was in his mouth, and injustice was not found on his lips; he walked with Me in peace and with fairness, and turned many away from iniquity."[59] The reference to *Torat emet* is meant to signify that Aharon would teach the masses what was in his heart, he did not say one thing and mean another.[60] There was clarity of message which allowed for both righteousness and justice to prevail in his life and in the lives of the people. The Talmudic Sages give as an example of this type of truth that one should not say something is impure if it is pure or pure if it is impure. This is different than "injustice not found on one's lips," which they attribute to things permitted and prohibited.[61] The importance of this distinction is that, in contradistinction to that which is permitted and prohibited, the Talmudic Sages describe legal aspects of purity and impurity as not being explicit in the written Torah, yet as having a strong foundation on which to rely.[62] Therefore, in spite of the possibility for error in the details, *Torat emet* provides clarity where misunderstanding may arise.

The relationship between truth and peace is emphasized by the Sages, who use the verse in Malachi to support their assertion that Aharon loved peace and pursued peace, and made peace between man and his fellow."[63] Yet the truth of the Torah which Aharon spoke came from Moses' authority, and, say the Sages, hearing the Torah from Moses was like hearing directly from God.[64] Moreover, this was the case not only for Aharon but also for every leader to whom Moses told the Torah. The Jerusalem Talmud describes this as follows:

Rabbi Yohanan in the name of Rav Benaya, "As Hashem commanded Moses His servant, so did Moses command Joshua; and so did Joshua; he left nothing undone of all that Hashem commanded Moses."[65] It does not say, "[commanded] him Moses (*oto Moshe*)" but rather "that Hashem commanded Moses (*et Moshe*)," [meaning] even that which was not heard explicitly he agreed to [follow], as we say "to Moses from Sinai." [So says] Rabbi Yohanan in the name of Rav Benaya [and] Rabbi Huna in the name of Rebbi, "The teaching of truth (*Torat emet*) was in his mouth," [these are] things heard explicitly from his master, "and injustice was not found on his lips," even that which was not said explicitly [he agreed to follow].[66]

Moses' truth, therefore, is due to the fact that his communication possesses a matter of clarity and understanding, not only in things that were explicit but rather also in that which is inferred.[67]

Moses' truth of clarity allows for the second part of the phrase to become apparent, namely that his Torah's message conveys the true way to live. This is supported by the verse in Psalms which states, "Your righteousness is an everlasting righteousness, and Your Torah is truth."[68] In the context of the psalm, which is to instruct its reader that fulfilling the Torah should be one's supreme concern, the juxtaposition of truth with righteousness implies that the commandments are just, and that they are meant to maintain social life through their adherence. Despite any inclinations to the contrary, one should trust in the Torah and it will not deceive him or her.[69] In this sense, the truth of the Torah is not in the propositions it contains but rather in directing a person to live a good and just life. The Talmudic Sages recognize this form of truth as the Torah's truth in the following exchange:

> Rabbi Shimon said, "Those who lend on interest lose more than they gain. And not only that, they impute wisdom[70] to Moses, our Teacher, and to his Torah of truth, saying, 'Had Moses our Teacher known that there is profit in this thing [i.e. lending on interest], he would not have prohibited it.'"[71]

This account gives two pieces of information. The first is that transgressing the Torah provides less benefit to a person than observing it, as a matter of course. The second is that the truth of the Torah is in the fact that it provides a means for personal success in a way that minimizes social disharmony. While lending on interest may seem to allow for personal profit without personal exertion, in fact, the person who lends money loses more than he gains in two respects, namely in terms of wealth and in terms of social harmony.[72]

A midrashic discussion similarly emphasizes the communal nature of the Torah's truth, and how its focus is in how people live together socially, even if to do so a person must accept certain grounding premises that can be seen as propositions. It states,

> Aquila said to the Emperor Hadrian, "I wish to convert and to become an Israelite." He replied: "You seek [to join] that people? See how I have debased them, and how many of them I have killed. You wish to ally yourself with the lowliest of peoples—what do you see in them that you wish

to convert?" [Aquila] told him: "The least among them knows how the Blessed Holy One created the world: what was created on the first day and what on the second day, how long it has been since the world was created, and on what the world stands. And their Torah is true." [Hadrian] said to him, "Go study their Torah, but do not get circumcised." Aquila told him, "Not even the wisest in your kingdom nor an elder one hundred years old could study their Torah unless he is circumcised!" Thus it is written, "[*God*] *issued His commands to Jacob, His statutes and rules to Israel. He did not do so with any other nation*" except with the children of Israel.[73]

What is interesting about this midrash is that it bases itself on the verses "*These are the mishpatim*,"[74] and "[*God*] *issued His commands* (*devarav*) *to Jacob*."[75] Aquila explained to Hadrian what even the least among the Jews knows in terms of beliefs or propositional information, yet the midrash makes it clear that those propositions are not the truth of the Torah to which Aquila refers. If they were, he would not need to convert, since he already knew them and even told Hadrian about them before converting. Moreover, it is difficult to differentiate between an uncircumcised elder who is 100 years old and someone who is circumcised with respect to their ability to know that God exists and that He created the world, especially since Noahides, who are commanded to know this information, are not commanded to be circumcised. The necessity of conversion must therefore lie in the ability to know the knowledge that was given uniquely to the Jewish people. This truth is to what the two initial verses of the midrash refer, namely in the *mishpatim* and the commandments, or simply the way of life that the Torah commands Jews to follow. Only those who live such a life can understand the truth of it, since its acquisition must come through experience and reflection. As Aquila explains, learning by observation or passive study is different than learning by participation.

In the Middle Ages and the early Modern period, these two ways of conceiving truth in the phrase *Moshe emet v'Torato emet* continued. For example, Rabbi Yehuda haLevi (1075–1141) uses the term *Torat emet* (קח העירש' in Judeo-Arabic) in distinguishing between knowledge gained through astrology versus that gained from the Torah. Astrologers, he writes, claim that they know the particulars of the influence the heavenly spheres have on the earth, yet, in truth, such knowledge cannot be known. However, the wisdom which they do possess which relies on the Divine wisdom of the Torah should be accepted, since we consider it as if it was received by the Divine power and thus true. In this juxtaposition, truth is a function of being reliable, and the source of the truth ultimately is the Divine power, even if it takes a circuitous route. Moreover, Rabbi Yehuda haLevi writes that followers of other religions, even if they believe in the narratives described in the Torah, since their actions contradict their claims that the Torah is true, are like converts who accept only the fundamental principles found in the Torah but not its entirety. They are as far from Judaism as the philosophers in their service of God, since knowledge of the Divine truth comes with following the Torah and not through speculation alone.[76] In a similar vein, Rabbi Shlomo ben Avraham ben Aderet (1235–1310) juxtaposes two groups of faith. The first consists of the philosophers, who only justify knowledge that they base on their own intellect. In terms of practical knowledge, this group possesses only ethics and social convention. The second group consists of those who recognize that religion was given by God and that Moses is true and his Torah is true. This group contains Jews, Christians, and Muslims, yet the group itself is divided in that each religion considers the authority and meaning of the commandments differently.[77]

In the thirteenth-century work *Sefer HaHinukh*, the author provides a meaning of *Torat emet* that is similar to the one found in the Talmudic literature. On the commandment not to rebel against the *Bet Din HaGadol* (mitzvah 391), he writes that the root of the commandment is to maintain the unity of the Torah, for if each person were given the ability to interpret the Torah according to his own understanding, there would be great disagreement in understanding the commandments, and the Torah would become many *Torot*. The Torah remains true, however, through the observance of it as understood by the Sages of the tradition.[78]

Rabbi Judah Loew of Prague (1525–1609), on the other hand, uses the expression *Torat emet* to distinguish the Torah from common sense and from social ethics. As truth, the Torah obligates a person to perform acts or refrain from acting according to a higher standard. He gives, as an example, that the obligation to return a lost object to a person who has despaired of ever finding it has a greater threshold in the Torah than it does according to social norms, since the Torah also considers what should constitute as an obligation from the viewpoint of loving-kindness (*hesed*) and not just from the viewpoint of social peace.[79] Elsewhere, Rabbi Loew calls the truth of the Torah a necessary and essential truth, rather than a truth of contingently correct propositions.[80]

Traditionalist rabbis of the nineteenth century also used the expression *Moshe emet v'Torato emet* in the same way as it is expressed in the Talmudic literature and by medieval and early modern rabbinic scholars. For example, in the introduction to his commentary on Leviticus, Rabbi Meir Leibush ben Jehiel Michel Wisser (Malbim, 1809–1879) writes that the Sages had possession of vast storehouses and treasures full of wisdom and knowledge, which contained overarching principles and fixed rules concerning grammar, linguistics and logic. Therefore, the rabbinic interpretation of the Torah is actually its simple understanding (*pshat*) and should not be considered as exegesis. The understanding of the Biblical text by those who only look at the written word (Karaim) and of those who reject the tradition of the Sages, on the other hand, is incorrect. Malbim's commentary intends to show that "Moses is true and his Torah is true and its reception is true, all were given from one shepherd." What Malbim means by this sentence is that the Torah, as attributed to Moses' authority, in providing the correct explanation of the Torah, and as passed on through tradition by the Sages, is true. In justifying the legitimacy of the tradition as well, Rabbi Samson Raphael Hirsch attributes the truth of Moses and his Torah to the fact that it has kept the Jewish people through the ages. He writes, "The historic path we have traveled through the ages, weak as we were, with nothing but the Torah in our arms, is reliable testimony forever that Moses and his Torah are true."[81]

Rabbi Yoseph Dov Baer haLevi Soloveitchik (1820–1892) uses the midrash about Korah and his men to support his claim that there are two purposes for Gehinnom, namely that it is used either to punish and avenge the evils done in a person's lifetime or as a place to remove the impurities of sin from a person so that he or she may merit a place in *Gan Eden*. For those who sin out of desire or lust, *Gehinnom* will be a temporary interlude so as to remove the dross of sin; however for those people, such as the *Apikorisim*, who deride the words of the Sages, *Gehinnom* is an eternal punishment. Rabbi Soloveitchik explains that in exclaiming that Moses and his Torah is true, it shows that the purpose of *Gehinnom* for Korah and his men is to purify them, and that once they are removed of their pride and materialism, they will ascend to their place in *Gan Eden*.[82] This understanding of the midrash provides support for both meanings of *Moshe emet v'Torato emet* that we have found. First, with respect to *Moshe emet*, it supports the idea that denial of Moses' authority is a result of pride and materialism rather than a pure challenge to its truth. Second, with respect to *Torato emet*, it supports the idea that proper obedience to the

Torah purifies the soul whereas transgression dirties it, that is, that obedience of the Torah is true in the sense that it is the best way to live.

Moshe emet v'Torato emet seems to be true on many levels. Not only is it an affirmation of the Torah as given from God to Moses at Sinai but also the meaning of its truth is two-fold. *Moshe emet*—Moses is true in reliably conveying God's Torah to the people in a way that both that which is explicit and that which is implied can be readily understood and passed down through the ages; *v'Torato emet*—and the Torah which Moses gave to the people is true in providing the means to live a life of truth. That two-fold truth, and the two pillars which it supports, namely justice and peace, is what makes the world stand,[83] as the prophet states, "Speak the truth each one with his neighbor; truth and judgment of peace you shall judge in your cities."[84]

NOTES

1. *Lifnim mishurat hadin* is usually translated as "supererogation," either acting "beyond the letter of the law" or acting "within the limits of the law." The difference between the latter two translations is a consequence of which perspective to take vis-à-vis the law when translating the phrase, that is, is the law the limit of what is acceptable or the limit of what is required.
2. Aharon Lichtenstein, "Does Jewish Tradition Recognize an Ethic Independent of Halakha?" *Contemporary Jewish Ethics*, ed. Menachem Kellner (New York: Sanhedrin Press, 1978) 106.
3. They were two renowned money changers in those days.
4. The reason that experts, such as Danko and Isser, would be exempt if they erred in saying that a bad coin was valid is that because their expertise is so great error could only result as a consequence of factors outside their control, such as if the government recently began stamping new coins and had just declared the old coins invalid.
5. BT *Bava Kama* 99b.
6. In recounting this passage, Louis Newman writes that this is a case of a privileged individual, for whom acting *lifnim mishurat hadin* means voluntarily foregoing exemption and, with self-sacrifice, applying a standard which applies to the ordinary person, with the motivation simply to redress the woman's grievance. Saul Berman, on the other hand, posits that Rabbi Hiyya was acting according to what he saw was the law, and that the notion of *lifnim mishurat*

hadin was a means for the Amoraim to understand Rabbi Hiyya's actions in light of the exemption that had later developed.

See Louis E. Newman, "Law, Virtue and Supererogation in the Halakha: The Problem of 'Lifnim Mishurat Hadin' Reconsidered," *Journal of Jewish Studies*, 40 (1989); Saul Berman, "*Lifnim Mishurat Hadin I*," *Journal of Jewish Studies*, 26 (1975).

7. *Braitot* (sing. *braita*) are Tannaitic statements or passages found in the Talmud that are not found in the Mishna.

8. Their relationship is demonstrated by the fact that the legal codes put the decisions of the two Talmudic discussions into the same statue. See *Mishne Torah, Hilkhot Sekhirot* 10:5; *Shulhan Arukh, Hoshen Mishpat* 306:4.

9. Though there is a commandment to help another with his load, a Sage and an elder are exempt from this obligation, since it is undignified for them to help. Rabbi Ishmael therefore declared the load ownerless so that there was no longer an obligation *de jure* to help the person, despite the fact that he was exempt de facto.

10. Rabbi Ishmael declared it ownerless for all but the original owner so that he could not acquire them and then ask Rabbi Ishmael for assistance. We will not be examining the legal principles that make this declaration effective.

11. BT *Bava Metsia* 30b.

12. Exodus 23:5; there is another positive commandment to lift up the animal together with its owner, and reload the animal's burden upon it, as it states: "You shall certainly lift it up (Deuteronomy 22:4)."

13. Although a year of 12 months sounds redundant according to the Gregorian calendar; according to the Jewish calendar, a leap year has 13 months.

14. BT *Bava Metsia* 24b.

15. The question over the presumption of despair is resolved as follows: If a person loses an object in a place that is frequented primarily by Jews, he will assume that a Jew will find it and announce its discovery so that he can claim it. He will therefore not despair of its return. If a person loses an object in a place that is frequented primarily by heathens, he will not assume that it will be found by a Jew, nor will the heathen announce its discovery so that he can claim it. He will therefore despair of the object. By the time a Jew then finds it, it is presumed that the original owner would have

relinquished ownership. In a place that is populated half by Jews and half by heathens, a Jew who finds an object must announce it; therefore, it is assumed that the owner will not despair of it.

16. *Tosafot HaRosh, Bava Metsia* 24b, s.v. *b'shukha d'daissa*; *Bet Yosef, Hoshen Mishpat* 259:3.

17. Moreover, because despairing of an object has less legal efficacy in causing one to lose possession of an object than if one were to announce it ownerless (especially when the object has identifying marks which diminishes the presumption of despair in the first place), the original owner would still have a claim of ownership over the purse to some degree, even if it could be overridden by the legal presumption. See *Tosafot, Bava Kama* 66a, s.v. *motze aveda lav keivan d'miya'ash marah minah*.

18. In fact, rather than being seen as an act of supererogation, Rabbi Karo adopts Shmuel's argument and writes that although, according to the law (*din*), in a place where the majority of people are idolaters, even if a Jew gives identification marks, a person is not *obligated to return* [a lost object], it is *good and proper to return* it *lifnim mishurat hadin* to the Jew who gives identification marks (*Shulhan Arukh, Hoshen Mishpat* 259:5). Compare this to the ruling of Maimonides, "Although a person is entitled to keep a lost article that he discovers, *one who wishes to follow a good and an upright path* should go *lifnim mishurat hadin* and return the lost article to a Jew, if he describes marks with which the object can be identified" (*Hilkhot Gezelah v'Aveda* 11:7). Rabbi Moshe Isserles adds that if the person who finds it is poor, then *he does not need to act lifnim mishurat hadin*, implying that it is a requirement for everyone else.

19. *Tosafot HaRosh, Bava Metsia* 24b, s.v. *ahadrinhu l'maryaihu batar tresar yarhei shata*. Rashi, however, has a different understanding of the case.

The Talmud does not state whether Shmuel's father was compensated for his efforts, yet this omission need not force us to assume that Shmuel's father lost money by fulfilling the commandment in the way that he did. He was permitted to work the animals, and that may have covered the costs of feeding them. Alternatively, the original owner could have reimbursed him for his expenses, even if the Talmud does not mention it.

20. It is common knowledge that the man was selling his property in order to raise capital, yet he did not verbalize his intention at the time of the sale. Had it not been common knowledge, his unexpressed intention would not be recognized since *devarim she' b' lev ainam devarim*—words of the heart are not words. Alternatively, he did make his intention known, but he did not formally stipulate it at the time of the sale.

21. The famine caused massive inflation, so the people needed to sell their houses to afford food.

22. Because the wheat was in transit, the sale of the mansions were voided because they erroneously relied on a mistaken assumption, that is, that there was no more wheat coming to be bought at cheaper prices. The sale was obviously conditioned on the presumption that people were selling them in order to pay for wheat.

23. BT *Ketubot* 97a.

24. *Shulhan Arukh, Hoshen Mishpat* 206:3.

25. Whether the presumption was explicitly discussed or not prior to the sale is subject to debate among the *Rishonim*.

26. There is one more case in the Talmud where a person's actions are described as being *lifnim mishurat hadin*. In that case, a person chooses to recognize an individual over and above what is required, yet in a way that is still within the realm of what is legally permissible. Because it is a case that deals with ritual law, however, it is more difficult to demonstrate the social versus societal nature of the action. See BT *Berakhot* 45b.

27. Exodus 18:20.

28. BT *Bava Metsia* 30b; see also *Mekhilta d' Rabbi Shimon bar Yohai* (Exodus 18:20); *Mekhilta d' Rabbi Ishmael* (*Masekhta d' Amalek, Yitro* 2).

29. Rashi, *Bava Metsia* 30b, s.v. *zeh bet hayyim*.

30. JT *Peah* 1:5.

31. Deuteronomy 30:19–20.

32. BT *Kiddushin* 30b.

33. For example, a true *hesed* is one that is performed for a person after he or she has already died, such as the *hesed* done for Joseph when the Jews brought his bones from Egypt to Israel (Genesis Rabba, *Parshat Vayehi*, 96).

34. BT *Bava Metsia* 30b.

35. BT *Yoma* 9b.

36. *Tosafot, Bava Metsia* 30b, s.v. *lo harva*.

37. Compare Kant, who writes, "The object of respect is the law only, that is, the law which we impose on ourselves, and yet recognize as necessary in itself. As a law, we are subjected to it without consulting self-love; as imposed by us on ourselves, it is a result of our will…Respect for a person is properly only respect for the law of which he gives us an example (*Fundamental Principles*, 19)."

38. The explanation of *lifnim mishurat hadin* as an extension of the command to love another by considering him or her as a person and not only as he or she stands under the law can also explain the situations in the Talmud where acting *lifnim mishurat hadin* is applied to God's actions. See BT *Berakhot* 7a, 20b; BT *Avodah Zara* 4b.

39. Turnus Rufus the wicked once asked Rabbi Akiva, "Whose works are superior, those of God or those of man?" He answered him, "Those of man are superior." Answered Turnus Rufus, "But look at heaven and earth, can man make their like?" Rabbi Akiva replied, "Do not draw on what is above human experience and control, but rather on that which is within our range." He said to him, "Why do you circumcise?" He answered, "I knew you would ask this question, and so I anticipated you by declaring that human works are superior to those of God." Thereupon Rabbi Akiva brought him ears of corn and cakes. He said to him, "The former are the works of God, the latter of man. Are not the latter superior to the ears of corn?" Turnus Rufus, however countered, "If He requires circumcision, why does not the child leave the mother's womb circumcised?" Rabbi Akiva replied, "Why indeed, does the umbilical cord come out with him and he is suspended by his navel and his mother cuts it? As for your query why he is not born circumcised, this is because the Holy One blessed be He has given the commandments for the sole purpose of refining our character through them. This is why David declared: 'The word of the Lord refined' (*Tanhuma, Tazria* 5)."

40. Deuteronomy 6:18.

41. *Shemonah Perakaim*, Chapter 4.

42. The Talmudic passage is as follows: "He said to me: Come, I will show you the men of Korah that were swallowed up. I saw two cracks that emitted smoke. I took a piece of clipped wool, dipped it in water, attached it to the point of a spear and let it in there. And when I took it out it was singed. [Thereupon] he said to me: Listen

attentively [to] what you [are about to] hear. And I heard them say: Moses and his Torah are truth and we are liars. He said to me: Every thirty days Gehenna causes them to turn back here as [one turns] flesh in a pot, and they say thus: Moses and his law are truth and we are liars (BT *Bava Batra* 74a)."

43. Obviously, it is a situation where the sons were not readily known so that there was a presumption that he did not have sons. Similarly, there was a presumption that he did not have brothers, but it was not known in fact.

44. He can divorce her rather than say that he has sons or that he has no brothers, so making the statement has no benefit on its own.

45. BT *Kiddushin* 64b.

46. BT *Bava Metsia* 81b; BT *Ketubot* 27b.

47. BT *Shevout* 21a.

48. BT *Yevamot* 55b, where it states regarding the reporting of a teaching, "When Rav Dimi came, he stated in the name of Rav Yohanan: The first stage is constituted by the insertion of the corona. They said to him: But, surely, Rabbah bar Bar Hana did not say so! He replied: Then either he is the liar or I lied."

49. BT *Sotah* 35a.

50. BT *Sanhedrin* 89b.

51. BT *Kiddushin* 49a.

52. Tractate *Derek Eretz* 2:1.

53. Exodus 11:4.

54. BT *Berakhot* 4b.

55. Numbers 16.

56. Exodus 19:6; 22:30; Leviticus 11:44; 19:2; 20:7; Numbers 15:40.

57. *Tanhuma* 4.

58. *Midrash Rabba*, Korah 16:3.

59. Malachi 2:5–6.

60. Radak, Malachi 2:6.

61. *Sifra Shemini* 1:38.

62. BT *Hagiga* 10a.

63. BT *Sanhedrin* 6b.

64. *Sifra, Aharei Mot* 5:10.

65. Joshua 11:15.

66. JT *Peah* 1:1. This is in line with the exegetical technique that assumes that every "et" in the Torah is meant to add to the meaning of the verse. See Kiddushin 57a.

67. It is true that Aharon and Moses are contrasted in that Aharon is said to pursue peace (*shalom*) while Moses is said to pursue truth (*emet*), which would seem to contradict that idea that Aharon followed Moses' instructions completely. However, one must recognize that this contradistinction in the Talmud is also accompanied with a differentiation between when a person is a judge, who must then pursue truth, and when a person is not a judge, so that he is permitted to pursue peace and compromise. Aharon was not a judge as Moses was; he therefore had the ability to pursue peace more often. However, in their own personal lives and as leaders, the Bible oftentimes gives similar accounts of how Moses and Aharon pursued peace. See *Tosafot, Sanhedrin* 6b.

68. Psalms 119:142.

69. Radak, Psalms 119:142.

70. A euphemism for folly.

71. BT *Bava Metsia* 75b.

72. This is exemplified by the preceding discussion in the Talmud which states that if a man lends to his neighbor, the latter must not afterwards extend a greeting to him first, if such was not the usual practice (meaning that the lender usually extended a greeting first), since it would be considered as a type of usury. This shows that even in permitted form of lending, social relations become strained.

73. Exodus Rabbah 30:12.

74. Exodus 21:1.

75. Psalm 147:19.

76. *Kuzari* 4:9–17.

77. *Teshuvot HaRashba*, 368. He, of course, continues to show that the Jewish understanding of the meaning and authority of the commandments is the correct one.

78. Rabbi Yosef Babad (1800–1874), in the *Minhat Hinukh*, a commentary on the *Sefer HaHinukh*, underlines this point by asserting that the truth of the matter is that the majority of the commandments are only known through tradition, from one mouth to another all the way to Moses. Even though the commandments are mentioned in the written Torah, very little of the details as to how one should fulfill the commandments are explicit, thus the great difference in understanding between traditional Jews and other factions of Judaism.

79. *Be'er HaGola, Be'er Sheini*.

80. *Tiferet Israel*, Chapter 19.
81. Commentary on Shemot 4:1.
82. *Teshuvot Bet HaLevi, Derushim, Derush* 13. This explanation is supported by Psalm 49.
83. *Avot* 1:18.
84. Zekharia 8:16.

BIBLIOGRAPHY

Abravanel, Isaac, and Menachem Marc Kellner. 1982. *Principles of Faith = Rosh Amanah*. East Brunswick: Associated University Presses.

Adams, Robert M. 2006. *A Theory of Virtue: Excellence in Being for the Good*. Oxford: Clarendon Press.

Allen, William T. 1993. Contracts and Communities in Corporation Law. *Washington and Lee Law Review* 50: 1395–1407.

Altmann, Alexander. 1974. Free will and Predestination in Saadia, Bahya and Maimonides. In *Religion in a Religious Age*, ed. S.D. Goiten. Cambridge: Harvard University Press.

Altmann, Alexander. 2000. Defining Maimonides' Aristotelianism. In *Maimonides and the Sciences*, ed. R.S. Cohen and Levine Hillel. Dordrecht: Kluwer.

Annas, Julia. 2008. The Phenomenology of Virtue. *Phenomenology and the Cognitive Sciences* 7(1): 21–34.

Anscombe, Gertrude E.M. 1958. Modern Moral Philosophy. *Philosophy* 33(124): 1–19.

Aristotle, and Barnes Jonathan. 1984. *The Complete Works of Aristotle: The Revised Oxford Translation*. Princeton: Princeton University Press.

Aristotle, and Oswald Martin. 1999. *Nicomachean Ethics*. Upper Saddle River: Prentice Hall, Inc.

Arnold, Magda B. 1960. *Emotion and Personality*. New York: Columbia University Press.

Arriaga, Ximena B., and Christopher R. Agnew. 2001. Being Committed: Affective, Cognitive, and Conative Components of Relationship Commitment. *Personality and Social Psychology Bulletin* 27(9): 1190–1203.

Avicenna, and Michael E. Marmura. 2004. *The Metaphysics of the Healing: A Parallel English-Arabic Text*. Provo: Brigham Young University Press.

© The Author(s) 2017

I. Bedzow, *Maimonides for Moderns*,

DOI 10.1007/978-3-319-44573-1

Avicenna, and F. Rahman. 1952. *Avicenna's Psychology*. London: Oxford University Press.

Badhwar, Neera K. 1996. The Limited Unity of Virtue. *Noûs* 30(3): 306–329.

Baehr, Jason S. 2011. *The Inquiring Mind: On Intellectual Virtues and Virtue Epistemology*. Oxford: Oxford University Press.

Balme, D.M. 1941. Greek Science and Mechanism: II. The Atomists. *The Classical Quarterly* 35(1/2): 23–28.

Balme, D.M. 1980. Aristotle's Biology was Not Essentialist. *Archiv für Geschichte der Philosophie*. 62(1): 1–12.

Barfield, Owen. 1967. *History in English Words*. Grand Rapids: W.B. Eerdmans.

Bargh, John A. 2006. What Have We Been Priming All These Years? On the Development, Mechanisms, and Ecology of Nonconscious Social Behavior. *European Journal of Social Psychology* 36(2): 147–68.

Baumeister, Roy F., F. Todd, and Dianne M. Heatherton. 1994. *Losing Control: How and Why People Fail at Self-Regulation*. San Diego: Academic Press.

Baumeister, Roy F., Kathleen D. Vohs, and Dianne M. Tice. 2007. The Strength Model of Self-Control. *Current Directions in Psychological Science* 16(6): 351–355.

Bedzow, Ira. 2009. *Halakhic Man, Authentic Jew: Moderns Expressions of Orthodox Thought from Rabbi Joseph B. Soloveitchik and Rabbi Eliezer Berkovits*. Jerusalem: Urim.

Bedzow, Ira, and Michael Broyde. 2013. The Multifarious Models for Jewish Marriage. *AJS Perspectives*. 52–53.

Ben-Menahem, Hanina. 2002. Reconsidering the 'Guide for the Perplexed' III:34. *Journal of Law and Religion* 17(1/2): 19–48.

Benveniste, Emile. 1973. *Indo-European Language and Society*. London: University of Miami Press.

Berger, Peter L., and Luckmann Thomas. 1967. *The Social Construction of Reality: A Treatise in the Sociology of Knowledge*. Garden City: Doubleday.

Berkovits, Eliezer. 1969. *Man and God: Studies in Biblical Theology*. Detroit: Wayne State University Press.

Berkovits, Eliezer. 1970. Authentic Judaism and Halakha. *Judaism* 19(1): 66–76.

Berlin, Isaiah. 1969. *Four Essays on Liberty*. London: Oxford University Press.

Bleich, J. 1977. *Contemporary Halakhic Problems Volume 1*. New York: Ktav.

Bleich, J. David. 1987. Hasgarat Posh'a Yehudi sheBarach LeEretz Yisrael. *Or Hamizrach* 35:247–269.

Bleich, J. David. 2010. The Metaphysics of Property Interests in Jewish law: An Analysis of 'Kinyan'. *Tradition* 43(2): 49–67.

Bleich, J. David. Mishpat Mavet Bedenai Benai Noach. *Jubilee Volume in Honor of Rabbi Joseph D. Soloveitchik* 1:193–208.

Blustein, Jeffrey. 1992. *Care and Commitment: Taking the Personal Point of View*. New York: Oxford University Press.

Bradie, Michael, and Fred D. Miller Jr. 1984. Teleology and Natural Necessity in Aristotle. *History of Philosophy Quarterly* 1(2): 75–89.

Brady, Michael, and Duncan Pritchard. 2003. *Moral and Epistemic Virtues.* Malden: Blackwell.

Breuer, Isaac. 1974. *Concepts of Judaism.* New York: Israel Universities Press.

Broadie, Sarah. 1991. *Ethics with Aristotle.* New York: Oxford University Press.

Broadie, Alexander. 1993. Medical Categories in Maimonidean Ethics. In *Moses Maimonides: Physician, Scientist, and Philosopher*, ed. Rosner Fred and Kottek Samuel. Northvale: Jason Aronson, Inc.

Brockman, John. 2013. *Thinking: The New Science of Decision-Making, Problem-Solving, and Prediction.* New York: Harper Perennial.

Brooks, Arnold. 2006. *Who Really Cares: The Surprising Truth About Compassionate Conservatism.* New York: Basic Books.

Broyde, Michael. 1997. The Obligation of Jews to Seek Observance of Noachide Laws by Gentiles: A Theoretical Review. In *Tikkun Olam: Social Responsibility in Jewish Thought and Law*, ed. Shatz David, Chaim I. Waxman, and Nathan J. Diament. Northvale: Jason Aronson.

Broyde, Michael, and Ira Bedzow. 2014. *The Codification of Jewish law and an Introduction to the Jurisprudence of the Mishna Berura.* Boston: Academic Studies Press.

Charles, David. 1988. Aristotle on Hypothetical Necessity and Irreducibility. *Pacific Philosophical Quarterly* 69: 1–53.

Cohen, Abraham. 1927. *The Teaching of Maimonides.* London: Routledge.

Csikszentmihalyi, Mihaly. 1990. *Flow: The Psychology of Optimal Experience.* New York: Harper & Row.

Cunningham, Michael R. 1979. Weather, Mood, and Helping Behavior: Quasi Experiments with the Sunshine Samaritan. *Journal of Personality and Social Psychology* 37(11): 1947–1956.

Damasio, Antonio. 2005. *Descartes' Error: Emotion, Reason, and the Human Brain.* London\New York: Penguin.

Dancy, Jonathan. 1993. *Moral Reasons.* Oxford: Basil Blackwell.

Darley, John M., and C. Daniel Batson. 1973. "From Jerusalem to Jericho": A Study of Situational and Dispositional Variables in Helping Behavior. *Journal of Personality and Social Psychology* 27: 100–108.

Darwall, Stephen. 1992. Internalism and Agency. *Philosophical Perspectives* 6: 155–174.

Davidson, Herbert A. 1992. *Alfarabi, Avicenna, and Averroes on Intellect: Their Cosmologies, Theories of the Active Intellect, and Theories of Human Intellect.* New York: Oxford University Press.

Davidson, Herbert A. 2001. The Authenticity of Works Attributed to Maimonides. *Me'ah She'arim: Studies in Medieval Jewish Spiritual Life in Memory of Isadore Twersky.* Jerusalem:118–125.

Davidson, Richard J., Klaus R. Scherer, and H.H. Goldsmith. 2003. *Handbook of Affective Sciences.* New York: Oxford University Press.

DePaul, Michael R., and Linda T. Zagzebski. 2003. *Intellectual Virtue: Perspectives from Ethics and Epistemology.* Oxford: Clarendon.

Dewey, John. 2008. *Human Nature and Conduct.* New York: Barnes & Noble, Inc.

Doris, John. 2002. Persons, Situations, and Virtue Ethics. *Noûs* 32(4): 505–10.

Duhigg, Charles. 2012. *The Power of Habit: Why We Do What We Do in Life and Business.* New York: Random House.

Dworkin, Ronald. 1985. *A Matter of Principle.* Cambridge: Harvard University Press.

Ekman, Paul. 1992. Argument for Basic Emotions. *Cognition and Emotion* 6(3–4): 169–200.

Ekman, Paul, and Wallace V. Friesen. 1971. Constants Across Cultures in the Face and Emotion. *Journal of Personality and Social Psychology* 17(2): 124–129.

Ekman, Paul, Richard Sorenson, and Wallace V. Friesen. 1969. Pan-Cultural Elements in Facial Displays of Emotion. *Science* 164(3875): 86–88.

Ellsworth, Phoebe C. 1994. Sense, Culture, and Sensibility. In *Emotion and Culture: Empirical Studies of Mutual Influence*, ed. Hazel R. Markus and Kitayama Shinobu. Washington: DC: American Psychological Association.

Emmons, Robert A., and Michael E. McCullough. 2003. Counting Blessings Versus Burdens: An Experimental Investigation of Gratitude and Subjective Well-Being in Daily Life. *Journal of Personality and Social Psychology* 84(2): 377–89.

Falk, W. David. 1947. 'Ought' and Motivation. *Proceedings of the Aristotelian Society*, Vol. 48. The Aristotelian Society; Blackwell Publishing.

Farabi, Abu Nasr, and Charles E. Butterworth. 2001. *Alfarabi, the Political Writings: Selected Aphorisms and Other Texts.* Ithaca: Cornell University Press.

Farabi, Abu Nasr, and Richard Walzer. 1985. *Al-Farabi on the Perfect State: A Revised Text with Introduction, Translation, and Commentary.* Oxford: Clarendon Press.

Faur, José. 1986. *Golden Doves with Silver Dots: Semiotics and Textuality in Rabbinic Tradition.* Bloomington: Indiana University Press.

Felten, Eric. 2011. *Loyalty: The Vexing Virtue.* New York: Simon & Schuster.

Fleeson, William. 2001. Toward a Structure- and Process-Integrated View of Personality: Traits as Density Distributions of States. *Journal of Personality and Social Psychology* 80(6): 1011–27.

Forgas, Joseph P. 1995. Mood and Judgment: The Affect Infusion Model (AIM). *Psychological Bulletin* 117(1): 39–66.

Francis Luce, Mary, and James Bettman. 1997. Choice Processing in Emotionally Difficult Decisions. *Journal of Experimental Psychology: Learning Memory and Cognition* 23: 384–405.

Frank, Daniel. 2000a. 'With All Your Heart and With All Your Soul…': The Moral Psychology of the Shemonah Peraqim. In *Maimonides and the Sciences*, ed. R.S. Cohen and H. Levine. London: Kluwer Academic Publishers.

Frank, Daniel. 2000b. Maimonides and Medieval Jewish Aristotelianism. In *Maimonides and the Sciences*, ed. Daniel Frank and Oliver Leaman. London: Kluwer Academic Publishers.

Frankfurt, Harry. 1969. Alternate Possibilities and Moral Responsibility. *Journal of Philosophy* LXVI(23): 829–839.

Frankfurt, Harry. 1975. Three Concepts of Free Action. *Proceedings of the Aristotelian Society*, supplementary volume.

Frege, Gottlob. 1980. *The Foundations of Arithmetic: A Logico-Mathematical Enquiry into the Concept of Number*. Evanston: Northwestern University Press.

Freundenthal, Gad. 1993. Maimonides' Stance on Astrology in Context: Cosmology, Physics, Medicine, and Providence. In *Moses Maimonides: Physician, Scientist, and Philosopher*, ed. Rosner Fred and Samuel S. Kottek. Northvale: Jason Aronson Press.

Froh, Jeffrey J., William J. Sefick, and Robert A. Emmons. 2008. Counting Blessings in Early Adolescents: An Experimental Study of Gratitude and Subjective Well-Being. *Journal of School Psychology* 46(2): 213–233.

Fuller, Lon L. 1964. *The Morality of Law*. New Haven: Yale University Press.

Fuller, Lon L. 1967. *Legal Fictions*. Stanford: Stanford University Press.

Funder, David C. 2009. Persons, Behaviors and Situations: An Agenda for Personality Psychology in the Postwar Era. *Journal of Research in Personality* 43: 120–126.

Gadamer, Hans-Georg. 1989. *Truth and Method*. New York: Crossroad.

Gadamer, Hans-Georg, and David E. Linge. 2004. *Philosophical Hermeneutics*. Berkeley: University of California Press.

Galston, Miriam. 1978. The Purpose of the Law According to Maimonides. *The Jewish Quarterly Review, New Series* 69(1): 27–51.

Geary, James. 2011. *I Is an Other: The Secret Life of Metaphor and how it Shapes the Way We See the World*. New York: HarperCollins.

Geertz, Clifford. 1973. *The Interpretation of Cultures: Selected Essays*. New York: Basic Books.

Gelfand, Donna M., et al. 1973. Who Reports Shoplifters? A Field-Experimental Study. *Journal of Personality and Social Psychology* 25(2): 276–285.

Gigerenzer, Gerd and Peter M. Todd. 1999. Fast and Frugal Heuristics: The Adaptive Toolbox. In *Simple Heuristics That Make Us Smart*. 3–34.

Gilhooly, K.J., and E. Fioratou. 2013. Motivation, Goals, Thinking and Problem Solving. In *Cognition and Motivation: Forging an Interdisciplinary Perspective*, ed. Kreitler Shulamit. Cambridge: Cambridge University Press.

Goodman, Lenn E. 1991. *On Justice: An Essay in Jewish Philosophy*. New Haven: Yale University Press.

Goodman, Lenn E. 1993. Rational Law/Ritual Law. In *A People Apart: Chosenness and Ritual in Jewish Philosophical Thought*, ed. Daniel H. Frank. Albany: State University of New York Press.

Goodman, Lenn E. 1996. *God of Abraham*. New York: Oxford University Press.

Goodman, Lenn E. 2005. God and the Good Life: Maimonides' Virtue Ethics and the Idea of Perfection. In *The Trias of Maimonides: Jewish, Arabic, and Ancient Culture of Knowledge*, ed. Georges Tamer. Berlin: De Gruyter.

Goodman, Lenn E. 2009. Happiness. In *The Cambridge History of Medieval Philosophy*, vol. 1, ed. Pasnau Robert and Dyke Christina. Cambridge: Cambridge University Press.

Goodman, Lenn E. 2011a. Ethics and God. *Philosophical Investigations* 34(2): 135–150.

Goodman, Lenn E. 2011b. Individuality. In *Judaic Sources and Western Thought: Jerusalem's Enduring Presence*, ed. Jacobs Jonathan. Oxford: Oxford University Press.

Gotthelf, Allan. 1987. Aristotle's Conception of Final Causality. In *Philosophical Issues in Aristotle's Biology*, ed. Gotthelf Allan and James G. Lennox. Cambridge: Cambridge University Press.

Granovetter, Mark S. 1973. The Strength of Weak Ties. *American Journal of Sociology* 78: 1360–1380.

Granovetter, Mark S. 1983. The Strength of Weak Ties: A Network Theory Revisited. *Sociological Theory* 1(1): 201–233.

Greco, John. 2008. Virtues and Vices of Virtue Epistemology. In *Epistemology: An Anthology*. eds. Matthew McGrath, Ernest Sosa, and Jaegwon Kim Matthew. Malden: Blackwell Publishing.

Greco, John. 2009. *Achieving Knowledge*. Cambridge: Cambridge University Press.

Gu, Yangie, Botti Simona, and Faro David. 2013. Turning the Page: The Impact of Choice Closure on Satisfaction. *Journal of Consumer Research* 40: 268–83.

Halberstam, Chaya T. 2009. *Law and Truth in Biblical and Rabbinic Literature*. Bloomington: Indiana University Press.

Hansen, Jochim, Susanne Winzeler, and Sascha Topolinski. 2010. When the Death Makes you Smoke: A Terror Management Perspective on the Effectiveness of Cigarette On-Pack Warnings. *Journal of Experimental Social Psychology* 46(1): 226–228.

Hardie, W.F.R. 1968. *Aristotle's Ethical Theory*. Oxford: The Clarendon Press.

Harman, Gilbert. 1999. Moral Psychology Meets Social Psychology. *Proceedings of the Aristotelian Society*, XCIX, 316–8.

Hart, James. 1990. Divine Truth in Husserl and Kant: Some Issues in Phenomenological Theology. In *Phenomenology of the Truth Proper to Religion: Critical Essays and Interviews*, ed. Guerrière Daniel. New York: SUNY Press.

Hartman, David. 2009. *Maimonides: Torah and Philosophic Quest*. Philadelphia: Jewish Publication Society.

Hayyim of Volozhin and Eliezer Lipa (Leonard) Moskowitz. 2012. *The Soul of Life: The Complete Neffesh Ha-chayyim*. Teaneck: New Davar Publications.

Hazony, Yoram. 2012. *The Philosophy of Hebrew Scripture*. Cambridge, UK: Cambridge University Press.

Heller, Daniel. 2009. The Future of Person–Situation Integration in the Interface Between Traits and Goals: A Bottom-Up Framework. *Journal of Research in Personality* 43(2): 171–178.

Hirsch, Samson Raphael. 1960. *The Psalms*. New York: Published for the Samson Raphael Hirsch Publications Society by P. Feldheim.

Hirsch, Samson Raphael. 1984. *The Collected Writings*. New York: P. Feldheim.

Hirsch, Eli. 1999. Identity in the Talmud. *Midwest Studies in Philosophy* 23: 166–180.

Hirsch, Samson Raphael, and Joseph Elias. 1995. *The Nineteen Letters*. New York: Feldheim Publishers.

Hirsch, Samson Raphael, and Daniel Haberman. 2000. *The Hirsch Chumash: The Five Books of Torah*. Jerusalem: Feldheim.

Hookway, Christopher. 2001. Cognitive Virtues and Epistemic Evaluations. *International Journal of Philosophical Studies* 2: 211–27.

Hulsen, Peter. 1998. Back to Basics: A Theory of the Emergence of Institutional Facts. *Law and Philosophy* 17(3): 271–299.

Hume, David, and L.A. Selby-Bigge. 1928. *A Treatise of Human Nature*. Oxford: Clarendon Press.

Hume, David, L.A. Selby-Bigge, and P.H. Nidditch. 1975. *Enquiries Concerning Human Understanding and Concerning the Principles of Morals*, 3rd ed. Oxford: Clarendon Press.

Hurka, Thomas. 2001. *Virtue, Vice, and Value*. Oxford: Oxford University Press.

Hutner, Yitzhak. 2003. *Pahad Yitzhak: Hanukah*. Brooklyn: Gur Aryeh Institute for Advanced Jewish Scholarship.

Hyman, Arthur. A Note on Maimonides' Classification of Law. *Proceedings of the American Academy for Jewish Research*, Vol. 46/47, Jubilee Volume (1928–29/1978–79).

Inzlicht, Michael, and Jennifer Gutsell. 2007. Running on Empty: Neural Signals for Self-Control Failure. *Psychological Science* 18(11): 933–937.

Isen, Alice M. 2004. *Positive Affect and Decision Making*. Handbook of Emotions. Eds. M. Lewis and JM Havieland. London: Guilford Press.

Ivry, Alfred. 1991. Neoplatonic Currents in Maimonides' Thought. In *Perspectives on Maimonides: Philosophical and Historical Studies*, ed. Kraemer Joel. Oxford: Littman Library of Jewish Civilization.

Ivry, Alfred. 2008. Moses Maimonides: An Averroist Avant La Lettre? In *Maimonidean Studies*, vol. 5, ed. Hyman Arthur and Ivry Alfred. New York: Yeshiva University Press.

Jacobs, Jonathan. 1997. Plasticity and Perfection: Maimonides and Aristotle on Character. *Religious Studies* 33(4): 443–54.

Jacobs, Jonathan. 2010. *Law, Reason, and Morality in Medieval Jewish Philosophy.* Oxford: Oxford University Press.

Jacobson-Horowitz, Hilla. 2006. Motivational Cognitivism and the Argument from Direction of Fit. *Philosophical Studies an International Journal for Philosophy in the Analytic Tradition* 127(3): 561–580.

James, William. 1905. *The Sentiment of Rationality.* London: Longmans, Green and Co.

James, William. 2000. *Pragmatism and Other Writings.* New York: Penguin Group US.

James, William, and Kuklick Bruce. 1987. *Writings, 1902–1910.* New York: Literary Classics of the United States.

James, William, and Bruce Kuklick. 1992. *Writings, 1878–1899.* New York: Library of America.

Joachim, H.H. 1999. The Nature of Truth. In *Truth*, ed. Blackburn Simon and Simmons Keith. New York: Oxford University Press.

Johnson, Mark. 2007. *The Meaning of the Body.* Chicago: University of Chicago Press.

Johnson, Devon, and Kent Grayson. 2005. Cognitive and Affective Trust in Service Relationships. *Journal of Business Research* 58(4): 500–507.

Johnson-Laird, Phillip, and Keith Oatley. 1992. Basic Emotions, Rationality, and Folk Theory. *Cognition & Emotion* 6(3–4): 201–223.

Joseph, Saadia ben., and Rosenblatt Samuel. 1976. *The Book of Beliefs and Opinions.* New Haven: Yale University Press.

Kahneman, Dan. 2003. A Perspective on Judgment and Choice: Mapping Bounded Rationality. *American Psychologist* 58: 697–720.

Ḳalonimus, Ḳalmish E., and Aharon Sorski. 2011. *[ḥovat Ha-Talmidim] =: Chovas Hatalmidim = the Students' Obligation; and [sheloshah Ma'amarim] = Sheloshah Ma'amarim = Three Discourses.* Jerusalem: Feldheim.

Kant, Immanuel. 1949. *Fundamental Principles of the Metaphysics of Morals.* Upper Saddle River: Prentice Hall.

Kant, Immanuel. 1970. *"What is Enlightenment?" Kant's Political Writings.* Cambridge: Cambridge University Press.

Kant, Immanuel, and Lewish White Beck. 1993. *Critique of Practical Reason.* Upper Saddle River: Prentice-Hall, Inc.

Kant, Immanuel, Allen W. Wood, and George Di Giovanni. 1998. *Religion Within the Boundaries of Mere Reason and Other Writings. Cambridge Texts in the History of Philosophy.* Cambridge/New York: Cambridge University Press.

Kasher, Hannah. 1993. Well-Being of the Body or Welfare of the Soul: The Maimonidean Explanation of the Dietary Laws. In *Moses Maimonides: Physician, Scientist, and Philosopher*, ed. Rosner Fred and Samuel S. Kottek. Northvale: Jason Aronson.

Kelley, Donald R. 1978. The Metaphysics of Law: An Essay on the Very Young Marx. *The American Historical Review* 83(2): 350–67.

Kellner, Menachem. 1979. Maimonides, Crescas, and Abravanel on Exod. 20: 2. A Medieval Jewish Exegetical Dispute. *The Jewish Quarterly Review* 69(3): 129–157.

Kellner, Menachem. 1990. *Maimonides on Human Perfection*. Atlanta: Scholars Press.

Kellner, Menachem. 2006. *Must a Jew Believe Anything?* London/Portland: Littman Library of Jewish Civilization.

Kellner, Menachem. 2009. Philosophical Themes in Maimonides' Sefer Ahavah. In *Maimonides and His Heritage*. Albany: State University of New York Press.

Keltner, Dache, Phoebe C. Ellsworth, and Edwards Kari. 1993. Beyond Simple Pessimism: Effects of Sadness and Anger on Social Perception. *Journal of Personality and Social Psychology* 64(5): 740–52.

Komter, Aafke, and Vollebergh Wilma. 1997. Gift Giving and the Emotional Significance of Family and Friends. *Journal of Marriage and Family* 59(3): 747–757.

Korsgaard, Christine. 1996. *Sources of Normativity*. Cambridge: Cambridge University Press.

Korsgaard, Christine. 2008. *The Constitution of Agency: Essays on Practical Reason and Moral Psychology*. Oxford: Oxford University Press.

Kreisel, Howard. 1988. The Practical Intellect in the Philosophy of Maimonides. *HUCA* 59: 189–215.

Kreisel, Howard. 1989. *"Intellectual Perfection and the Role of the Law"*. From *Ancient Israel to Modern Judaism: Intellect in Quest of Understanding*, vol. 3. Atlanta: Georgia Scholars Press.

Kreisel, Howard. 1999. *Maimonides' Political Thought: Studies in Ethics, Law, and the Human Ideal*. Albany: State University of New York Press.

Kreitler, Shulamith. 2013. *Cognition and Motivation: Forging an Interdisciplinary Perspective*. Cambridge: Cambridge University Press.

Kristjánsson, Kristján. 2010. *The Self and Its Emotions*. Cambridge: Cambridge University Press.

Kristjánsson, Kristján. 2013. *Virtues and Vices in Positive Psychology: A Philosophical Critique*. New York: Cambridge University Press.

Kupperman, Joel. 2001. The Indispensability of Character. *Philosophy* 76: 239–50.

Kvanvig, Jonathan L. 1992. *The Intellectual Virtues and the Life of the Mind: On the Place of the Virtues in Epistemology*. Savage: Rowman & Littlefield Publishers.

Kvanvig, Jonathan L. 2003. *The Value of Knowledge and the Pursuit of Understanding*. Cambridge: Cambridge University Press.

Lakatos, Imre. 1998. Science and Pseudoscience. In *Philosophy of Science: The Central Issues*, ed. Curd Martin and J.A. Cover. New York: W.W. Norton.

Lakoff, George, and Mark Johnson. 1999. *Philosophy in the Flesh: The Embodied Mind and Its Challenge to Western Thought*. New York: Basic Books.

Lakoff, George, and Johnson Mark. 1993. The Contemporary Theory of Metaphor. In *Metaphor and Thought*, ed. Ortony Andrew. Cambridge: Cambridge University Press.

Landau, Mark J., Brian P. Meier, and Lucas A. Keefer. 2010. A Metaphor-Enriched Social Cognition. *Psychological Bulletin* 136(6): 1045–67.

Larmore, Charles. 2008. *The Autonomy of Morality*. New York: Cambridge University Press.

Lazarus, Richard S. 1991. Progress on a Cognitive-Motivational-Relational Theory of Emotion. *American Psychologist* 46(8): 819–834.

LeDoux, Joseph. 1998. *The Emotional Brain: The Mysterious Underpinnings of Emotional Life*. New York: Simon and Schuster.

Leibowitz, Nehama, and Aryeh Newman. 1996. *Studies in Shemot (Exodus)*. Jerusalem: Dept. for Torah Education and Culture in the Diaspora.

Lerner, Ralph, and Muhsin Mahdi. 1963. *Medieval Political Philosophy: A Sourcebook*. New York: Free Press of Glencoe.

Lewis, Marc D. 1996. Self-Organising Cognitive Appraisals. *Cognition & Emotion* 10(1): 1–26.

Lichtenstein, Aaron. 1978. Does Jewish Tradition Recognize an Ethic Independent of Halakha? In *Contemporary Jewish Ethics*, ed. Kellner Menachem. New York: Sanhedrin Press.

Lichtenstein, Aaron. 1981. *The Seven Laws of Noah*. New York: Rabbi Jacob Joseph School Press.

Little, Margaret Olivia. 1997. Virtue as Knowledge: Objections from the Philosophy of Mind. *Noûs* 31: 59–79.

Locke, John. 1959. *An Essay Concerning Human Understanding*. New York: Dover Publications.

Locke, John. 1983. *A Letter Concerning Toleration*. Indianapolis: Hackett Publishing Company.

Lowenstein, George, and Jennifer S. Lerner. 2003. The Role of Affect in Decision Making. In *Handbook of Affective Sciences*, ed. Richard J. Davidson, Klaus R. Scherer, and H.H. Goldsmith. Oxford: Oxford University Press.

MacIntyre, Alasdair C. 1984. *After Virtue: A Study in Moral Theory*, 2nd ed. Notre Dame: University of Notre Dame Press.

MacIntyre, Alasdair C. 1988. *Whose Justice? Which Rationality?* Notre Dame: University of Notre Dame Press.

Mackie, J.L. 1977. *Ethics: Inventing Right and Wrong*. New York: Penguin.

Maimonides, Moses, and Arthur David. 1968. *The Commentary to Mishnah Aboth*. New York: Bloch Pub. Co.

Maimonides, Moses, and Israel Efros. 1938. *Maimonides' Treatise on Logic: Critically Ed. On the Basis of Mss. And Early Ed. and Transl. into English*. New York: American Acad. for Jewish Research.

Maimonides, Moses, and Shlomo Pines. 1963. *The Guide of the Perplexed*. Chicago: University of Chicago Press.

Maimonides, Moses, and Isadore Twersky. 1972. *A Maimonides Reader*. New York: Behrman House.

Maimonides, Moses, Raymond L. Weiss, and Charles E. Butterworth. 1983. *Ethical Writings of Maimonides*. New York: Dover Publications.

Marx, Karl. 1964. *Economic and Philosophic Manuscripts of 1844*. New York: International Publishers.

Mathews, Kenneth E., and Lance K. Canon. 1975. Environmental Noise Level as a Determinant of Helping Behavior. *Journal of Personality and Social Psychology* 32(4): 571–577.

McDowell, John. 1979. Virtue and Reason. *The Monist* 62: 331–50.

McDowell, John. 1998. *Mind, Value, and Reality*. Cambridge, Mass: Harvard University Press.

McFall, Lynne. 1987. Integrity. *Ethics* 98(1): 5–20.

McNaughton, David. 1988. *Moral Vision: An Introduction to Ethics*. Oxford: Basil Blackwell.

Mendelssohn, Moses, and Allan Arkush. 1983. *Jerusalem, or, on Religious Power and Judaism*. Hanover: Published for Brandeis University Press by University Press of New England.

Meyer, Susan Sauve. 1992. Aristotle, Teleology and Reduction. *Philosophical Review* 101: 791–825.

Milgram, Stanley. 2009. *Obedience to Authority: An Experimental View*. New York: Harper Perennial Modern Classics.

Miller, Christian. 2003. Social Psychology and Virtue Ethics. *The Journal of Ethics* 7(4): 365–392.

Miller, Arthur H., and Vicki L. Hesli. 1997. Conceptions of Democracy Among Mass and Elite in Post-soviet Societies. *British Journal of Political Science* 27(2): 163–4.

Mirus, Christopher V. 2004. The Metaphysical Roots of Aristotle's Teleology. *The Review of Metaphysics* 57(4): 699–724.

Mischel, Walter. 1968. *Personality and Assessment*. New York: John Wiley and Sons, Inc.

Mischel, Walter, and Shoda Yuichi. 1995. A Cognitive-Affective System Theory of Personality: Reconceptualizing Situations, Dispositions, Dynamics, and Invariance in Personality Structure. *Psychological Review* 102: 246–68.

Muraven, Mark, and R.F. Baumeister. 2000. Self-Regulation and Depletion of Limited Resources: Does Self-Control Resemble a Muscle? *Psychological Bulletin* 126: 247–259.

Muraven, Mark, Roy F. Baumeister, and Dianne M. Tice. 1999. Longitudinal Improvement of Self-Regulation Through Practice: Building Self-Control Strength Through Repeated Exercise. *The Journal of Social Psychology* 139(4): 446–457.

Nagel, Thomas. 1970. *The Possibility of Altruism*. Oxford: Oxford University Press.

Nahmanides. 1963. *Kitve Ramban I*. Jerusalem: Mosad Harav Kook.

Nahmanides, and Chavel Ber Charles. 1971. *Commentary on the Torah: Genesis*. New York: Shilo Pub. House.

Nahmanides, and Chavel B. Charles. 1978. *Writings & Discourses*. New York: Shilo Pub. House.

Newman, Louis E. 1989. Virtue and Supererogation in the Halakha: The Problem of 'Lifnim Mishurat Hadin' Reconsidered. *Journal of Jewish Studies* 40: 61–88.

Niedenthal, Paula, and Halberstadt Jaiman. 2000. Grounding Categories in Emotional Response. In *Feeling and Thinking: The Role of Affect in Social Cognition*, ed. Joseph P. Forgas. New York: Cambridge University Press.

Niedenthal, Paula M., and Shinobu Ed Kitayama. 1994. *The Heart's Eye: Emotional Influences in Perception and Attention*. San Diego: Academic Press.

Novak, David. 1998. *Natural Law in Judaism*. New York: Cambridge University Press.

Novak, David. 2009. Can We Be Maimonideans Today? In *Maimonides and His Heritage*, ed. Dobbs-Weinstein Idit, Goodman Lenn Evan, and Grady James Allen. Albany: State University of New York Press.

Nussbaum, Martha. 1999. Virtue Ethics: A Misleading Category? *The Journal of Ethics* 3(3): 163–201.

Nussbaum, Martha. 2011. *Creating Capabilities: The Human Development Approach*. Cambridge: Harvard University Press.

Pakuda, Bahya ben Joseph ibn, Yehudah ibn Tibbon, and Daniel Haberman. 1996. *Sefer Torat Hovot HaLevovot*. New York: Feldheim

Pakuda, Bahya ibn, Yehudah Tibon, and Moses Hyamson. 1925. *Duties of the Heart*. New York: Bloch Pub. Co.

Panksepp, Jaak. 1998. *Affective Neuroscience: The Foundations of Human and Animal Emotions*. New York: Oxford University Press.

Peirce, Charles S. 1992. *The Essential Peirce: Selected Philosophical Writings*, vol. 1. Bloomington: Indiana University Press.

Peller, Gary. 1985. The Metaphysics of American Law. *California Law Review* 73(4): 1151.

Pettit, Phillip. 1987. Humeans, Anti-Humeans, and Motivation. *Mind* 96(384): 530–533. New Series.

Phelps, Elizabeth A., Sam Ling, and Marisa Carrasco. 2006. Emotion Facilitates Perception and Potentiates the Perceptual Benefits of Attention. *Psychological Science* 17(4): 292–299.

Pines, Shlomo. 1960. Studies in Abul-Barakat al-Baghdadi's Poetics and Metaphysics. In *Studies in Philosophy, Scripta Hierosolymitana*, vol. 6. Jerusalem: Magnes Press.

Pinker, Steven. 2007. *The Stuff of Thought: Language as a Window into Human Nature*. New York: Viking.

Plantinga, Alvin. 1993. *Warrant and Proper Function*. Oxford: Oxford University Press.

Plantinga, Alvin. 1996. Respondeo. In *Warrant in Contemporary Epistemology: Essays in Honor of plantinga's Theory of Knowledge*, ed. Plantinga Alvin and Jonathan L. Kvanvig. Lanham: Rowman & Littlefield Publishers.

Platts, Mark B. 1979. *Ways of Meaning: An Introduction to a Philosophy of Language*. London: Routledge & K. Paul.

Platts, Mark. 1980. Moral Reality and the End of Desire. In *Reference, Truth, and Reality*, ed. Platts Mark. London: Routledge and Kegan Paul.

Posner, Eric A. 1998. Symbols, Signals, and Social Norms in Politics and the Law. *The Journal of Legal Studies* 27(S2): 765–797.

Putnam, Hilary. 2002. *The Collapse of the Fact/Value Dichotomy*. Cambridge: Harvard University Press.

Raffel, Charles. 1987. Maimonides' Theory of Providence. *AJS Review* 12(1): 25–71.

Rakover, Nahum. 1991. Jewish Law and the Noahide Obligation to Preserve Social Order. *Cardozo Law Review* 12: 1073–1136.

Ramsey, F.P. 2010. Truth and Probability. In *Philosophy of Probability: Contemporary Readings*, ed. Eagle Antony. New York: Routledge.

Rawls, John. 2000. *A Theory of Justice*. Cambridge, Mass: Belknap Press of Harvard Univ. Press.

Raz, Joseph. 1975. *Practical Reason and Norms*. London: Hutchinson.

Raz, Joseph. 1999. *Engaging Reason*. New York: Oxford University Press.

Raz, Joseph. 2001. *Ethics in the Public Domain: Essays in the Morality of Law and Politics*. Oxford: Clarendon Press.

Raz, Joseph. 2009. *Between Authority and Interpretation: On the Theory of Law and Practical Reason*. Oxford: Oxford University Press.

Raz, Joseph. 2011. *From Normativity to Responsibility*. New York: Oxford University Press.

Reis, Harry T. 2008. Reinvigorating the Concept of Situation in Social Psychology. *Personality and Social Psychology Review* 12(4): 311–329.

Riggs, Wayne. 2002. Reliability and the Value of Knowledge. *Philosophy and Phenomenological Research* 64.

Rosenberg, Shalom. 1987. Ethics. In *Contemporary Jewish Religious Thought*, ed. Arthur A. Cohen and Mendes-Flohr Paul. New York: Scribner.

Rosenbloom, Noah H., and Samuel D. Luzatto. 1965. *Luzzatto's Ethico-Psychological Interpretation of Judaism: A Study in the Religious Philosophy of Samuel David Luzzatto*. New York: Yeshiva University, Department of Special Publications.

Royce, Josiah. 1995. *The Philosophy of Loyalty.* Nashville: Vanderbilt University Press.

Russell, James A., and Merry Bullock. 1985. Multidimensional Scaling of Emotional Facial Expressions: Similarity from Preschoolers to Adults. *Journal of Personality and Social Psychology* 48(5): 1290–8.

Russell, James A., Lewicka Maria, and Niit Toomas. 1989. A Cross-Cultural Study of a Circumplex Model of Affect. *Journal of Personality and Social Psychology* 57(5): 848–856.

Samuelson, Norbert. 1991. Maimonides' Doctrine of Creation. *The Harvard Theological Review* 84(3): 249–271.

Sandis, Constantine. 2009. *New Essays on the Explanation of Action.* New York: Palgrave Macmillan.

Sapir, Edward, and David G. Mandelbaum. 1949. *Selected Writings in Language, Culture and Personality.* Berkeley: University of California Press.

Scanlon, Thomas. 1998. *What We Owe to Each Other.* Cambridge: Harvard University Press.

Scheenwind, J.B. 1998. *The Invention of Autonomy.* Cambridge: Cambridge University Press.

Scherer, Klaus R., Angela Schorr, and Tom Johnstone. 2001. *Appraisal Processes in Emotion: Theory, Methods, Research.* Oxford: Oxford University Press.

Schlosberg, Harold. 1954. Three Dimensions of Emotion. *Psychological Review* 61(2): 81–8.

Searle, John. 1995. *The Construction of Social Reality.* New York: Simon and Schuster.

Searle, John. 2001. *Rationality in Action.* Cambridge: MIT Press.

Seeman, Don. 2013. Reasons for the Commandments as Contemplative Practice in Maimonides. *The Jewish Quarterly Review* 103(3): 321–2.

Segerstrom, Suzanne C., Jaime K. Hardy, Daniel R. Evans, and Natalie F. Winters. 2012. Pause and Plan: Self-Regulation and the Heart. In *How Motivation Affects Cardiovascular Response: Mechanisms and Applications,* ed. Rex A. Wright and H.E. Guido. Washington, DC: American Psychological Association.

Seidman, Jeffrey. 2005. Two Sides of 'Silencing'. *The Philosophical Quarterly* 55(218): 68–77.

Seligman, Martin. 2011. *Flourish: A Visionary Understanding of Happiness and Well-Being.* New York: Free Press.

Shafer-Landau, Russ. 2003. *Moral Realism: A Defence.* Oxford: Clarendon Press.

Shaffer, David R., Mary Rogle, and Clyde Hendrlck. 1975. Intervention in the Library: The Effect of Increased Responsibility on Bystanders' Willingness to Prevent a Theft. *Journal of Applied Social Psychology* 5(4): 303–319.

Shapiro, Marc. 2008. *Studies in Maimonides and His Interpreters.* Scranton: University of Scranton Press.

Shatz, David. 2005. *Maimonides' Moral Theory*. The Cambridge Companion to Maimonides. Ed. Kenneth Seeskin. Cambridge: Cambridge University Press.

Shneur Zalman of Liadi, Nissan Mindel, Nissen Mangel, Zalman I. Posner, and Jacob I. Schochet. 1973. *Liḳuṭe Amarim: Tanya*. London: "Kehot" Publication Society by the Soncino Press.

Slovic, Paul, Finucane Melissa, Peters Ellen, and Donald G. MacGregor. 2002. The Affect Heuristic. In *Heuristics and Biases: The Psychology of Intuitive Judgment*, ed. Gilovich Thomas, Griffin Dale, and Kahneman Dan. Cambridge: Cambridge University Press.

Slovic, Paul, et al. 2007. The Affect Heuristic. *European Journal of Operational Research* 177(3): 1333–1352.

Smith, Michael. 1987. The Humean Theory of Motivation. *Mind. New Series* 96(381): 36–61.

Snow, Nancy E. 2010. *Virtue as Social Intelligence: An Empirically Grounded Theory*. New York: Routledge.

Sokol, Moshe. 1993. Mitzvah as Metaphor. In *A People Apart: Chosenness and Ritual in Jewish Philosophical Thought*. Albany: State University of New York Press.

Soloveitchik, Joseph Dov. 1983. *Halakhic Man*. Philadelphia: Jewish Publication Society of America.

Sosa, Ernest. 1991a. *Intellectual Virtue in Perspective*. Knowledge in Perspective. Cambridge: Cambridge University Press.

Sosa, Ernest. 1991b. *Reliabilism and Intellectual Virtue*. Knowledge in Perspective. Cambridge: Cambridge University Press.

Sosa, Ernest. 1996. Proper Functioning and Virtue Epistemology. In *Warrant in Contemporary Epistemology: Essays in Honor of plantinga's Theory of Knowledge*, ed. Plantinga Alvin and Jonathan L. Kvanvig. Lanham: Rowman & Littlefield Publishers.

Sosa, Ernest. 2007. *A Virtue Epistemology*. Oxford: Oxford University Press.

Stern, Joseph. 2005. *Maimonides' Epistemology*. The Cambridge Companion to Maimonides. Ed. Kenneth Seeskin. Cambridge: Cambridge University Press.

Svavarsdottir, Sigrun. 1999. Moral Cognitivism and Motivation. *The Philosophical Review* 108(2): 161–219.

Svenson, Ola. 1992. Differentiation and Consolidation Theory of Human Decision Making: A Frame of Reference for the Study of pre- and Post-decision Processes. *Acta Psychologica* 80(1): 143–168.

Svenson, Ola. 2003. Values, Affect, and Processes in Human Decision Making: A Differentiation and Consolidation Theory Perspective. In *Emerging Perspectives on Judgment and Decision Research*, ed. Sandra L. Schneider and Shanteau James. Cambridge: Cambridge University Press.

Swann, William B., and Conor Seyle. 2005. Personality Psychology's Comeback and Its Emerging Symbiosis with Social Psychology. *Personality and Social Psychology Bulletin* 31(2): 155–165.

Swinburne, Richard. 1986. *The Evolution of the Soul*. Oxford: Clarendon Press.

Taylor, Charles. 2007. What's Wrong with Negative Liberty. In *Law and Morality: Readings in Legal Philosophy*, ed. Dyzenhaus David, Moreau S. Reibetanz, and Ripstein Arthur. Toronto: University of Toronto Press.

Taylor, Gabriele, and Raimond Gaita. 1981. Integrity. *Proceedings of the Aristotelian Society*, Supplementary Volumes, Vol. 55, 143–159, 161–176.

Taylor, C., Charles G. Lord, and Charles F. Bond Jr. 2009. Embodiment, Agency, and Attitude Change. *Journal of Personality and Social Psychology* 97(6): 946–62.

Thagard, Paul. 1998. Why Astrology Is a Pseudoscience. In *Philosophy of Science: The Central Issues*, ed. Curd Martin and J.A. Cover. New York: W.W. Norton.

Tomkins, Silvan, and Robert McCarter. 1964. What and Where Are the Primary Affects? Some Evidence for a Theory. *Perceptual and Motor Skills* 18(1): 119–158.

Tönnies, Ferdinand. 1887. *Gemeinschaft und Gesellschaft*. Leipzig: Fues.

Toussaint, Loren, and Philip Friedman. 2009. Forgiveness, Gratitude, and Well-Being: The Mediating Role of Affect and Beliefs. *Journal of Happiness Studies* 10(6): 635–654.

Twersky, Isadore. 1980. *Introduction to the Code of Maimonides (Mishneh Torah)*. New Haven: Yale University Press.

Vohs, K.D., R.F. Baumeister, B.J. Schmeichel, J.M. Twenge, N.M. Nelson, and D.M. Tice. 2008. Making Choices Impairs Subsequent Self-Control: A Limited Resource Account of Decision Making, Self-Regulation, and Active Initiative. *Journal of Personality and Social Psychology* 94: 883–898.

Volozhiner, Hayyim, and Chanoch Levi. 2002. *Ruach Chayim: Rav Chaim Volozhiner's Classic Commentary on Pirke Avos*. Targum: Southfield.

Wagerman, Seth A., and David C. Funder. 2009. Personality Psychology of Situations. In *The Cambridge Handbook of Personality Psychology*, ed. Philip J. Corr and Matthews Gerald. Cambridge: Cambridge University Press.

Walzer, Michael. 1983. *Spheres of Justice: A Defense of Pluralism and Equality*. New York: Basic Books.

Walzer, Michael. 1987. *Interpretation and Social Criticism*. Cambridge: Harvard University Press.

Watkins, Philip C., et al. 2003. Gratitude and Happiness: Development of a Measure of Gratitude, and Relationships with Subjective Well-Being. *Social Behavior and Personality: An International Journal* 31(5): 431–451.

Watson, Gary. 1982. *Free Will*. Oxford: Oxford University Press.

Waxman, Meyer. 1919. The Philosophy of Don Hasdai Crescas: Chapter V. *The Jewish Quarterly Review, New Series* 10(1): 25–47.

Weil, Simone. 1951. *Waiting for God*. New York: Putnam.

Weiss, Raymond. 1991. *Maimonides' Ethics: The Encounter of Philosophic and Religious Morality*. Chicago: University of Chicago Press.

Wierzbicka, Anna. 1999. *Emotions Across Languages and Cultures: Diversity and Universals*. Cambridge: Cambridge University Press.

Williams, Bernard. 1981. Internal and External Reasons. In *Moral Luck*. Cambridge: Cambridge University Press.

Witte, John, and Thomas C. Arthur. 1994. The Three Uses of the Law: A Protestant Source of the Purposes of Criminal Punishment?". *Journal of Law and Religion* 10(2): 433.

Wolfson, H.A. 1925. Classification of Sciences in Medieval Jewish Philosophy. In *Hebrew Union College Jubilee Volume*. Cincinnati: HUC Press.

Wolfson, Elliot R. 1988. Light Through Darkness: The Ideal of Human Perfection in the Zohar. *The Harvard Theological Review* 81(1): 73–95.

Wurzburger, Walter. 1994. *Ethics of Responsibility: Pluralistic Approaches to Covenantal Ethics*. Philadelphia: Jewish Publication Society.

Zadra, Jonathan R., and Gerald L. Clore. 2011. Emotion and Perception: The Role of Affective Information. *Wiley Interdisciplinary Reviews: Cognitive Science* 2(6): 676–685.

Zagzebski, Linda. 1996. *Virtues of the Mind: An Inquiry into the Nature of Virtue and the Ethical Foundations of Knowledge*. New York: Cambridge University Press.

Zagzebski, Linda. 2001. Must Knowers be Agents? In *Virtue Epistemology: Essays on Epistemic Virtue and Responsibility*, ed. Fairweather Abrol and Zagzebski Linda. New York: Oxford University Press.

Zemore, Sarah E. 2007. A Role for Spiritual Change in the Benefits of 12-Step Involvement. *Alcoholism, Clinical and Experimental Research* 31: 76s–79s.

Zhang, Meng, and Xiuping Li. 2012. From Physical Weight to Psychological Significance: The Contribution of Semantic Activations. *Journal of Consumer Research* 38(6): 1063–75.

Zimbardo, Philip G. 1971. *Stanford Prison Experiment*. Stanford, CA: Stanford University.

Index

Note: Page number followed by 'n' refers to notes.